D1226298

APR 1 9 2010

SIXTY

Dark AVENGERS
ASSEMBLE

WRITER: **BRIAN MICHAEL BENDIS**
ARTIST: **MIKE DEODATO**
WITH **WILL CONRAD** (ISSUE #6)
COLOR ART: **RAIN BEREDO**
LETTERER: **VIRTUAL CALLIGRAPHY'S CORY PETIT**
COVER ART: **MIKE DEODATO & RAIN BEREDO**
ASSOCIATE EDITOR: **JEANINE SCHAEFER**
EDITOR: **TOM BREVOORT**

COLLECTION EDITOR: **JENNIFER GRÜNWALD**
EDITORIAL ASSISTANT: **ALEX STARBUCK**
ASSISTANT EDITOR: **JOHN DENNING**
EDITOR, SPECIAL PROJECTS: **MARK D. BEAZLEY**
SENIOR EDITOR, SPECIAL PROJECTS: **JEFF YOUNGQUIST**
SENIOR VICE PRESIDENT OF SALES: **DAVID GABRIEL**
BOOK DESIGNER: **RODOLFO MURAGUCHI**
EDITOR IN CHIEF: **JOE QUESADA**
PUBLISHER: **DAN BUCKLEY**
EXECUTIVE PRODUCER: **ALAN FINE**

PREVIOUSLY

And there came a day, a day unlike any other, when Earth's Mightiest Heroes found themselves united against a common threat! On that day, the Avengers were born, to fight the foes no single super hero could withstand!

The shape-shifting alien race known as the Skrulls recently invaded Earth through a well-planned secret invasion, using their shape-shifting ability to seed mistrust among the Avengers and other heroes around the world.

All seemed lost, but the Skrulls' plans quickly unraveled when the mighty Thor summoned both the humans and the Skrulls to a battle on the fields of Central Park. For the first time in years, the original Avengers were united and Nick Fury was back on the battlefield. And for the first time ever, with the help of super-villain kingpin The Hood, heroes and villains fought as one.

The turning point came when Norman Osborn, once the villainous Green Goblin and most recently the leader of the Thunderbolts, stepped up and made the kill-shot that took out the Skrull Queen.

The humans prevailed, barely, over the alien army.

In the aftermath, Tony Stark took the blame for the invasion and was stripped of his roles as leader of the Avengers and director of a now defunct S.H.I.E.L.D. Norman Osborn, Thunderbolts leader and former super villain Green Goblin, has risen to power and was appointed to replace Stark. Secretly, Norman has been meeting with some of the most malevolent figures in the world today, including Latverian dictator Doctor Doom.

DARK AVENGERS #1

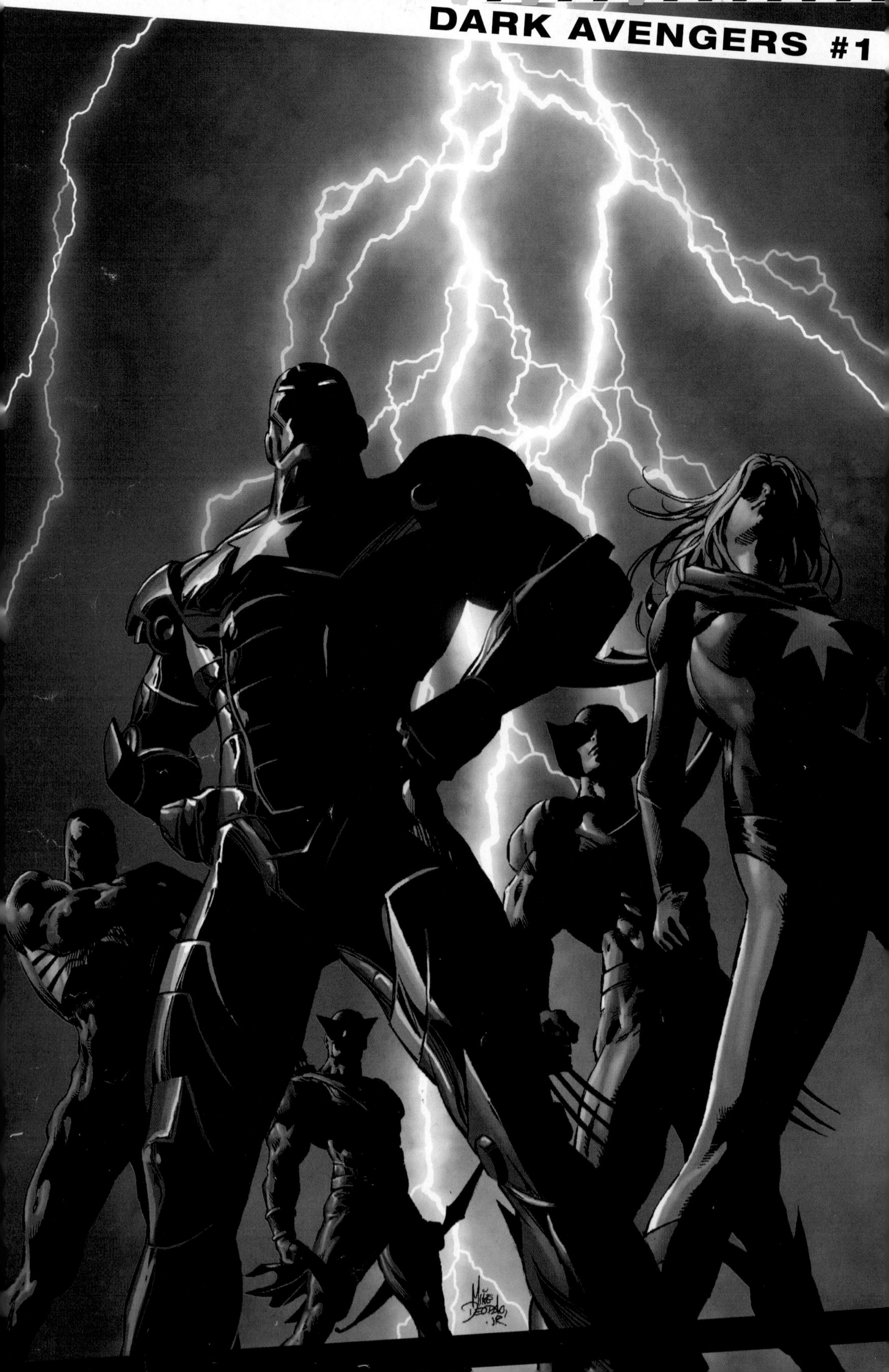

DARK AVENGERS #1 VARIANT

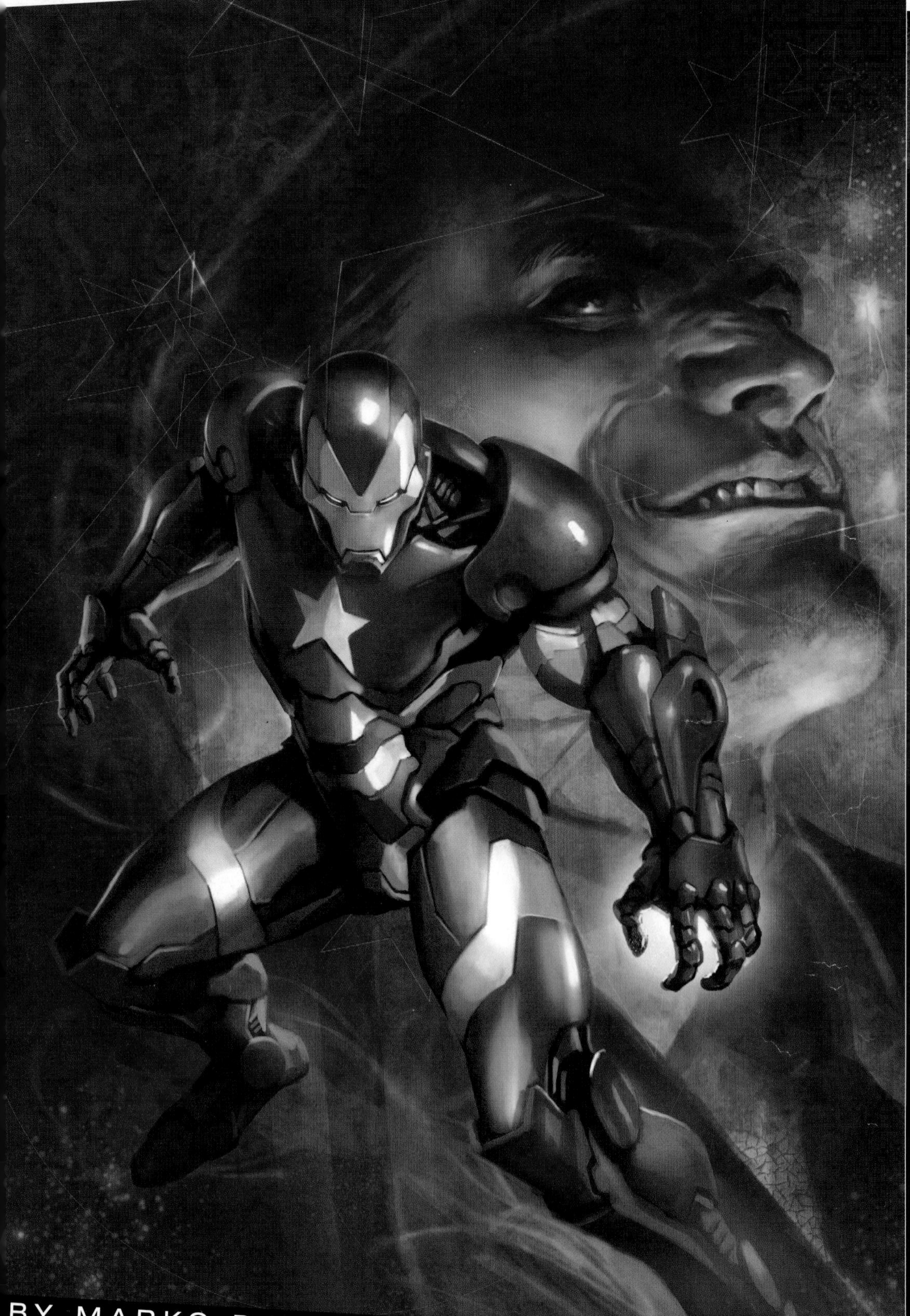

BY MARKO DJURDJEVIC

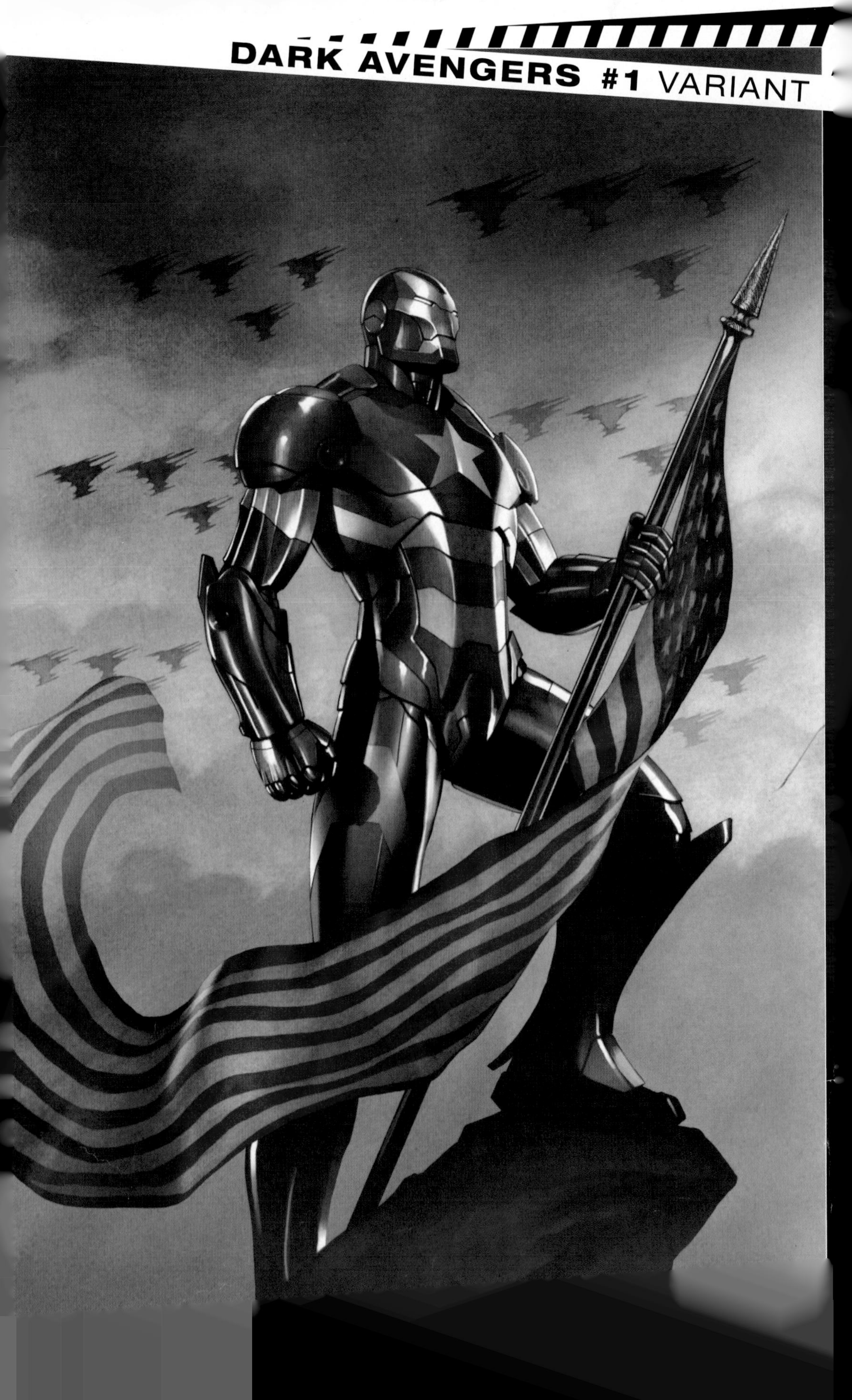
DARK AVENGERS #1 VARIANT

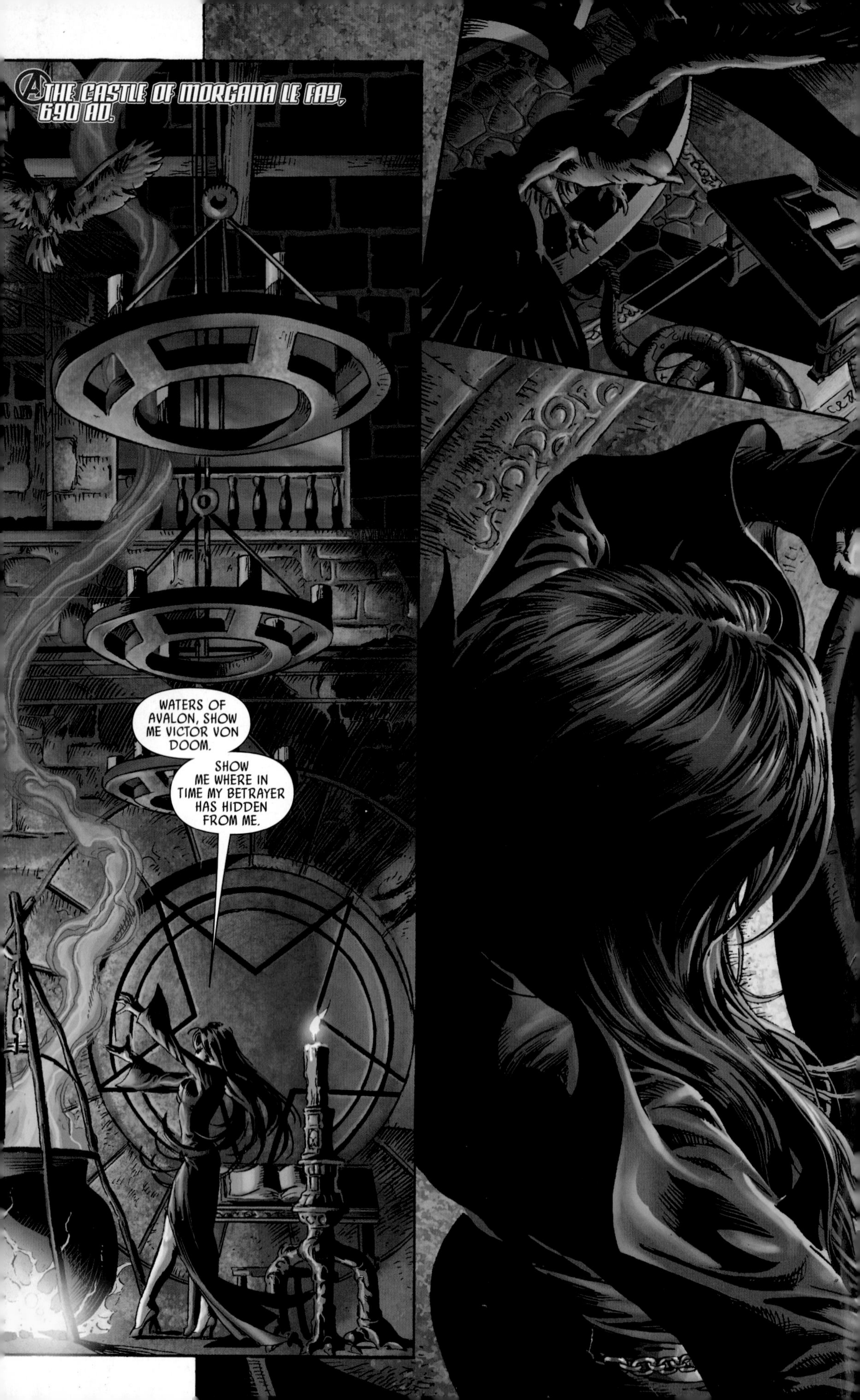
THE CASTLE OF MORGANA LE FAY, 690 AD.
WATERS OF AVALON, SHOW ME VICTOR VON DOOM.
SHOW ME WHERE IN TIME MY BETRAYER HAS HIDDEN FROM ME.

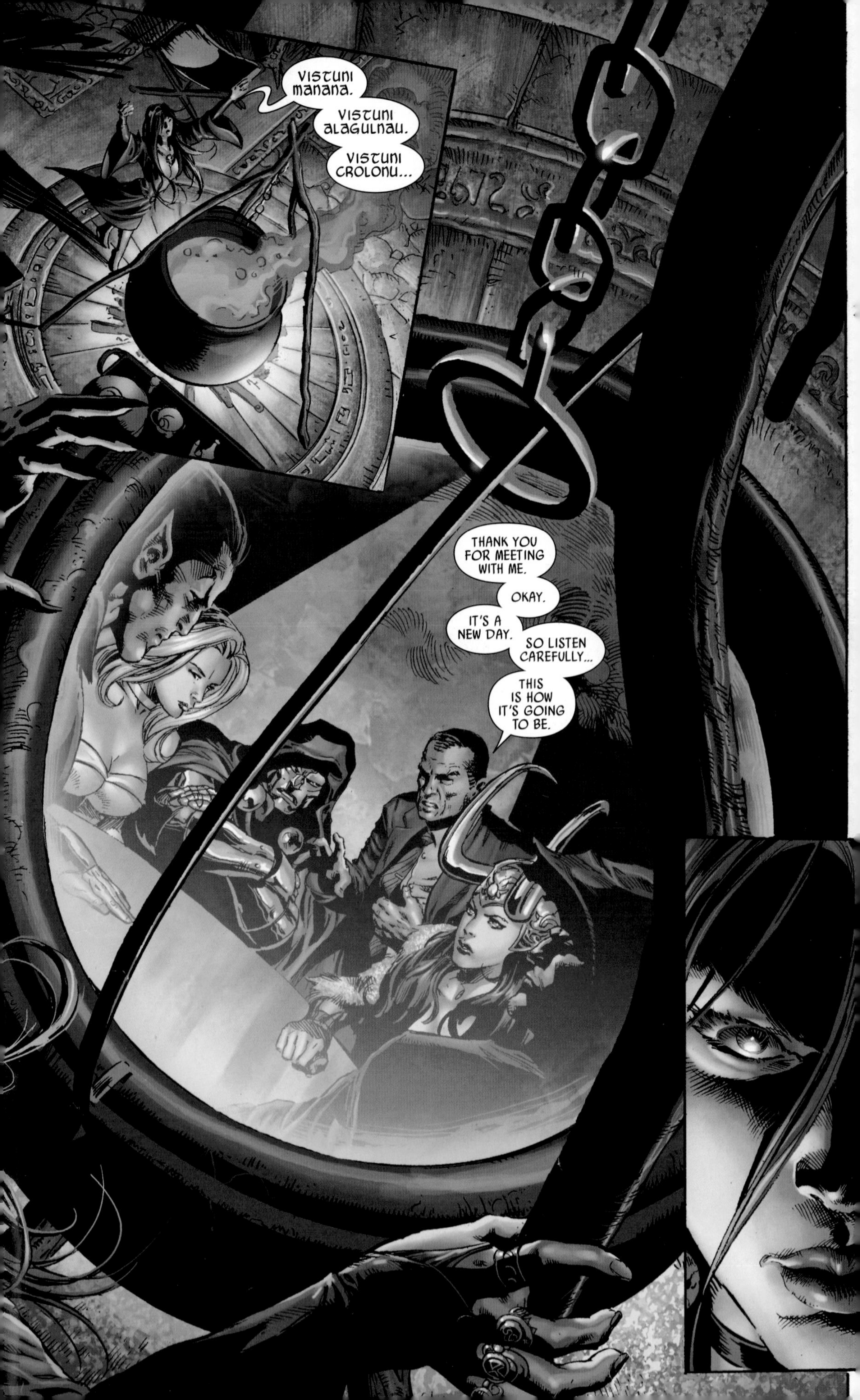
VISTUNI MANANA.
VISTUNI ALAGULNAU.
VISTUNI CROLONU...
THANK YOU FOR MEETING WITH ME.
OKAY.
IT'S A NEW DAY.
SO LISTEN CAREFULLY...
THIS IS HOW IT'S GOING TO BE.

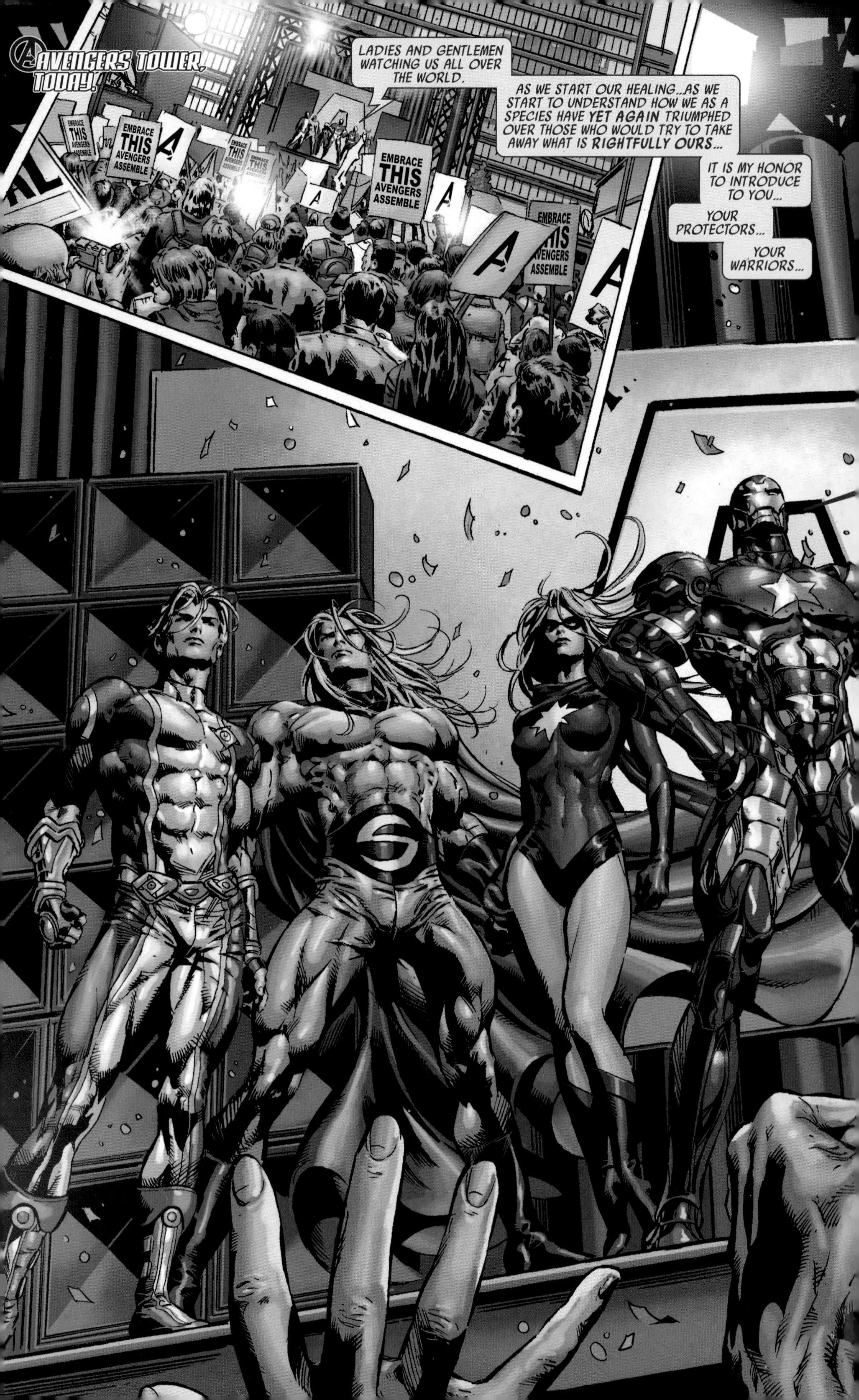
AVENGERS TOWER, TODAY!
LADIES AND GENTLEMEN WATCHING US ALL OVER THE WORLD.
AS WE START OUR HEALING...AS WE START TO UNDERSTAND HOW WE AS A SPECIES HAVE YET AGAIN TRIUMPHED OVER THOSE WHO WOULD TRY TO TAKE AWAY WHAT IS RIGHTFULLY OURS...
IT IS MY HONOR TO INTRODUCE TO YOU...
YOUR PROTECTORS...
YOUR WARRIORS...
EMBRACE THIS AVENGERS ASSEMBLE

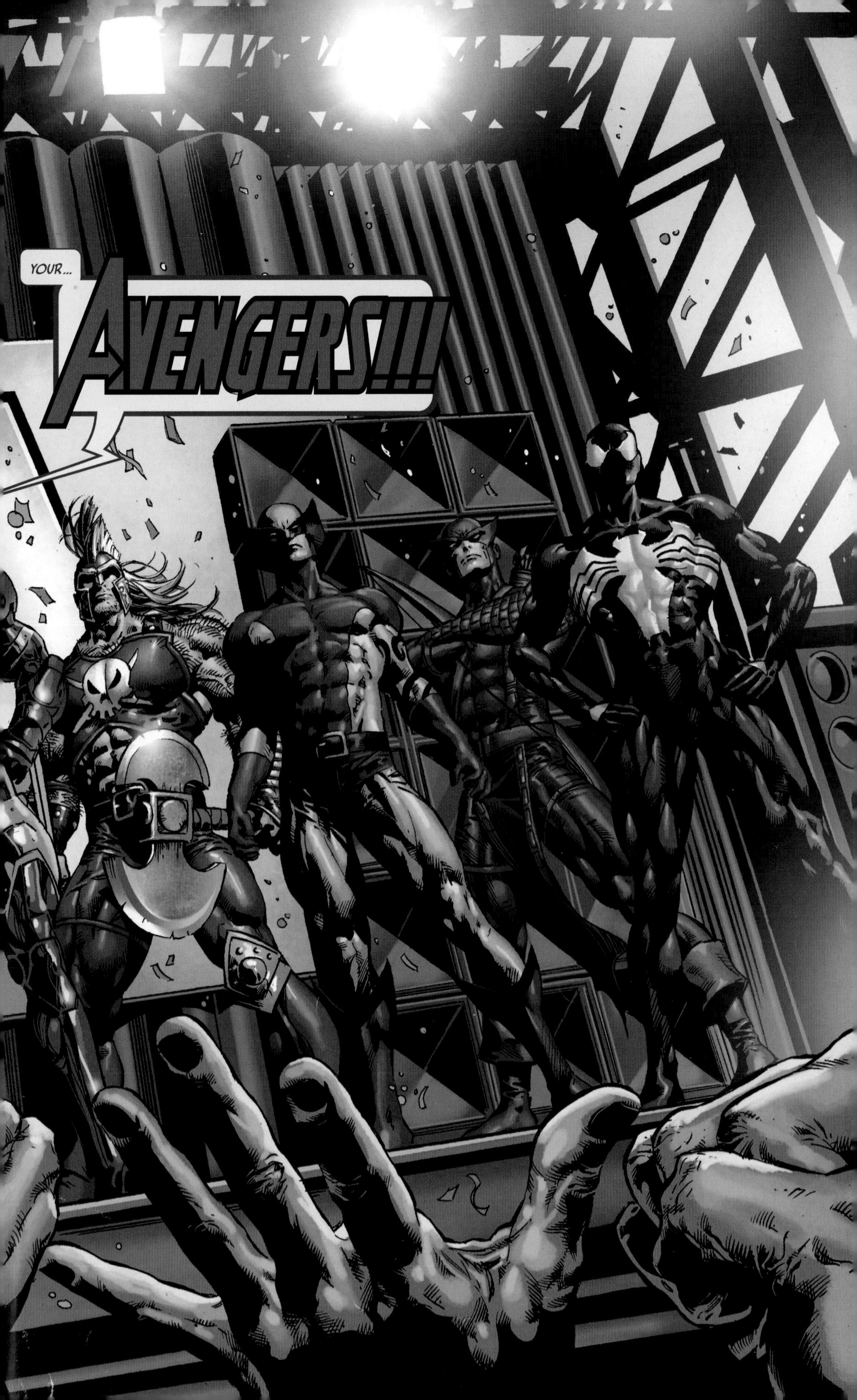
YOUR...
AVENGERS!!!

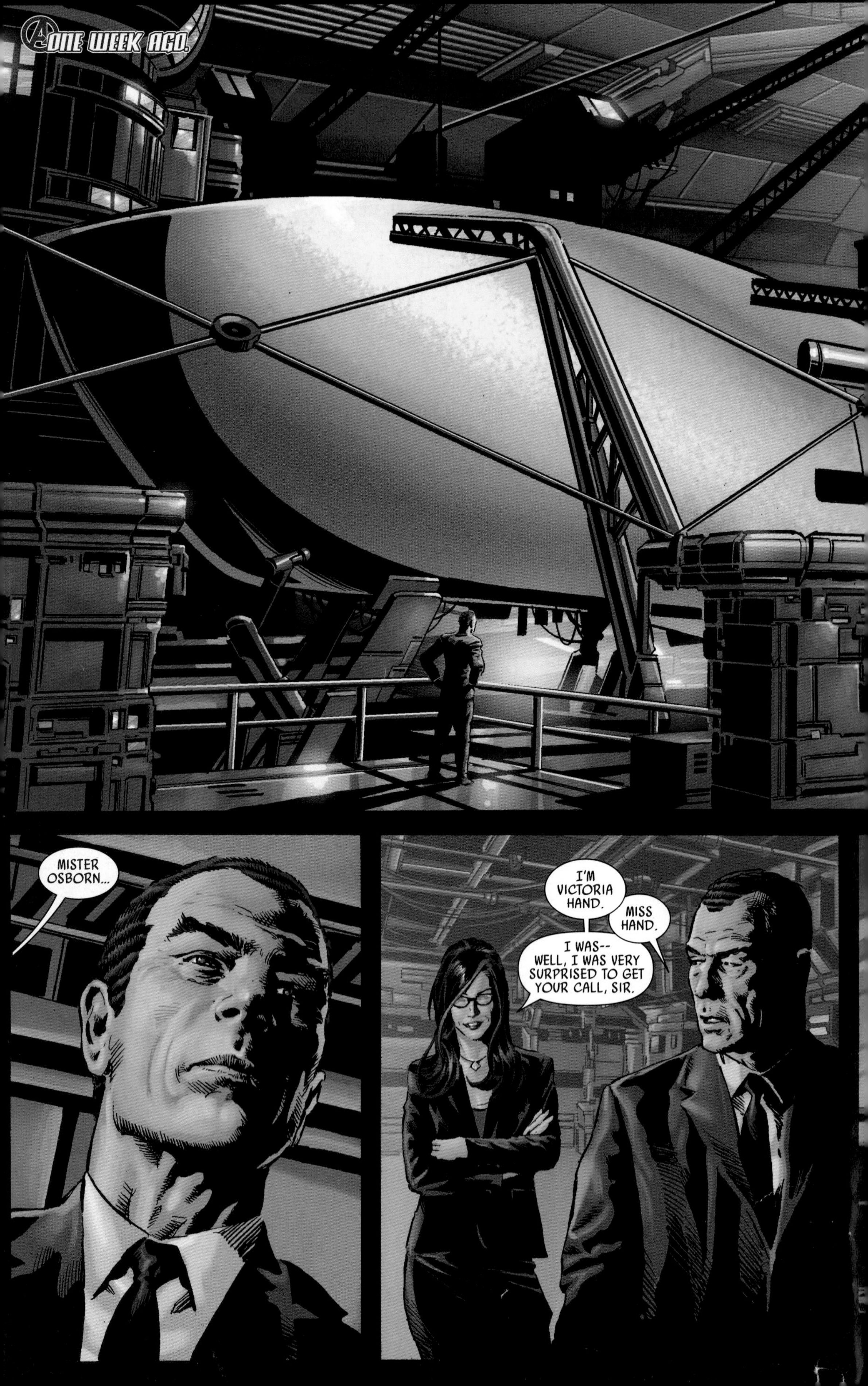
ONE WEEK AGO.
MISTER OSBORN...
I'M VICTORIA HAND.
MISS HAND.
I WAS-- WELL, I WAS VERY SURPRISED TO GET YOUR CALL, SIR.

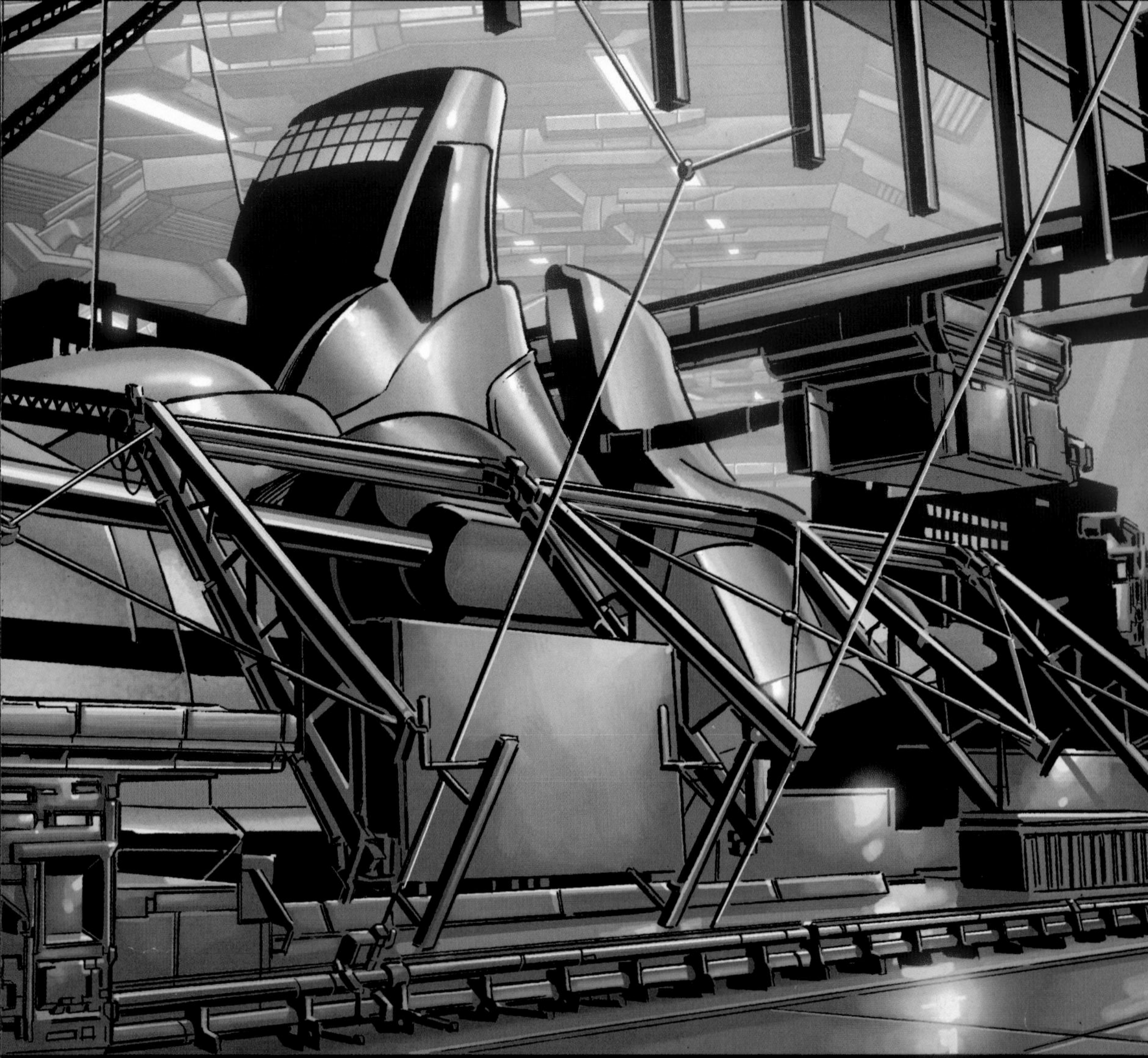

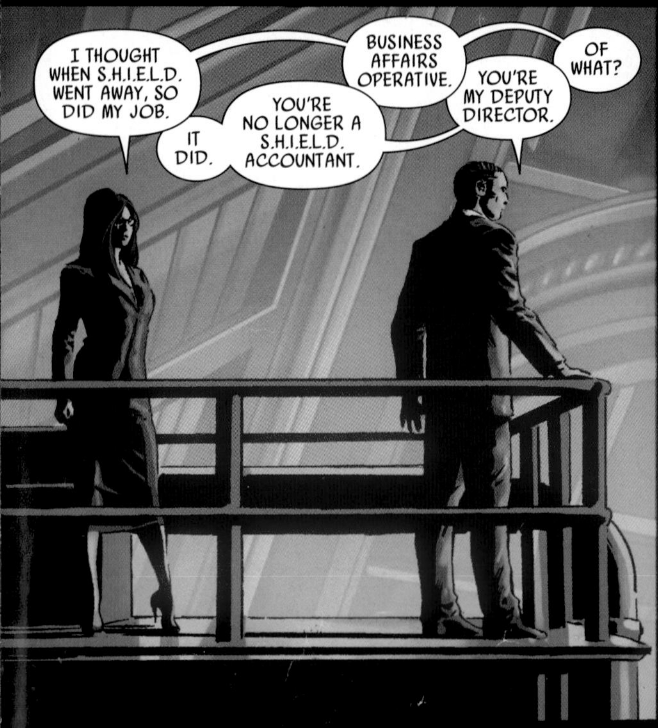
I THOUGHT WHEN S.H.I.E.L.D. WENT AWAY, SO DID MY JOB.
IT DID.
YOU'RE NO LONGER A S.H.I.E.L.D. ACCOUNTANT.
BUSINESS AFFAIRS OPERATIVE.
YOU'RE MY DEPUTY DIRECTOR.
OF WHAT?

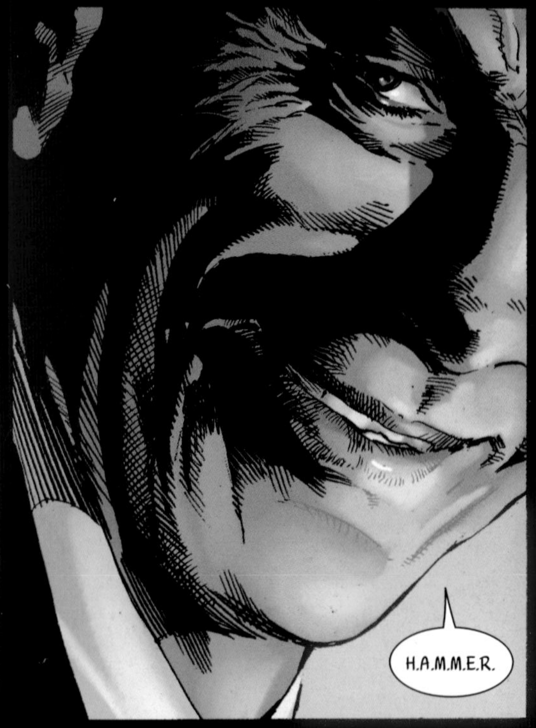
H.A.M.M.E.R.

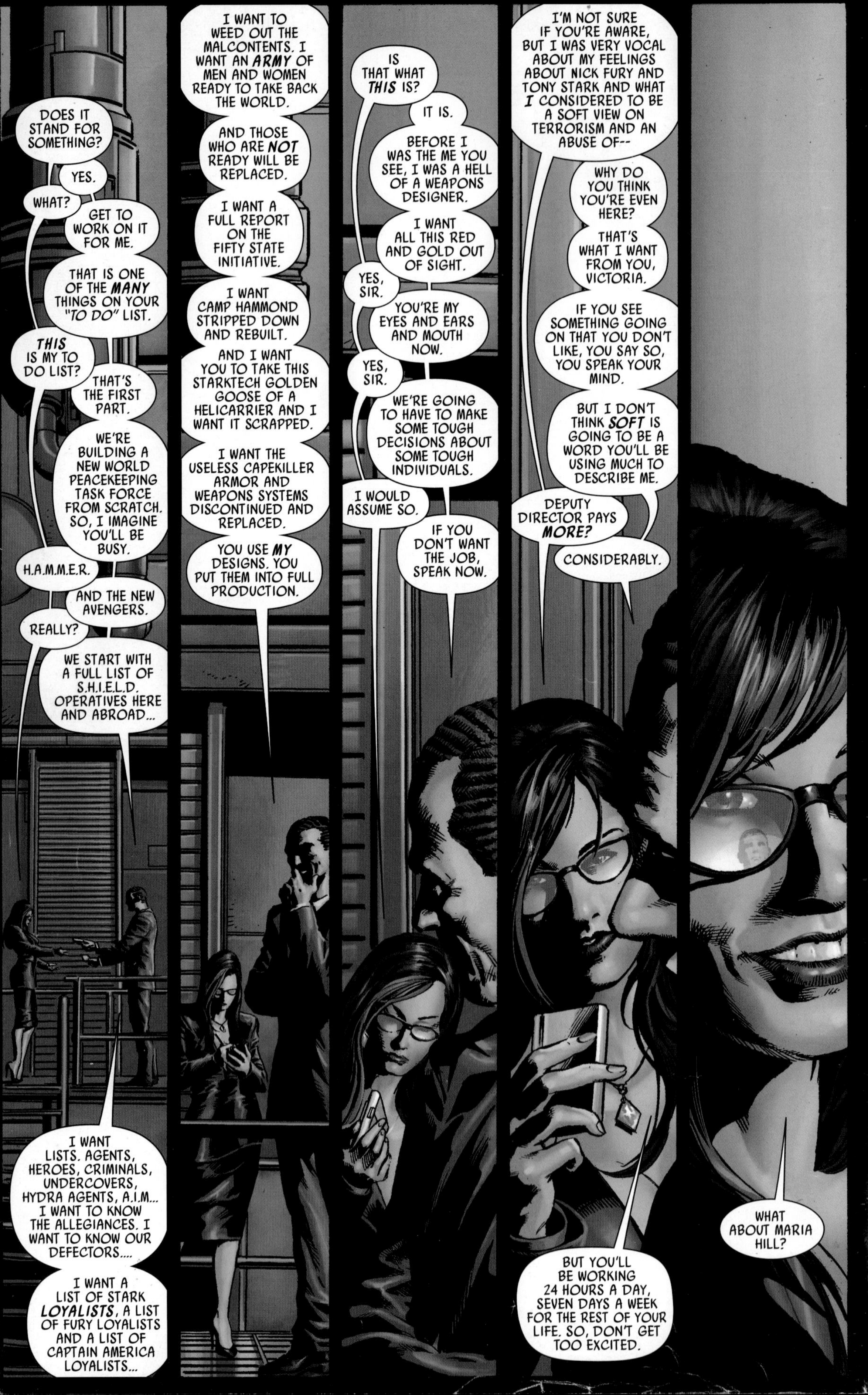
DOES IT STAND FOR SOMETHING?
YES.
WHAT?
GET TO WORK ON IT FOR ME.
THAT IS ONE OF THE MANY THINGS ON YOUR "TO DO" LIST.
THIS IS MY TO DO LIST?
THAT'S THE FIRST PART.
WE'RE BUILDING A NEW WORLD PEACEKEEPING TASK FORCE FROM SCRATCH. SO, I IMAGINE YOU'LL BE BUSY.
H.A.M.M.E.R.
AND THE NEW AVENGERS.
REALLY?
WE START WITH A FULL LIST OF S.H.I.E.L.D. OPERATIVES HERE AND ABROAD...
I WANT LISTS. AGENTS, HEROES, CRIMINALS, UNDERCOVERS, HYDRA AGENTS, A.I.M... I WANT TO KNOW THE ALLEGIANCES. I WANT TO KNOW OUR DEFECTORS....
I WANT A LIST OF STARK LOYALISTS, A LIST OF FURY LOYALISTS AND A LIST OF CAPTAIN AMERICA LOYALISTS...
I WANT TO WEED OUT THE MALCONTENTS. I WANT AN ARMY OF MEN AND WOMEN READY TO TAKE BACK THE WORLD.
AND THOSE WHO ARE NOT READY WILL BE REPLACED.
I WANT A FULL REPORT ON THE FIFTY STATE INITIATIVE.
I WANT CAMP HAMMOND STRIPPED DOWN AND REBUILT.
AND I WANT YOU TO TAKE THIS STARKTECH GOLDEN GOOSE OF A HELICARRIER AND I WANT IT SCRAPPED.
I WANT THE USELESS CAPEKILLER ARMOR AND WEAPONS SYSTEMS DISCONTINUED AND REPLACED.
YOU USE MY DESIGNS. YOU PUT THEM INTO FULL PRODUCTION.
IS THAT WHAT THIS IS?
IT IS.
BEFORE I WAS THE ME YOU SEE, I WAS A HELL OF A WEAPONS DESIGNER.
I WANT ALL THIS RED AND GOLD OUT OF SIGHT.
YES, SIR.
YOU'RE MY EYES AND EARS AND MOUTH NOW.
YES, SIR.
WE'RE GOING TO HAVE TO MAKE SOME TOUGH DECISIONS ABOUT SOME TOUGH INDIVIDUALS.
I WOULD ASSUME SO.
IF YOU DON'T WANT THE JOB, SPEAK NOW.
I'M NOT SURE IF YOU'RE AWARE, BUT I WAS VERY VOCAL ABOUT MY FEELINGS ABOUT NICK FURY AND TONY STARK AND WHAT I CONSIDERED TO BE A SOFT VIEW ON TERRORISM AND AN ABUSE OF--
WHY DO YOU THINK YOU'RE EVEN HERE?
THAT'S WHAT I WANT FROM YOU, VICTORIA.
IF YOU SEE SOMETHING GOING ON THAT YOU DON'T LIKE, YOU SAY SO, YOU SPEAK YOUR MIND.
BUT I DON'T THINK SOFT IS GOING TO BE A WORD YOU'LL BE USING MUCH TO DESCRIBE ME.
DEPUTY DIRECTOR PAYS MORE?
CONSIDERABLY.
BUT YOU'LL BE WORKING 24 HOURS A DAY, SEVEN DAYS A WEEK FOR THE REST OF YOUR LIFE. SO, DON'T GET TOO EXCITED.
WHAT ABOUT MARIA HILL?

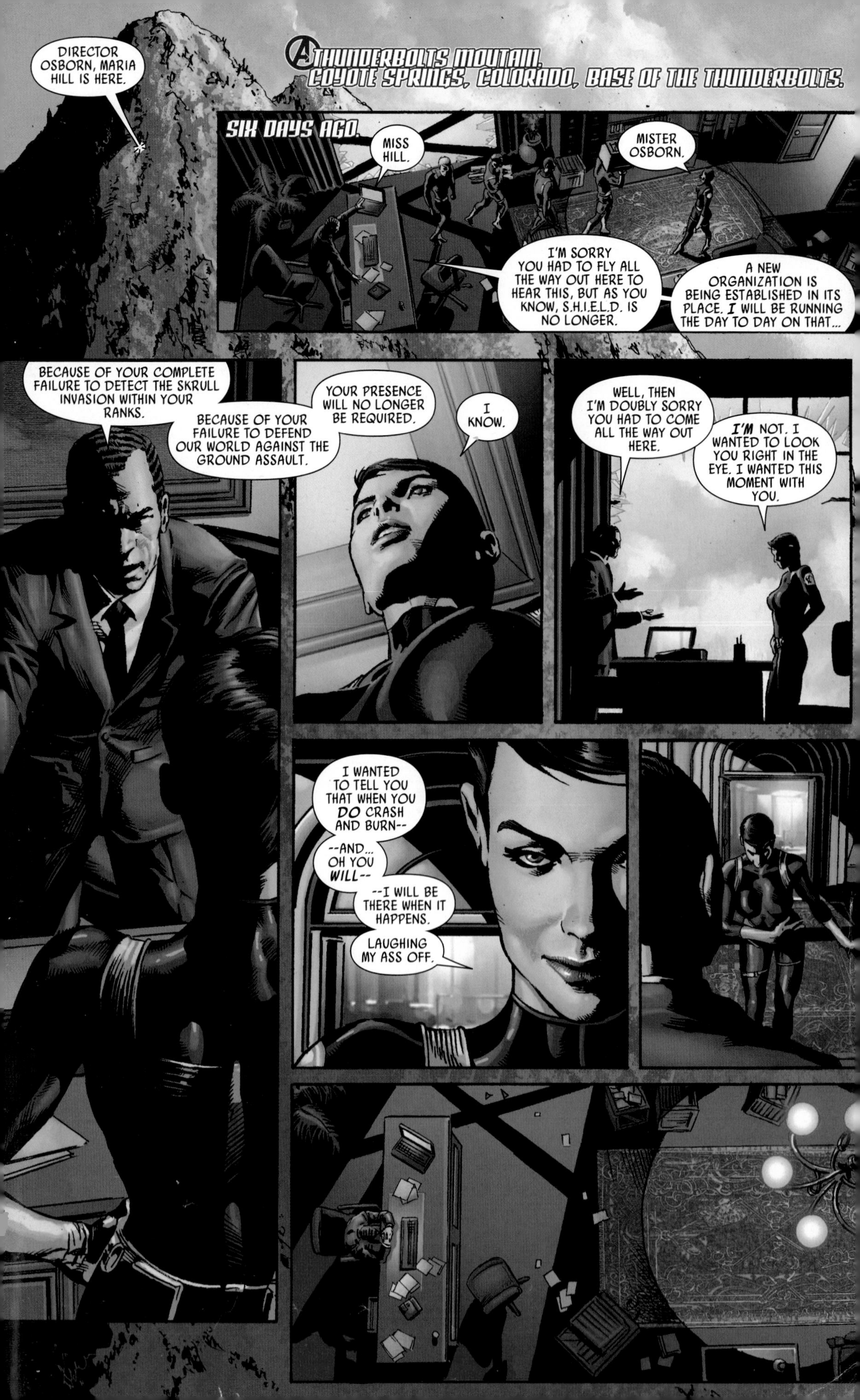

DIRECTOR OSBORN, MARIA HILL IS HERE.
THUNDERBOLTS MOUTAIN. COYOTE SPRINGS, COLORADO, BASE OF THE THUNDERBOLTS.
SIX DAYS AGO.
MISS HILL.
MISTER OSBORN.
I'M SORRY YOU HAD TO FLY ALL THE WAY OUT HERE TO HEAR THIS, BUT AS YOU KNOW, S.H.I.E.L.D. IS NO LONGER.
A NEW ORGANIZATION IS BEING ESTABLISHED IN ITS PLACE. I WILL BE RUNNING THE DAY TO DAY ON THAT...
BECAUSE OF YOUR COMPLETE FAILURE TO DETECT THE SKRULL INVASION WITHIN YOUR RANKS.
BECAUSE OF YOUR FAILURE TO DEFEND OUR WORLD AGAINST THE GROUND ASSAULT.
YOUR PRESENCE WILL NO LONGER BE REQUIRED.
I KNOW.
WELL, THEN I'M DOUBLY SORRY YOU HAD TO COME ALL THE WAY OUT HERE.
I'M NOT. I WANTED TO LOOK YOU RIGHT IN THE EYE. I WANTED THIS MOMENT WITH YOU.
I WANTED TO TELL YOU THAT WHEN YOU DO CRASH AND BURN--
--AND... OH YOU WILL--
--I WILL BE THERE WHEN IT HAPPENS.
LAUGHING MY ASS OFF.

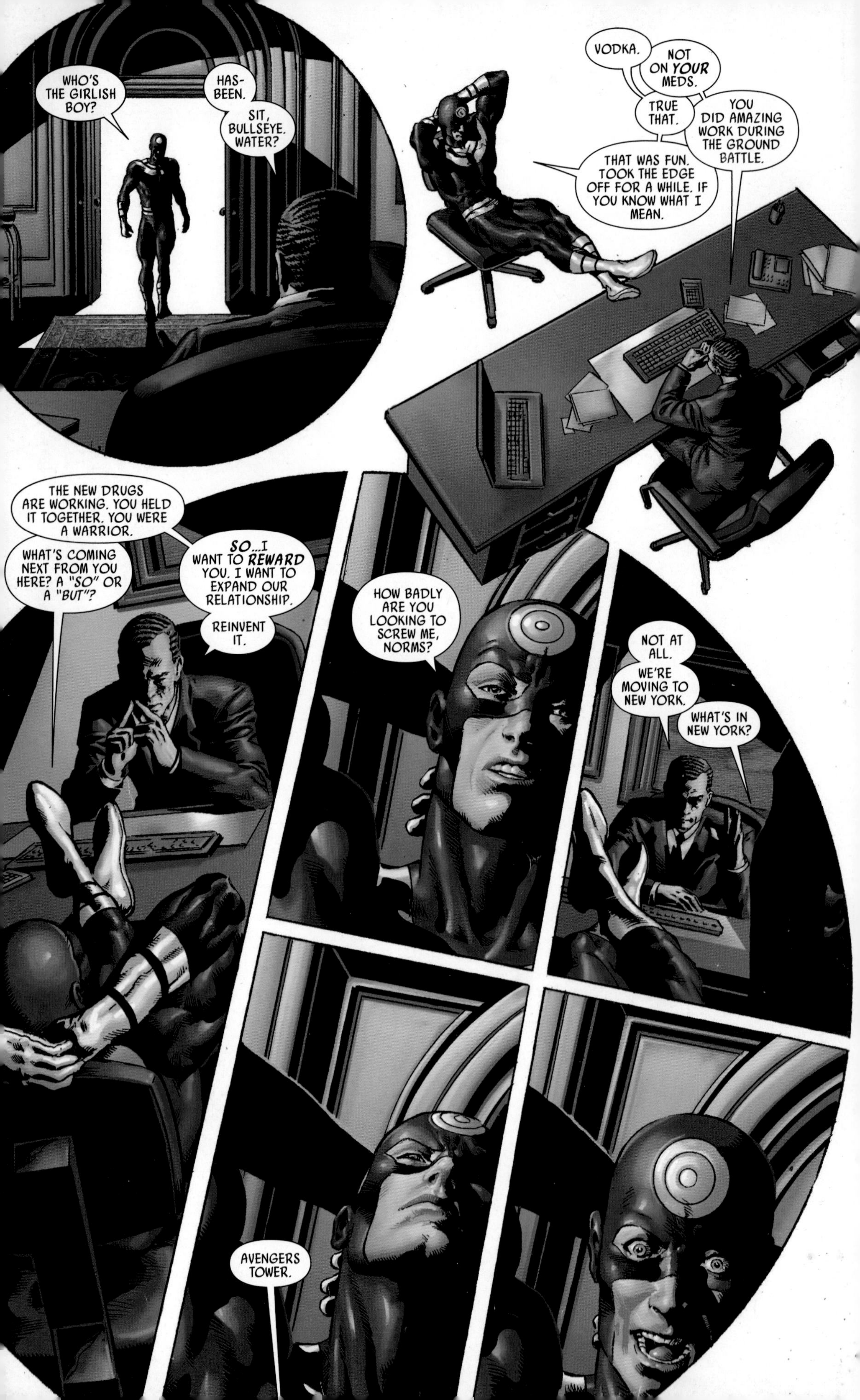
WHO'S THE GIRLISH BOY?
HAS-BEEN.
SIT, BULLSEYE. WATER?
VODKA.
NOT ON YOUR MEDS.
TRUE THAT.
YOU DID AMAZING WORK DURING THE GROUND BATTLE.
THAT WAS FUN. TOOK THE EDGE OFF FOR A WHILE. IF YOU KNOW WHAT I MEAN.
THE NEW DRUGS ARE WORKING. YOU HELD IT TOGETHER. YOU WERE A WARRIOR.
WHAT'S COMING NEXT FROM YOU HERE? A "SO" OR A "BUT"?
SO...I WANT TO REWARD YOU. I WANT TO EXPAND OUR RELATIONSHIP.
REINVENT IT.
HOW BADLY ARE YOU LOOKING TO SCREW ME, NORMS?
NOT AT ALL.
WE'RE MOVING TO NEW YORK.
WHAT'S IN NEW YORK?
AVENGERS TOWER.

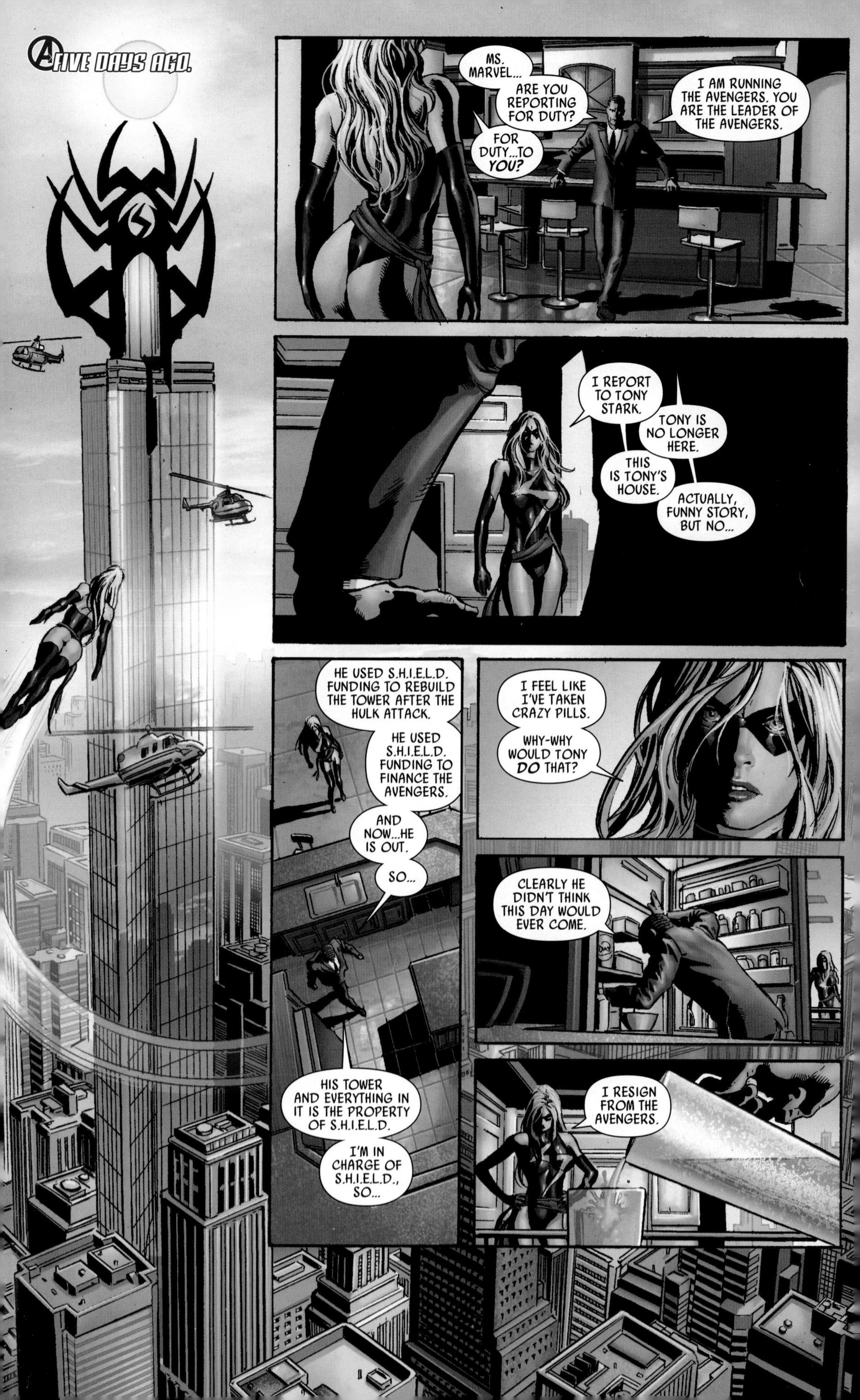
FIVE DAYS AGO.
MS. MARVEL...
ARE YOU REPORTING FOR DUTY?
FOR DUTY...TO YOU?
I AM RUNNING THE AVENGERS. YOU ARE THE LEADER OF THE AVENGERS.
I REPORT TO TONY STARK.
TONY IS NO LONGER HERE.
THIS IS TONY'S HOUSE.
ACTUALLY, FUNNY STORY, BUT NO...
HE USED S.H.I.E.L.D. FUNDING TO REBUILD THE TOWER AFTER THE HULK ATTACK.
HE USED S.H.I.E.L.D. FUNDING TO FINANCE THE AVENGERS.
AND NOW...HE IS OUT.
SO...
HIS TOWER AND EVERYTHING IN IT IS THE PROPERTY OF S.H.I.E.L.D.
I'M IN CHARGE OF S.H.I.E.L.D., SO...
I FEEL LIKE I'VE TAKEN CRAZY PILLS.
WHY-WHY WOULD TONY DO THAT?
CLEARLY HE DIDN'T THINK THIS DAY WOULD EVER COME.
I RESIGN FROM THE AVENGERS.

YOU ARE REGISTERED, YOU ARE MILITARY...

I HAVE THE RIGHT TO *ORDER* YOU TO TAKE YOUR POSITION, CAPTAIN.

THEN YOU ARE UNDER ARREST.

I RESIGN FROM THE AVENGERS.

NO ONE WORTH A *DAMN* WILL SIDE WITH YOU, NORMAN.

THERE WILL *BE NO* AVENGERS.

NONE.

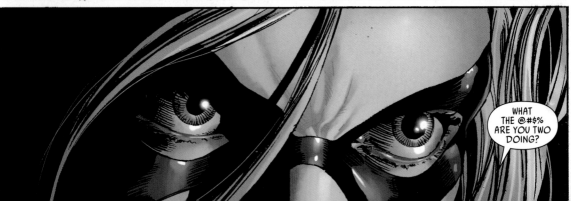

WHAT THE @#$% ARE YOU TWO DOING?

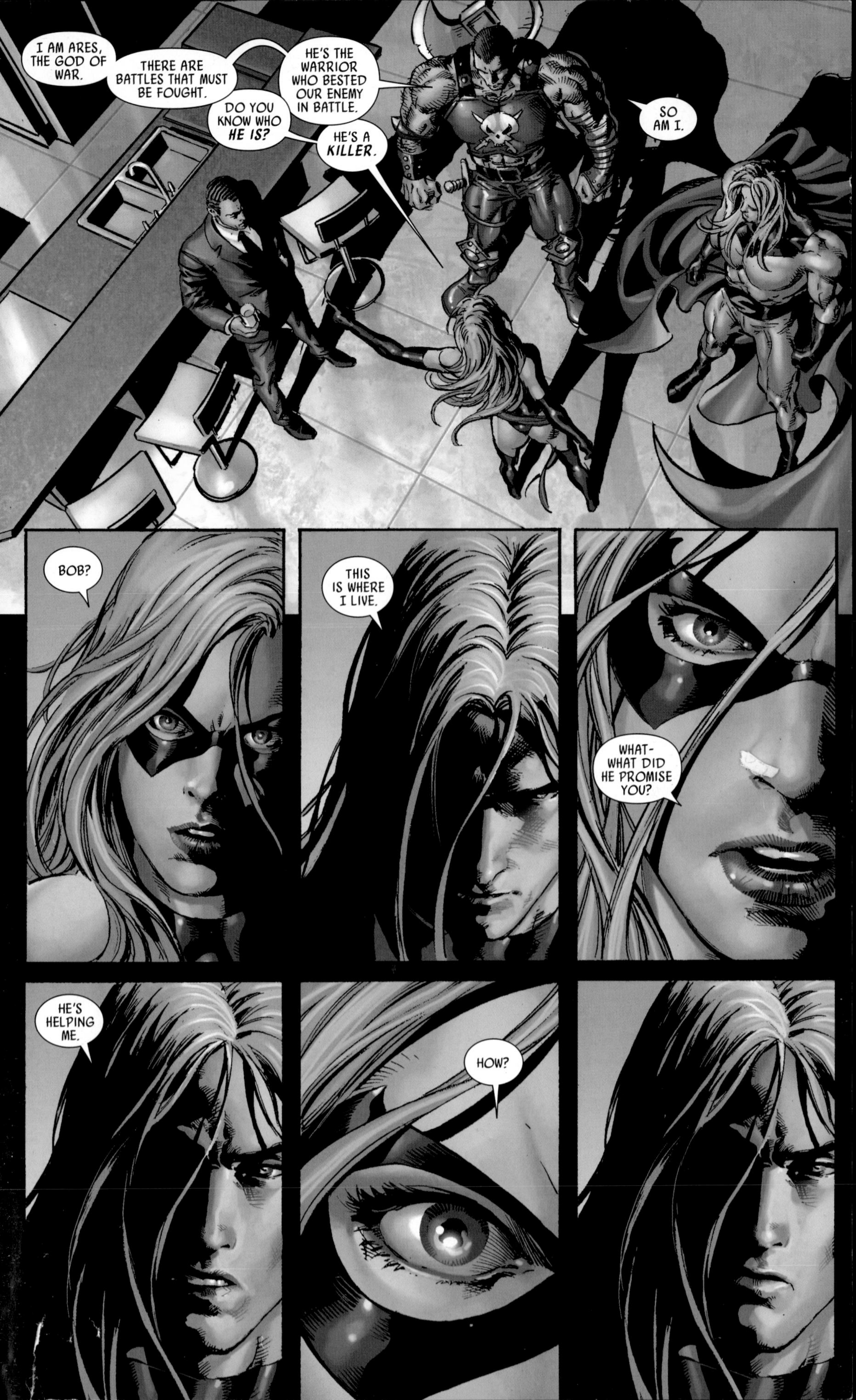
I AM ARES, THE GOD OF WAR.
THERE ARE BATTLES THAT MUST BE FOUGHT.
DO YOU KNOW WHO HE IS?
HE'S THE WARRIOR WHO BESTED OUR ENEMY IN BATTLE.
HE'S A KILLER.
SO AM I.
BOB?
THIS IS WHERE I LIVE.
WHAT- WHAT DID HE PROMISE YOU?
HE'S HELPING ME.
HOW?

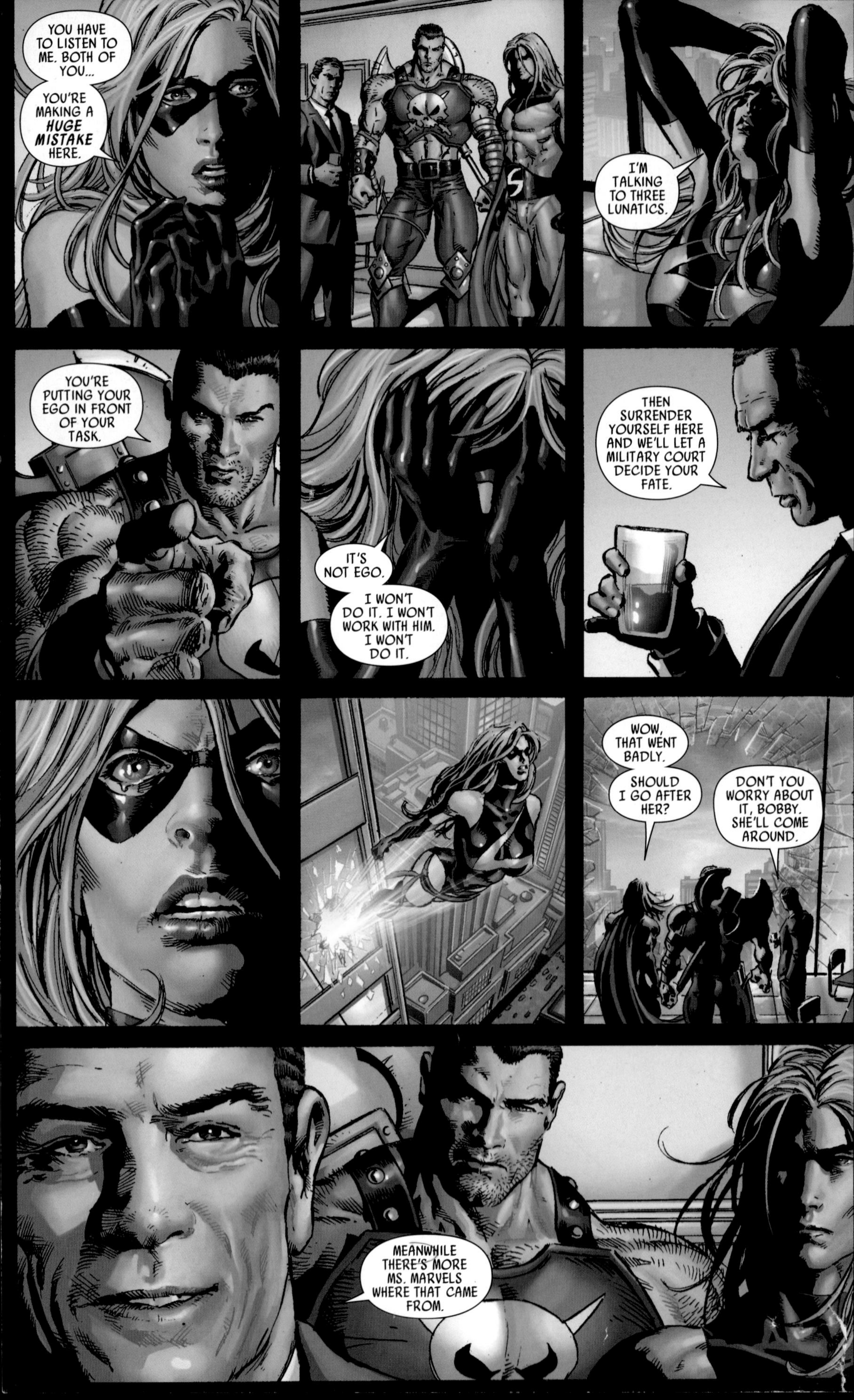
YOU HAVE TO LISTEN TO ME. BOTH OF YOU...
YOU'RE MAKING A *HUGE MISTAKE* HERE.
I'M TALKING TO THREE LUNATICS.
YOU'RE PUTTING YOUR EGO IN FRONT OF YOUR TASK.
IT'S NOT EGO.
I WON'T DO IT. I WON'T WORK WITH HIM. I WON'T DO IT.
THEN SURRENDER YOURSELF HERE AND WE'LL LET A MILITARY COURT DECIDE YOUR FATE.
WOW, THAT WENT BADLY.
SHOULD I GO AFTER HER?
DON'T YOU WORRY ABOUT IT, BOBBY. SHE'LL COME AROUND.
MEANWHILE THERE'S MORE MS. MARVELS WHERE THAT CAME FROM.

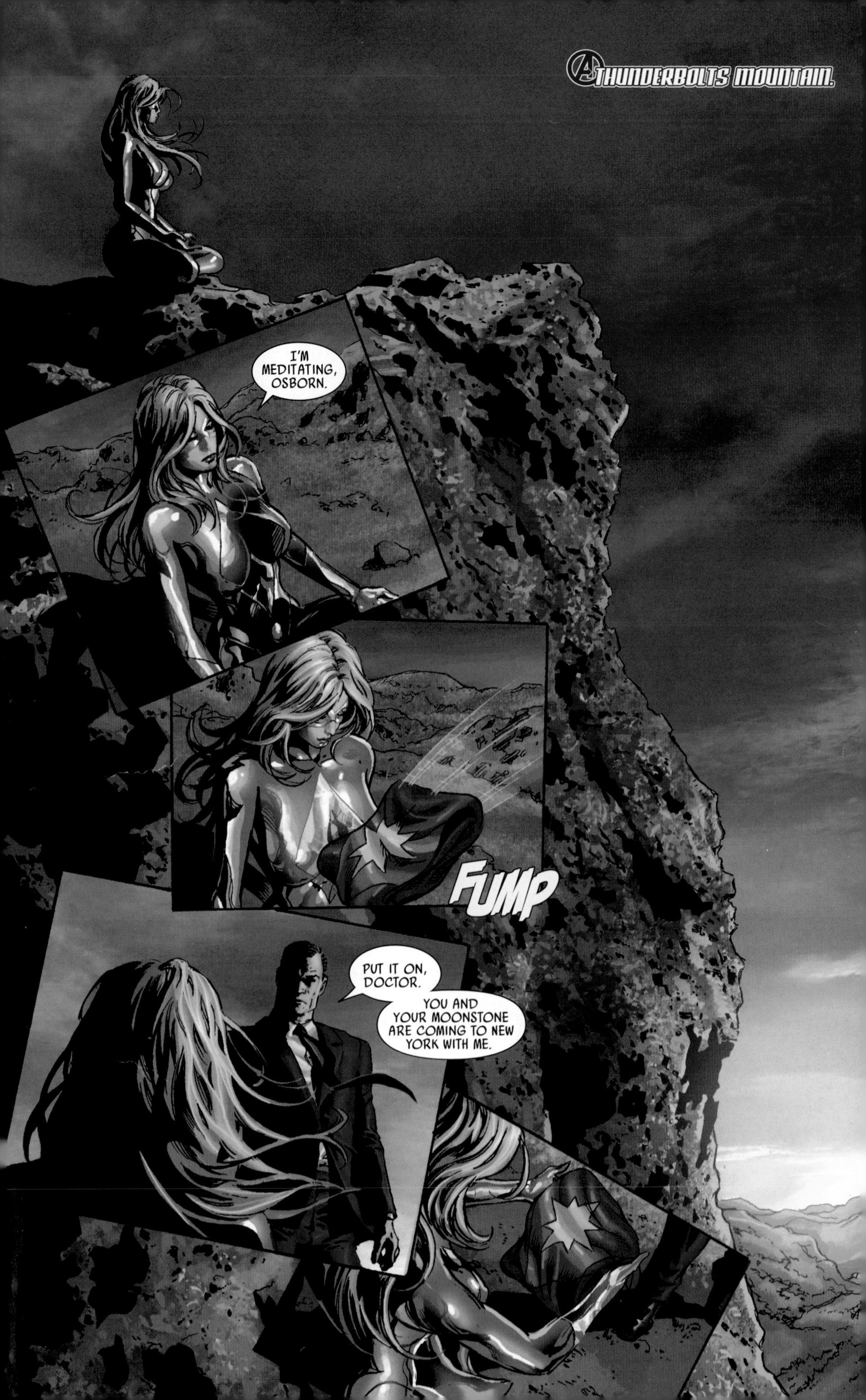
THUNDERBOLTS MOUNTAIN.
I'M MEDITATING, OSBORN.
FUMP
PUT IT ON, DOCTOR.
YOU AND YOUR MOONSTONE ARE COMING TO NEW YORK WITH ME.

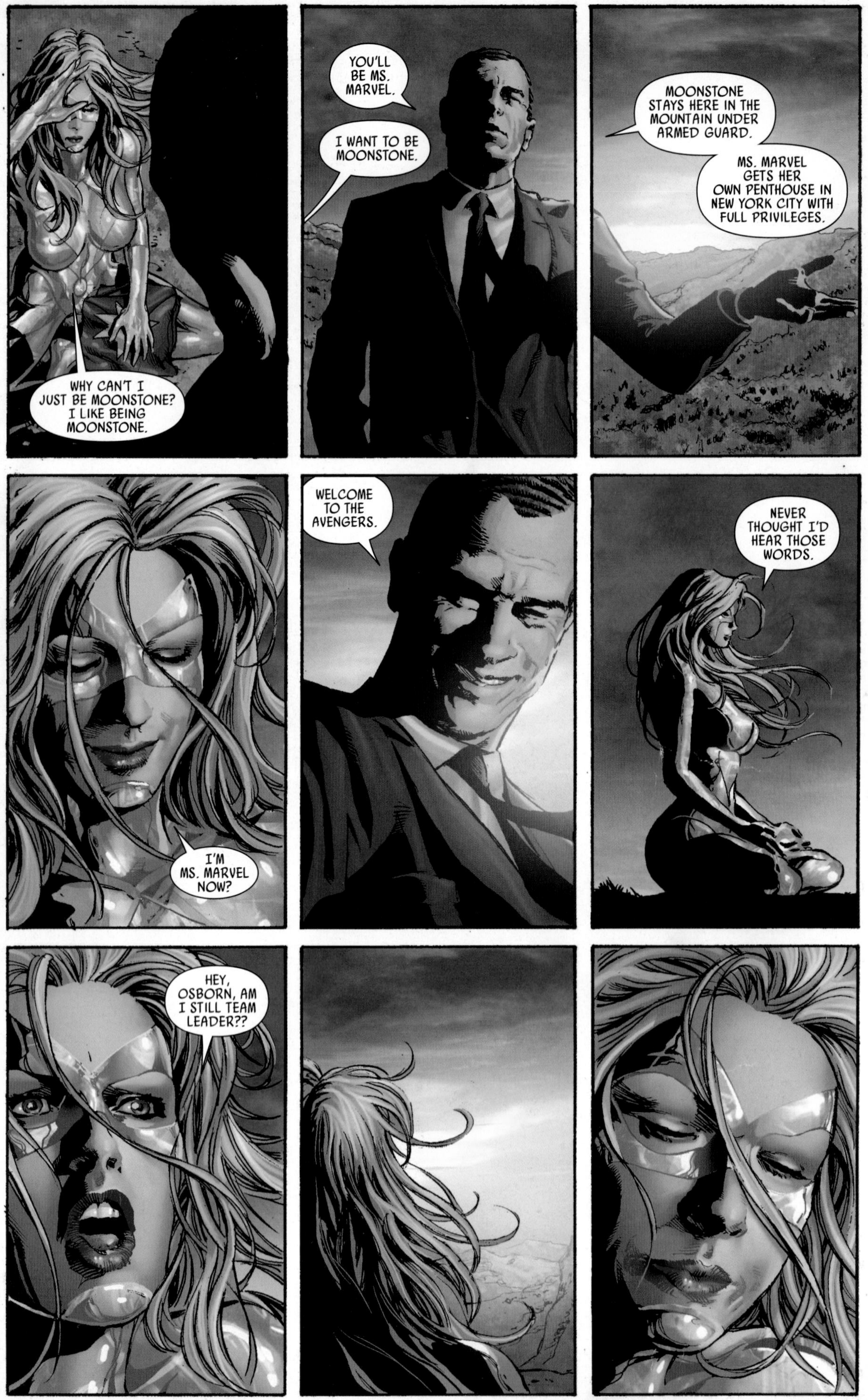
WHY CAN'T I JUST BE MOONSTONE? I LIKE BEING MOONSTONE.
YOU'LL BE MS. MARVEL.
I WANT TO BE MOONSTONE.
MOONSTONE STAYS HERE IN THE MOUNTAIN UNDER ARMED GUARD.
MS. MARVEL GETS HER OWN PENTHOUSE IN NEW YORK CITY WITH FULL PRIVILEGES.
I'M MS. MARVEL NOW?
WELCOME TO THE AVENGERS.
NEVER THOUGHT I'D HEAR THOSE WORDS.
HEY, OSBORN, AM I STILL TEAM LEADER??

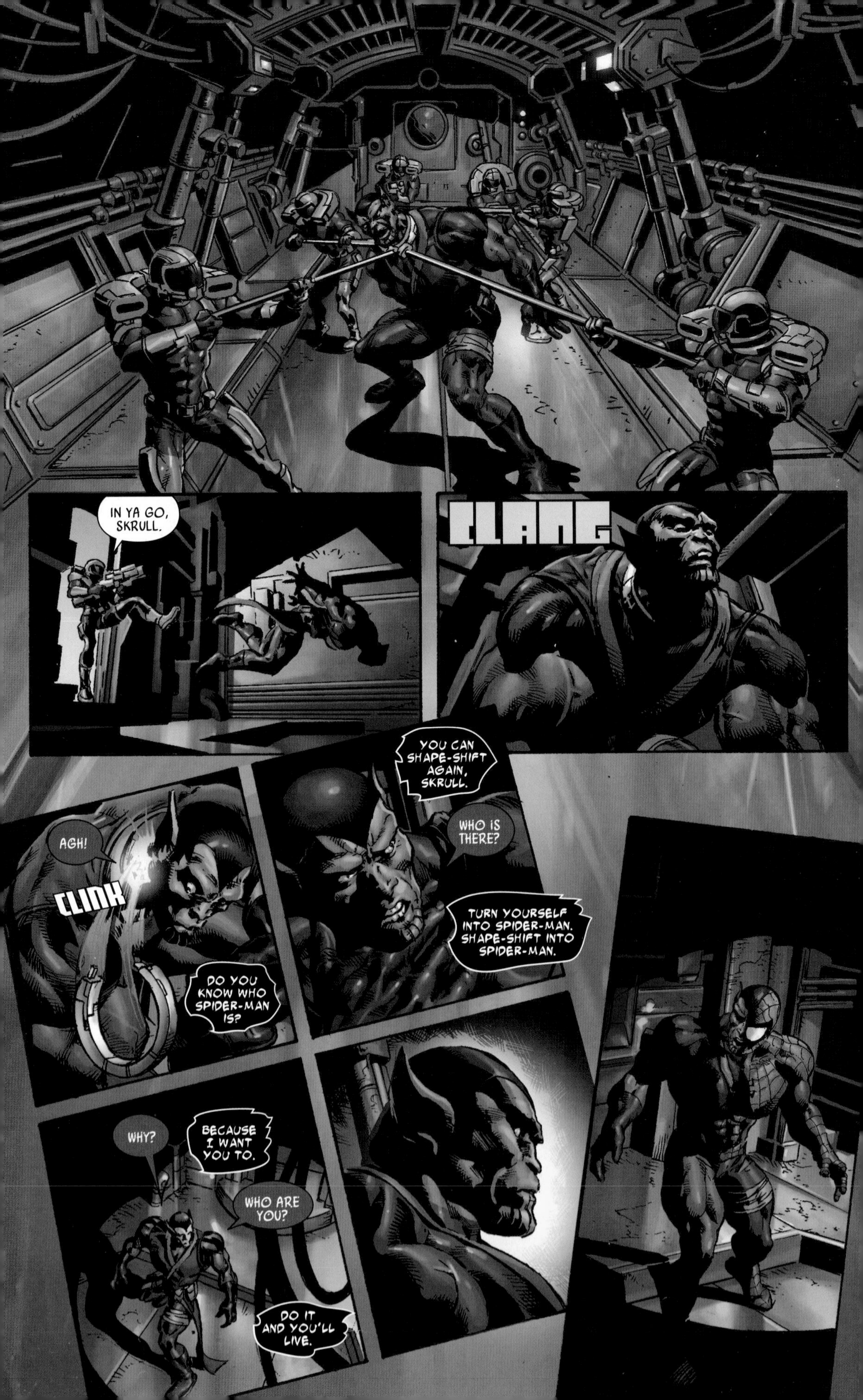

IN YA GO, SKRULL.
CLANG
AGH!
CLINK
DO YOU KNOW WHO SPIDER-MAN IS?
YOU CAN SHAPE-SHIFT AGAIN, SKRULL.
WHO IS THERE?
TURN YOURSELF INTO SPIDER-MAN. SHAPE-SHIFT INTO SPIDER-MAN.
WHY?
BECAUSE I WANT YOU TO.
WHO ARE YOU?
DO IT AND YOU'LL LIVE.

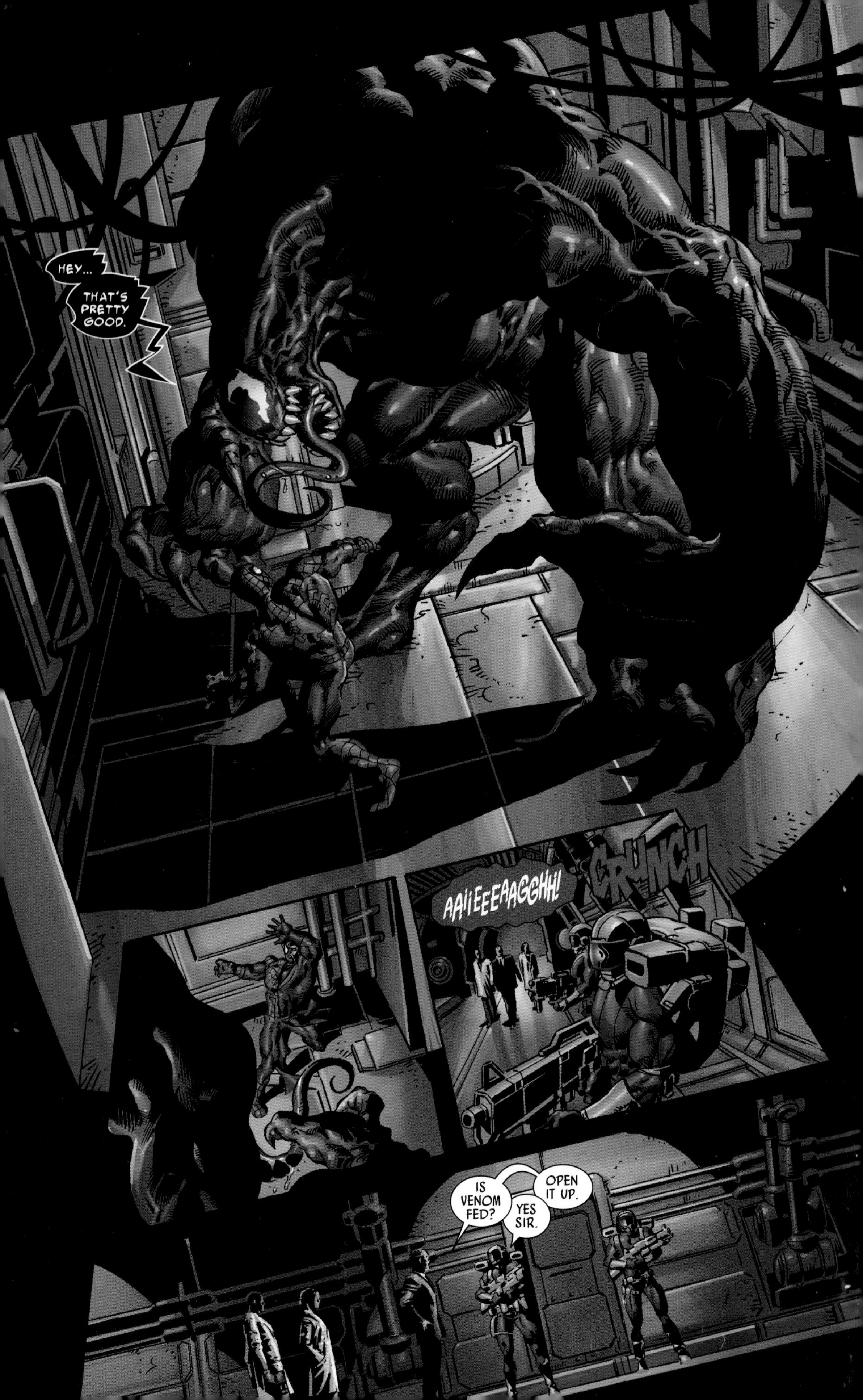
HEY...
THAT'S PRETTY GOOD.
AAIIEEEAAGGHH!
CRUNCH
IS VENOM FED?
OPEN IT UP.
YES SIR.

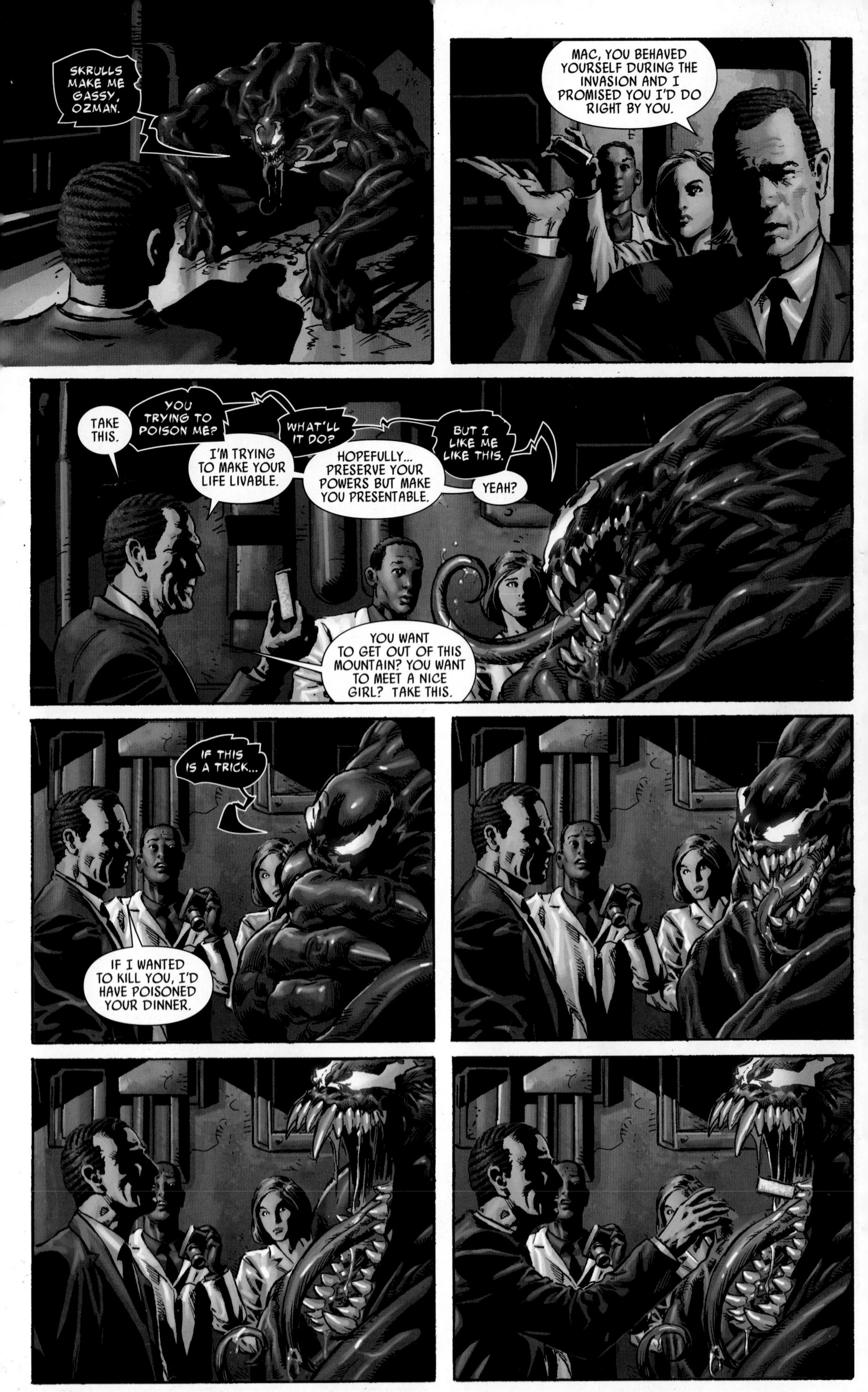
SKRULLS MAKE ME GASSY, OZMAN.
MAC, YOU BEHAVED YOURSELF DURING THE INVASION AND I PROMISED YOU I'D DO RIGHT BY YOU.
TAKE THIS.
YOU TRYING TO POISON ME?
I'M TRYING TO MAKE YOUR LIFE LIVABLE.
WHAT'LL IT DO?
HOPEFULLY... PRESERVE YOUR POWERS BUT MAKE YOU PRESENTABLE.
BUT I LIKE ME LIKE THIS.
YEAH?
YOU WANT TO GET OUT OF THIS MOUNTAIN? YOU WANT TO MEET A NICE GIRL? TAKE THIS.
IF THIS IS A TRICK...
IF I WANTED TO KILL YOU, I'D HAVE POISONED YOUR DINNER.

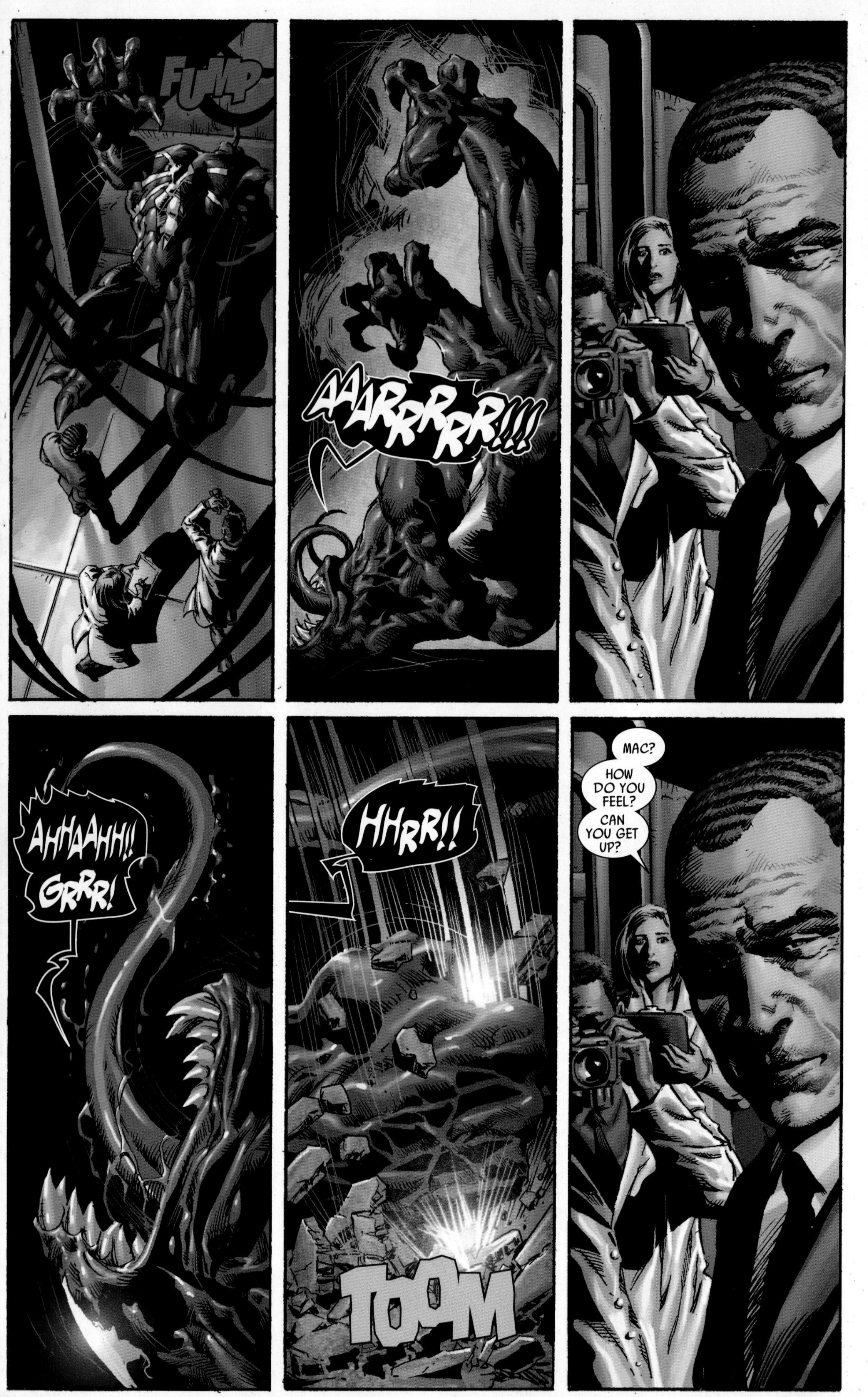
FUMP
AAARRRRRR!!!
AHHAAHH!! GRRR!
HHRR!!
TOOM
MAC?
HOW DO YOU FEEL?
CAN YOU GET UP?

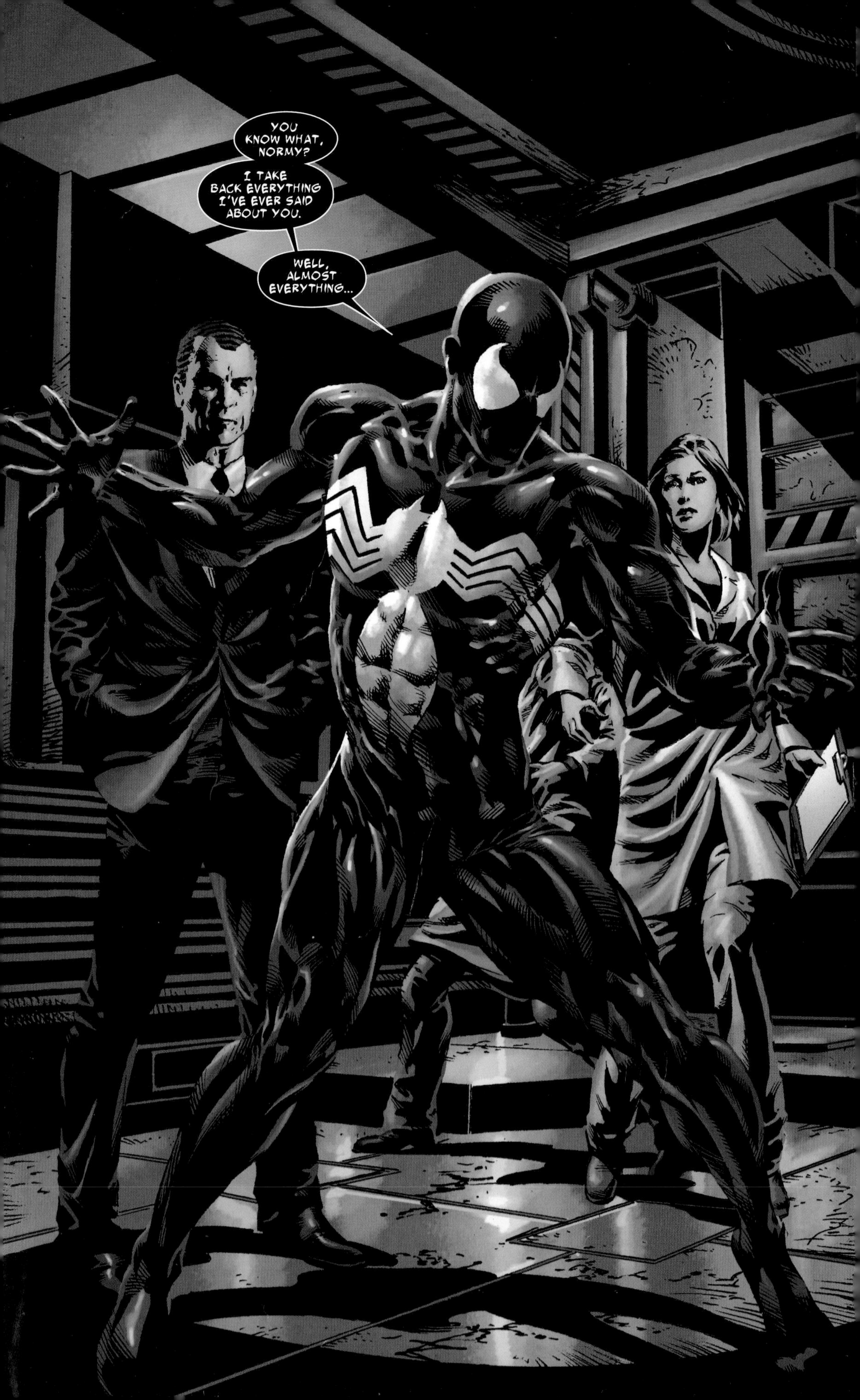
YOU KNOW WHAT, NORMY?
I TAKE BACK EVERYTHING I'VE EVER SAID ABOUT YOU.
WELL, ALMOST EVERYTHING...

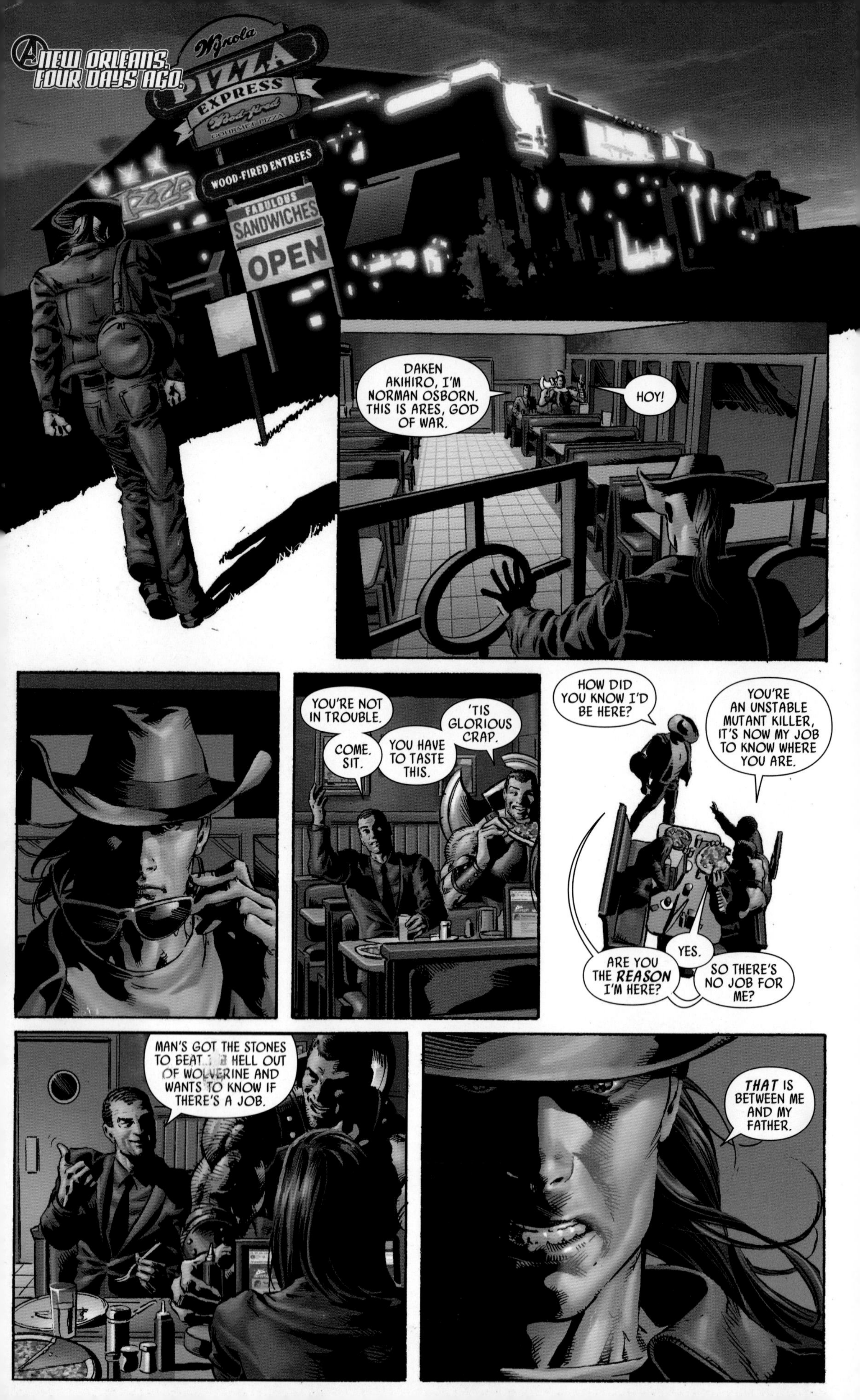
NEW ORLEANS, FOUR DAYS AGO.
Wyrola PIZZA EXPRESS
Wood-fired GOURMET PIZZA
WOOD-FIRED ENTREES
FABULOUS SANDWICHES
OPEN
DAKEN AKIHIRO, I'M NORMAN OSBORN. THIS IS ARES, GOD OF WAR.
HOY!
YOU'RE NOT IN TROUBLE.
COME. SIT.
YOU HAVE TO TASTE THIS.
'TIS GLORIOUS CRAP.
HOW DID YOU KNOW I'D BE HERE?
YOU'RE AN UNSTABLE MUTANT KILLER, IT'S NOW MY JOB TO KNOW WHERE YOU ARE.
ARE YOU THE REASON I'M HERE?
YES.
SO THERE'S NO JOB FOR ME?
MAN'S GOT THE STONES TO BEAT THE HELL OUT OF WOLVERINE AND WANTS TO KNOW IF THERE'S A JOB.
THAT IS BETWEEN ME AND MY FATHER.

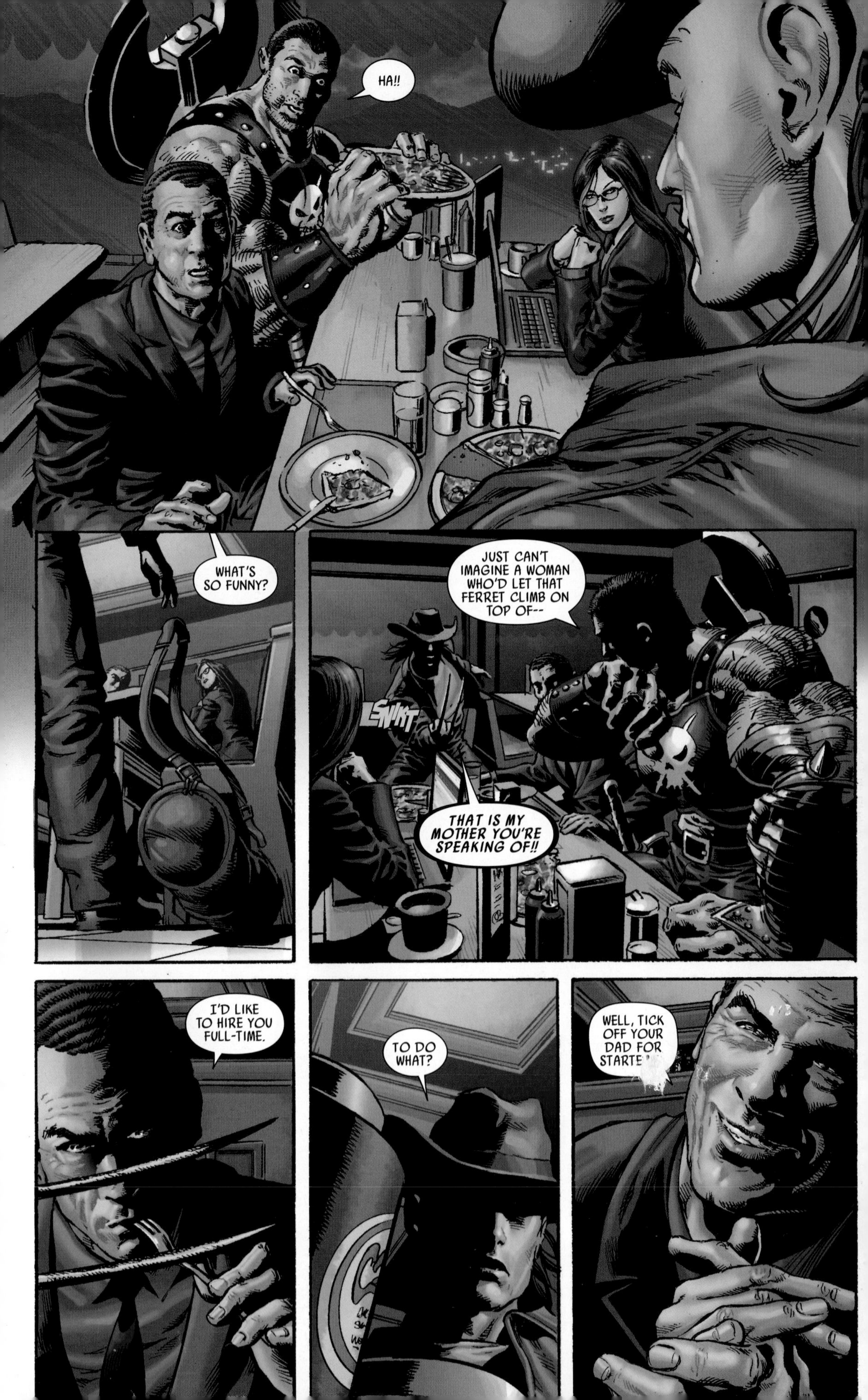
HA!!
WHAT'S SO FUNNY?
JUST CAN'T IMAGINE A WOMAN WHO'D LET THAT FERRET CLIMB ON TOP OF--
SNIKT
THAT IS MY MOTHER YOU'RE SPEAKING OF!!
I'D LIKE TO HIRE YOU FULL-TIME.
TO DO WHAT?
WELL, TICK OFF YOUR DAD FOR STARTE

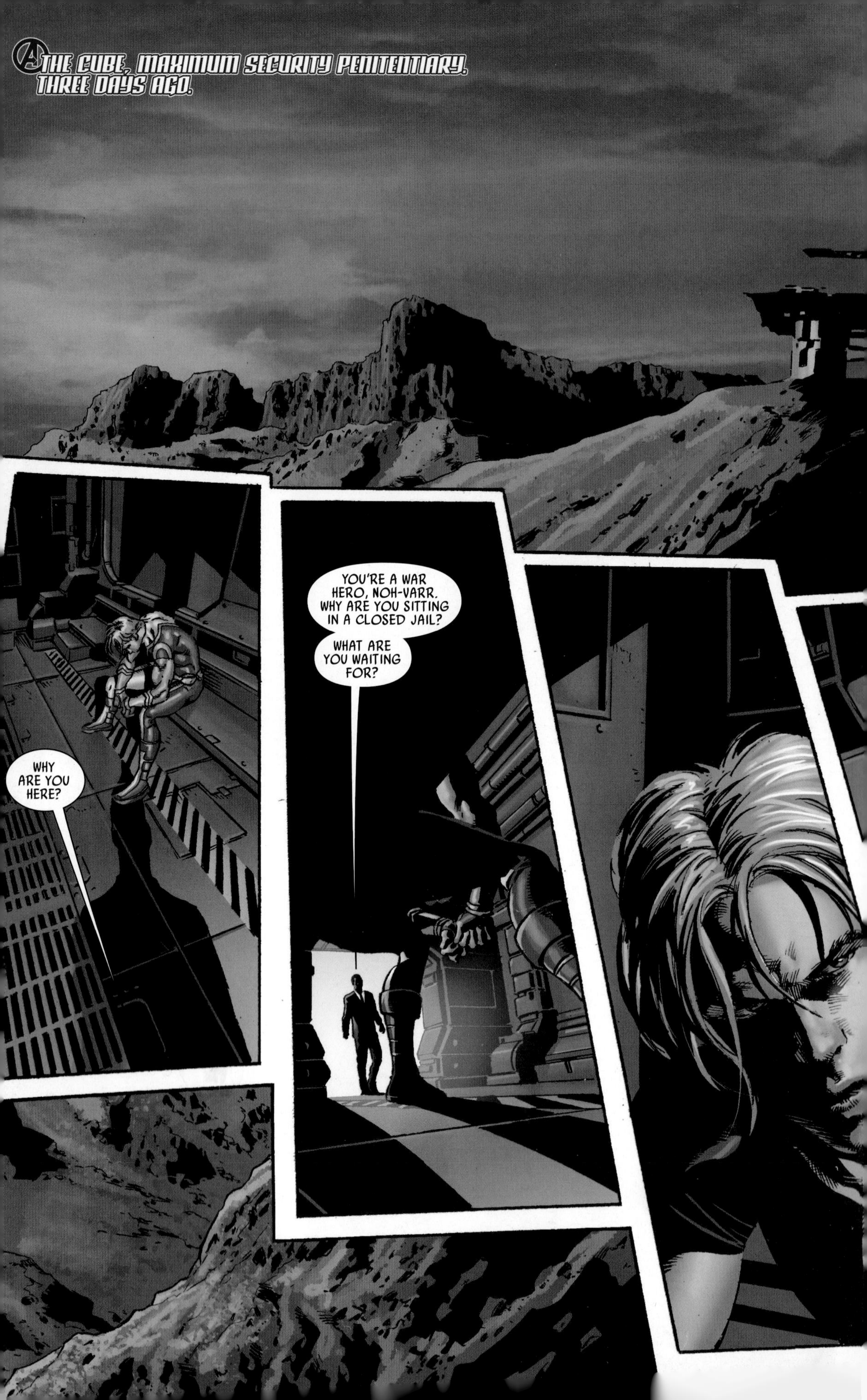
THE CUBE, MAXIMUM SECURITY PENITENTIARY. THREE DAYS AGO.
WHY ARE YOU HERE?
YOU'RE A WAR HERO, NOH-VARR. WHY ARE YOU SITTING IN A CLOSED JAIL?
WHAT ARE YOU WAITING FOR?

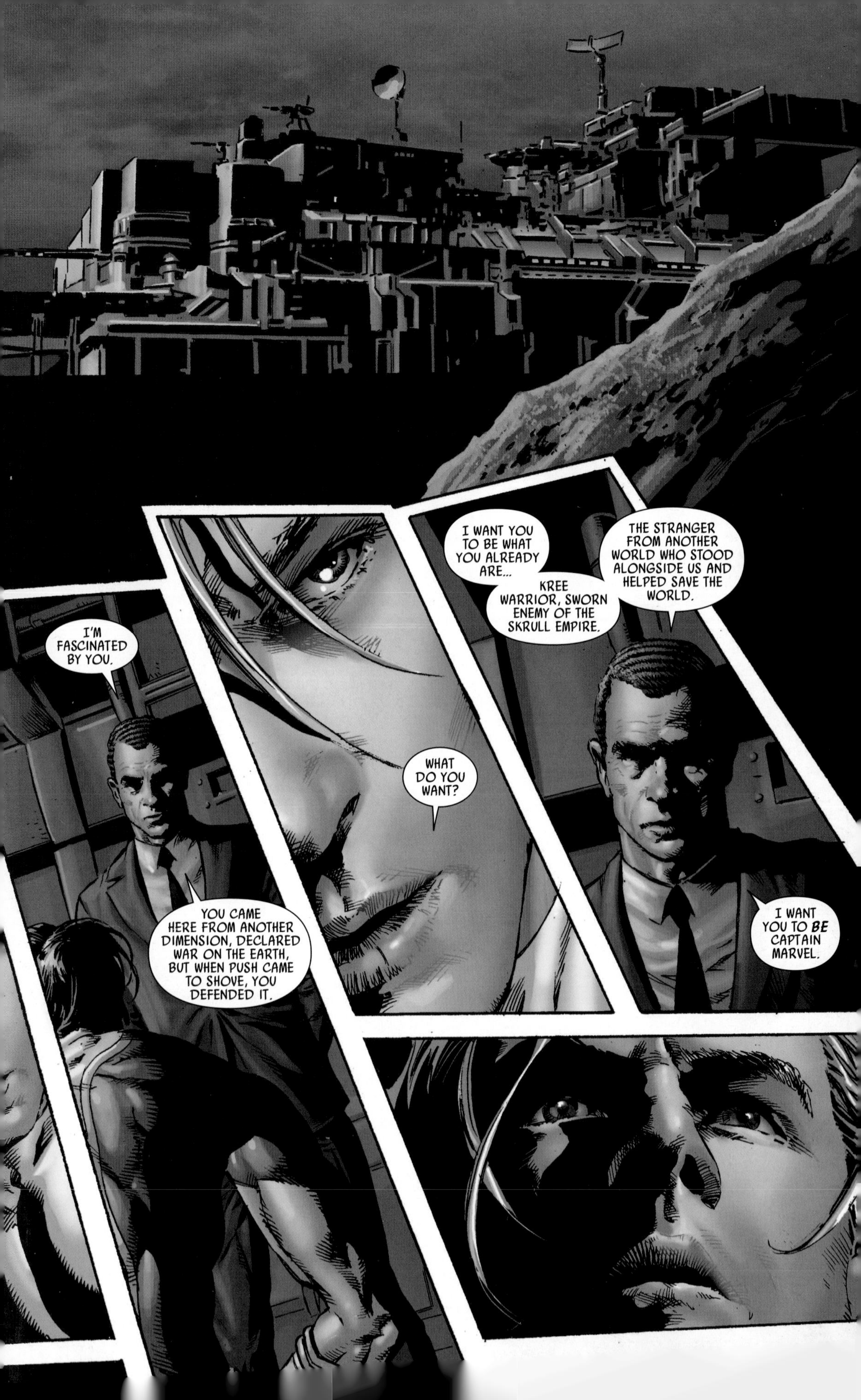
I'M FASCINATED BY YOU.
YOU CAME HERE FROM ANOTHER DIMENSION, DECLARED WAR ON THE EARTH, BUT WHEN PUSH CAME TO SHOVE, YOU DEFENDED IT.
WHAT DO YOU WANT?
I WANT YOU TO BE WHAT YOU ALREADY ARE...
KREE WARRIOR, SWORN ENEMY OF THE SKRULL EMPIRE.
THE STRANGER FROM ANOTHER WORLD WHO STOOD ALONGSIDE US AND HELPED SAVE THE WORLD.
I WANT YOU TO *BE* CAPTAIN MARVEL.

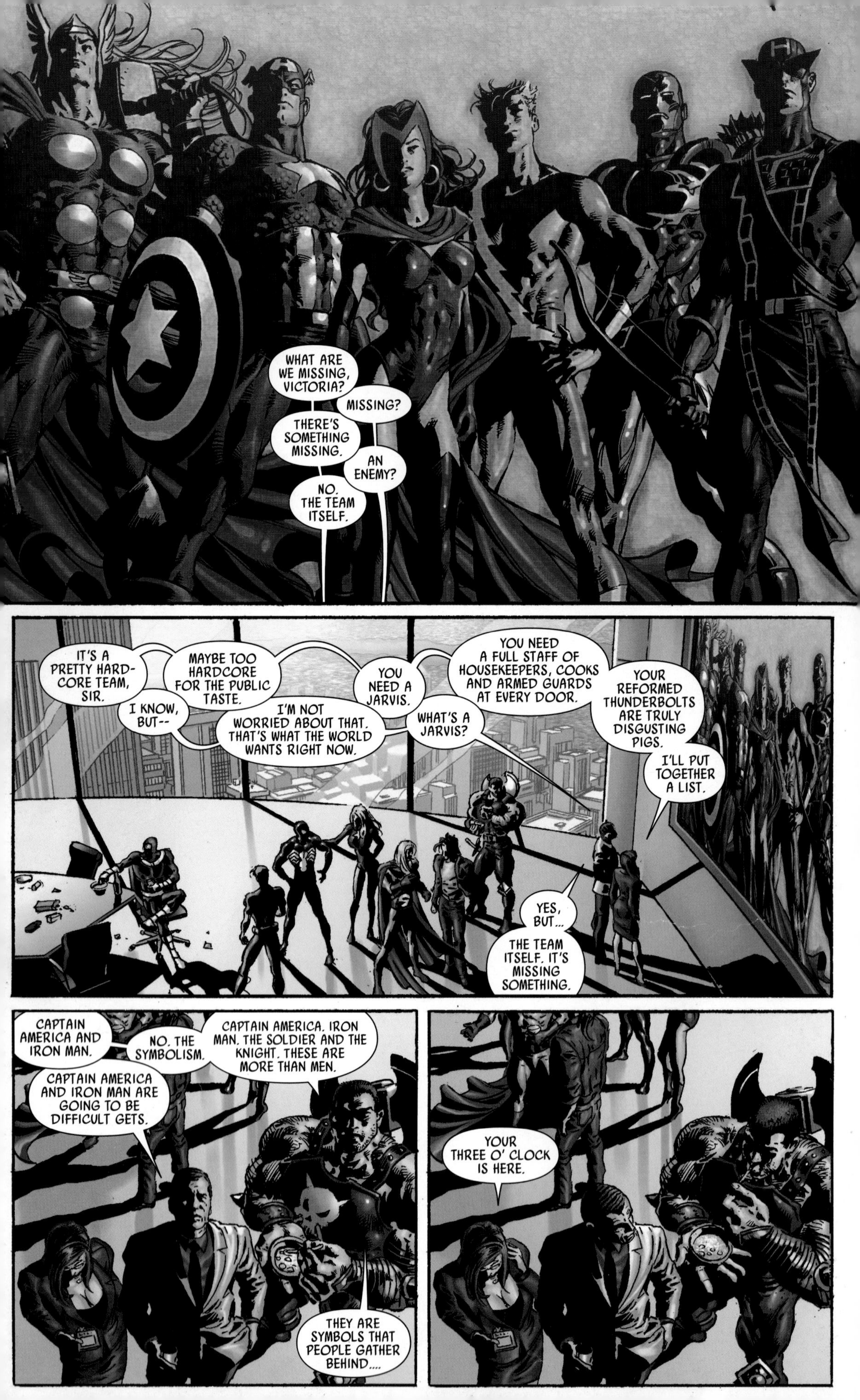
WHAT ARE WE MISSING, VICTORIA?
MISSING?
THERE'S SOMETHING MISSING.
AN ENEMY?
NO. THE TEAM ITSELF.
IT'S A PRETTY HARD-CORE TEAM, SIR.
I KNOW, BUT--
MAYBE TOO HARDCORE FOR THE PUBLIC TASTE.
I'M NOT WORRIED ABOUT THAT. THAT'S WHAT THE WORLD WANTS RIGHT NOW.
YOU NEED A JARVIS.
WHAT'S A JARVIS?
YOU NEED A FULL STAFF OF HOUSEKEEPERS, COOKS AND ARMED GUARDS AT EVERY DOOR.
YOUR REFORMED THUNDERBOLTS ARE TRULY DISGUSTING PIGS.
I'LL PUT TOGETHER A LIST.
YES, BUT...
THE TEAM ITSELF. IT'S MISSING SOMETHING.
CAPTAIN AMERICA AND IRON MAN.
NO. THE SYMBOLISM.
CAPTAIN AMERICA. IRON MAN. THE SOLDIER AND THE KNIGHT. THESE ARE MORE THAN MEN.
CAPTAIN AMERICA AND IRON MAN ARE GOING TO BE DIFFICULT GETS.
THEY ARE SYMBOLS THAT PEOPLE GATHER BEHIND....
YOUR THREE O' CLOCK IS HERE.

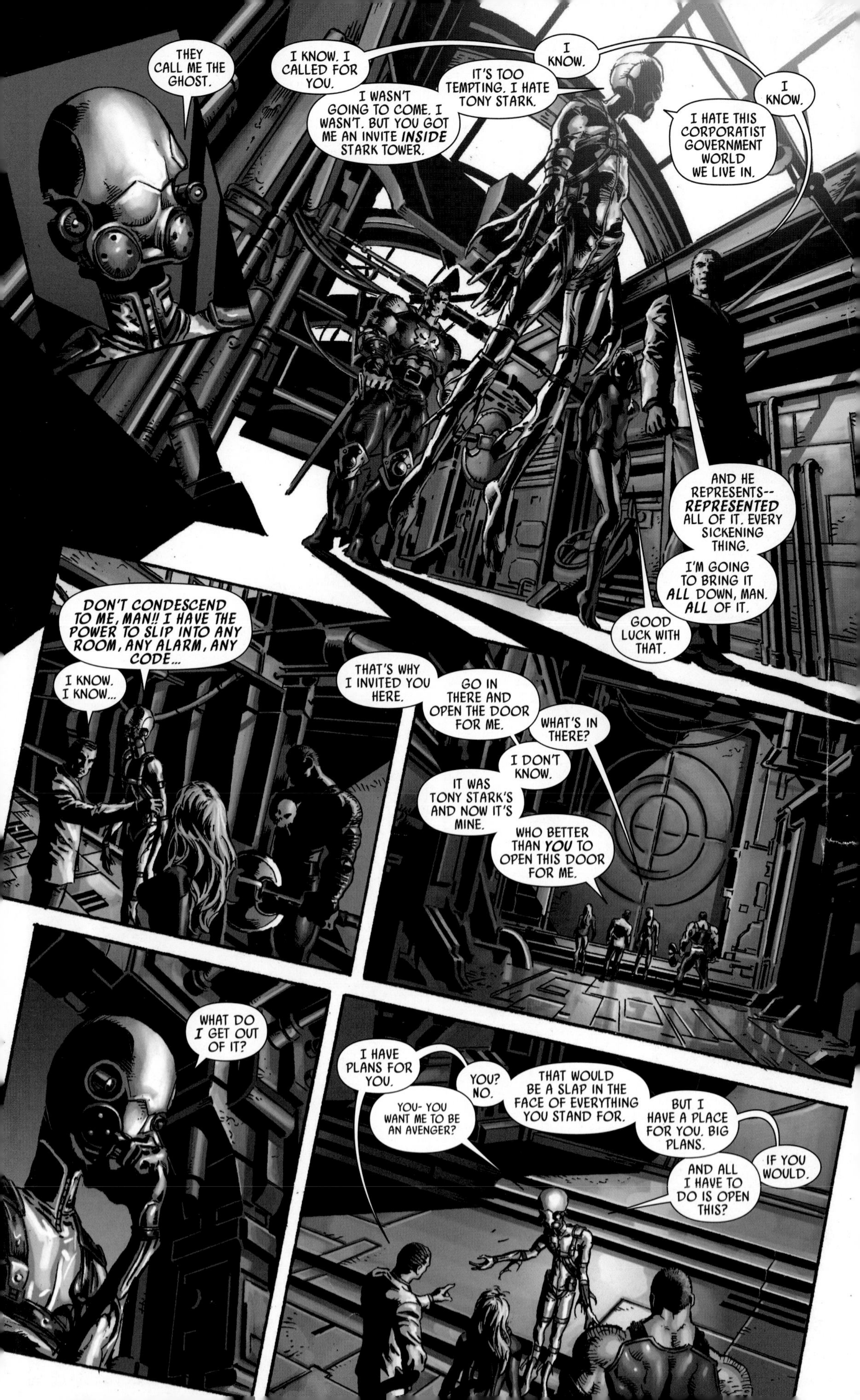
THEY CALL ME THE GHOST.
I KNOW. I CALLED FOR YOU.
I KNOW.
I WASN'T GOING TO COME. I WASN'T. BUT YOU GOT ME AN INVITE INSIDE STARK TOWER.
IT'S TOO TEMPTING. I HATE TONY STARK.
I KNOW.
I HATE THIS CORPORATIST GOVERNMENT WORLD WE LIVE IN.
AND HE REPRESENTS-- REPRESENTED ALL OF IT. EVERY SICKENING THING.
I'M GOING TO BRING IT ALL DOWN, MAN. ALL OF IT.
GOOD LUCK WITH THAT.
DON'T CONDESCEND TO ME, MAN!! I HAVE THE POWER TO SLIP INTO ANY ROOM, ANY ALARM, ANY CODE...
I KNOW. I KNOW...
THAT'S WHY I INVITED YOU HERE.
GO IN THERE AND OPEN THE DOOR FOR ME.
WHAT'S IN THERE?
I DON'T KNOW.
IT WAS TONY STARK'S AND NOW IT'S MINE.
WHO BETTER THAN YOU TO OPEN THIS DOOR FOR ME.
WHAT DO I GET OUT OF IT?
I HAVE PLANS FOR YOU.
YOU- YOU WANT ME TO BE AN AVENGER?
YOU? NO.
THAT WOULD BE A SLAP IN THE FACE OF EVERYTHING YOU STAND FOR.
BUT I HAVE A PLACE FOR YOU. BIG PLANS.
IF YOU WOULD.
AND ALL I HAVE TO DO IS OPEN THIS?

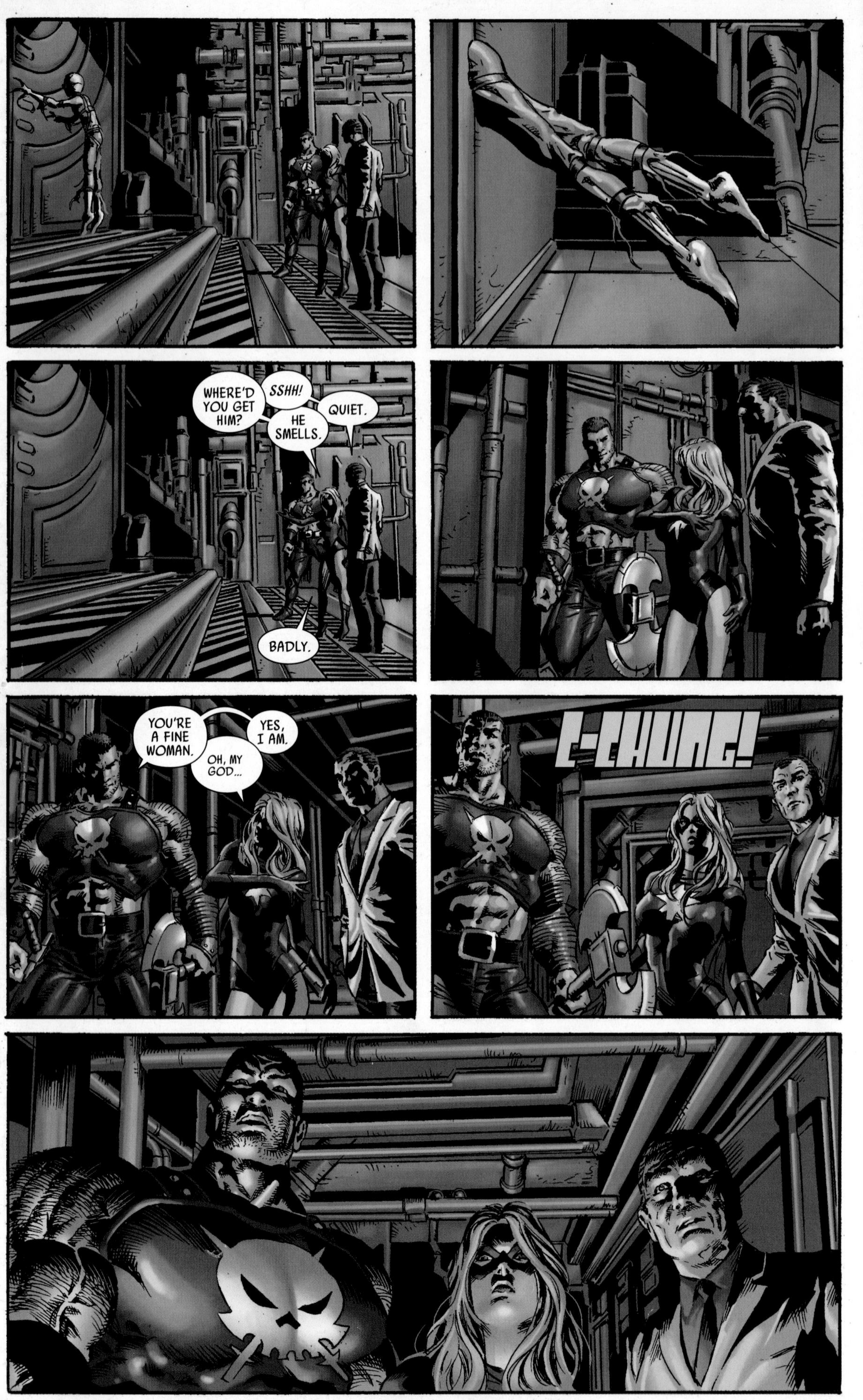
WHERE'D YOU GET HIM?
SSHH!
HE SMELLS.
QUIET.
BADLY.
YOU'RE A FINE WOMAN.
YES, I AM.
OH, MY GOD...
K-CHUNG!

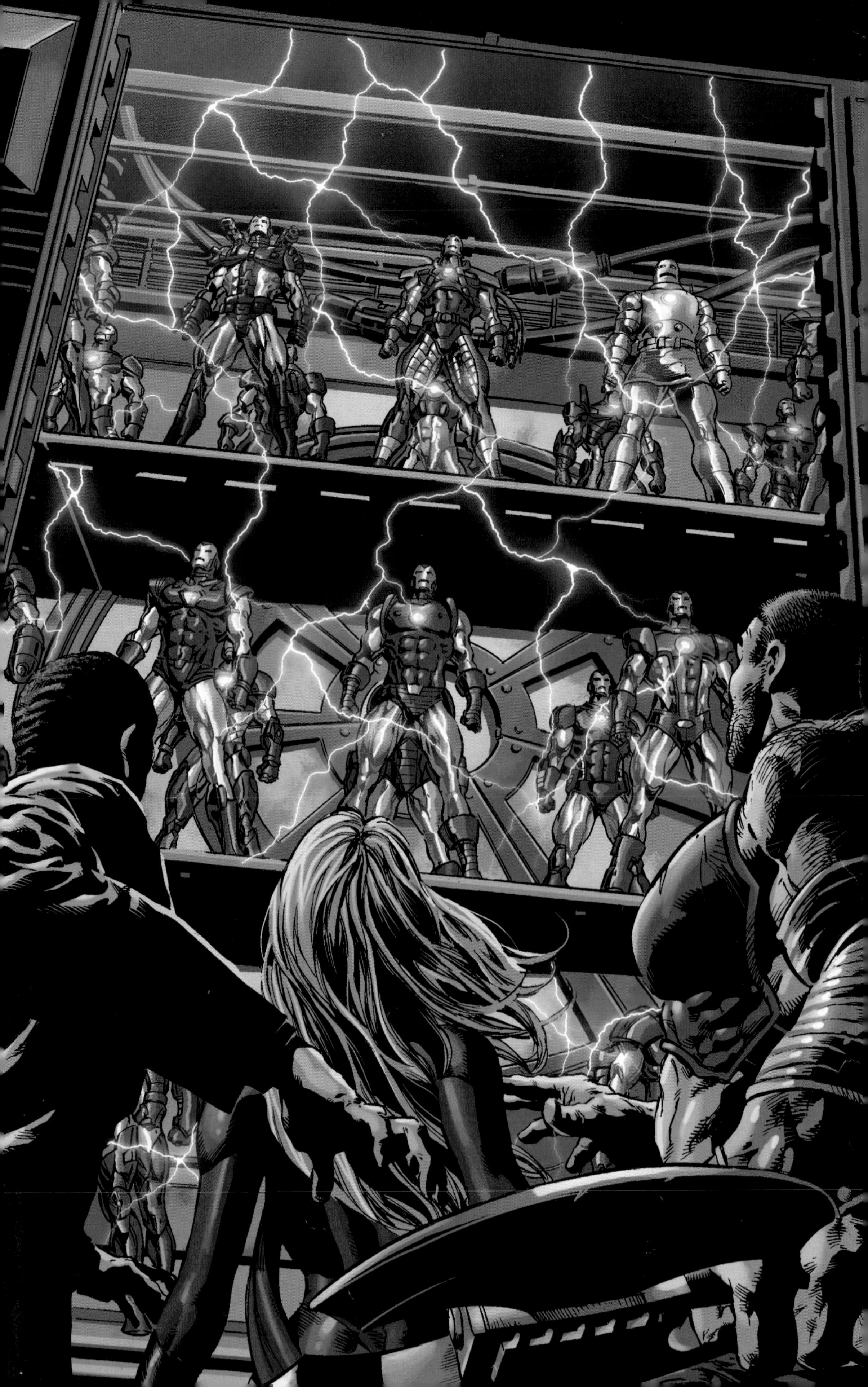

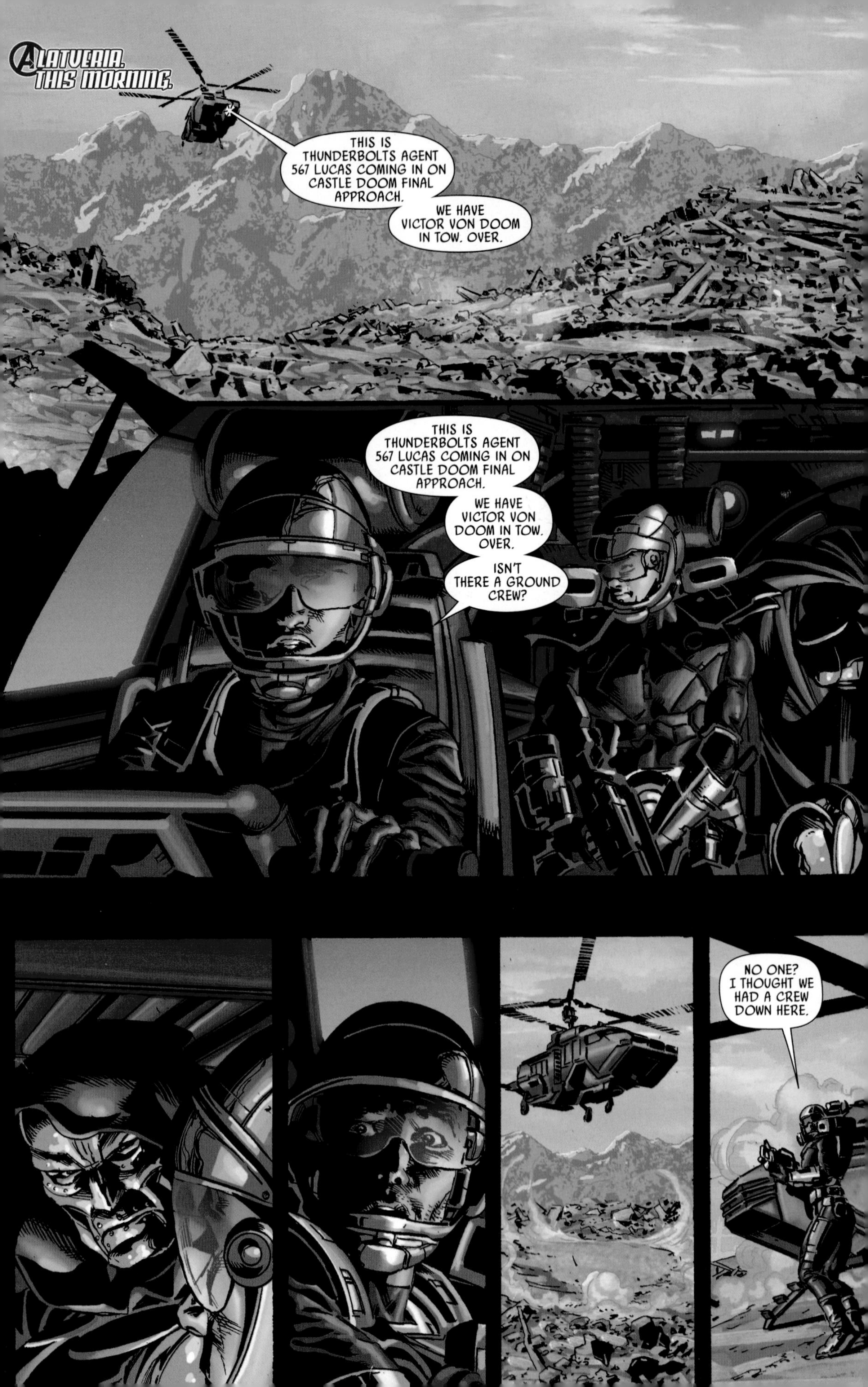
LATVERIA. THIS MORNING.
THIS IS THUNDERBOLTS AGENT 567 LUCAS COMING IN ON CASTLE DOOM FINAL APPROACH.
WE HAVE VICTOR VON DOOM IN TOW. OVER.
THIS IS THUNDERBOLTS AGENT 567 LUCAS COMING IN ON CASTLE DOOM FINAL APPROACH.
WE HAVE VICTOR VON DOOM IN TOW. OVER.
ISN'T THERE A GROUND CREW?
NO ONE? I THOUGHT WE HAD A CREW DOWN HERE.

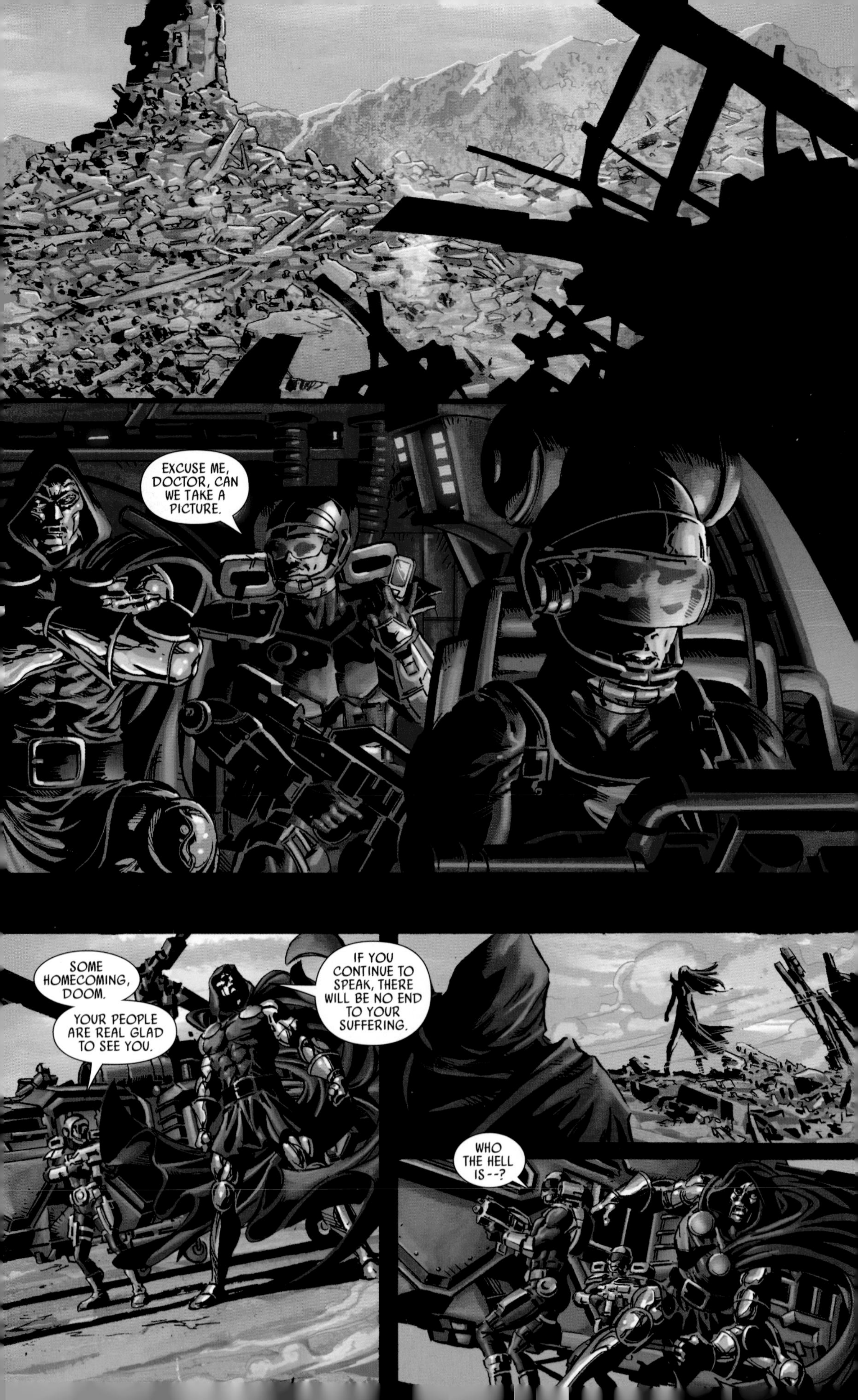
EXCUSE ME, DOCTOR, CAN WE TAKE A PICTURE.
SOME HOMECOMING, DOOM.
YOUR PEOPLE ARE REAL GLAD TO SEE YOU.
IF YOU CONTINUE TO SPEAK, THERE WILL BE NO END TO YOUR SUFFERING.
WHO THE HELL IS--?

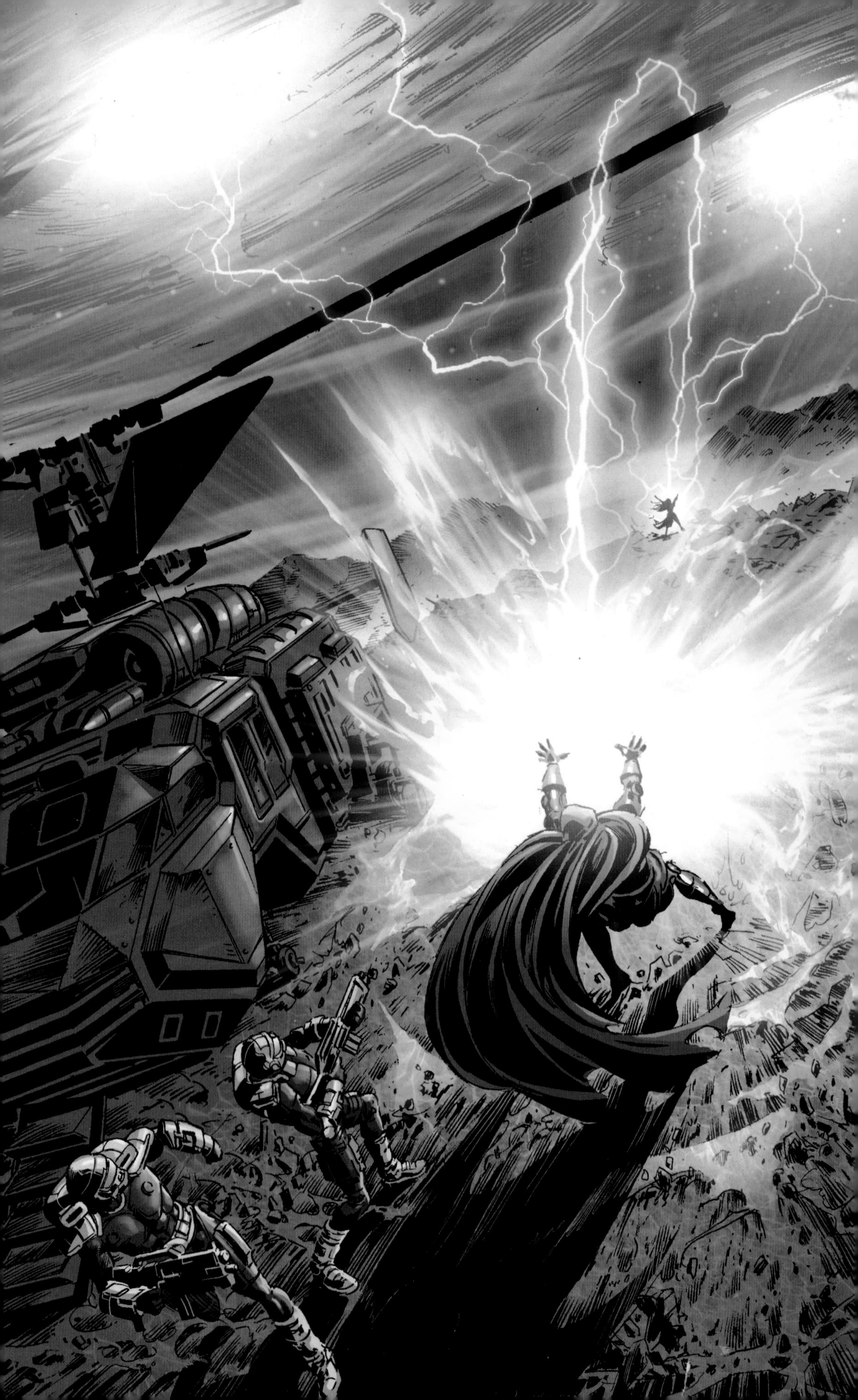

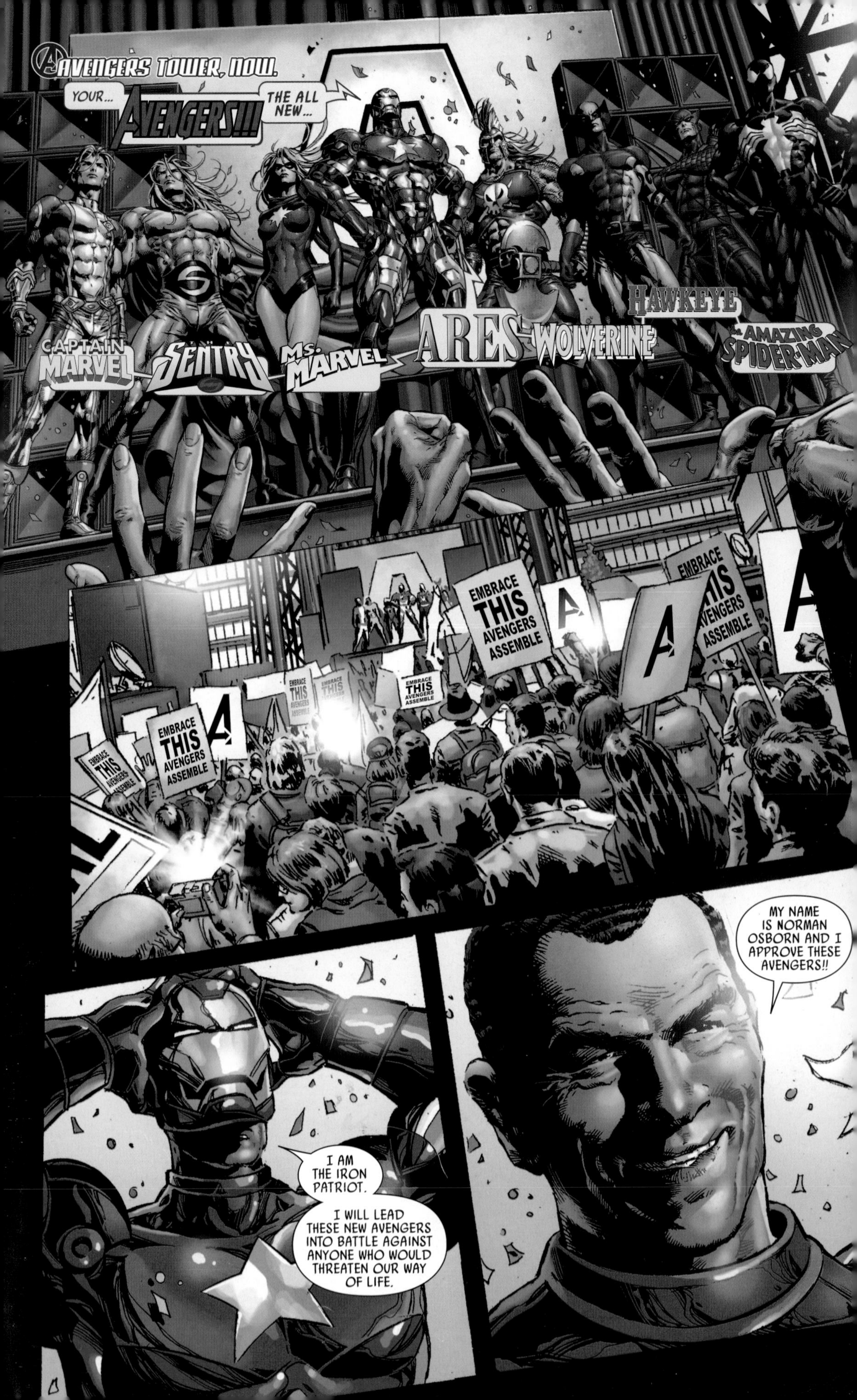
AVENGERS TOWER, NOW.
YOUR...
THE ALL NEW...
AVENGERS!!!
CAPTAIN MARVEL
SENTRY
Ms. MARVEL
ARES
WOLVERINE
HAWKEYE
THE AMAZING SPIDER-MAN
EMBRACE THIS AVENGERS ASSEMBLE
I AM THE IRON PATRIOT.
I WILL LEAD THESE NEW AVENGERS INTO BATTLE AGAINST ANYONE WHO WOULD THREATEN OUR WAY OF LIFE.
MY NAME IS NORMAN OSBORN AND I APPROVE THESE AVENGERS!!

DARK AVENGERS #2

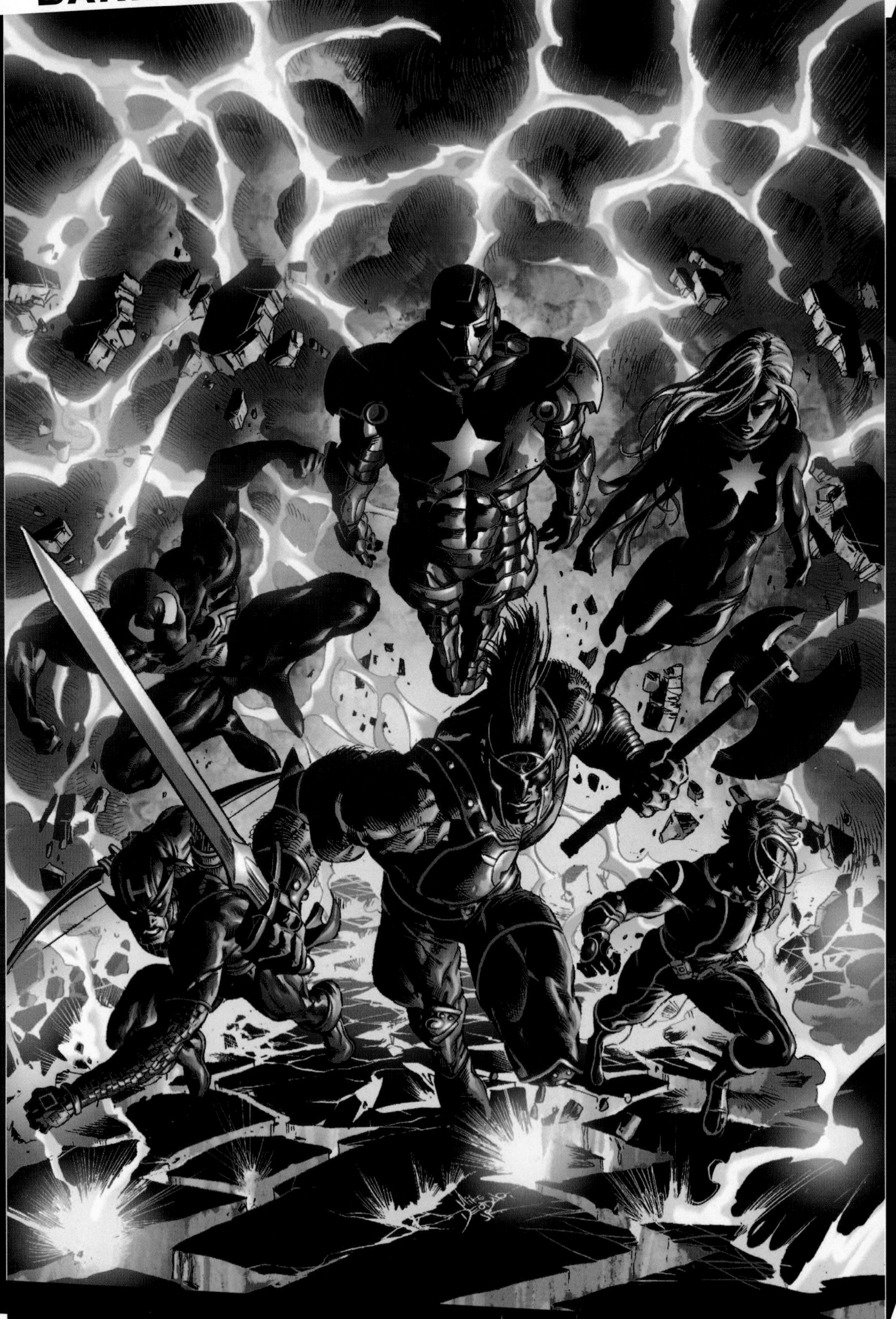

DARK AVENGERS #2 VARIANT

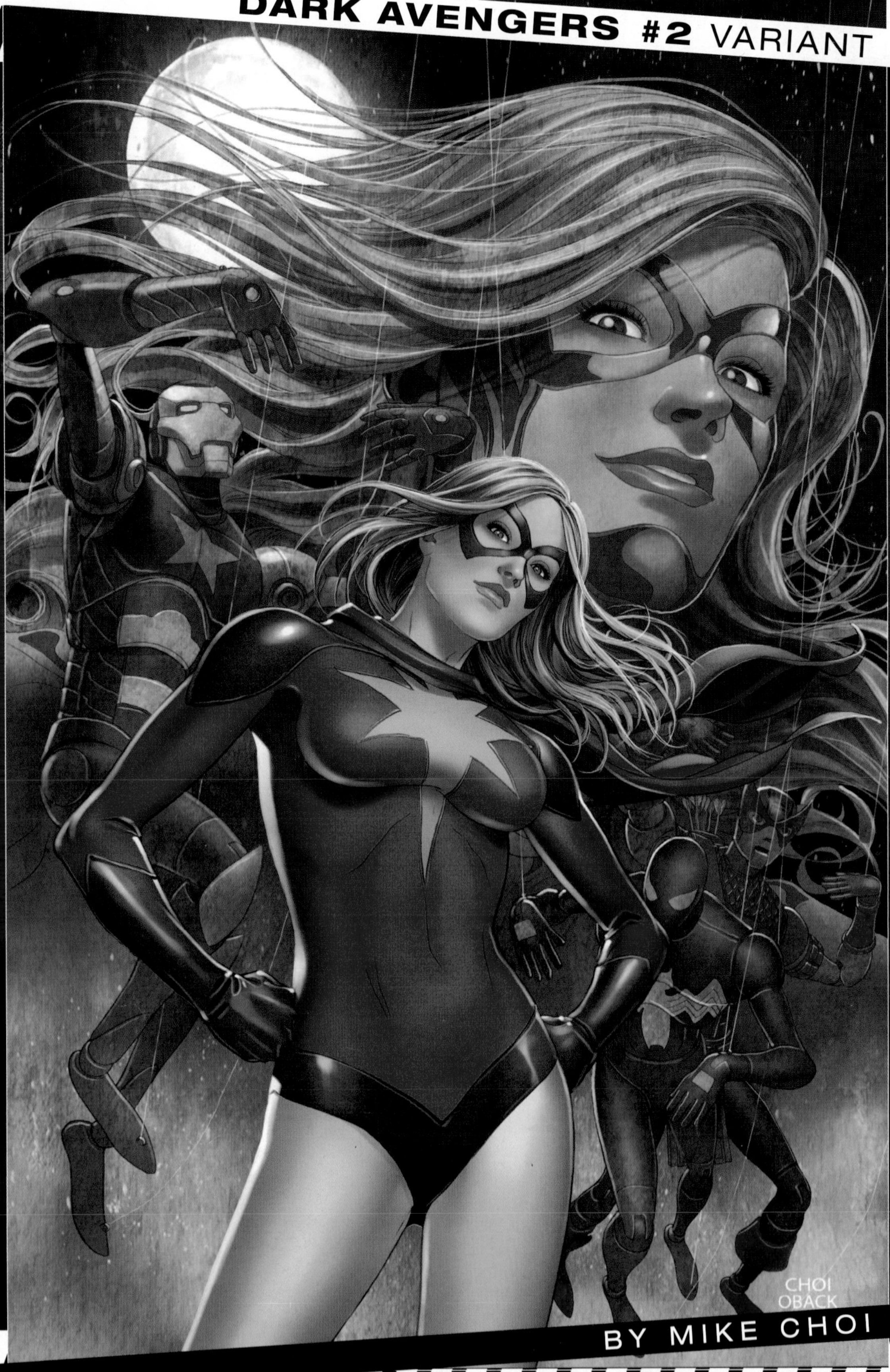
CHOI
OBACK

BY MIKE CHOI

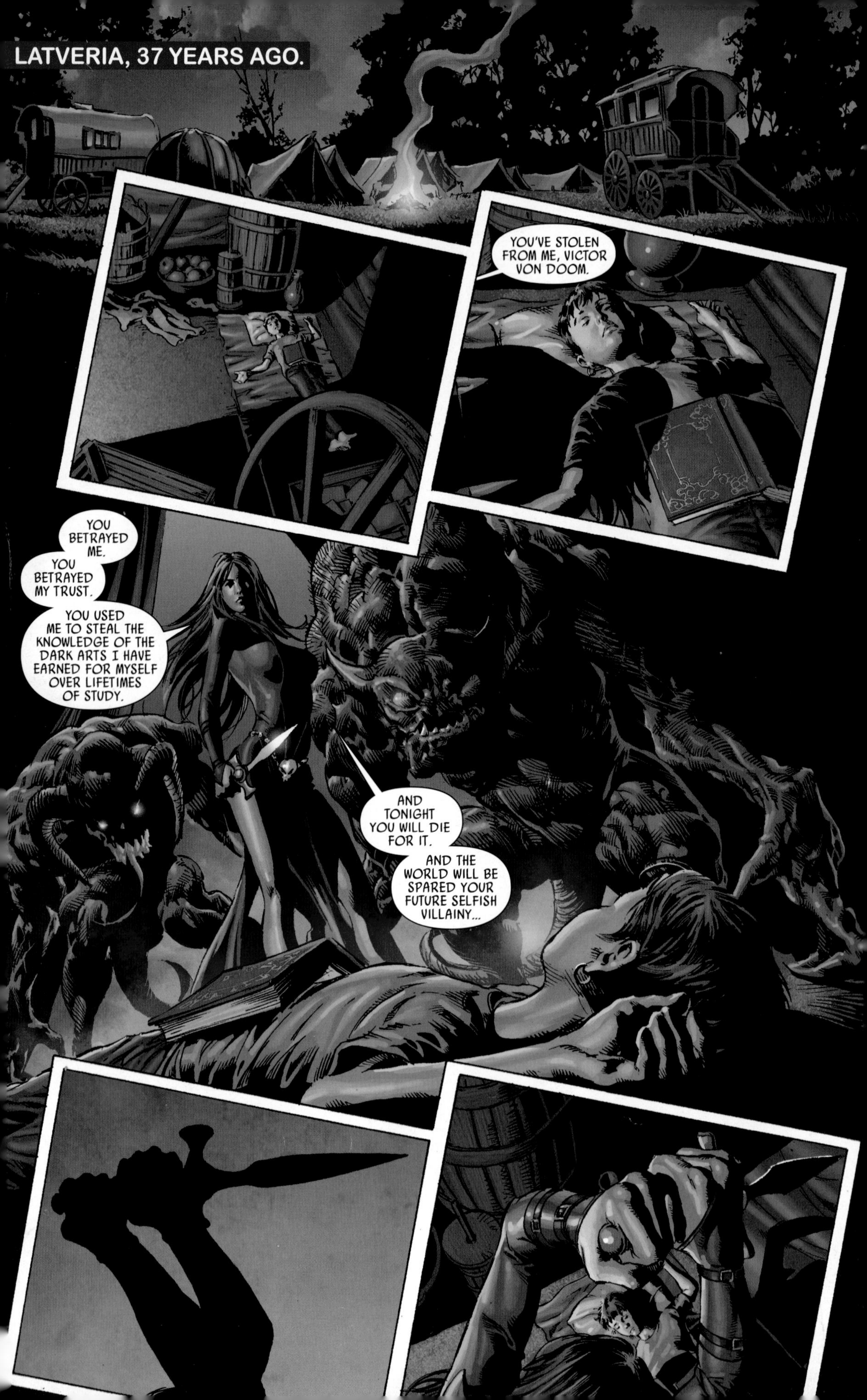
LATVERIA, 37 YEARS AGO.
YOU'VE STOLEN FROM ME, VICTOR VON DOOM.
YOU BETRAYED ME.
YOU BETRAYED MY TRUST.
YOU USED ME TO STEAL THE KNOWLEDGE OF THE DARK ARTS I HAVE EARNED FOR MYSELF OVER LIFETIMES OF STUDY.
AND TONIGHT YOU WILL DIE FOR IT.
AND THE WORLD WILL BE SPARED YOUR FUTURE SELFISH VILLAINY...

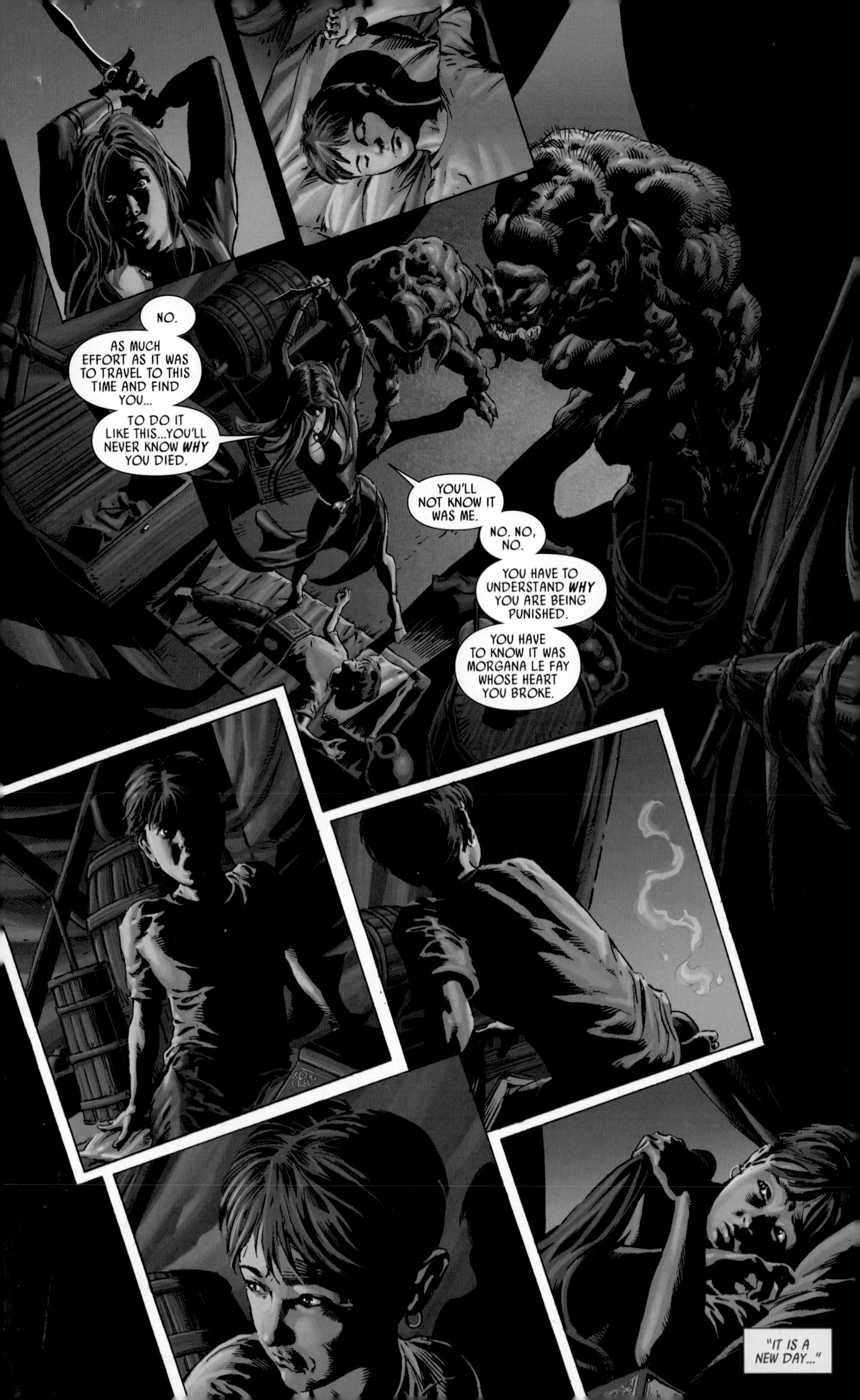

NO.
AS MUCH EFFORT AS IT WAS TO TRAVEL TO THIS TIME AND FIND YOU...
TO DO IT LIKE THIS...YOU'LL NEVER KNOW *WHY* YOU DIED.
YOU'LL NOT KNOW IT WAS ME.
NO. NO, NO.
YOU HAVE TO UNDERSTAND *WHY* YOU ARE BEING PUNISHED.
YOU HAVE TO KNOW IT WAS MORGANA LE FAY WHOSE HEART YOU BROKE.
"IT IS A NEW DAY..."

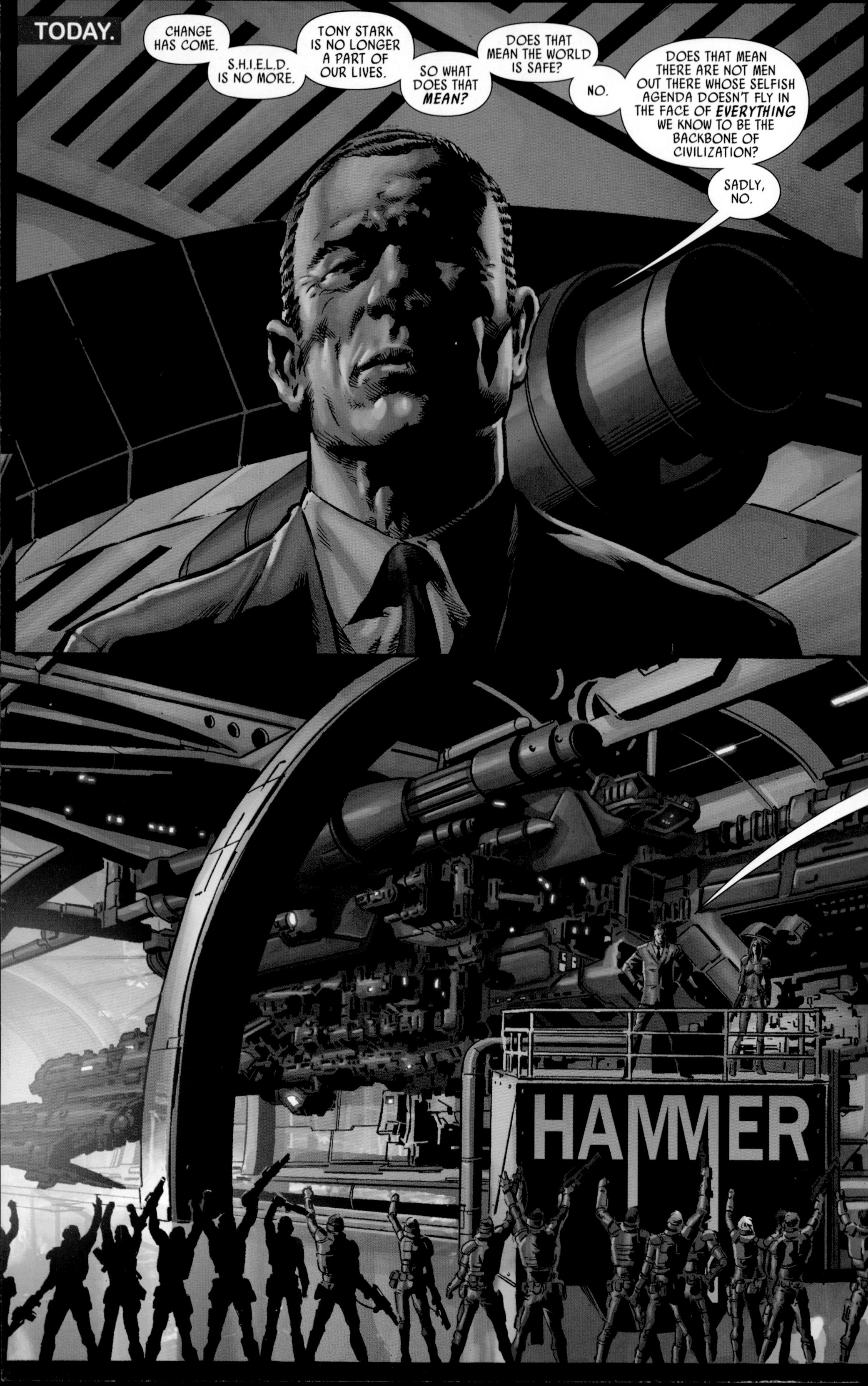
TODAY.
CHANGE HAS COME.
S.H.I.E.L.D. IS NO MORE.
TONY STARK IS NO LONGER A PART OF OUR LIVES.
SO WHAT DOES THAT *MEAN?*
DOES THAT MEAN THE WORLD IS SAFE?
NO.
DOES THAT MEAN THERE ARE NOT MEN OUT THERE WHOSE SELFISH AGENDA DOESN'T FLY IN THE FACE OF *EVERYTHING* WE KNOW TO BE THE BACKBONE OF CIVILIZATION?
SADLY, NO.
HAMMER

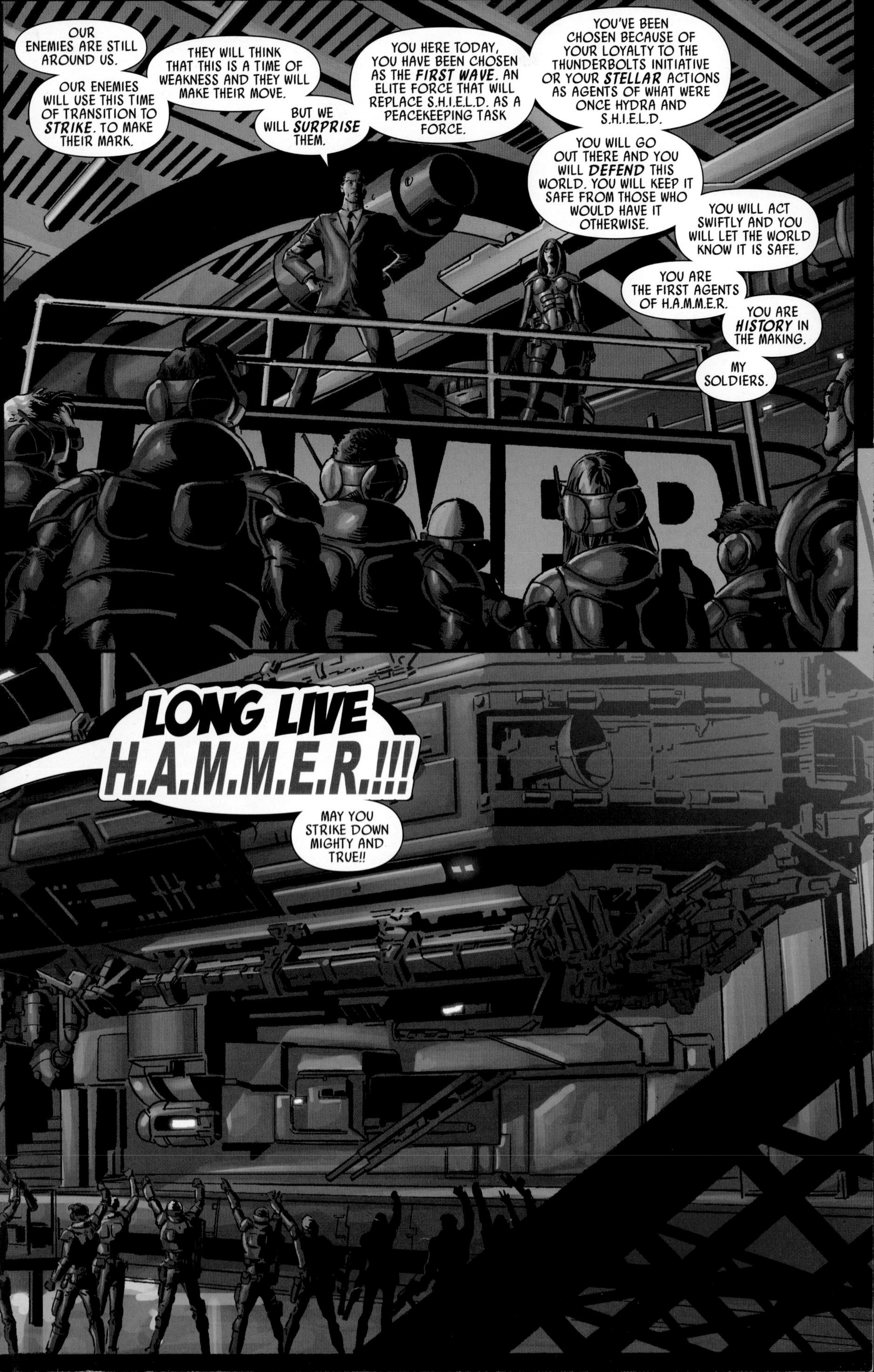
OUR ENEMIES ARE STILL AROUND US.
OUR ENEMIES WILL USE THIS TIME OF TRANSITION TO STRIKE. TO MAKE THEIR MARK.
THEY WILL THINK THAT THIS IS A TIME OF WEAKNESS AND THEY WILL MAKE THEIR MOVE.
BUT WE WILL SURPRISE THEM.
YOU HERE TODAY, YOU HAVE BEEN CHOSEN AS THE FIRST WAVE. AN ELITE FORCE THAT WILL REPLACE S.H.I.E.L.D. AS A PEACEKEEPING TASK FORCE.
YOU'VE BEEN CHOSEN BECAUSE OF YOUR LOYALTY TO THE THUNDERBOLTS INITIATIVE OR YOUR STELLAR ACTIONS AS AGENTS OF WHAT WERE ONCE HYDRA AND S.H.I.E.L.D.
YOU WILL GO OUT THERE AND YOU WILL DEFEND THIS WORLD. YOU WILL KEEP IT SAFE FROM THOSE WHO WOULD HAVE IT OTHERWISE.
YOU WILL ACT SWIFTLY AND YOU WILL LET THE WORLD KNOW IT IS SAFE.
YOU ARE THE FIRST AGENTS OF H.A.M.M.E.R.
YOU ARE HISTORY IN THE MAKING.
MY SOLDIERS.
LONG LIVE H.A.M.M.E.R.!!!
MAY YOU STRIKE DOWN MIGHTY AND TRUE!!

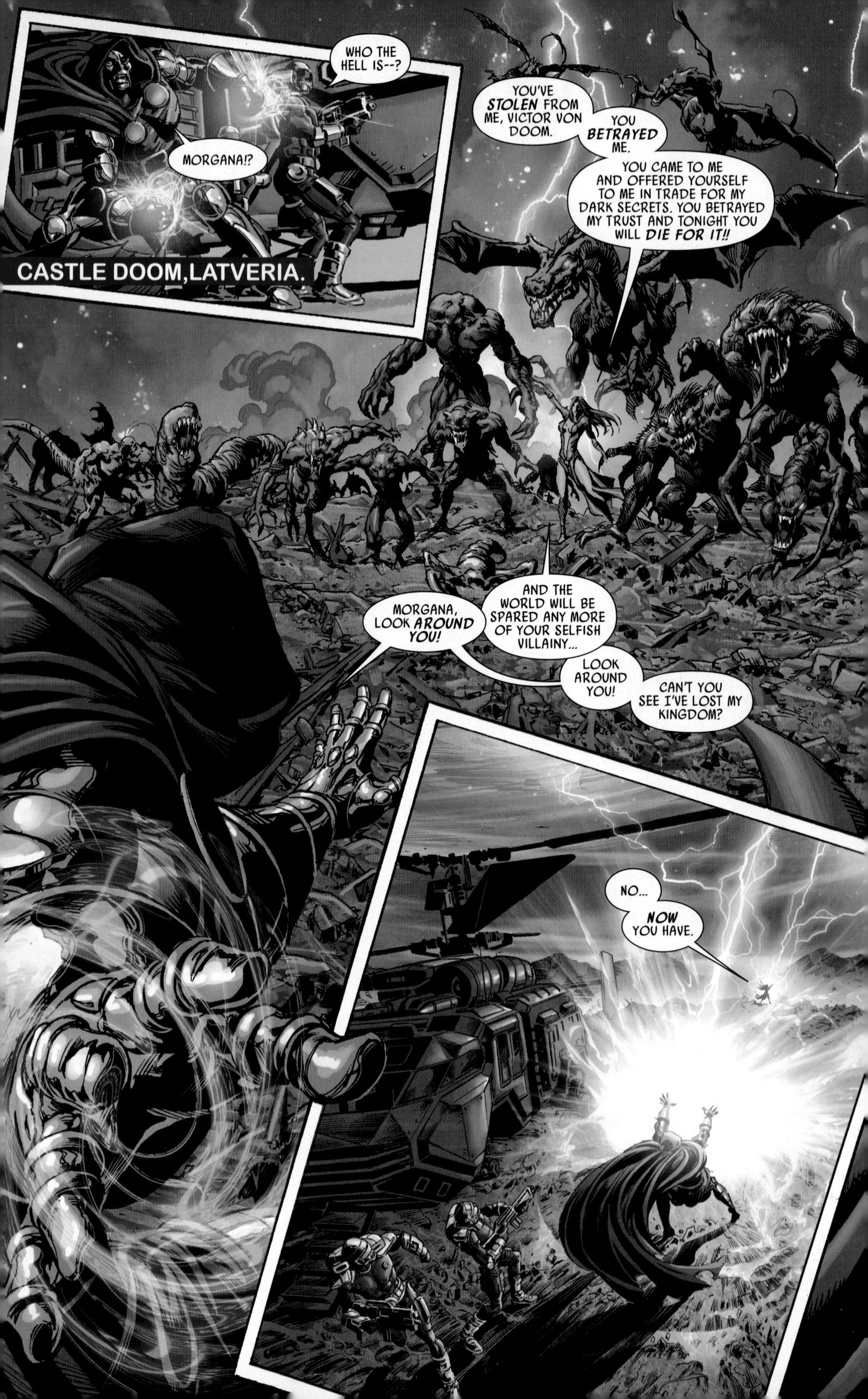
CASTLE DOOM, LATVERIA.
WHO THE HELL IS--?
MORGANA!?
YOU'VE STOLEN FROM ME, VICTOR VON DOOM.
YOU BETRAYED ME.
YOU CAME TO ME AND OFFERED YOURSELF TO ME IN TRADE FOR MY DARK SECRETS. YOU BETRAYED MY TRUST AND TONIGHT YOU WILL DIE FOR IT!!
AND THE WORLD WILL BE SPARED ANY MORE OF YOUR SELFISH VILLAINY...
MORGANA, LOOK AROUND YOU!
LOOK AROUND YOU!
CAN'T YOU SEE I'VE LOST MY KINGDOM?
NO...
NOW YOU HAVE.

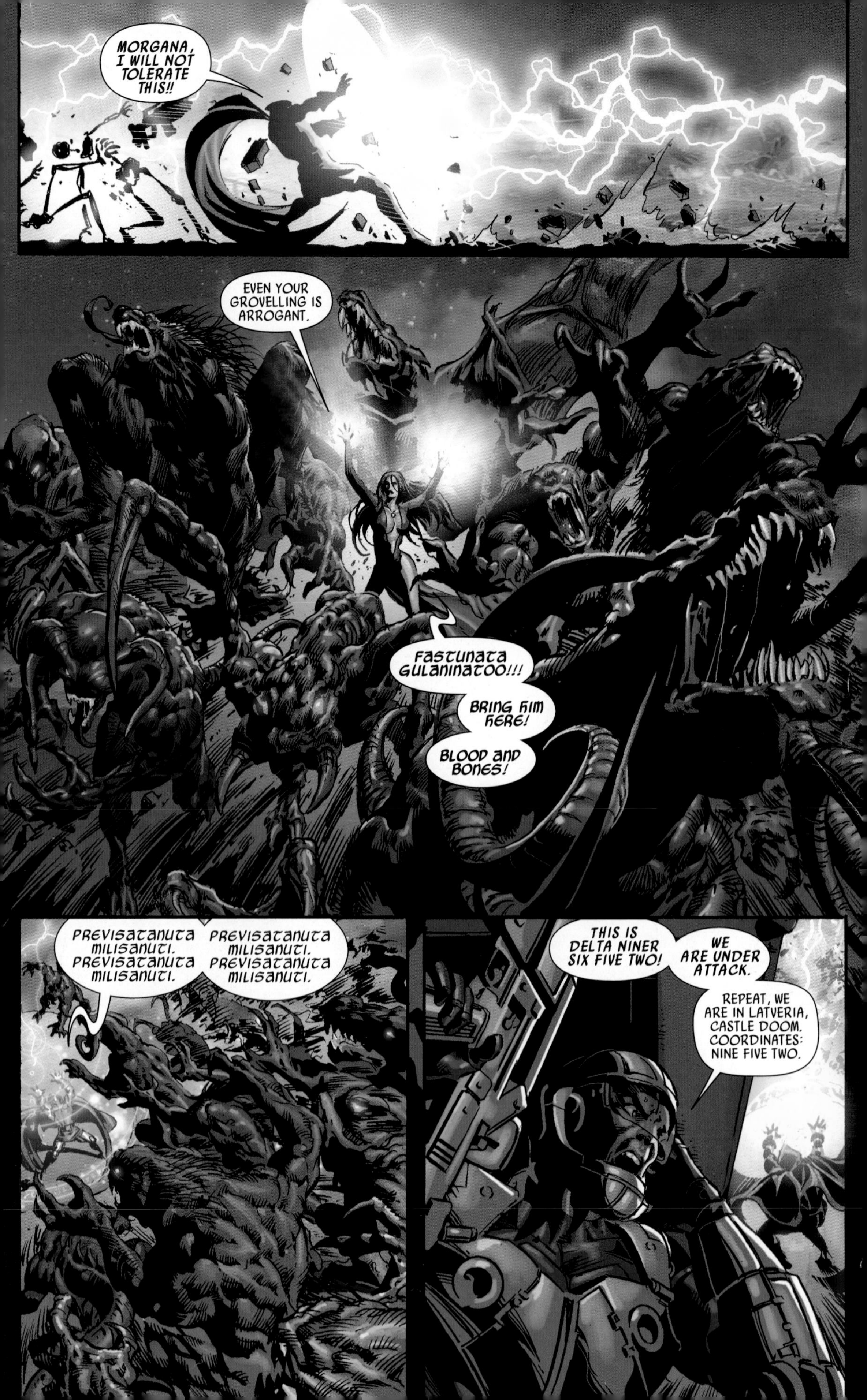
MORGANA, I WILL NOT TOLERATE THIS!!
EVEN YOUR GROVELLING IS ARROGANT.
FASTUNATA GULANINATOO!!!
BRING HIM HERE!
BLOOD AND BONES!
PREVISATANUTA MILISANUTI. PREVISATANUTA MILISANUTI.
PREVISATANUTA MILISANUTI. PREVISATANUTA MILISANUTI.
THIS IS DELTA NINER SIX FIVE TWO!
WE ARE UNDER ATTACK.
REPEAT, WE ARE IN LATVERIA, CASTLE DOOM. COORDINATES: NINE FIVE TWO.

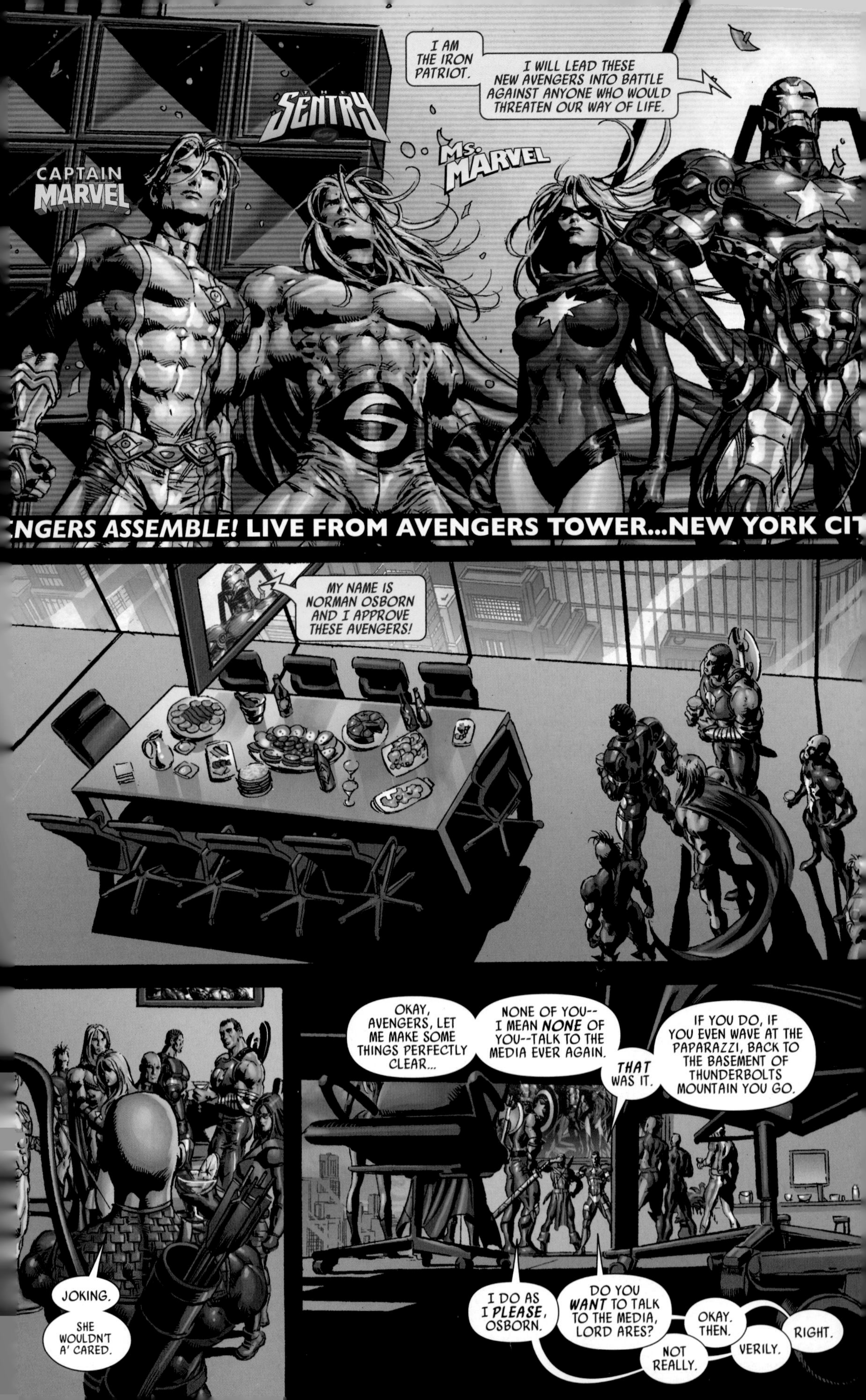
I AM THE IRON PATRIOT.
I WILL LEAD THESE NEW AVENGERS INTO BATTLE AGAINST ANYONE WHO WOULD THREATEN OUR WAY OF LIFE.
THE SENTRY
CAPTAIN MARVEL
MS. MARVEL
NGERS ASSEMBLE! LIVE FROM AVENGERS TOWER...NEW YORK CIT
MY NAME IS NORMAN OSBORN AND I APPROVE THESE AVENGERS!
OKAY, AVENGERS, LET ME MAKE SOME THINGS PERFECTLY CLEAR...
NONE OF YOU-- I MEAN NONE OF YOU--TALK TO THE MEDIA EVER AGAIN.
THAT WAS IT.
IF YOU DO, IF YOU EVEN WAVE AT THE PAPARAZZI, BACK TO THE BASEMENT OF THUNDERBOLTS MOUNTAIN YOU GO.
JOKING.
SHE WOULDN'T A' CARED.
I DO AS I PLEASE, OSBORN.
DO YOU WANT TO TALK TO THE MEDIA, LORD ARES?
NOT REALLY.
OKAY. THEN.
VERILY.
RIGHT.

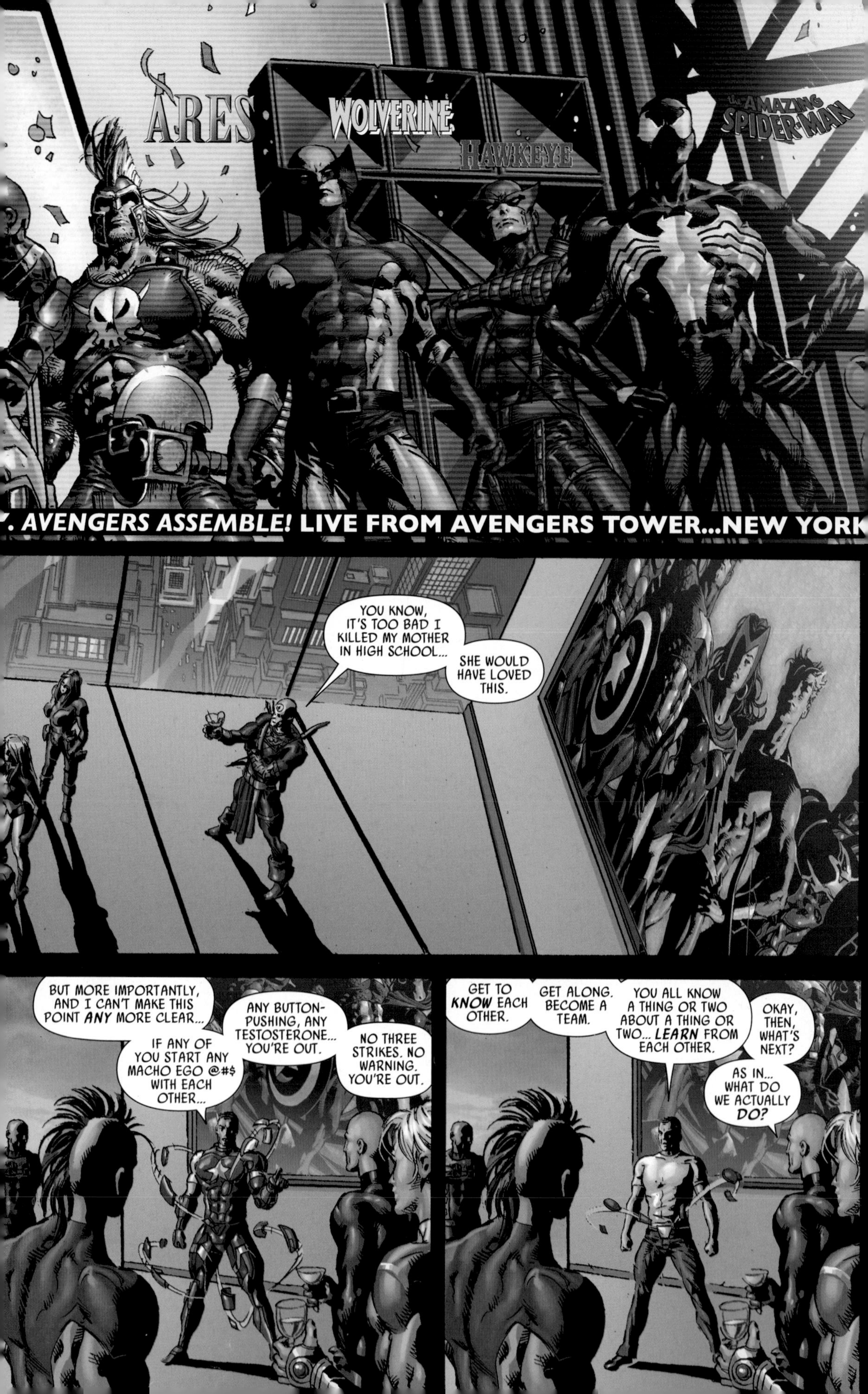
ARES
WOLVERINE
HAWKEYE
the AMAZING SPIDER-MAN
. AVENGERS ASSEMBLE! LIVE FROM AVENGERS TOWER...NEW YORK
YOU KNOW, IT'S TOO BAD I KILLED MY MOTHER IN HIGH SCHOOL...
SHE WOULD HAVE LOVED THIS.
BUT MORE IMPORTANTLY, AND I CAN'T MAKE THIS POINT ANY MORE CLEAR...
IF ANY OF YOU START ANY MACHO EGO @#$ WITH EACH OTHER...
ANY BUTTON-PUSHING, ANY TESTOSTERONE... YOU'RE OUT.
NO THREE STRIKES. NO WARNING. YOU'RE OUT.
GET TO KNOW EACH OTHER.
GET ALONG. BECOME A TEAM.
YOU ALL KNOW A THING OR TWO ABOUT A THING OR TWO... LEARN FROM EACH OTHER.
OKAY, THEN, WHAT'S NEXT?
AS IN... WHAT DO WE ACTUALLY DO?

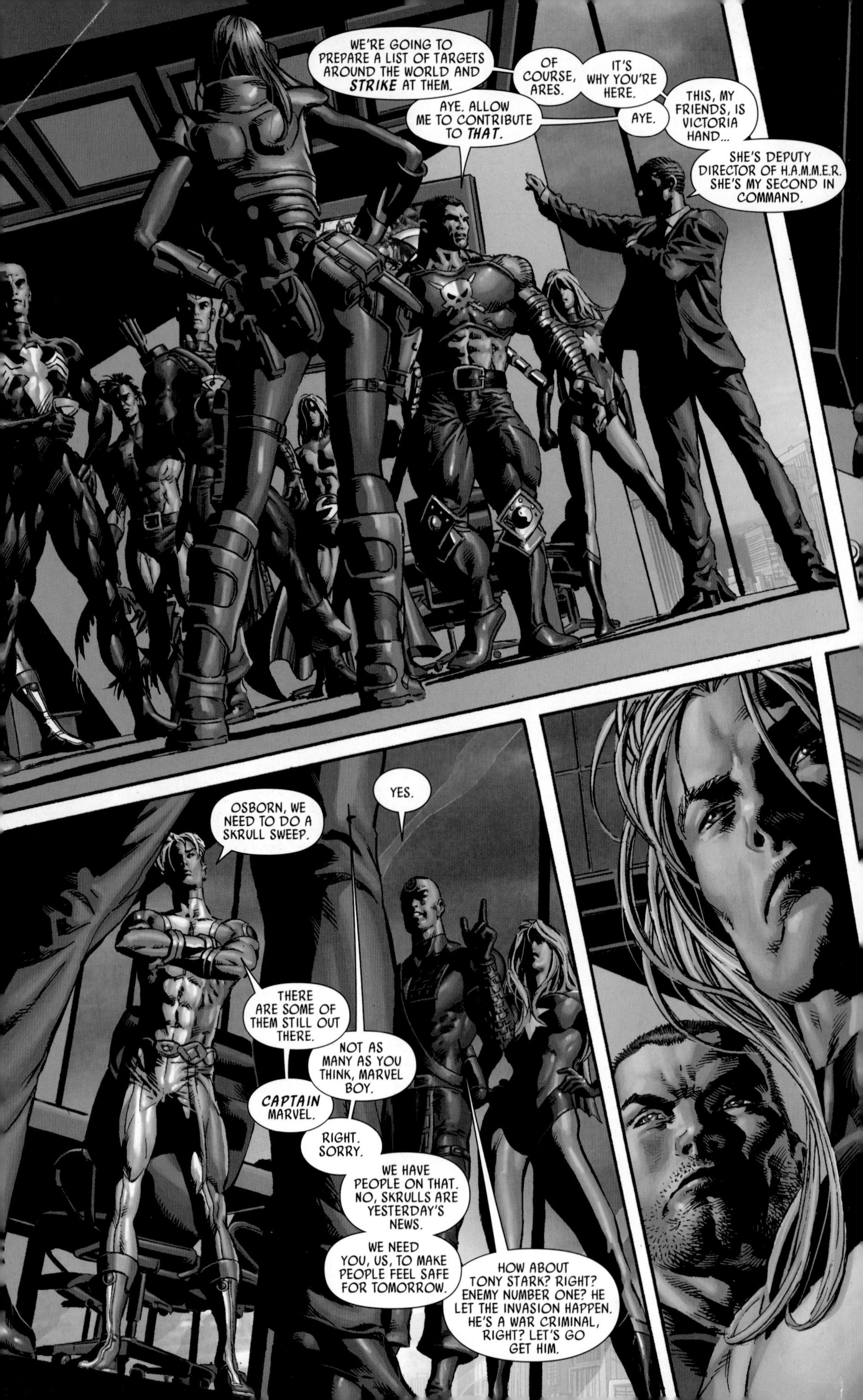
WE'RE GOING TO PREPARE A LIST OF TARGETS AROUND THE WORLD AND STRIKE AT THEM.
OF COURSE, ARES.
IT'S WHY YOU'RE HERE.
AYE. ALLOW ME TO CONTRIBUTE TO THAT.
AYE.
THIS, MY FRIENDS, IS VICTORIA HAND...
SHE'S DEPUTY DIRECTOR OF H.A.M.M.E.R. SHE'S MY SECOND IN COMMAND.
OSBORN, WE NEED TO DO A SKRULL SWEEP.
YES.
THERE ARE SOME OF THEM STILL OUT THERE.
NOT AS MANY AS YOU THINK, MARVEL BOY.
CAPTAIN MARVEL.
RIGHT. SORRY.
WE HAVE PEOPLE ON THAT. NO, SKRULLS ARE YESTERDAY'S NEWS.
WE NEED YOU, US, TO MAKE PEOPLE FEEL SAFE FOR TOMORROW.
HOW ABOUT TONY STARK? RIGHT? ENEMY NUMBER ONE? HE LET THE INVASION HAPPEN. HE'S A WAR CRIMINAL, RIGHT? LET'S GO GET HIM.

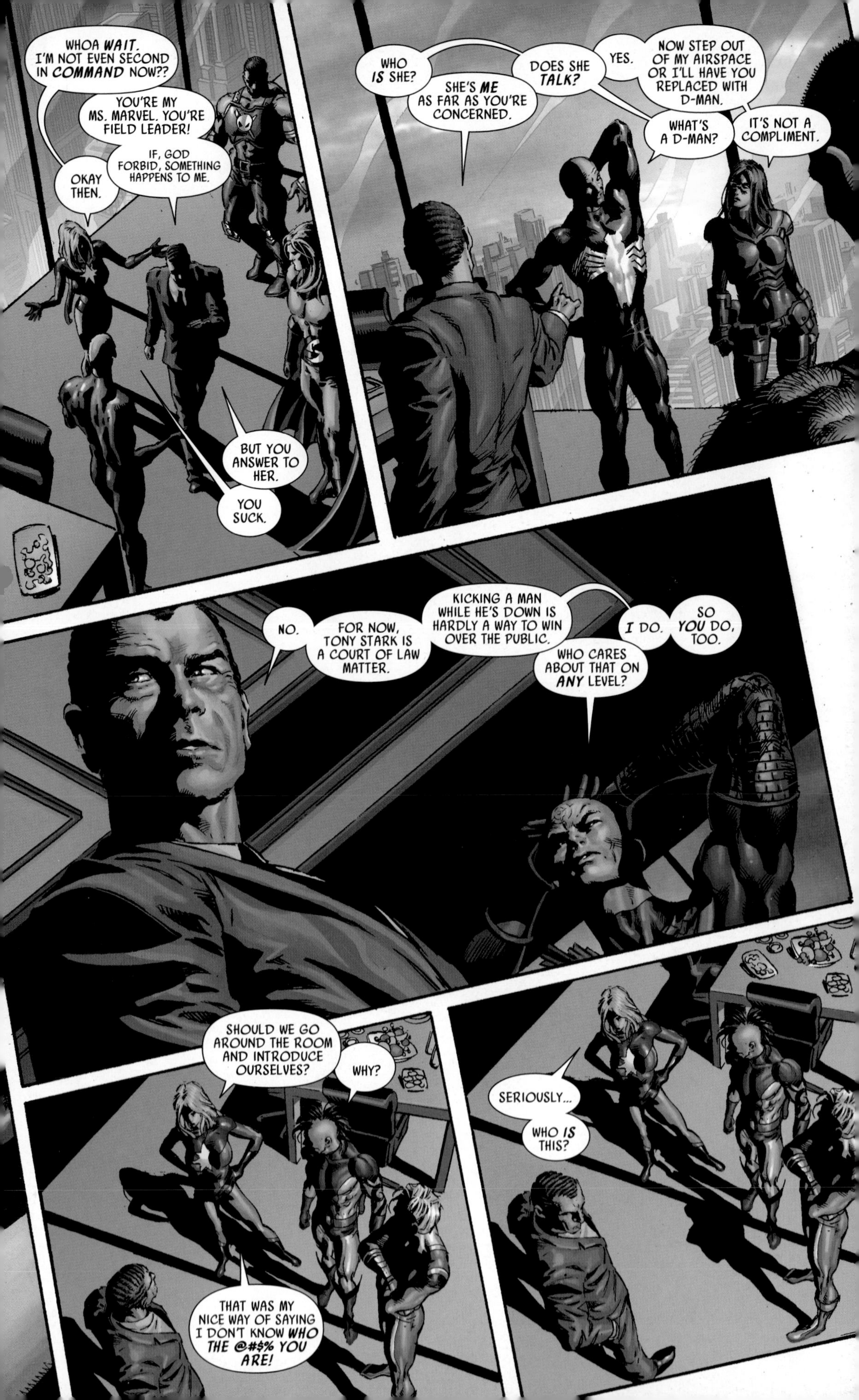
WHOA WAIT. I'M NOT EVEN SECOND IN COMMAND NOW??
YOU'RE MY MS. MARVEL. YOU'RE FIELD LEADER!
OKAY THEN.
IF, GOD FORBID, SOMETHING HAPPENS TO ME.
BUT YOU ANSWER TO HER.
YOU SUCK.
WHO IS SHE?
SHE'S ME AS FAR AS YOU'RE CONCERNED.
DOES SHE TALK?
YES.
NOW STEP OUT OF MY AIRSPACE OR I'LL HAVE YOU REPLACED WITH D-MAN.
WHAT'S A D-MAN?
IT'S NOT A COMPLIMENT.
NO.
FOR NOW, TONY STARK IS A COURT OF LAW MATTER.
KICKING A MAN WHILE HE'S DOWN IS HARDLY A WAY TO WIN OVER THE PUBLIC.
WHO CARES ABOUT THAT ON ANY LEVEL?
I DO.
SO YOU DO, TOO.
SHOULD WE GO AROUND THE ROOM AND INTRODUCE OURSELVES?
WHY?
THAT WAS MY NICE WAY OF SAYING I DON'T KNOW WHO THE @#$% YOU ARE!
SERIOUSLY...
WHO IS THIS?

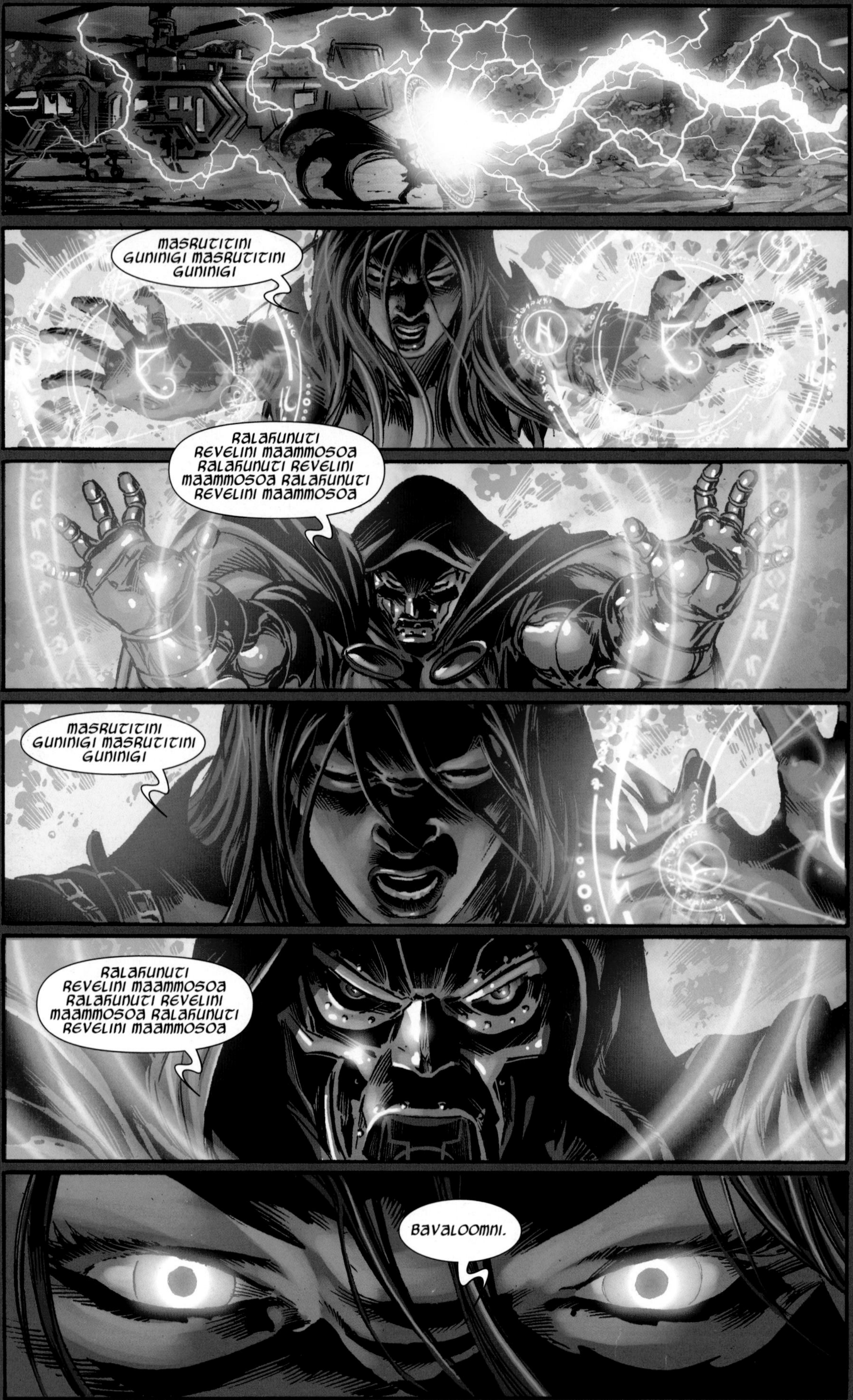
MASRUTITINI GUNINIGI MASRUTITINI GUNINIGI
RALAHUNUTI REVELINI MAAMMOSOA RALAHUNUTI REVELINI MAAMMOSOA RALAHUNUTI REVELINI MAAMMOSOA
MASRUTITINI GUNINIGI MASRUTITINI GUNINIGI
RALAHUNUTI REVELINI MAAMMOSOA RALAHUNUTI REVELINI MAAMMOSOA RALAHUNUTI REVELINI MAAMMOSOA
BAVALOOMNI.

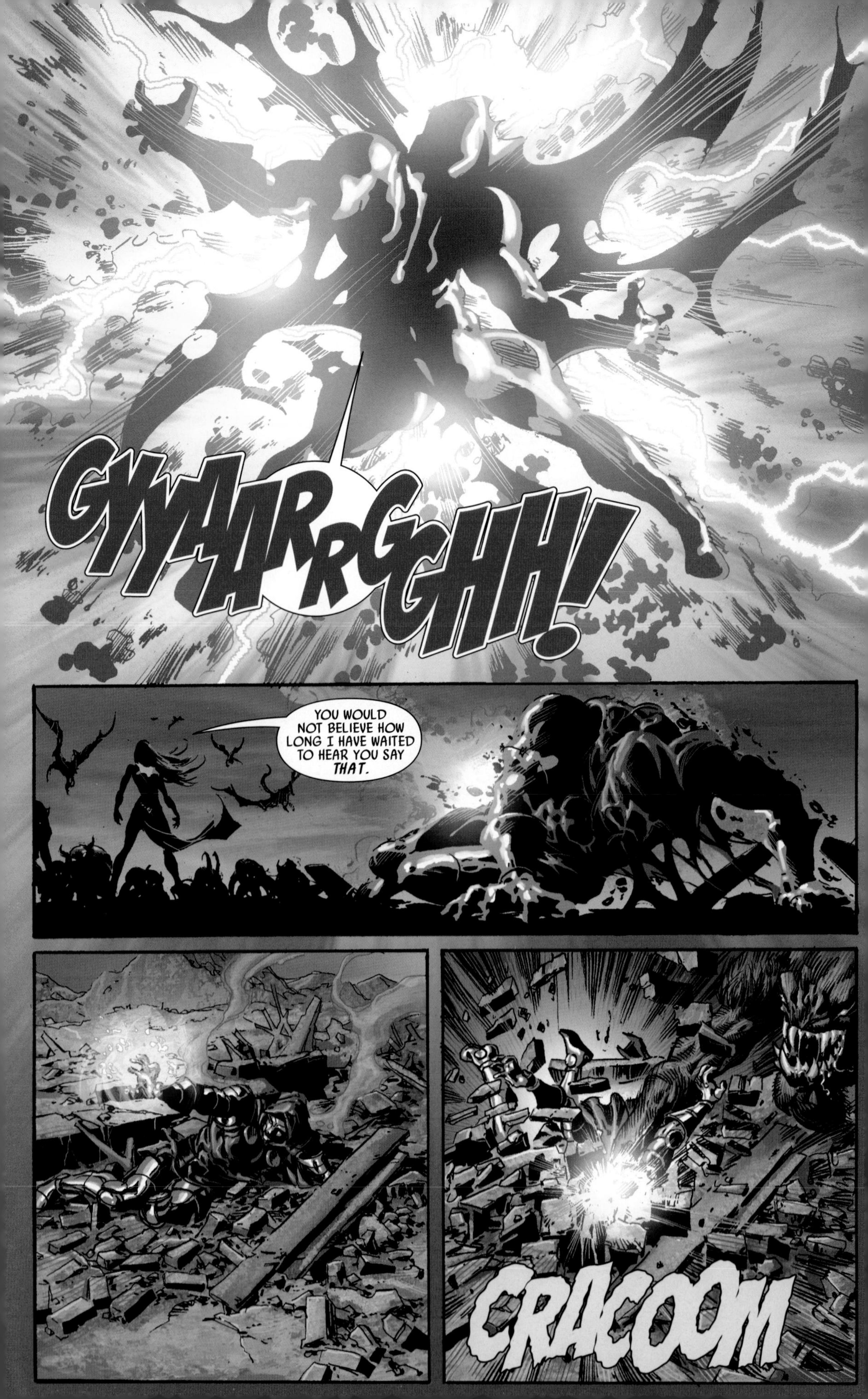
GYYAARRGGHH!
YOU WOULD NOT BELIEVE HOW LONG I HAVE WAITED TO HEAR YOU SAY *THAT*.
CRACOOM

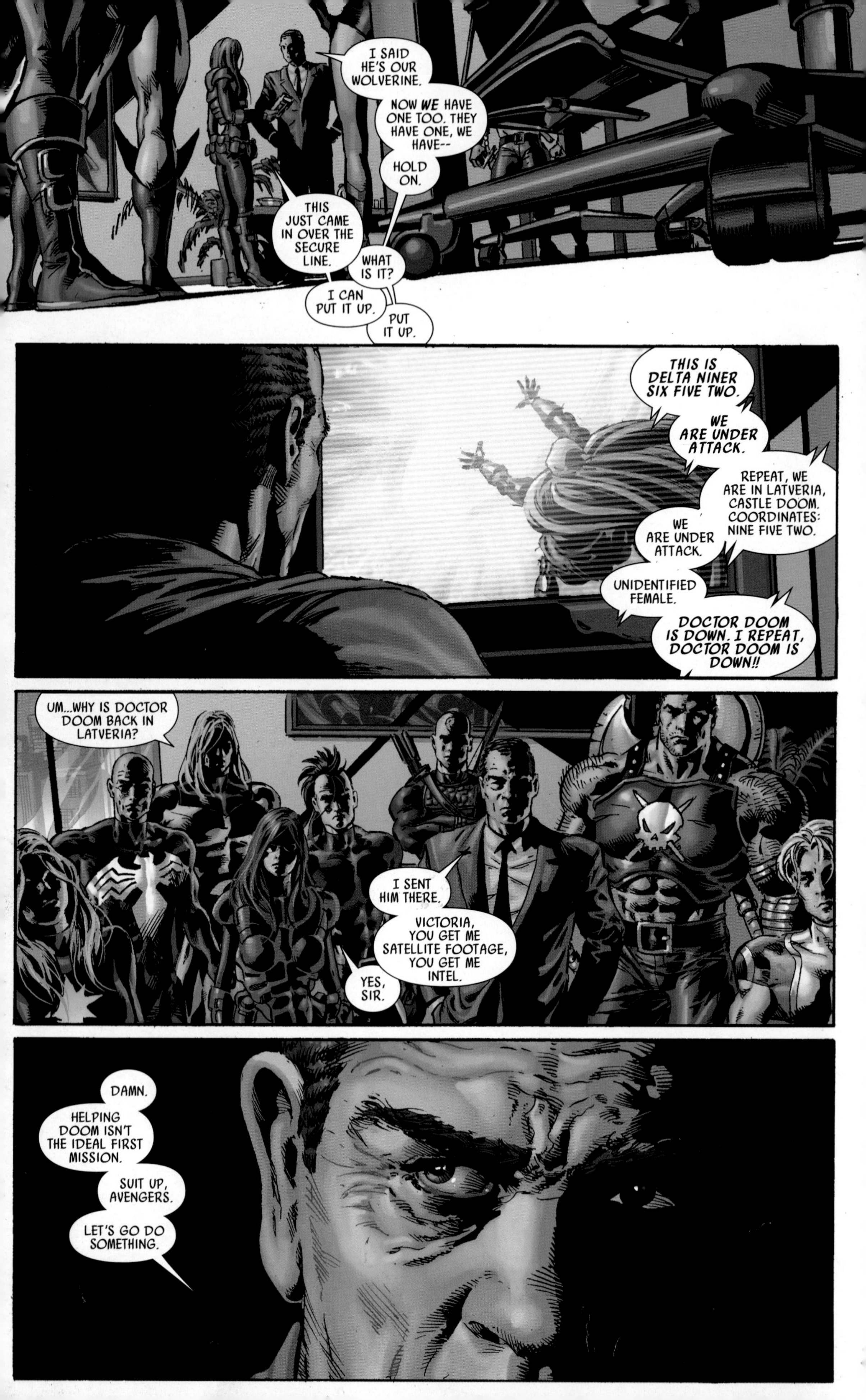
I SAID HE'S OUR WOLVERINE.
NOW **WE** HAVE ONE TOO. THEY HAVE ONE, WE HAVE--
HOLD ON.
THIS JUST CAME IN OVER THE SECURE LINE.
WHAT IS IT?
I CAN PUT IT UP.
PUT IT UP.
THIS IS DELTA NINER SIX FIVE TWO.
WE ARE UNDER ATTACK.
REPEAT, WE ARE IN LATVERIA, CASTLE DOOM. COORDINATES: NINE FIVE TWO.
WE ARE UNDER ATTACK.
UNIDENTIFIED FEMALE.
DOCTOR DOOM IS DOWN. I REPEAT, DOCTOR DOOM IS DOWN!!
UM...WHY IS DOCTOR DOOM BACK IN LATVERIA?
I SENT HIM THERE.
VICTORIA, YOU GET ME SATELLITE FOOTAGE, YOU GET ME INTEL.
YES, SIR.
DAMN.
HELPING DOOM ISN'T THE IDEAL FIRST MISSION.
SUIT UP, AVENGERS.
LET'S GO DO SOMETHING.

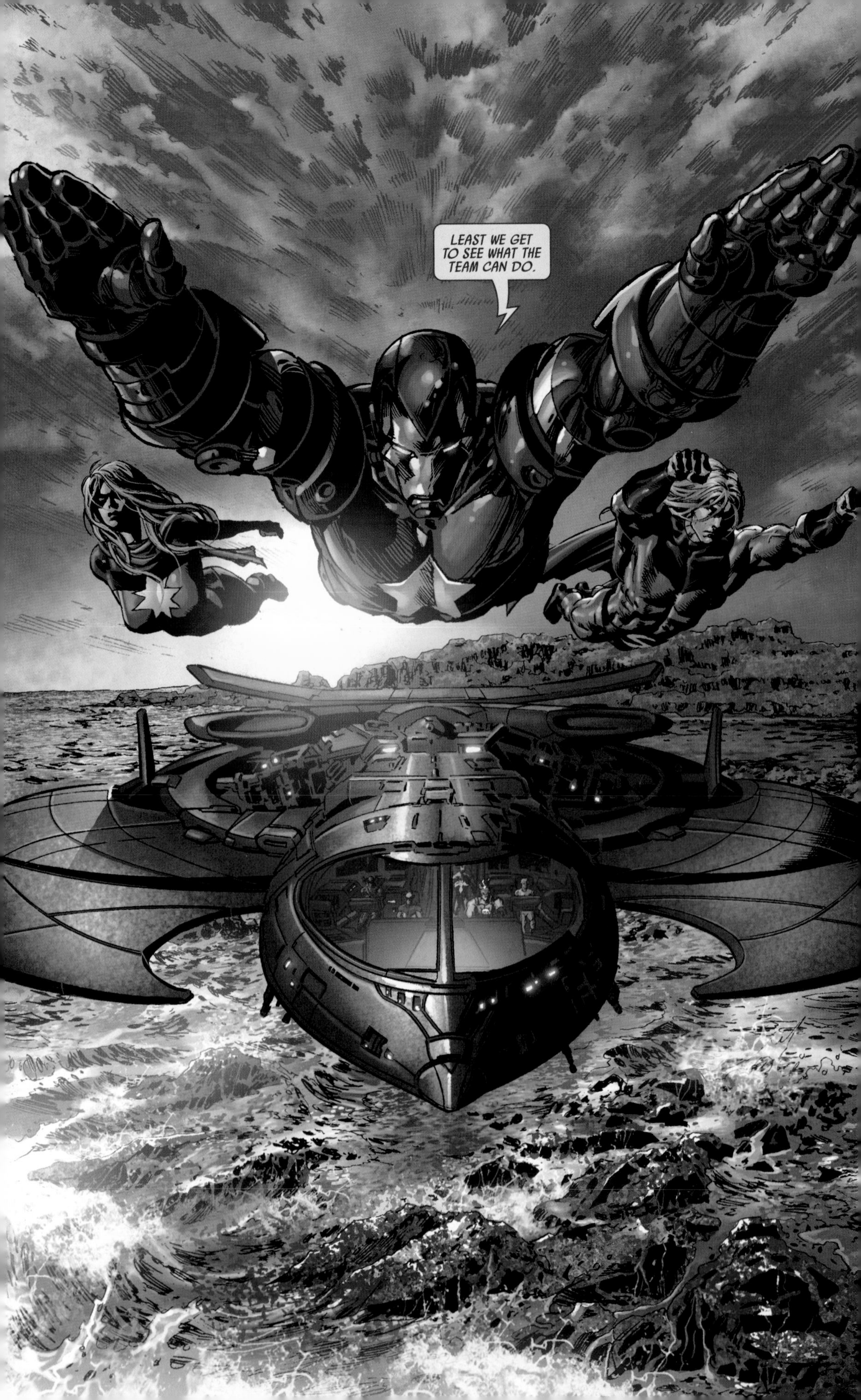
LEAST WE GET TO SEE WHAT THE TEAM CAN DO.

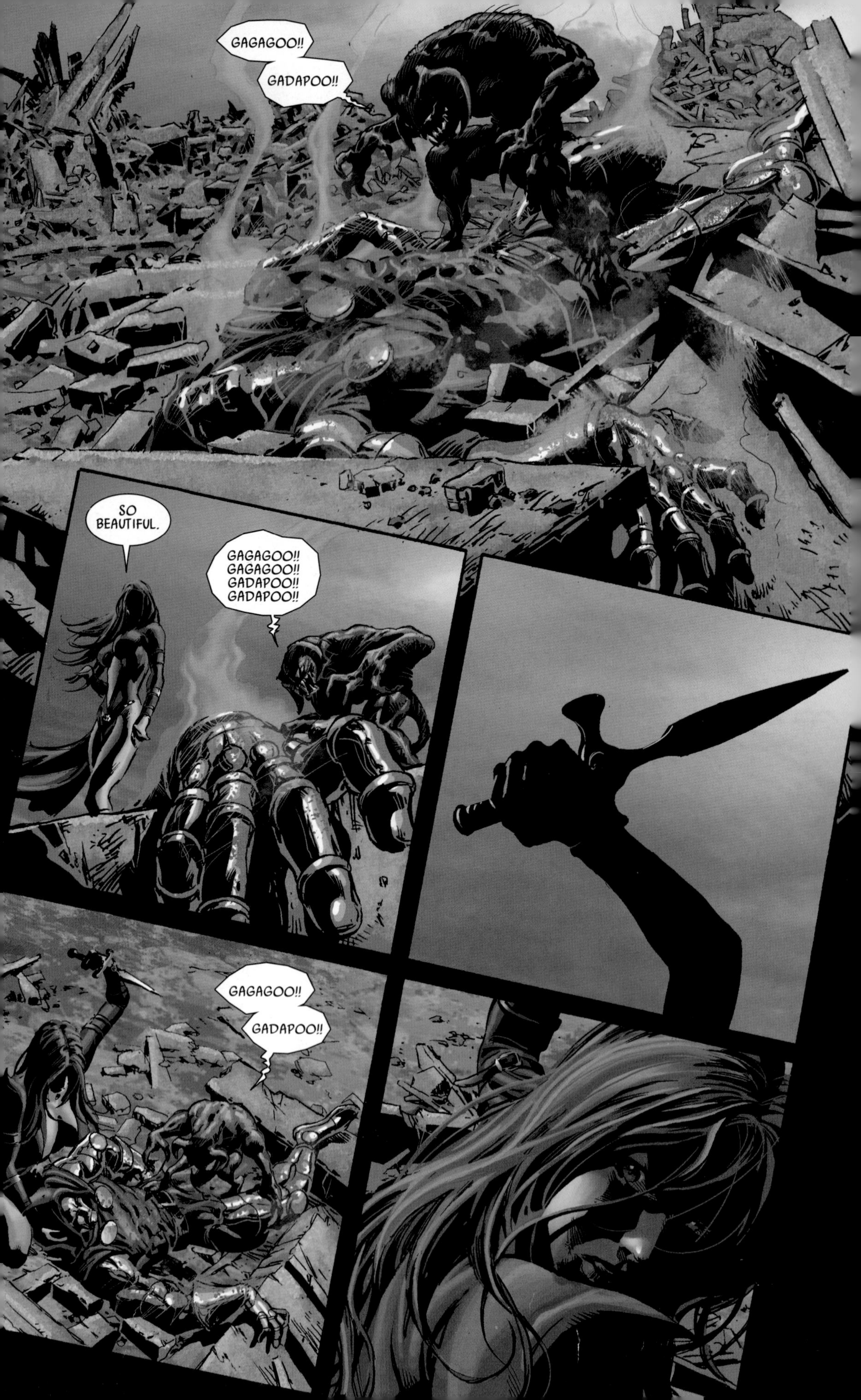
GAGAGOO!!
GADAPOO!!
SO BEAUTIFUL.
GAGAGOO!! GAGAGOO!! GADAPOO!! GADAPOO!!
GAGAGOO!!
GADAPOO!!

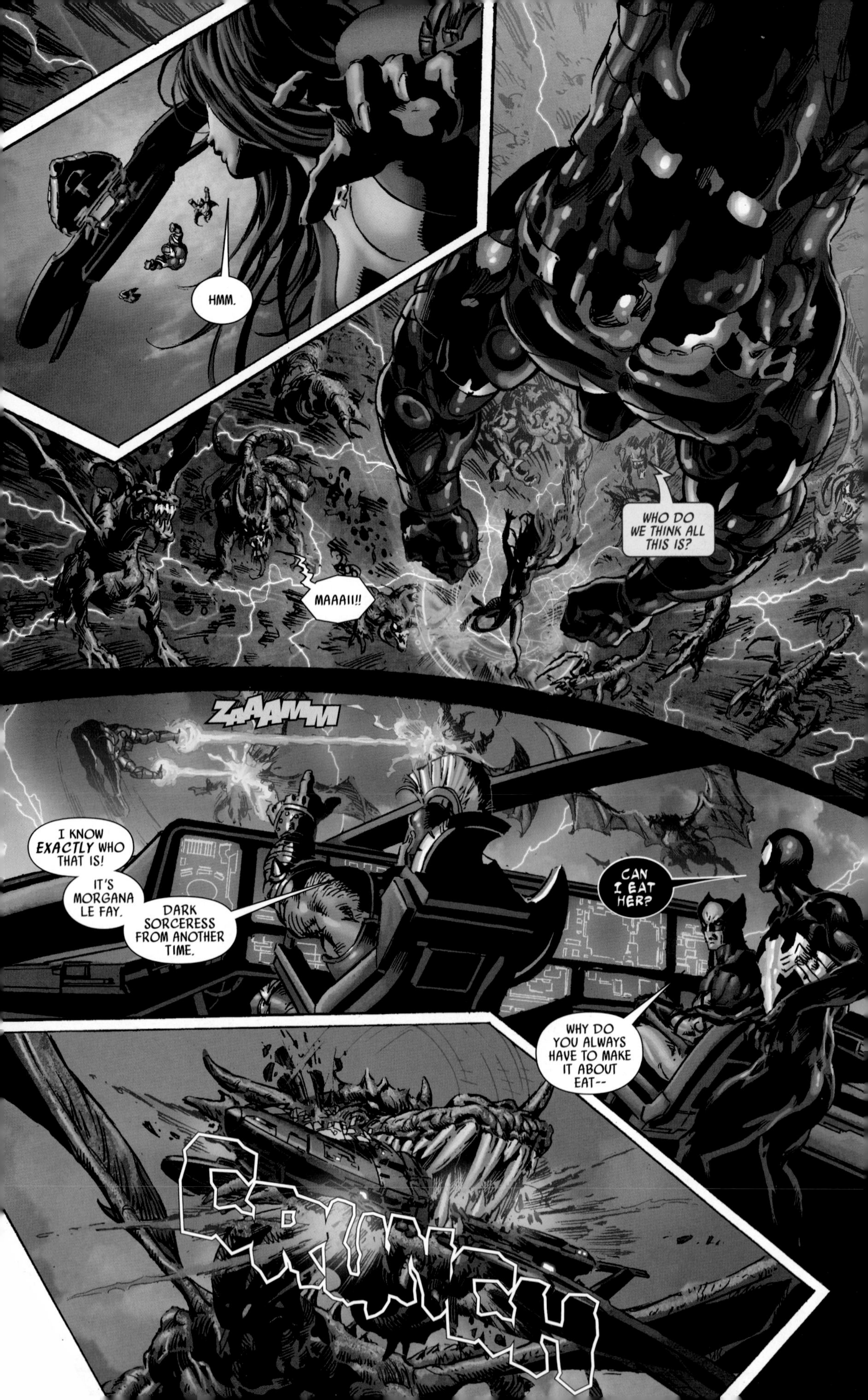
HMM.
WHO DO WE THINK ALL THIS IS?
MAAAII!!
ZAAAMMM
I KNOW EXACTLY WHO THAT IS!
IT'S MORGANA LE FAY.
DARK SORCERESS FROM ANOTHER TIME.
CAN I EAT HER?
WHY DO YOU ALWAYS HAVE TO MAKE IT ABOUT EAT--
CRUNCH

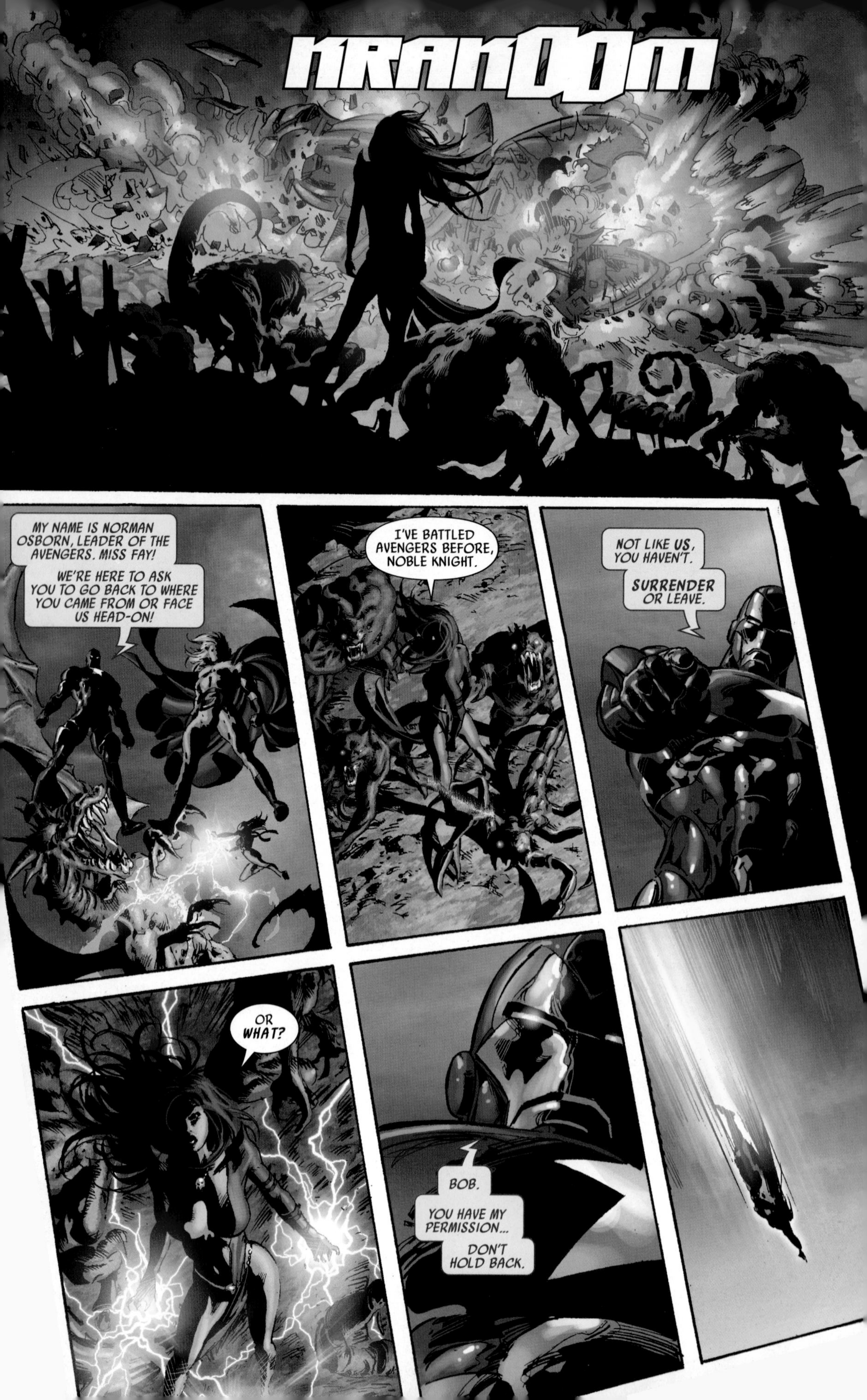
KRAKOOM
MY NAME IS NORMAN OSBORN, LEADER OF THE AVENGERS. MISS FAY!
WE'RE HERE TO ASK YOU TO GO BACK TO WHERE YOU CAME FROM OR FACE US HEAD-ON!
I'VE BATTLED AVENGERS BEFORE, NOBLE KNIGHT.
NOT LIKE US, YOU HAVEN'T.
SURRENDER OR LEAVE.
OR WHAT?
BOB.
YOU HAVE MY PERMISSION...
DON'T HOLD BACK.

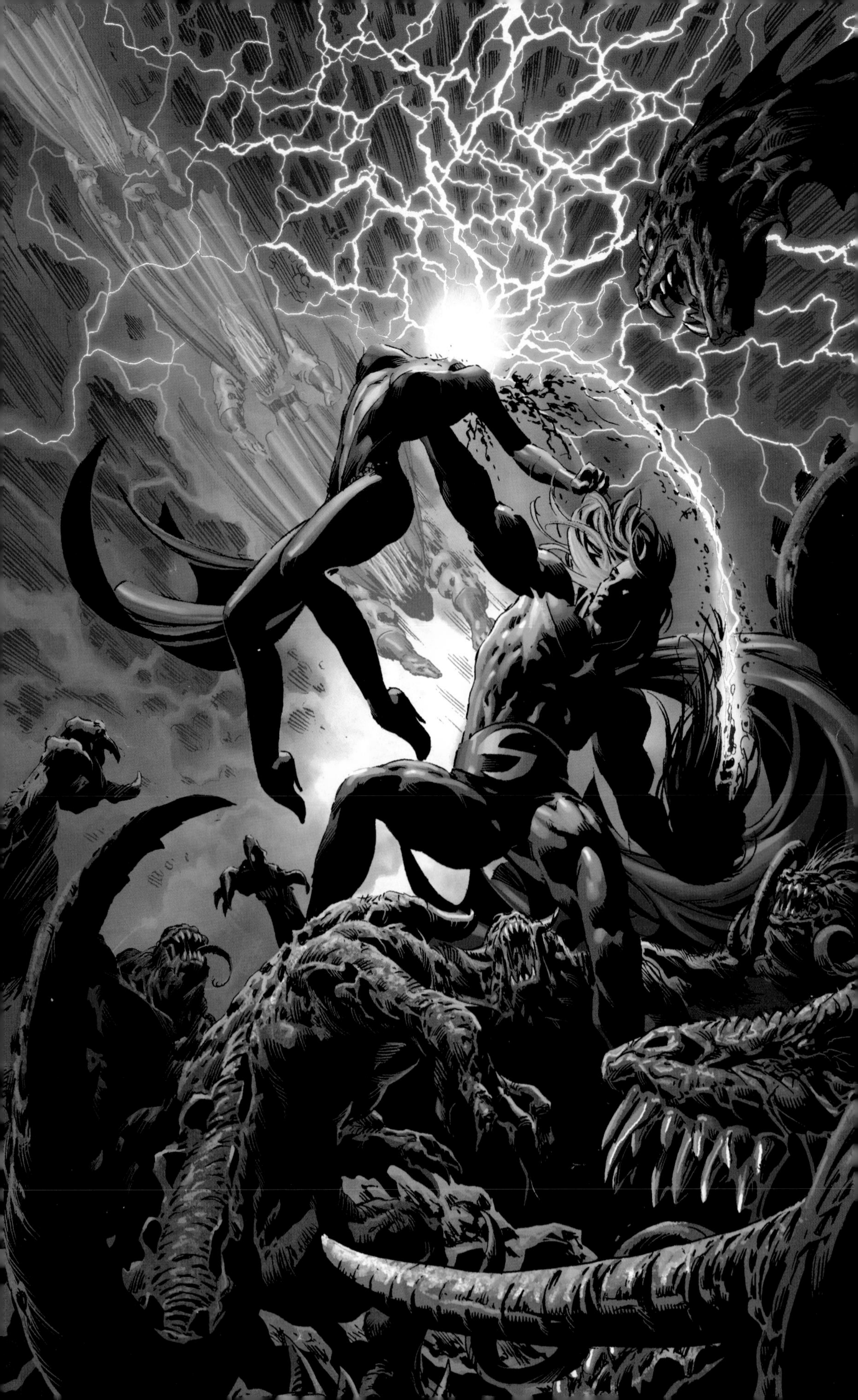

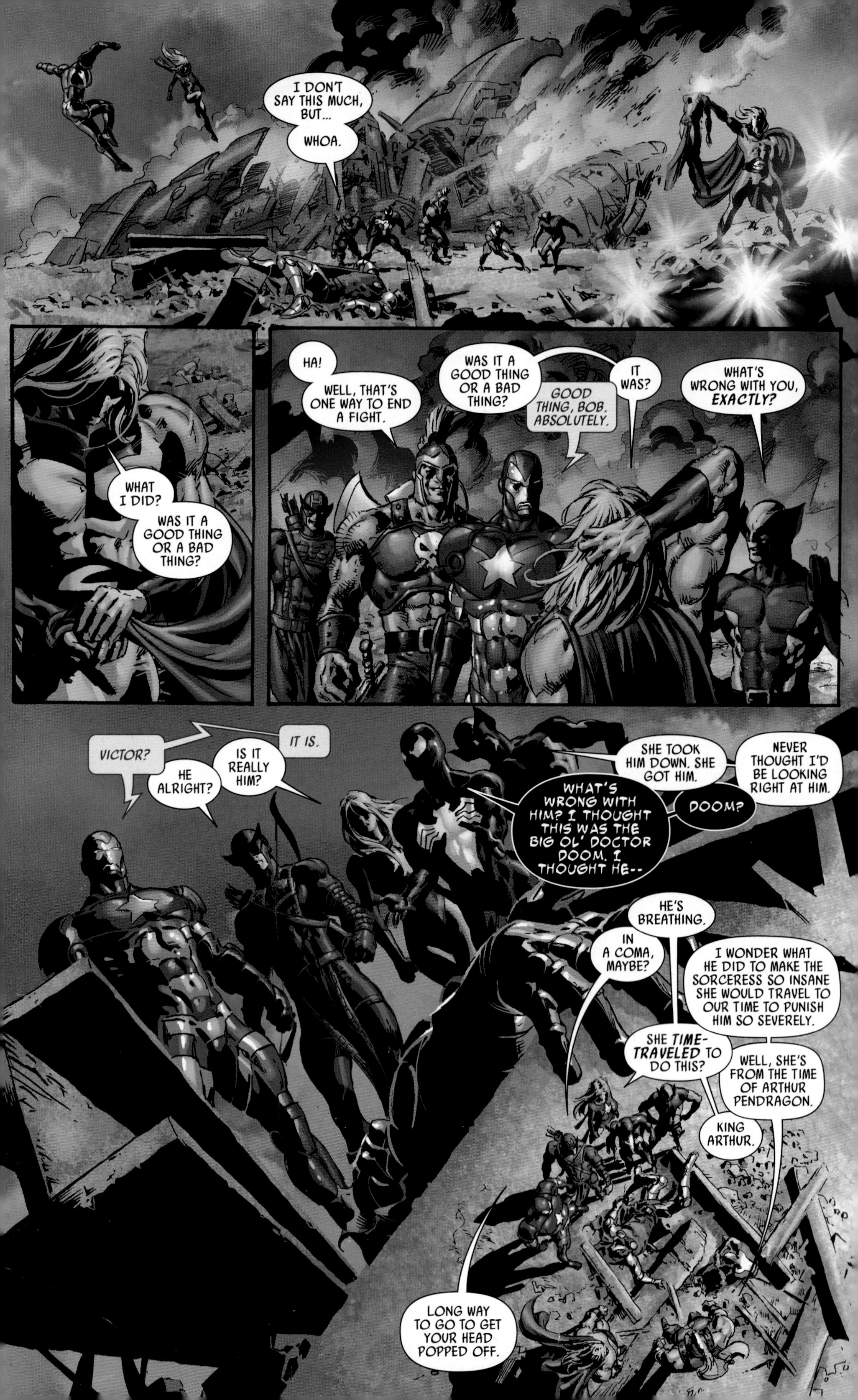
I DON'T SAY THIS MUCH, BUT...
WHOA.
WHAT I DID?
WAS IT A GOOD THING OR A BAD THING?
HA!
WELL, THAT'S ONE WAY TO END A FIGHT.
WAS IT A GOOD THING OR A BAD THING?
GOOD THING, BOB. ABSOLUTELY.
IT WAS?
WHAT'S WRONG WITH YOU, EXACTLY?
VICTOR?
HE ALRIGHT?
IS IT REALLY HIM?
IT IS.
WHAT'S WRONG WITH HIM? I THOUGHT THIS WAS THE BIG OL' DOCTOR DOOM. I THOUGHT HE--
SHE TOOK HIM DOWN. SHE GOT HIM.
DOOM?
NEVER THOUGHT I'D BE LOOKING RIGHT AT HIM.
HE'S BREATHING.
IN A COMA, MAYBE?
I WONDER WHAT HE DID TO MAKE THE SORCERESS SO INSANE SHE WOULD TRAVEL TO OUR TIME TO PUNISH HIM SO SEVERELY.
SHE TIME-TRAVELED TO DO THIS?
WELL, SHE'S FROM THE TIME OF ARTHUR PENDRAGON.
KING ARTHUR.
LONG WAY TO GO TO GET YOUR HEAD POPPED OFF.

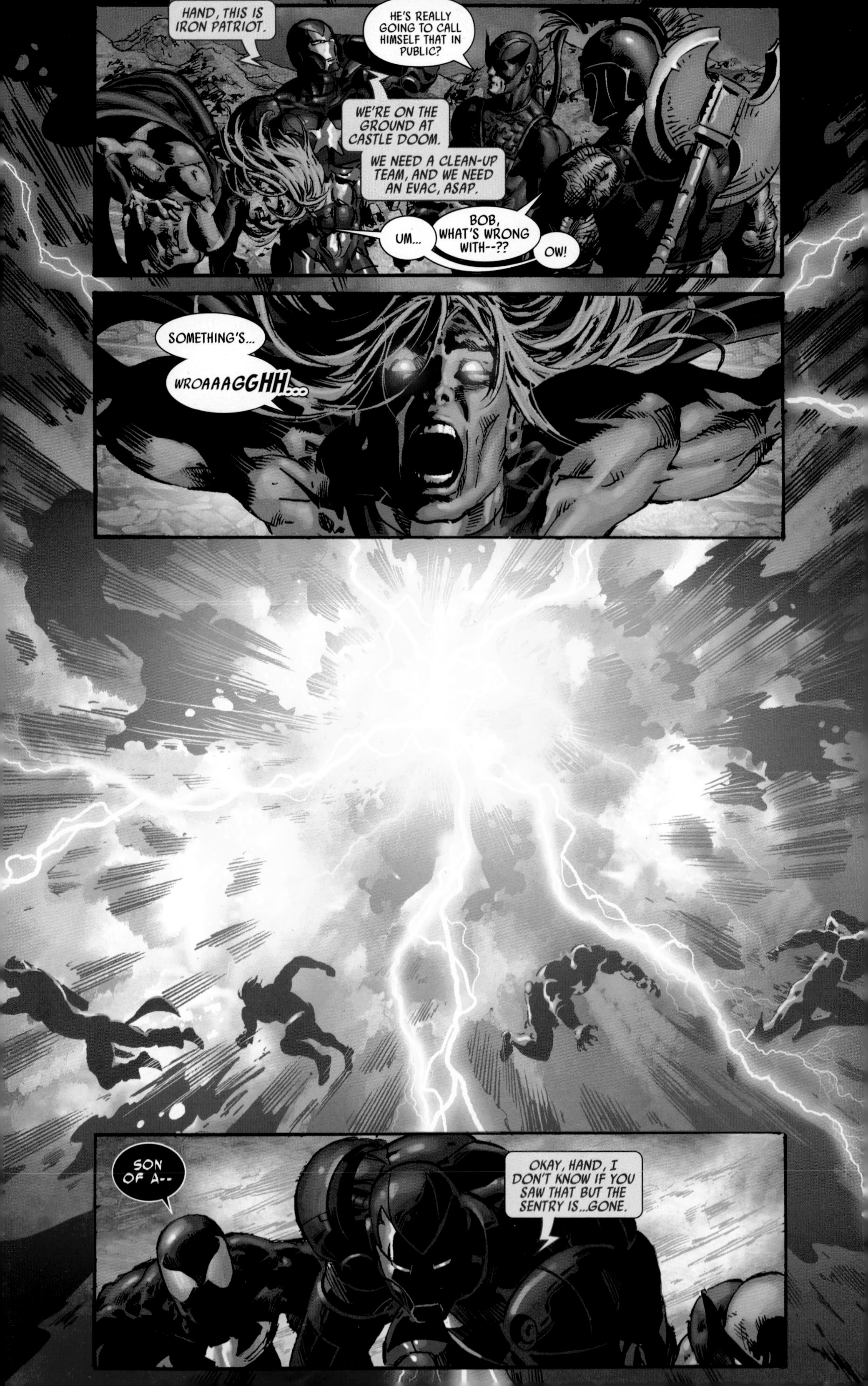
HAND, THIS IS IRON PATRIOT.
HE'S REALLY GOING TO CALL HIMSELF THAT IN PUBLIC?
WE'RE ON THE GROUND AT CASTLE DOOM.
WE NEED A CLEAN-UP TEAM, AND WE NEED AN EVAC, ASAP.
UM...
BOB, WHAT'S WRONG WITH--??
OW!
SOMETHING'S...
WROAAAGGHH...
SON OF A--
OKAY, HAND, I DON'T KNOW IF YOU SAW THAT BUT THE SENTRY IS...GONE.

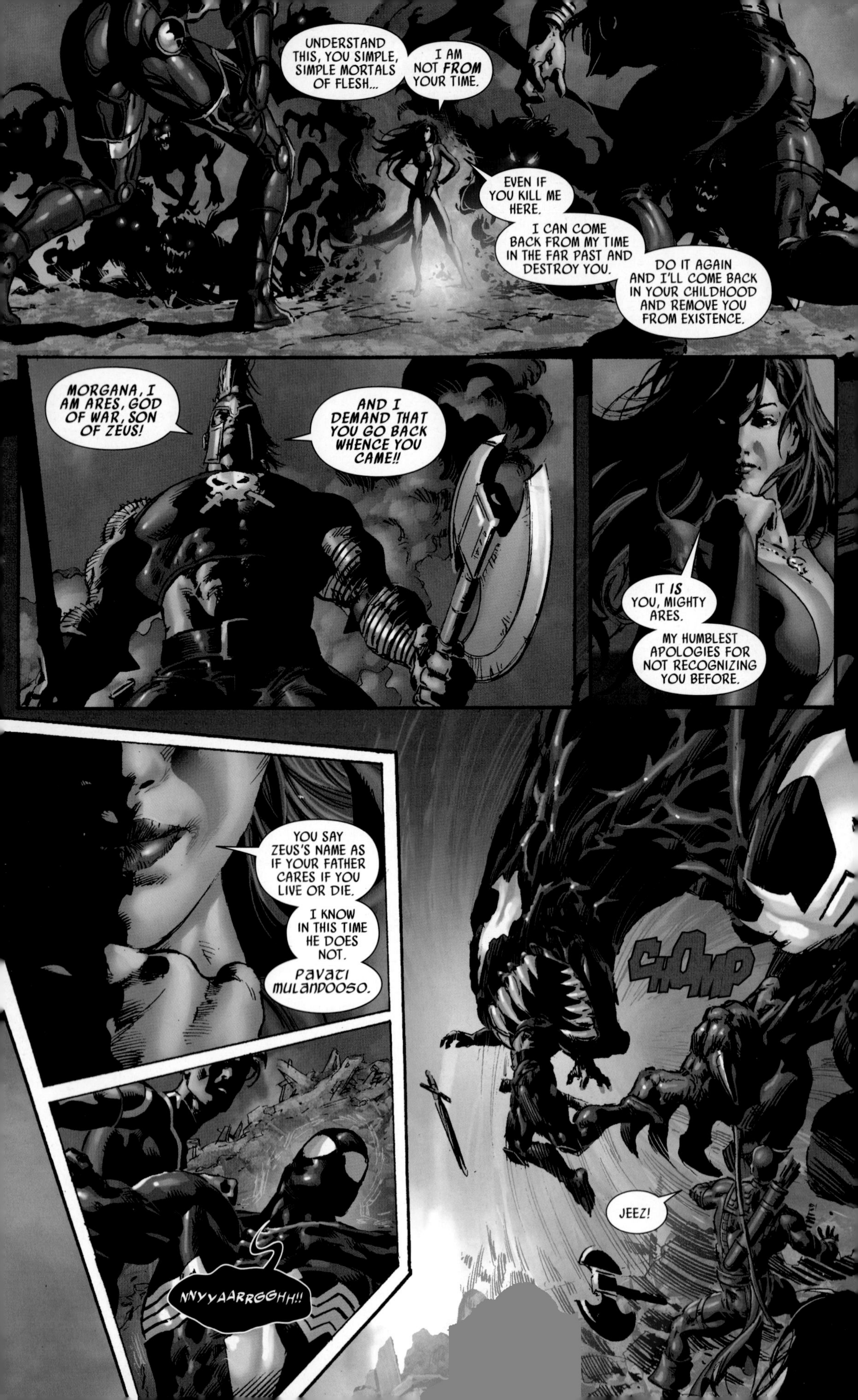
UNDERSTAND THIS, YOU SIMPLE, SIMPLE MORTALS OF FLESH...
I AM NOT FROM YOUR TIME.
EVEN IF YOU KILL ME HERE.
I CAN COME BACK FROM MY TIME IN THE FAR PAST AND DESTROY YOU.
DO IT AGAIN AND I'LL COME BACK IN YOUR CHILDHOOD AND REMOVE YOU FROM EXISTENCE.
MORGANA, I AM ARES, GOD OF WAR, SON OF ZEUS!
AND I DEMAND THAT YOU GO BACK WHENCE YOU CAME!!
IT IS YOU, MIGHTY ARES.
MY HUMBLEST APOLOGIES FOR NOT RECOGNIZING YOU BEFORE.
YOU SAY ZEUS'S NAME AS IF YOUR FATHER CARES IF YOU LIVE OR DIE.
I KNOW IN THIS TIME HE DOES NOT.
PAVATI MULANDOOSO.
NNYYAARRGGHH!!
CHOMP
JEEZ!

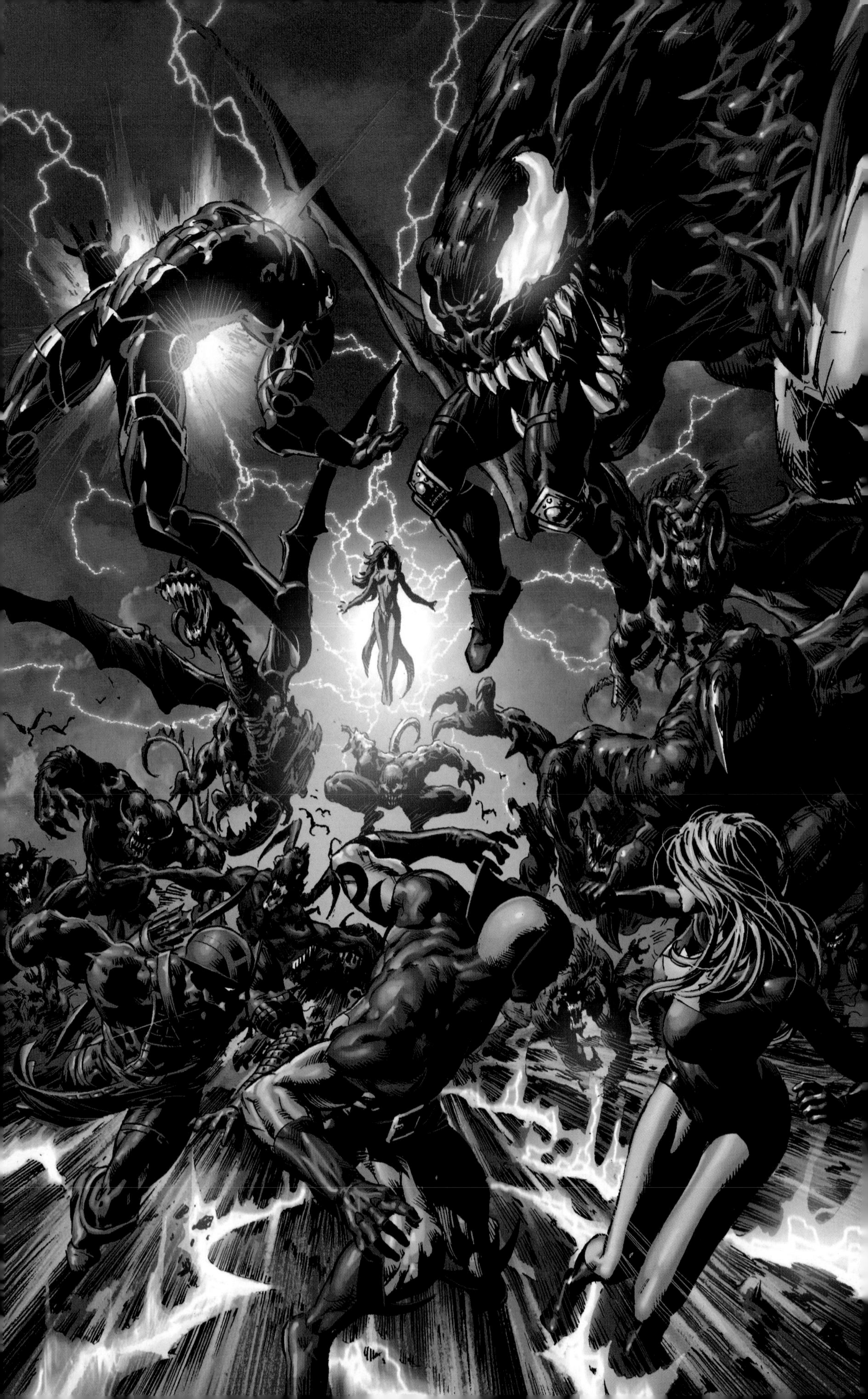

DARK AVENGERS #3

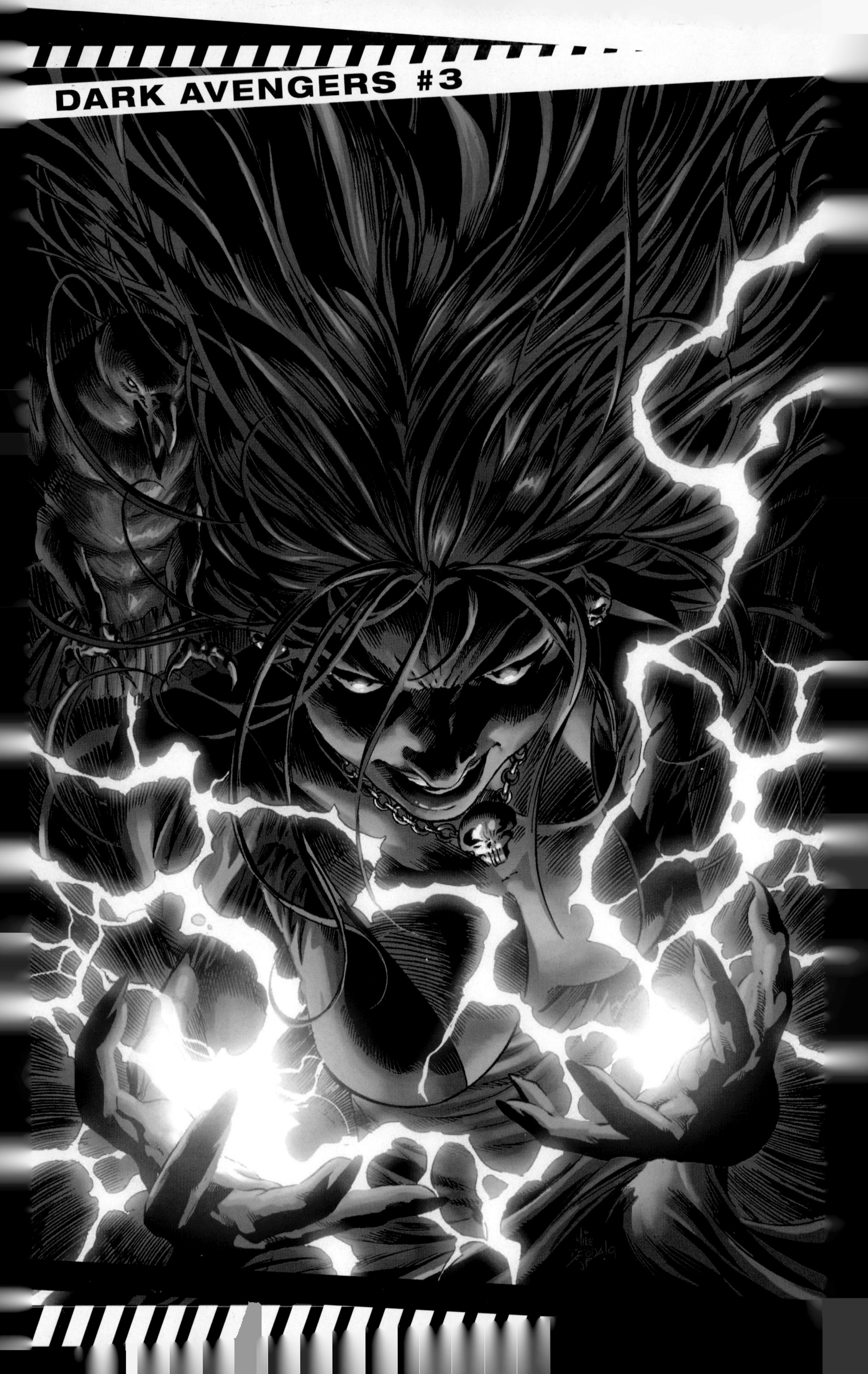

DARK AVENGERS #3 VARIANT

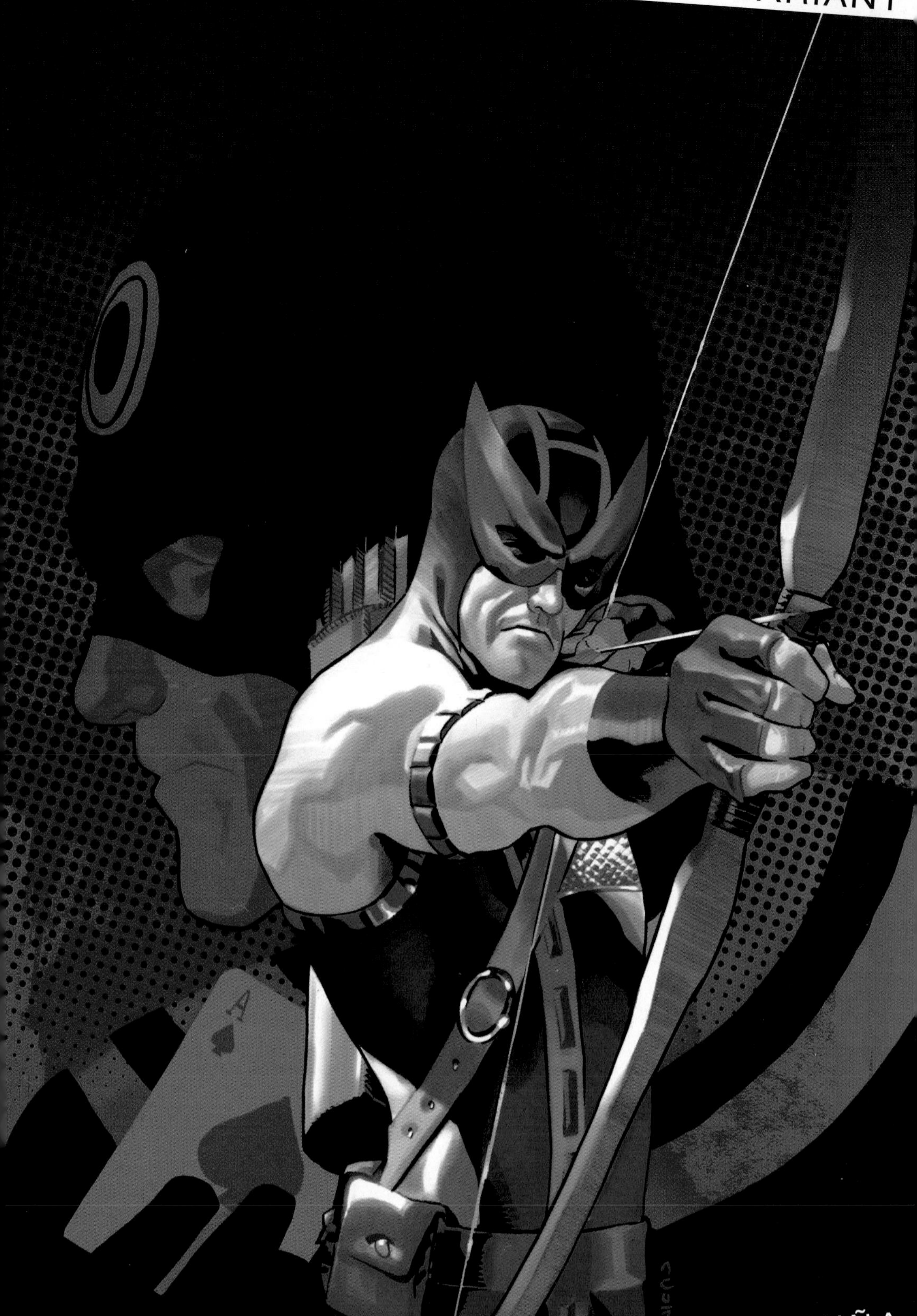

BY DANIEL ACUÑA

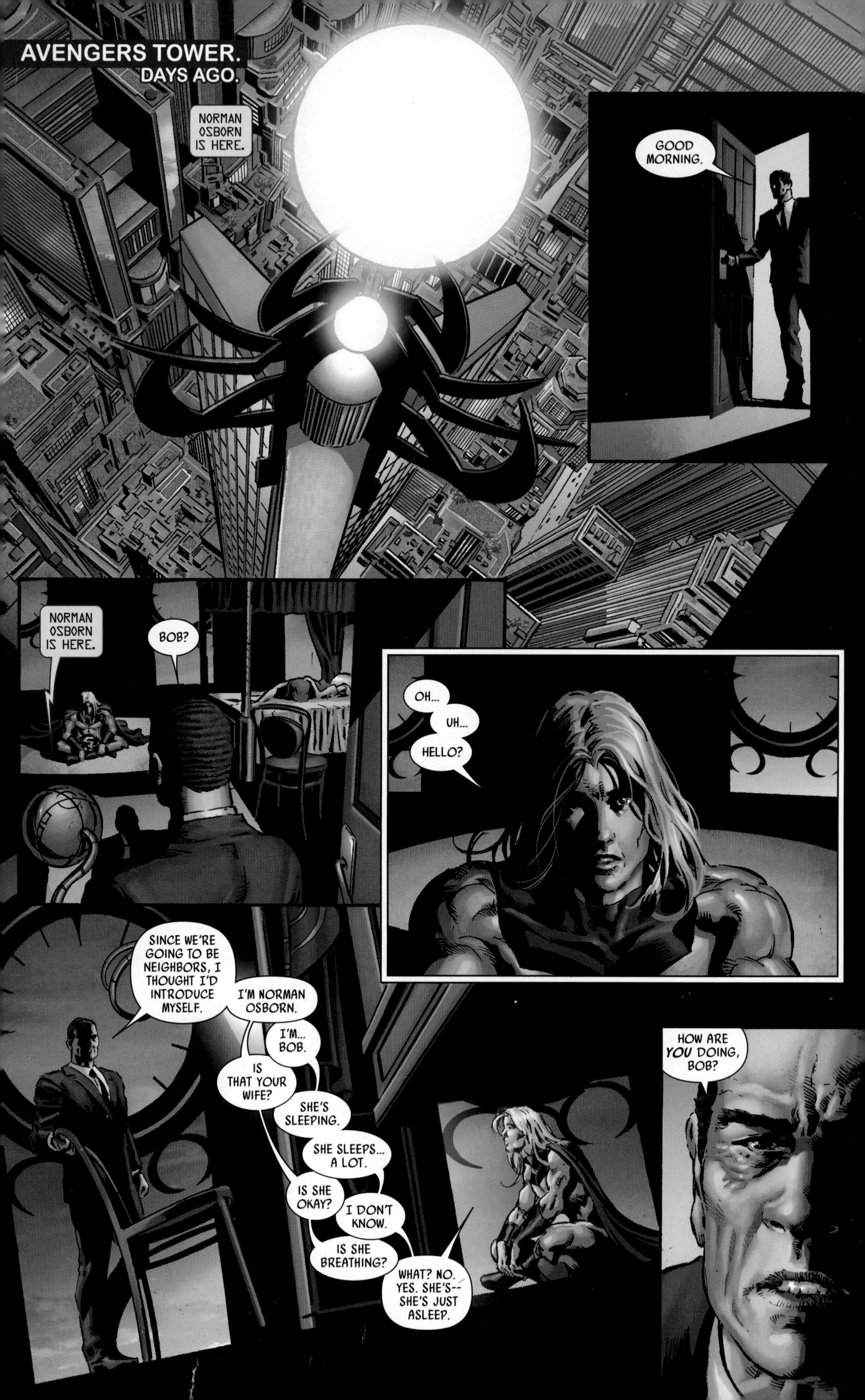
AVENGERS TOWER.
DAYS AGO.
NORMAN OSBORN IS HERE.
GOOD MORNING.
NORMAN OSBORN IS HERE.
BOB?
OH...
UH...
HELLO?
SINCE WE'RE GOING TO BE NEIGHBORS, I THOUGHT I'D INTRODUCE MYSELF.
I'M NORMAN OSBORN.
I'M... BOB.
IS THAT YOUR WIFE?
SHE'S SLEEPING.
SHE SLEEPS... A LOT.
IS SHE OKAY?
I DON'T KNOW.
IS SHE BREATHING?
WHAT? NO. YES. SHE'S-- SHE'S JUST ASLEEP.
HOW ARE YOU DOING, BOB?

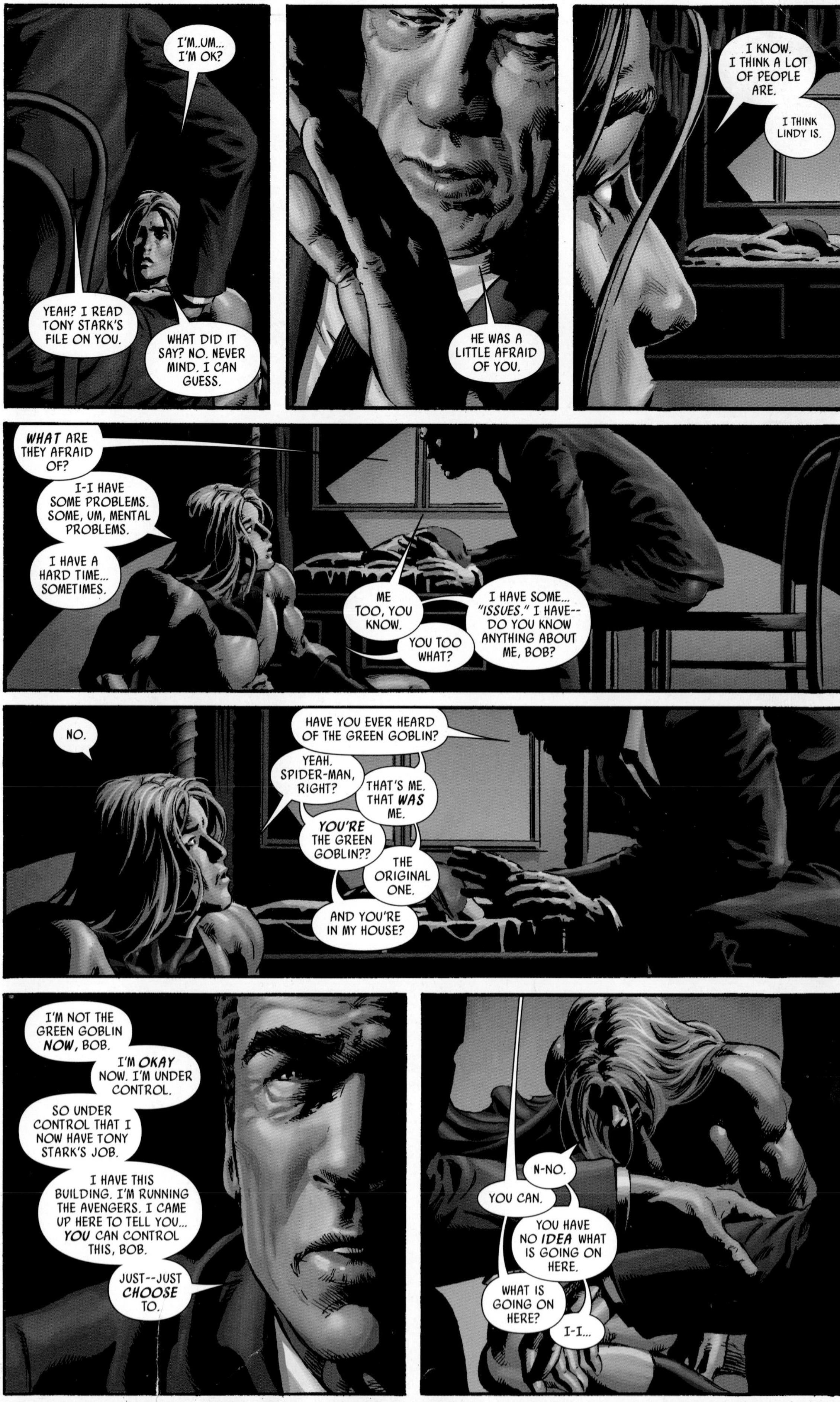
I'M..UM... I'M OK?
YEAH? I READ TONY STARK'S FILE ON YOU.
WHAT DID IT SAY? NO. NEVER MIND. I CAN GUESS.
HE WAS A LITTLE AFRAID OF YOU.
I KNOW. I THINK A LOT OF PEOPLE ARE.
I THINK LINDY IS.
WHAT ARE THEY AFRAID OF?
I-I HAVE SOME PROBLEMS. SOME, UM, MENTAL PROBLEMS.
I HAVE A HARD TIME... SOMETIMES.
ME TOO, YOU KNOW.
YOU TOO WHAT?
I HAVE SOME... "ISSUES." I HAVE-- DO YOU KNOW ANYTHING ABOUT ME, BOB?
NO.
HAVE YOU EVER HEARD OF THE GREEN GOBLIN?
YEAH. SPIDER-MAN, RIGHT?
THAT'S ME. THAT WAS ME.
YOU'RE THE GREEN GOBLIN??
THE ORIGINAL ONE.
AND YOU'RE IN MY HOUSE?
I'M NOT THE GREEN GOBLIN NOW, BOB.
I'M OKAY NOW. I'M UNDER CONTROL.
SO UNDER CONTROL THAT I NOW HAVE TONY STARK'S JOB.
I HAVE THIS BUILDING. I'M RUNNING THE AVENGERS. I CAME UP HERE TO TELL YOU... YOU CAN CONTROL THIS, BOB.
JUST--JUST CHOOSE TO.
N-NO.
YOU CAN.
YOU HAVE NO IDEA WHAT IS GOING ON HERE.
WHAT IS GOING ON HERE?
I-I...

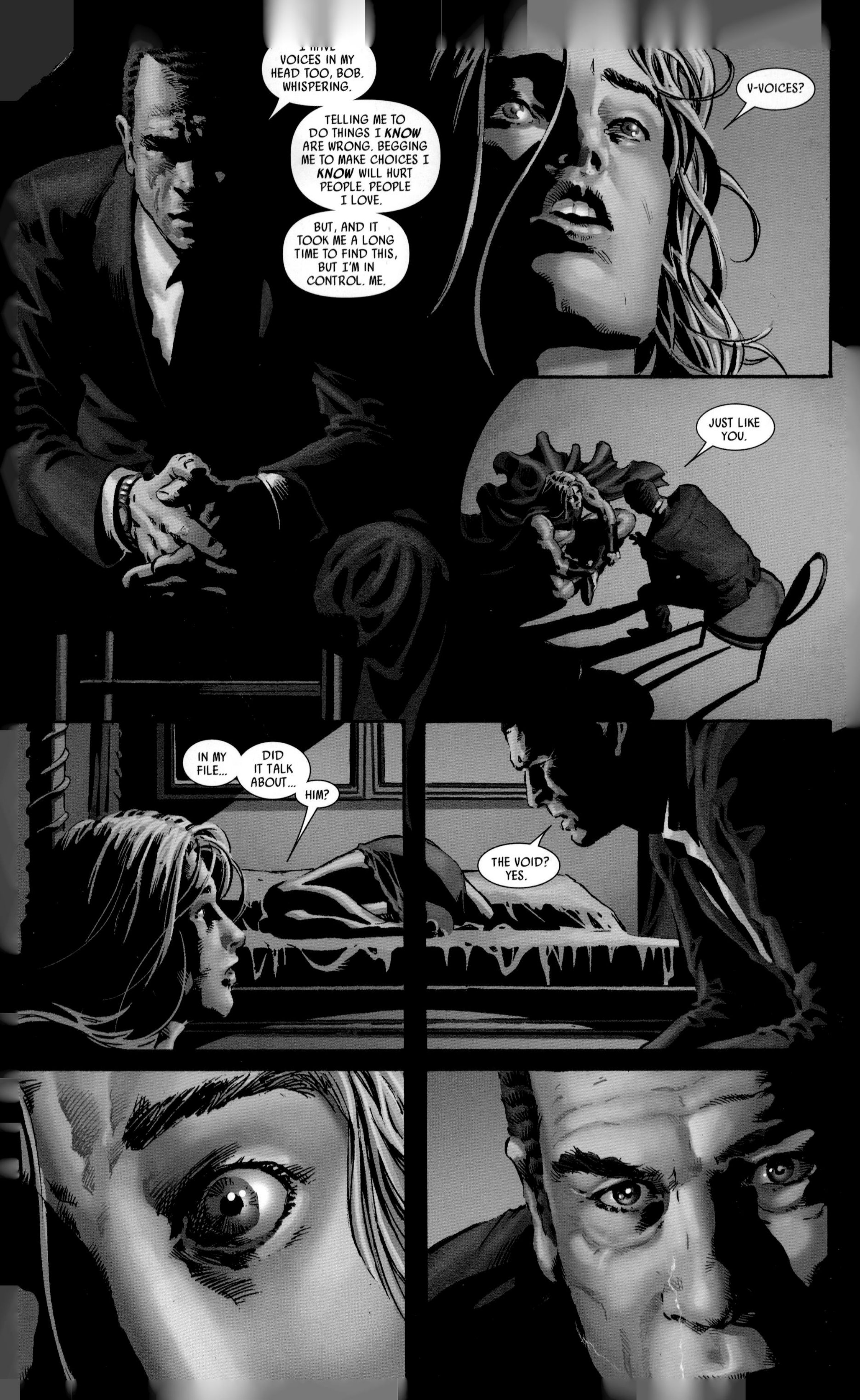
VOICES IN MY HEAD TOO, BOB. WHISPERING.
TELLING ME TO DO THINGS I **KNOW** ARE WRONG. BEGGING ME TO MAKE CHOICES I **KNOW** WILL HURT PEOPLE. PEOPLE I LOVE.
BUT, AND IT TOOK ME A LONG TIME TO FIND THIS, BUT I'M IN CONTROL. ME.
V-VOICES?
JUST LIKE YOU.
IN MY FILE...
DID IT TALK ABOUT...
HIM?
THE VOID? YES.

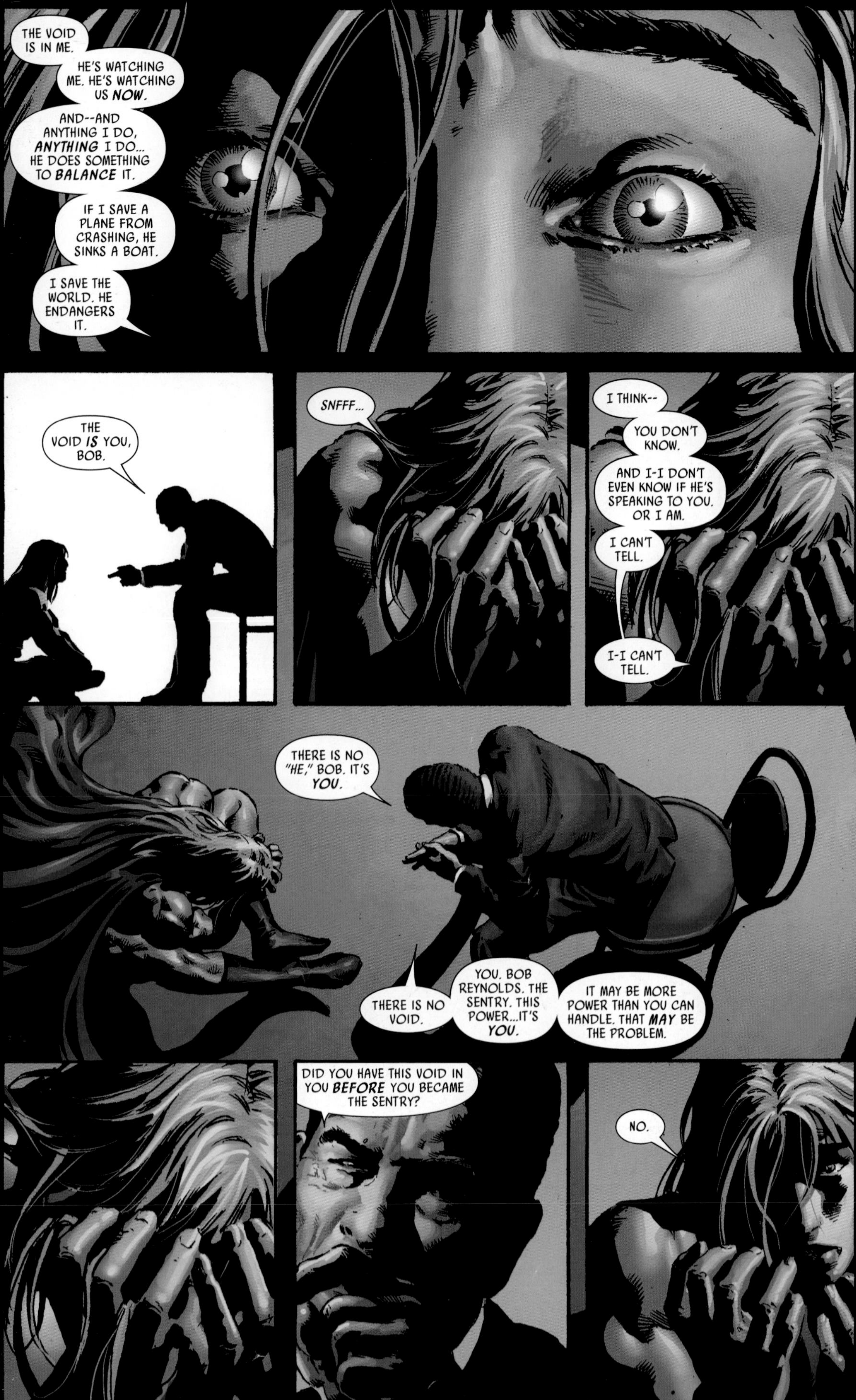
THE VOID IS IN ME.
HE'S WATCHING ME. HE'S WATCHING US NOW.
AND--AND ANYTHING I DO, ANYTHING I DO... HE DOES SOMETHING TO BALANCE IT.
IF I SAVE A PLANE FROM CRASHING, HE SINKS A BOAT.
I SAVE THE WORLD. HE ENDANGERS IT.
THE VOID IS YOU, BOB.
SNFFF...
I THINK--
YOU DON'T KNOW.
AND I-I DON'T EVEN KNOW IF HE'S SPEAKING TO YOU. OR I AM.
I CAN'T TELL.
I-I CAN'T TELL.
THERE IS NO "HE," BOB. IT'S YOU.
THERE IS NO VOID.
YOU. BOB REYNOLDS. THE SENTRY. THIS POWER...IT'S YOU.
IT MAY BE MORE POWER THAN YOU CAN HANDLE. THAT MAY BE THE PROBLEM.
DID YOU HAVE THIS VOID IN YOU BEFORE YOU BECAME THE SENTRY?
NO.

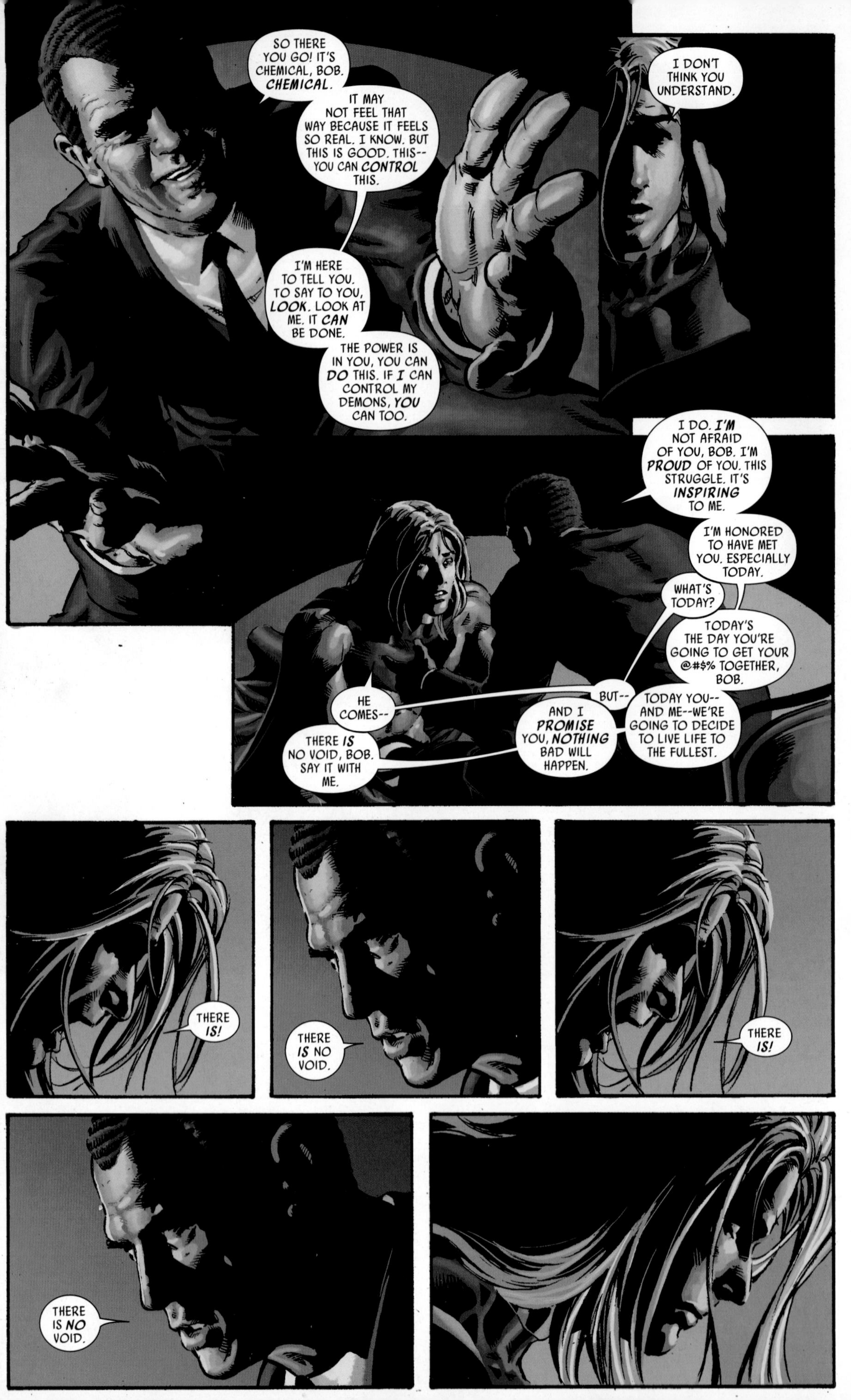
SO THERE YOU GO! IT'S CHEMICAL, BOB. CHEMICAL.
IT MAY NOT FEEL THAT WAY BECAUSE IT FEELS SO REAL. I KNOW. BUT THIS IS GOOD. THIS-- YOU CAN CONTROL THIS.
I'M HERE TO TELL YOU. TO SAY TO YOU, LOOK. LOOK AT ME. IT CAN BE DONE.
THE POWER IS IN YOU, YOU CAN DO THIS. IF I CAN CONTROL MY DEMONS, YOU CAN TOO.
I DON'T THINK YOU UNDERSTAND.
I DO. I'M NOT AFRAID OF YOU, BOB. I'M PROUD OF YOU. THIS STRUGGLE. IT'S INSPIRING TO ME.
I'M HONORED TO HAVE MET YOU. ESPECIALLY TODAY.
WHAT'S TODAY?
TODAY'S THE DAY YOU'RE GOING TO GET YOUR @#$% TOGETHER, BOB.
BUT--
TODAY YOU-- AND ME--WE'RE GOING TO DECIDE TO LIVE LIFE TO THE FULLEST.
AND I PROMISE YOU, NOTHING BAD WILL HAPPEN.
HE COMES--
THERE IS NO VOID, BOB. SAY IT WITH ME.
THERE IS!
THERE IS NO VOID.
THERE IS!
THERE IS NO VOID.

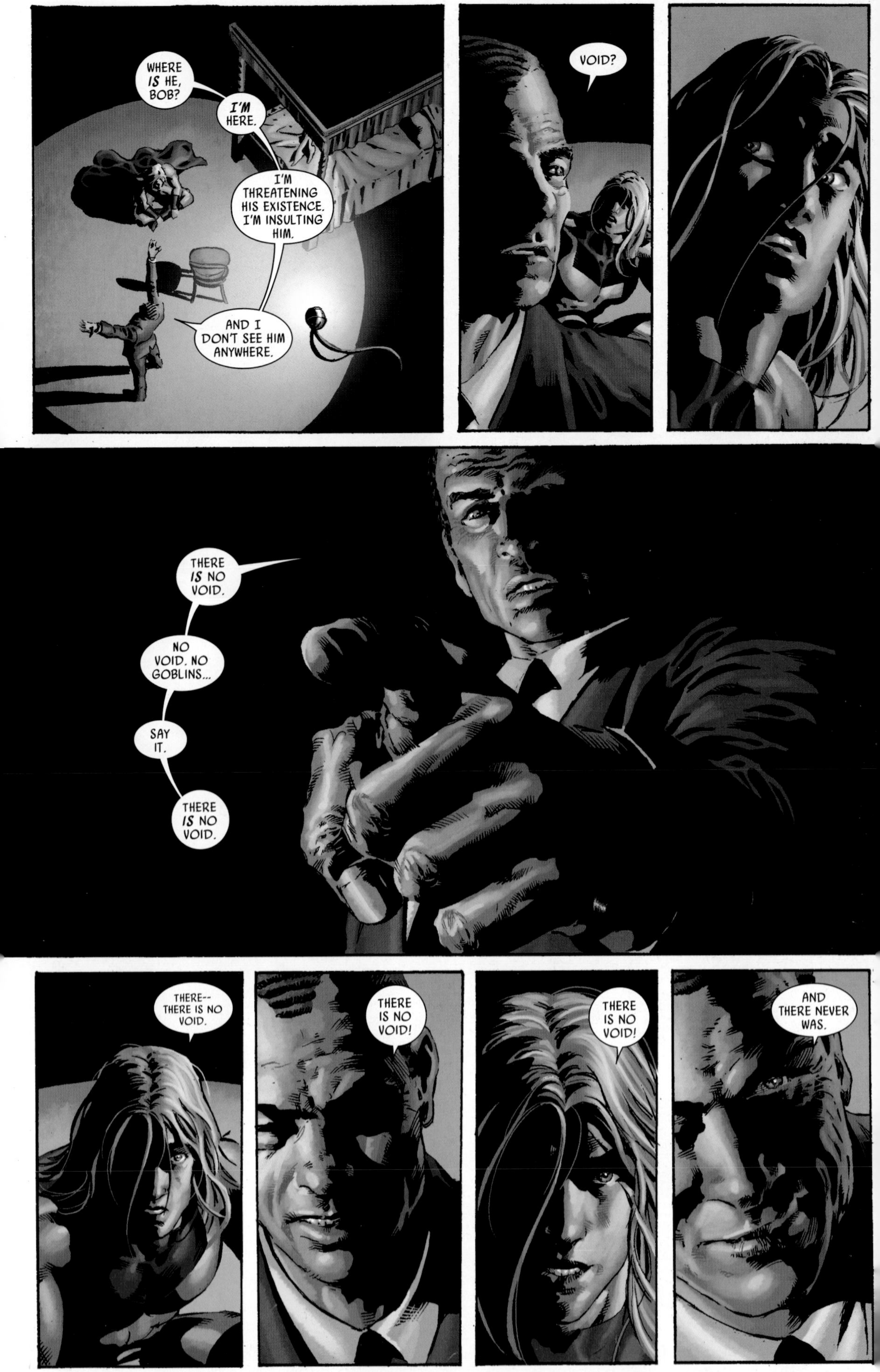
WHERE IS HE, BOB?
I'M HERE.
I'M THREATENING HIS EXISTENCE. I'M INSULTING HIM.
AND I DON'T SEE HIM ANYWHERE.
VOID?
THERE IS NO VOID.
NO VOID. NO GOBLINS...
SAY IT.
THERE IS NO VOID.
THERE-- THERE IS NO VOID.
THERE IS NO VOID!
THERE IS NO VOID!
AND THERE NEVER WAS.

IS HE TALKING TO YOU NOW?

WHO?

THE VOID.

DO YOU HEAR HIM?

NO.

DO YOU SEE HIM?

NO.

BECAUSE THERE IS NO VOID. AS LONG AS *YOU* SAY SO-- THERE IS *NO VOID.*

AS LONG AS *I* SAY SO?

HERE'S WHAT HAPPENS NEXT--WE'RE GOING TO USE OUR POWERS TO DO THAT WHICH TONY STARK AND NICK FURY AND CAPTAIN AMERICA COULD *NOT* DO.

WOULD YOU LIKE TO DO THAT WITH ME? WOULD YOU LIKE TO BE AN AVENGER? THE HERO YOU ARE?

TODAY?

NOW?

NOW?

NO.

NOW WE'RE GOING TO SHOWER AND SHAVE AND EAT AND SLEEP.

I DON'T THINK I HAVE TO DO THOSE THINGS ANYMORE. I DON'T SEEM TO NEED TO--

NOT BECAUSE YOU HAVE TO, BECAUSE YOU *WANT* TO. BECAUSE THEY MAKE YOU FEEL GOOD AND HUMAN.

THEY MAKE YOU FEEL LIKE... "BOB."

AND IF YOU *FEEL* LIKE BOB, YOU *ARE* BOB.

I THINK YOU'RE-- YOU KNOW WHAT?

I *DON'T* DO THOSE THINGS ANYMORE. YOU'RE RIGHT!

I LOVE A HOT SHOWER. I LOVE HAMBURGERS. I DO.

I HAVEN'T EATEN IN FOREVER.

AND WHEN YOU DENY YOURSELF YOUR HUMANITY...

YOU CREATE SOMETHING ELSE, YOU CREATE A...

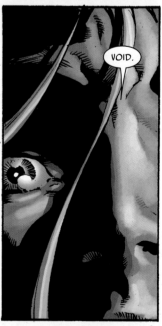

VOID.

EXACTLY.

OH MY GOD. YOU'RE RIGHT.

YOU'RE-- YOU'RE RIGHT.

YOU CRY, BOB.

BE HUMAN, FEEL THOSE FEELINGS.

I KNOW. YOU'RE RELIEVED.

I'M NOT SAD.

YOU KNOW WHY? BECAUSE YOU JUST REALIZED HOW GREAT YOUR LIFE IS GOING TO BE FROM NOW ON.

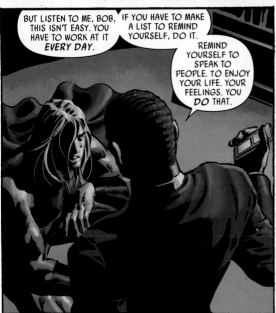

BUT LISTEN TO ME, BOB, THIS ISN'T EASY. YOU HAVE TO WORK AT IT *EVERY DAY.*

IF YOU HAVE TO MAKE A LIST TO REMIND YOURSELF, DO IT.

REMIND YOURSELF TO SPEAK TO PEOPLE. TO ENJOY YOUR LIFE. YOUR FEELINGS. YOU *DO* THAT.

JUST LIKE I DO. YOU TAKE THOSE VOID FEELINGS AND YOU PUSH THEM *DOWN.*

YOU FIGHT THEM DOWN AND YOU *BE* BOB REYNOLDS.

AND I'LL *HELP* YOU, BOB. EVERY DAY.

WE'LL HELP EACH OTHER.

YOU WILL?

DAMN RIGHT. WE'RE ROOMMATES NOW. *TEAMMATES* IF YOU WANT TO BE.

NO ONE HAS EVER TALKED TO ME LIKE THIS BEFORE.

DO YOU KNOW WHY?

BECAUSE NO ONE HAS UNDERSTOOD YOU LIKE I DO.

BELIEVE ME, THIS ROAD WE'RE ON, IT'S A TOUGH ONE, BUT WHEN IT WORKS...

WHEN THOSE MOMENTS HAPPEN...

IT'S *ALL* WORTH IT.

VICTORIA. I WANT YOU TO SEND SOMEONE OUT TO 5 GUYS BURGERS AND FRIES.

ORDER FOR EVERYONE, CHEESEBURGERS, SHAKES, FRIES, BACON BURGERS, ONION RINGS...

ORDER EVERYTHING THEY GOT. LET ME KNOW WHEN IT'S HERE.

WHAT? NO, I'M NOT JOKING.

5 GUYS BURGERS. YOU'RE GOING TO FAINT FROM HAPPINESS.

THANK YOU FOR THIS.

NO WORRIES.

VISTUNI MANANA.

VISTUNI ALAGULNAU.

VISTUNI CROLONU...

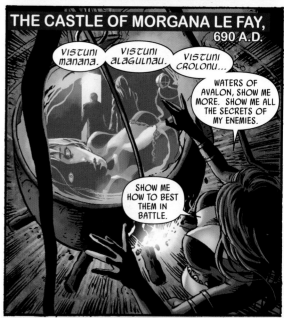

THE CASTLE OF MORGANA LE FAY, 690 A.D.

VISTUNI MANANA.

VISTUNI ALAGULNAU.

VISTUNI CROLONU...

WATERS OF AVALON, SHOW ME MORE. SHOW ME ALL THE SECRETS OF MY ENEMIES.

SHOW ME HOW TO BEST THEM IN BATTLE.

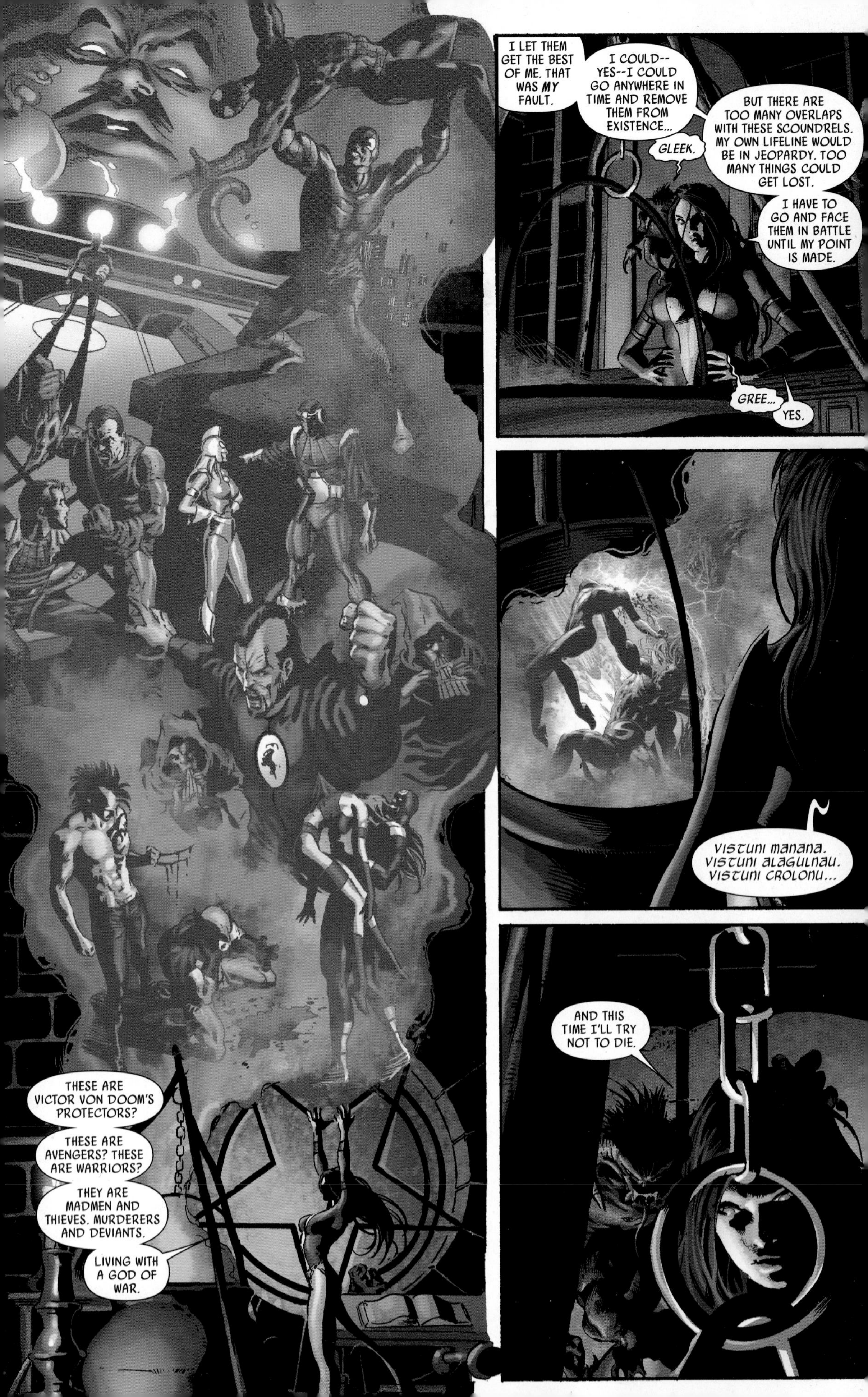
THESE ARE VICTOR VON DOOM'S PROTECTORS?
THESE ARE AVENGERS? THESE ARE WARRIORS?
THEY ARE MADMEN AND THIEVES. MURDERERS AND DEVIANTS.
LIVING WITH A GOD OF WAR.
I LET THEM GET THE BEST OF ME. THAT WAS MY FAULT.
I COULD-- YES--I COULD GO ANYWHERE IN TIME AND REMOVE THEM FROM EXISTENCE...
GLEEK.
BUT THERE ARE TOO MANY OVERLAPS WITH THESE SCOUNDRELS. MY OWN LIFELINE WOULD BE IN JEOPARDY. TOO MANY THINGS COULD GET LOST.
I HAVE TO GO AND FACE THEM IN BATTLE UNTIL MY POINT IS MADE.
GREE... YES.
VISTUNI MANANA. VISTUNI ALAGULNAU. VISTUNI CROLONU...
AND THIS TIME I'LL TRY NOT TO DIE.

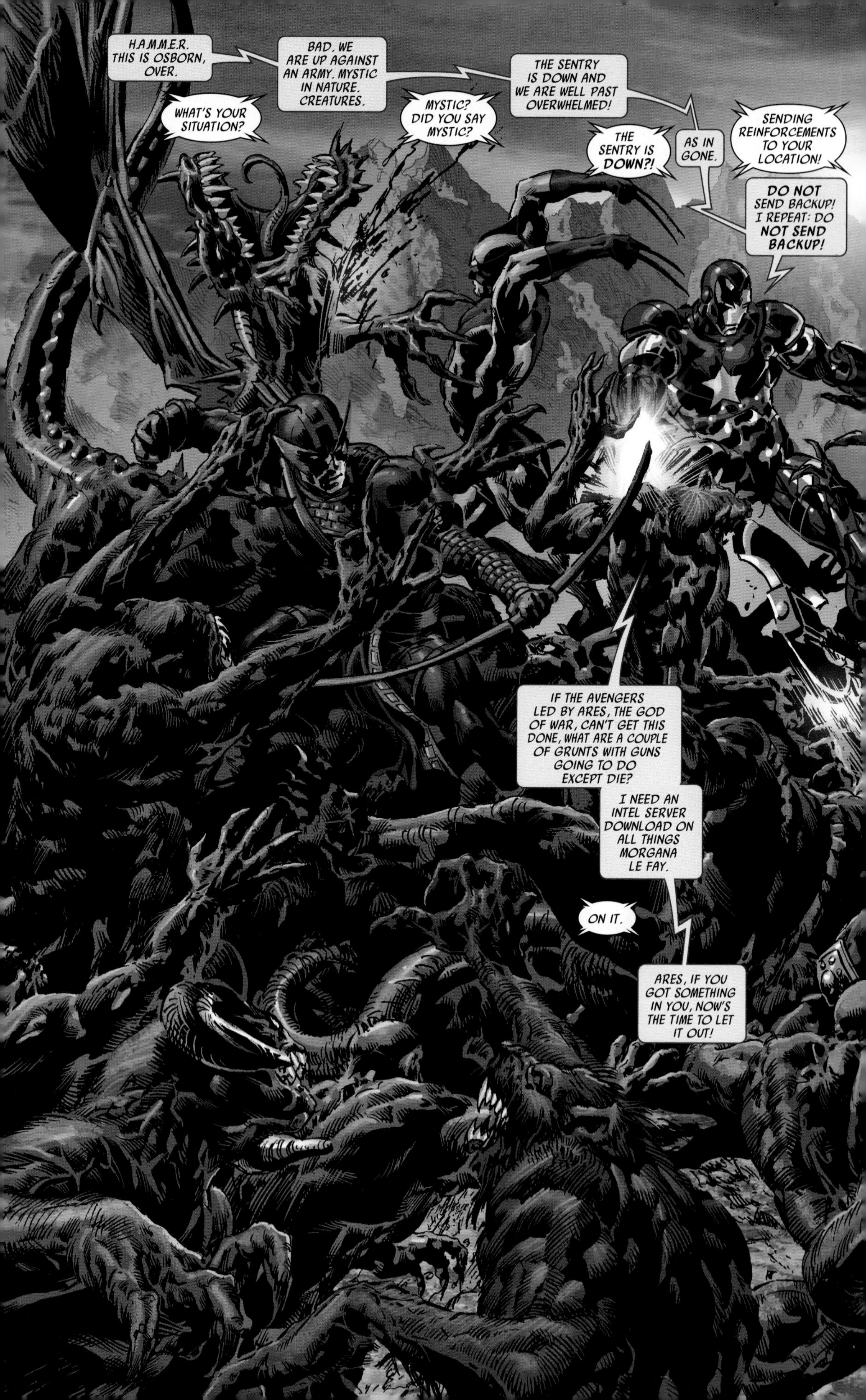
H.A.M.M.E.R. THIS IS OSBORN, OVER.
WHAT'S YOUR SITUATION?
BAD. WE ARE UP AGAINST AN ARMY. MYSTIC IN NATURE. CREATURES.
MYSTIC? DID YOU SAY MYSTIC?
THE SENTRY IS DOWN AND WE ARE WELL PAST OVERWHELMED!
THE SENTRY IS DOWN?!
AS IN GONE.
SENDING REINFORCEMENTS TO YOUR LOCATION!
DO NOT SEND BACKUP! I REPEAT: DO NOT SEND BACKUP!
IF THE AVENGERS LED BY ARES, THE GOD OF WAR, CAN'T GET THIS DONE, WHAT ARE A COUPLE OF GRUNTS WITH GUNS GOING TO DO EXCEPT DIE?
I NEED AN INTEL SERVER DOWNLOAD ON ALL THINGS MORGANA LE FAY.
ON IT.
ARES, IF YOU GOT SOMETHING IN YOU, NOW'S THE TIME TO LET IT OUT!

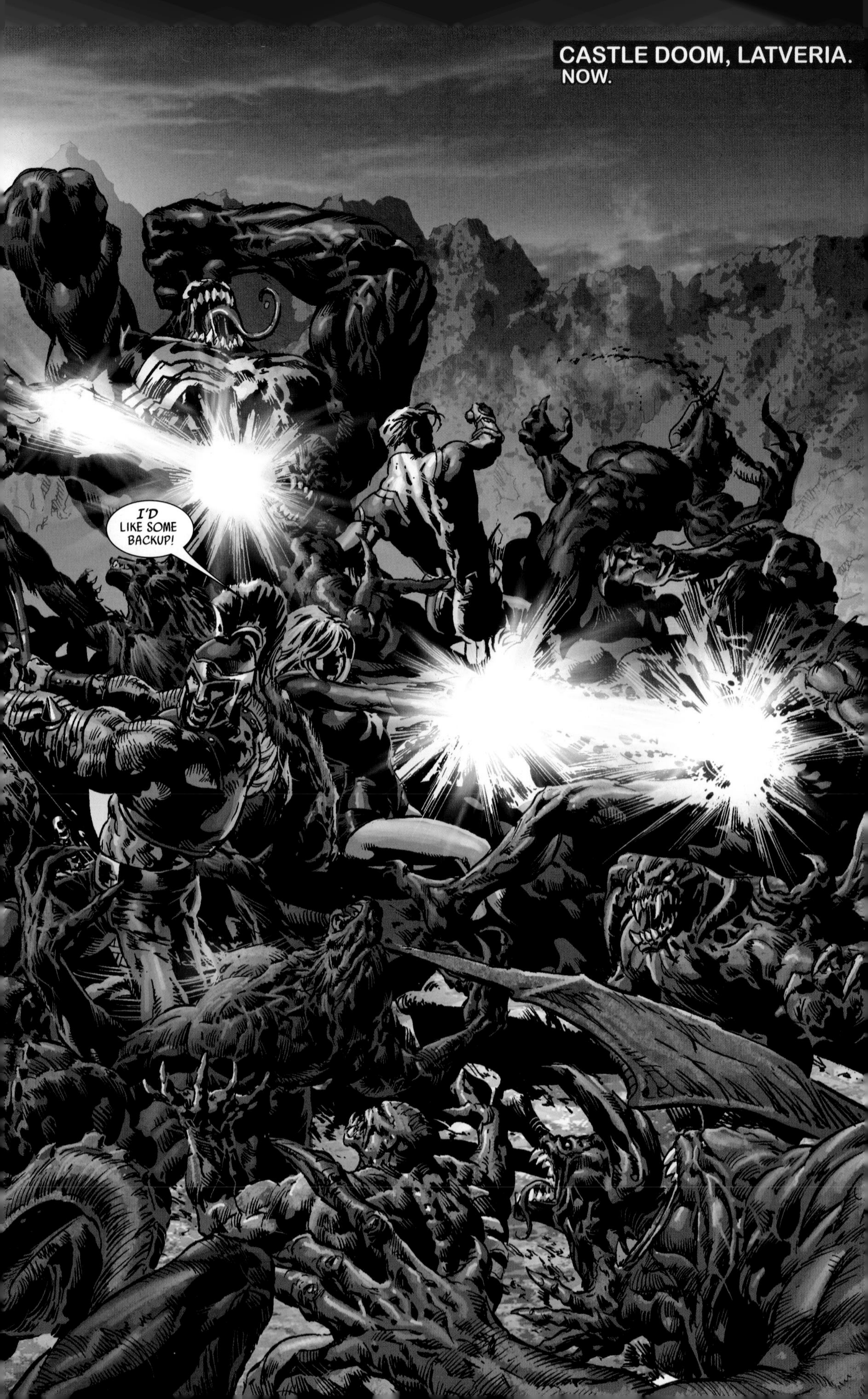
CASTLE DOOM, LATVERIA.
NOW.
I'D LIKE SOME BACKUP!

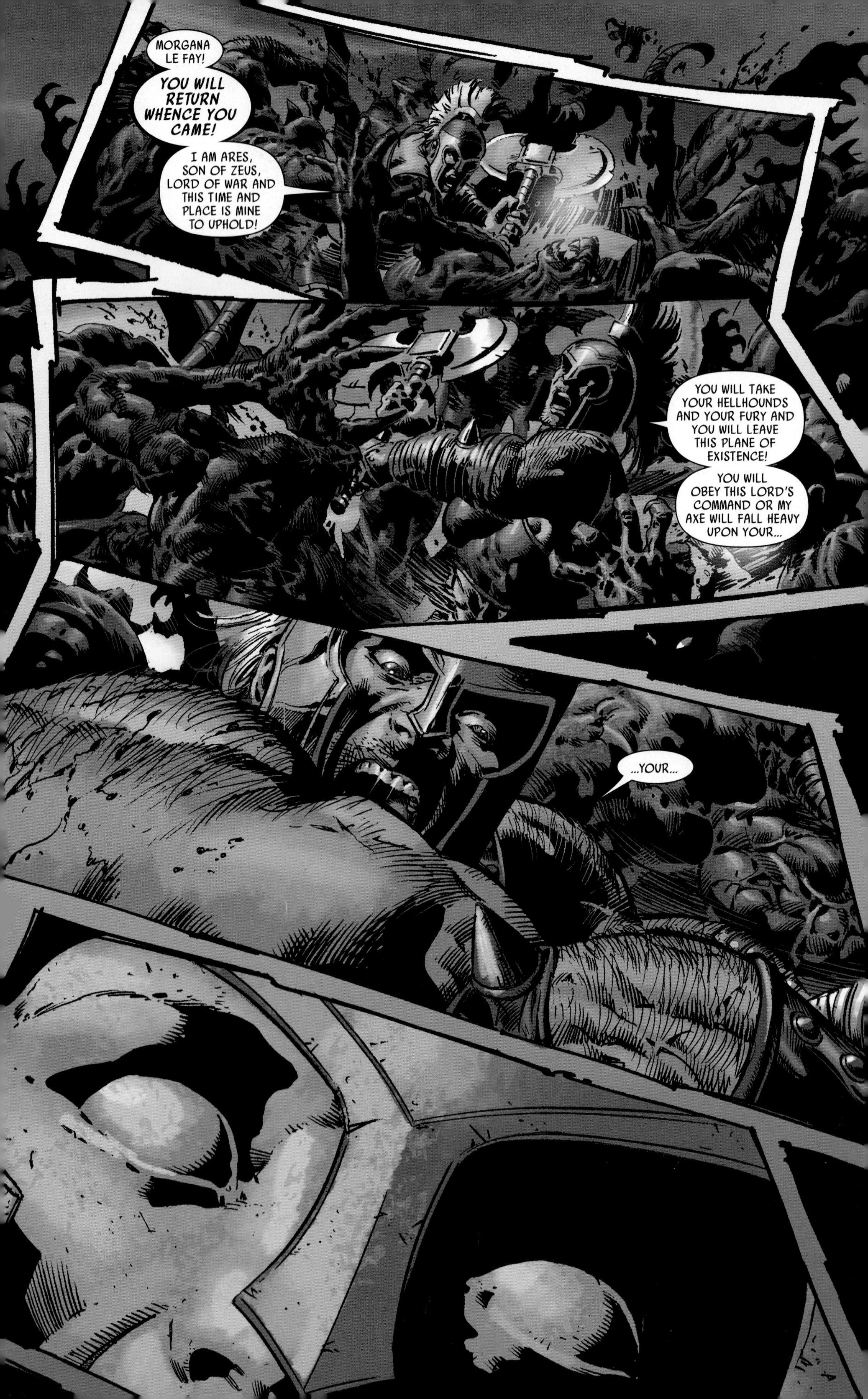
MORGANA LE FAY!
YOU WILL RETURN WHENCE YOU CAME!
I AM ARES, SON OF ZEUS, LORD OF WAR AND THIS TIME AND PLACE IS MINE TO UPHOLD!
YOU WILL TAKE YOUR HELLHOUNDS AND YOUR FURY AND YOU WILL LEAVE THIS PLANE OF EXISTENCE!
YOU WILL OBEY THIS LORD'S COMMAND OR MY AXE WILL FALL HEAVY UPON YOUR...
...YOUR...

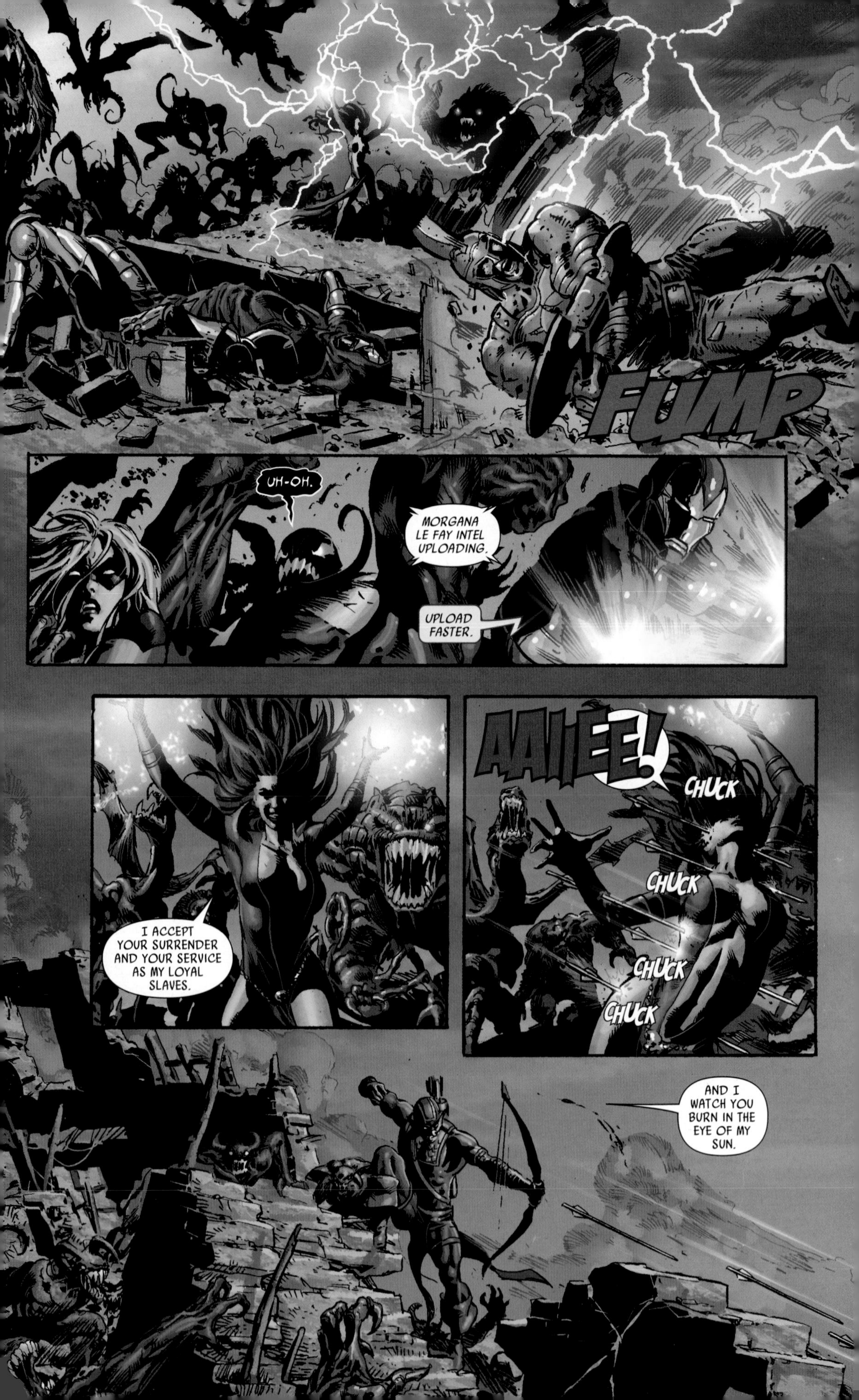
FUMP
UH-OH.
MORGANA LE FAY INTEL UPLOADING.
UPLOAD FASTER.
I ACCEPT YOUR SURRENDER AND YOUR SERVICE AS MY LOYAL SLAVES.
AAIIEE!
CHUCK
CHUCK
CHUCK
CHUCK
AND I WATCH YOU BURN IN THE EYE OF MY SUN.

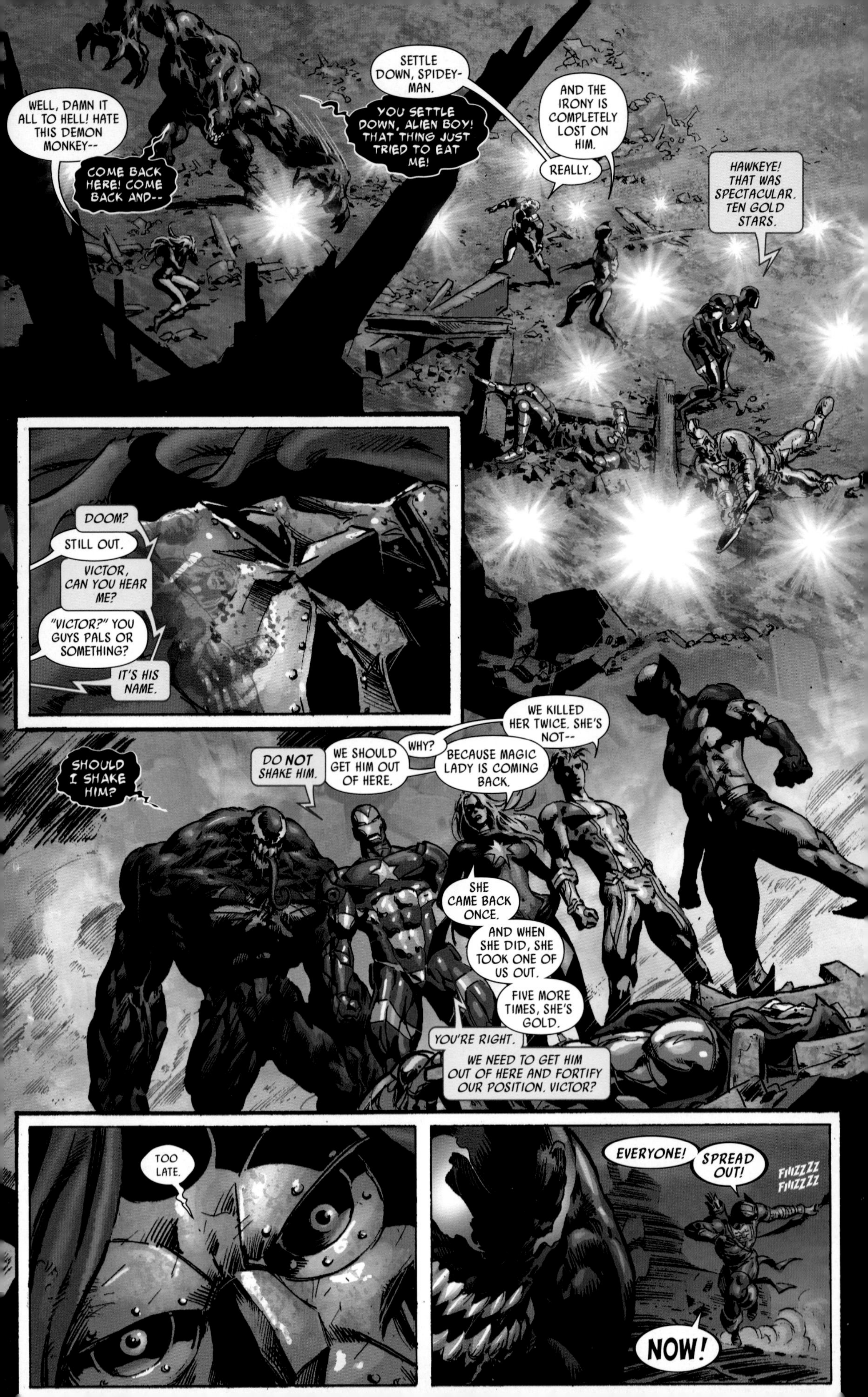

WELL, DAMN IT ALL TO HELL! HATE THIS DEMON MONKEY--
COME BACK HERE! COME BACK AND--
SETTLE DOWN, SPIDEY-MAN.
YOU SETTLE DOWN, ALIEN BOY! THAT THING JUST TRIED TO EAT ME!
AND THE IRONY IS COMPLETELY LOST ON HIM.
REALLY.
HAWKEYE! THAT WAS SPECTACULAR. TEN GOLD STARS.
DOOM?
STILL OUT.
VICTOR, CAN YOU HEAR ME?
"VICTOR?" YOU GUYS PALS OR SOMETHING?
IT'S HIS NAME.
SHOULD I SHAKE HIM?
DO NOT SHAKE HIM.
WE SHOULD GET HIM OUT OF HERE.
WHY?
WE KILLED HER TWICE. SHE'S NOT--
BECAUSE MAGIC LADY IS COMING BACK.
SHE CAME BACK ONCE.
AND WHEN SHE DID, SHE TOOK ONE OF US OUT.
FIVE MORE TIMES, SHE'S GOLD.
YOU'RE RIGHT.
WE NEED TO GET HIM OUT OF HERE AND FORTIFY OUR POSITION. VICTOR?
TOO LATE.
EVERYONE!
SPREAD OUT!
FIIIZZZZ FIIIZZZZ
NOW!

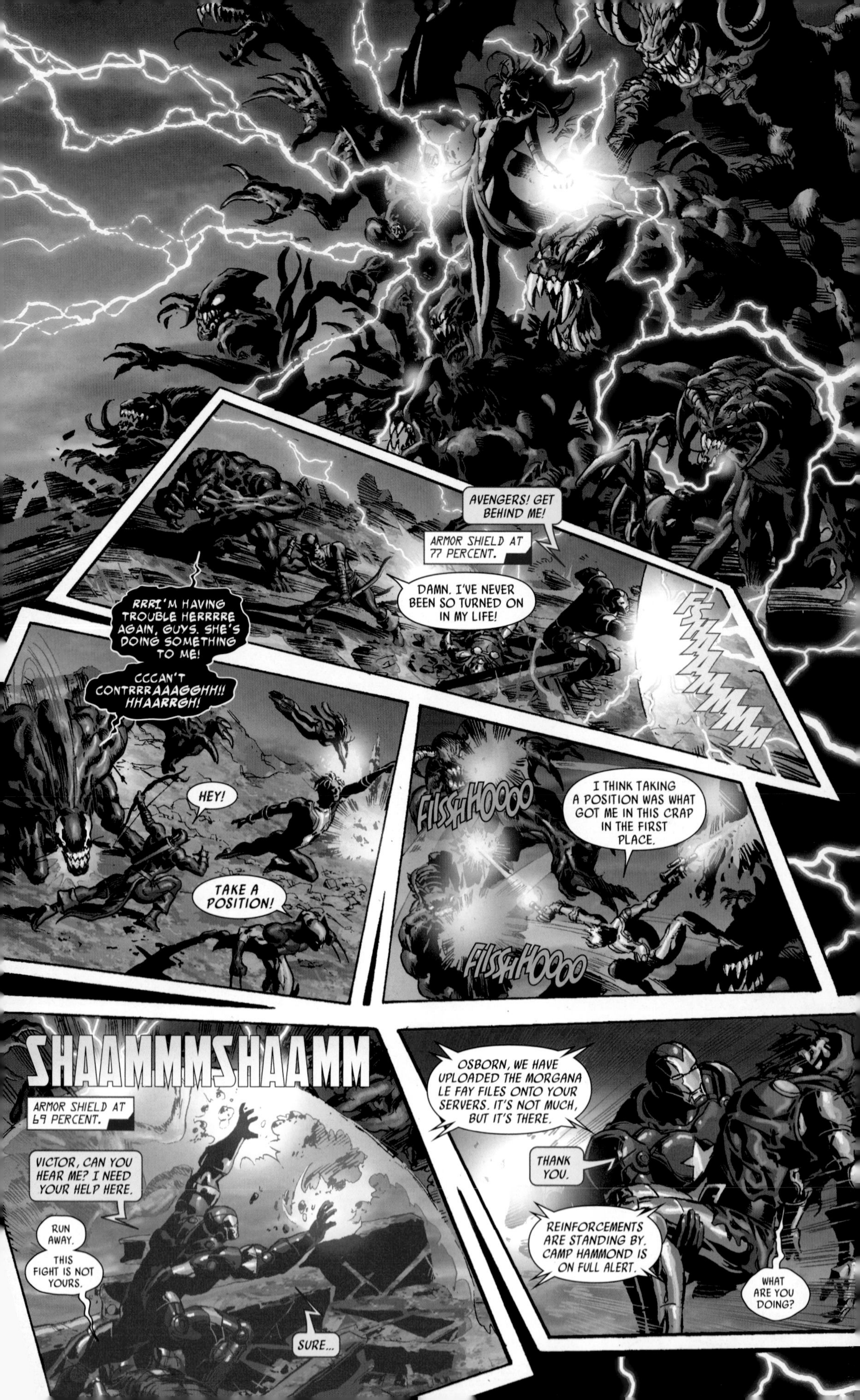
AVENGERS! GET BEHIND ME!
ARMOR SHIELD AT 77 PERCENT.
DAMN. I'VE NEVER BEEN SO TURNED ON IN MY LIFE!
RRRI'M HAVING TROUBLE HERRRRE AGAIN, GUYS. SHE'S DOING SOMETHING TO ME!
CCCAN'T CONTRRRAAAGGHH!! HHAARRGH!
HEY!
TAKE A POSITION!
FIISSHHOOOO
I THINK TAKING A POSITION WAS WHAT GOT ME IN THIS CRAP IN THE FIRST PLACE.
FIISSHHOOOO
SHAAMMMSHAAMM
ARMOR SHIELD AT 69 PERCENT.
VICTOR, CAN YOU HEAR ME? I NEED YOUR HELP HERE.
RUN AWAY.
THIS FIGHT IS NOT YOURS.
SURE...
OSBORN, WE HAVE UPLOADED THE MORGANA LE FAY FILES ONTO YOUR SERVERS. IT'S NOT MUCH, BUT IT'S THERE.
THANK YOU.
REINFORCEMENTS ARE STANDING BY. CAMP HAMMOND IS ON FULL ALERT.
WHAT ARE YOU DOING?

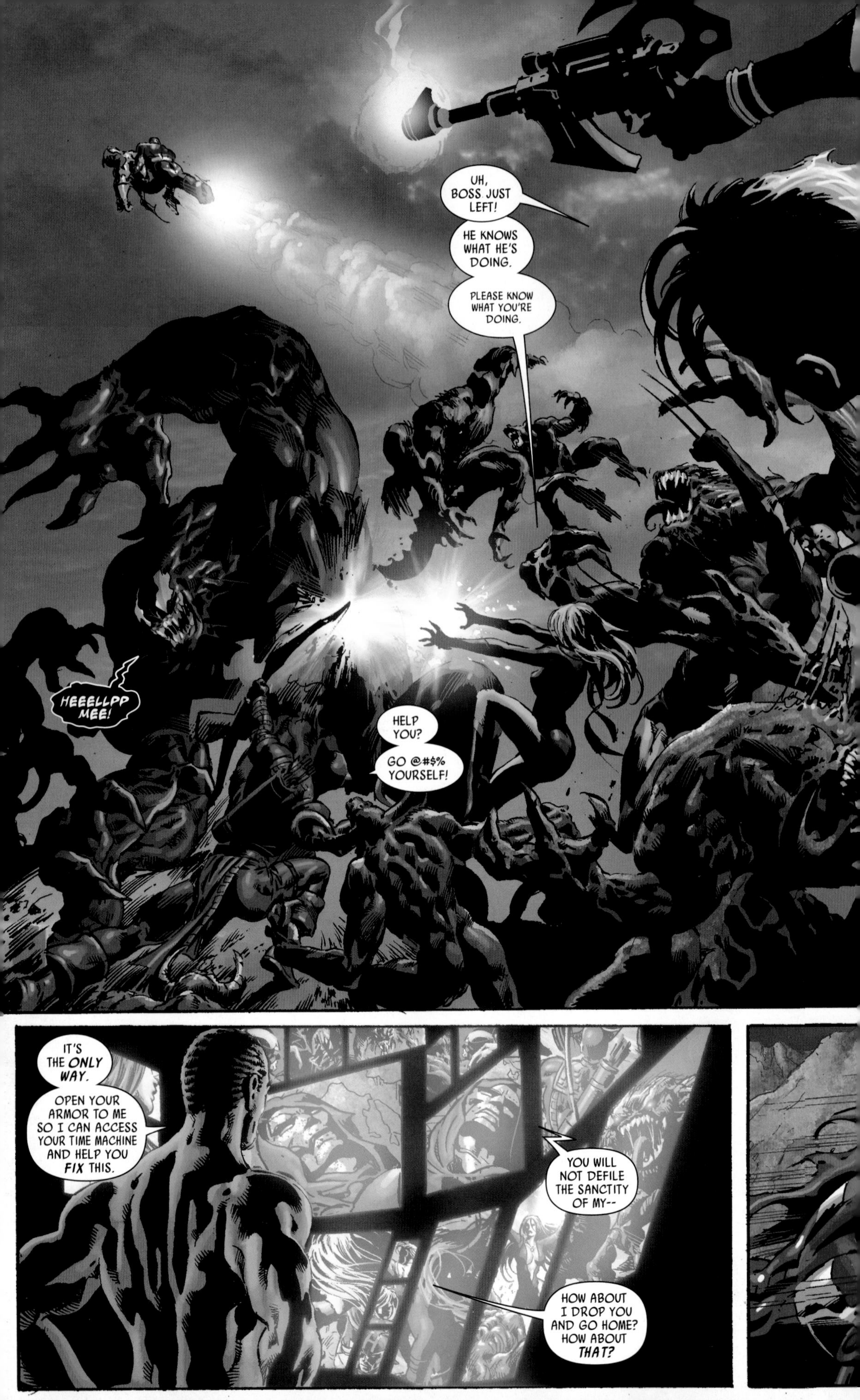
UH, BOSS JUST LEFT!
HE KNOWS WHAT HE'S DOING.
PLEASE KNOW WHAT YOU'RE DOING.
HEEELLPP MEE!
HELP YOU?
GO @#$% YOURSELF!
IT'S THE ONLY WAY.
OPEN YOUR ARMOR TO ME SO I CAN ACCESS YOUR TIME MACHINE AND HELP YOU FIX THIS.
YOU WILL NOT DEFILE THE SANCTITY OF MY--
HOW ABOUT I DROP YOU AND GO HOME? HOW ABOUT THAT?

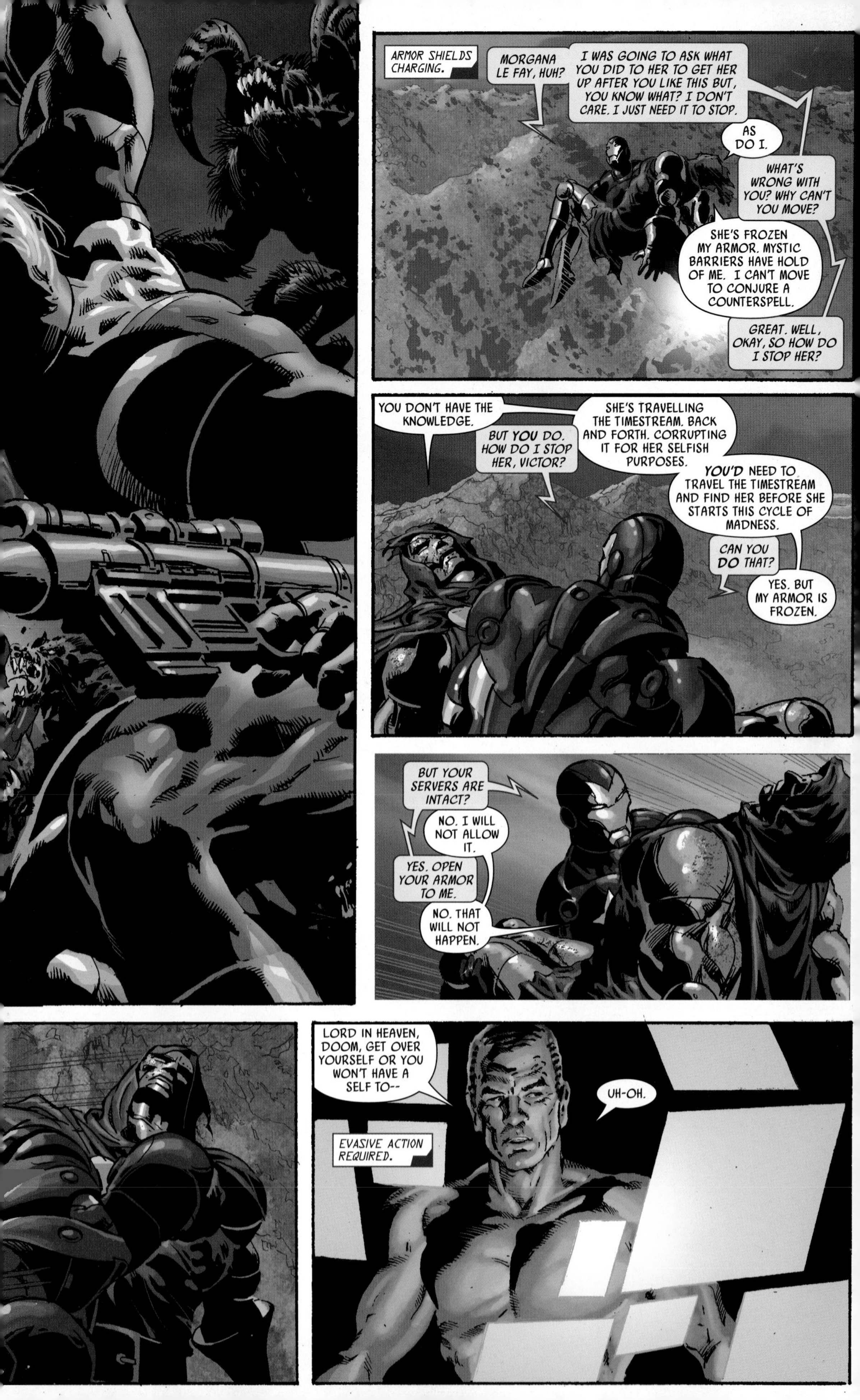
ARMOR SHIELDS CHARGING.
MORGANA LE FAY, HUH?
I WAS GOING TO ASK WHAT YOU DID TO HER TO GET HER UP AFTER YOU LIKE THIS BUT, YOU KNOW WHAT? I DON'T CARE. I JUST NEED IT TO STOP.
AS DO I.
WHAT'S WRONG WITH YOU? WHY CAN'T YOU MOVE?
SHE'S FROZEN MY ARMOR. MYSTIC BARRIERS HAVE HOLD OF ME. I CAN'T MOVE TO CONJURE A COUNTERSPELL.
GREAT. WELL, OKAY, SO HOW DO I STOP HER?
YOU DON'T HAVE THE KNOWLEDGE.
SHE'S TRAVELLING THE TIMESTREAM. BACK AND FORTH. CORRUPTING IT FOR HER SELFISH PURPOSES.
BUT YOU DO. HOW DO I STOP HER, VICTOR?
YOU'D NEED TO TRAVEL THE TIMESTREAM AND FIND HER BEFORE SHE STARTS THIS CYCLE OF MADNESS.
CAN YOU DO THAT?
YES. BUT MY ARMOR IS FROZEN.
BUT YOUR SERVERS ARE INTACT?
NO. I WILL NOT ALLOW IT.
YES. OPEN YOUR ARMOR TO ME.
NO. THAT WILL NOT HAPPEN.
LORD IN HEAVEN, DOOM, GET OVER YOURSELF OR YOU WON'T HAVE A SELF TO--
UH-OH.
EVASIVE ACTION REQUIRED.

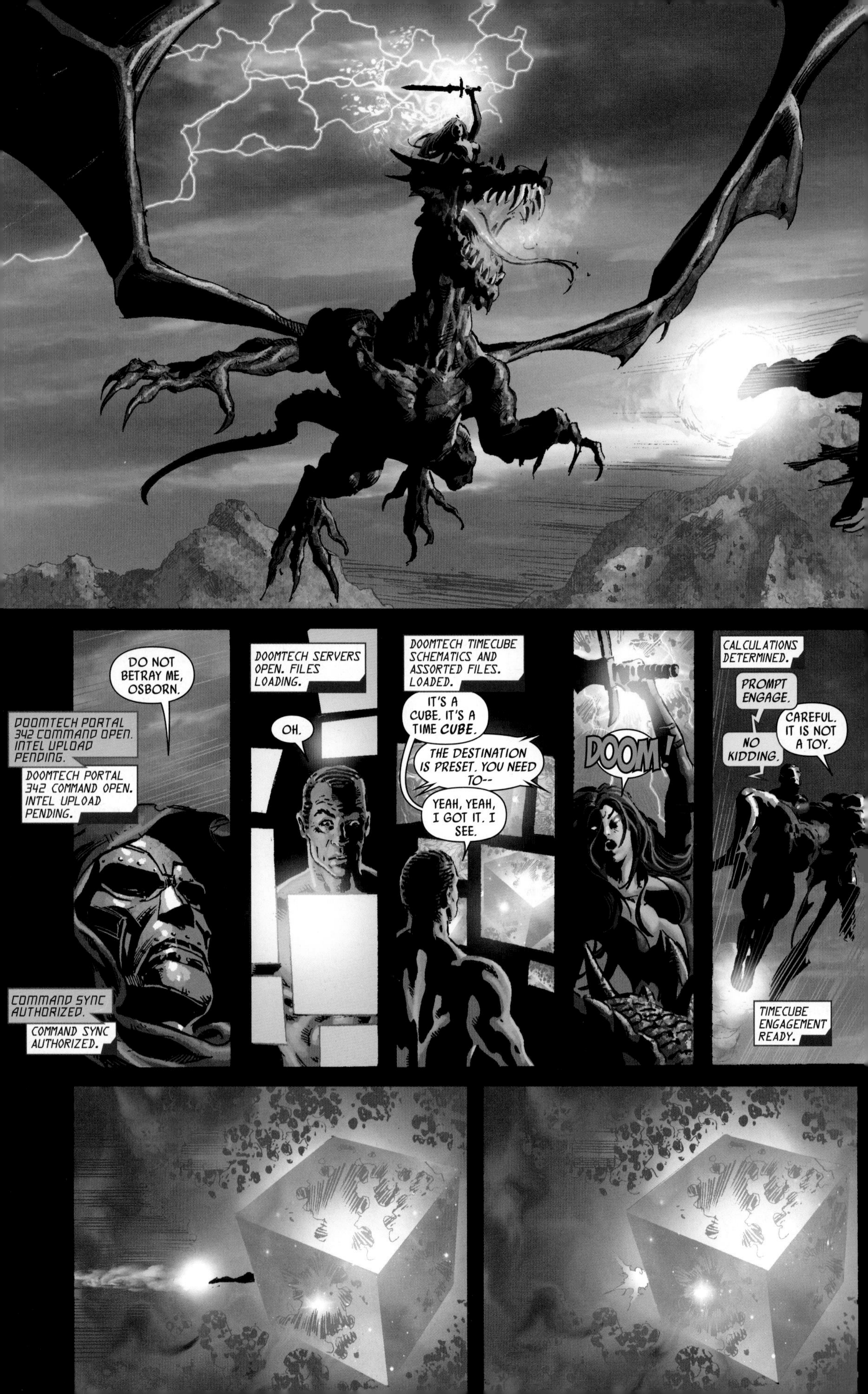
DO NOT BETRAY ME, OSBORN.
DOOMTECH PORTAL 342 COMMAND OPEN. INTEL UPLOAD PENDING.
DOOMTECH PORTAL 342 COMMAND OPEN. INTEL UPLOAD PENDING.
COMMAND SYNC AUTHORIZED.
COMMAND SYNC AUTHORIZED.
DOOMTECH SERVERS OPEN. FILES LOADING.
OH.
DOOMTECH TIMECUBE SCHEMATICS AND ASSORTED FILES. LOADED.
IT'S A CUBE. IT'S A TIME CUBE.
THE DESTINATION IS PRESET. YOU NEED TO--
YEAH, YEAH, I GOT IT. I SEE.
DOOM!
CALCULATIONS DETERMINED.
PROMPT ENGAGE.
NO KIDDING.
CAREFUL. IT IS NOT A TOY.
TIMECUBE ENGAGEMENT READY.

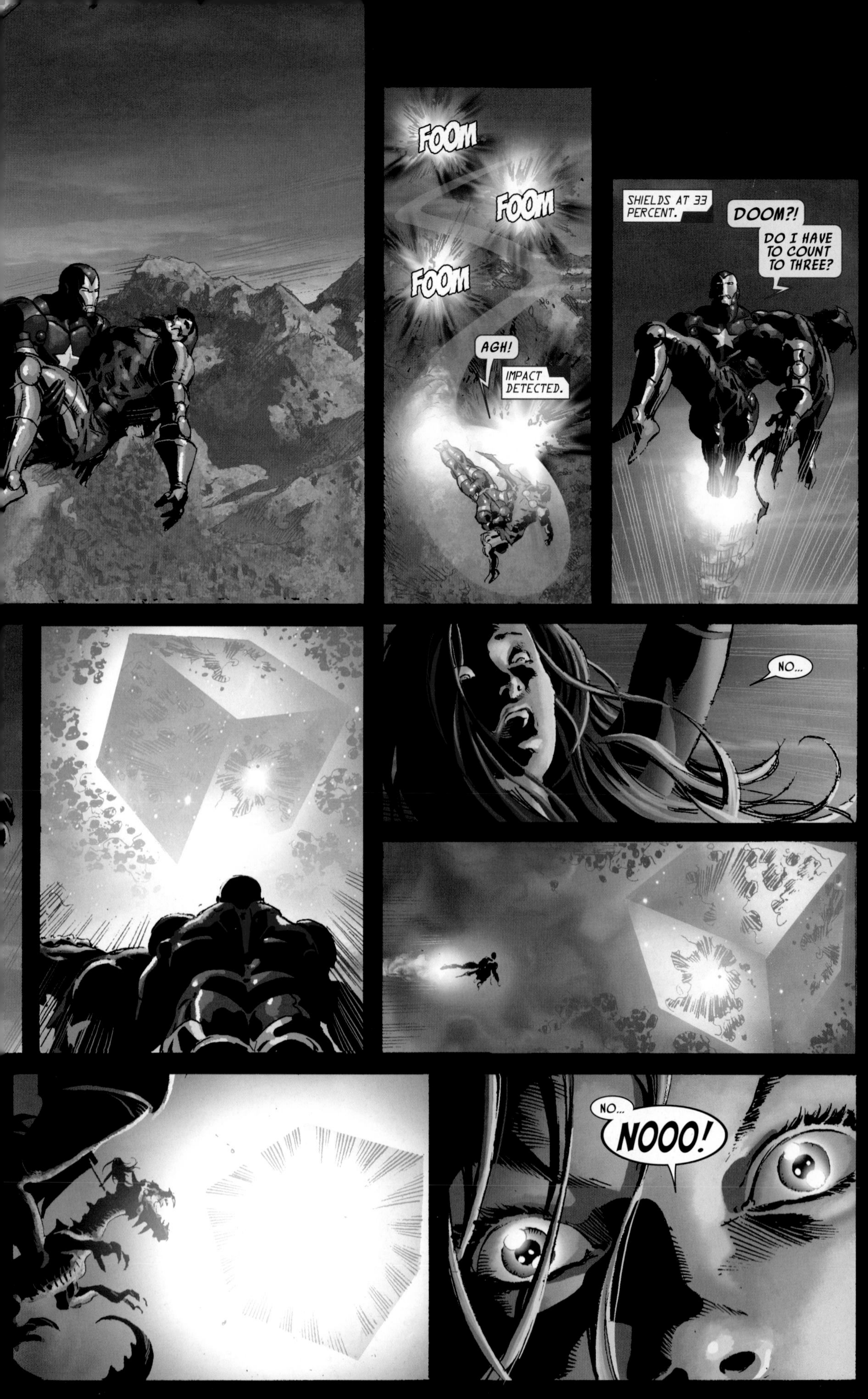
FOOM
FOOM
FOOM
AGH!
IMPACT DETECTED.
SHIELDS AT 33 PERCENT.
DOOM?!
DO I HAVE TO COUNT TO THREE?
NO...
NO...
NOOO!

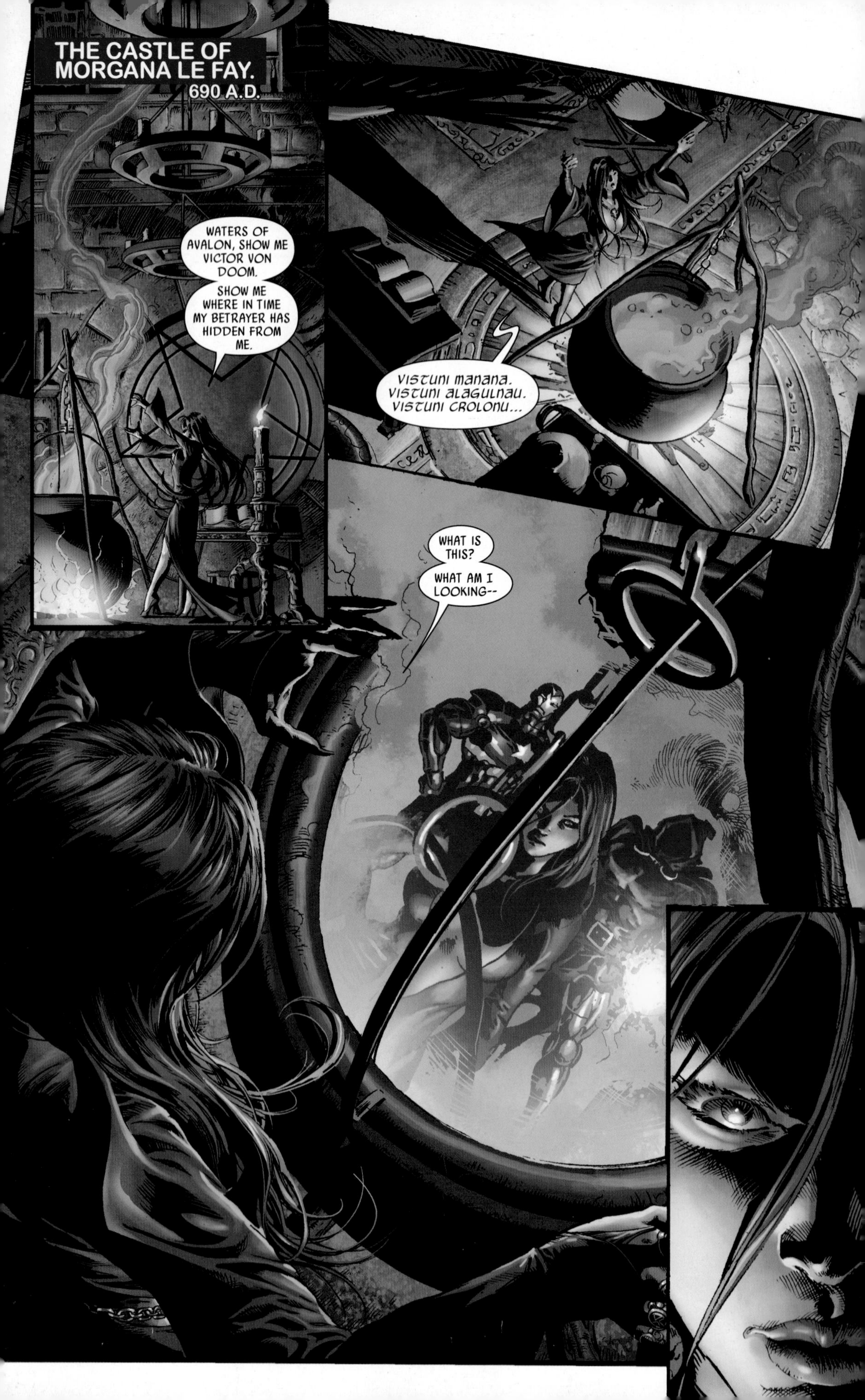
THE CASTLE OF MORGANA LE FAY.
690 A.D.
WATERS OF AVALON, SHOW ME VICTOR VON DOOM.
SHOW ME WHERE IN TIME MY BETRAYER HAS HIDDEN FROM ME.
VISTUNI MANANA. VISTUNI ALAGULNAU. VISTUNI CROLONU...
WHAT IS THIS?
WHAT AM I LOOKING--

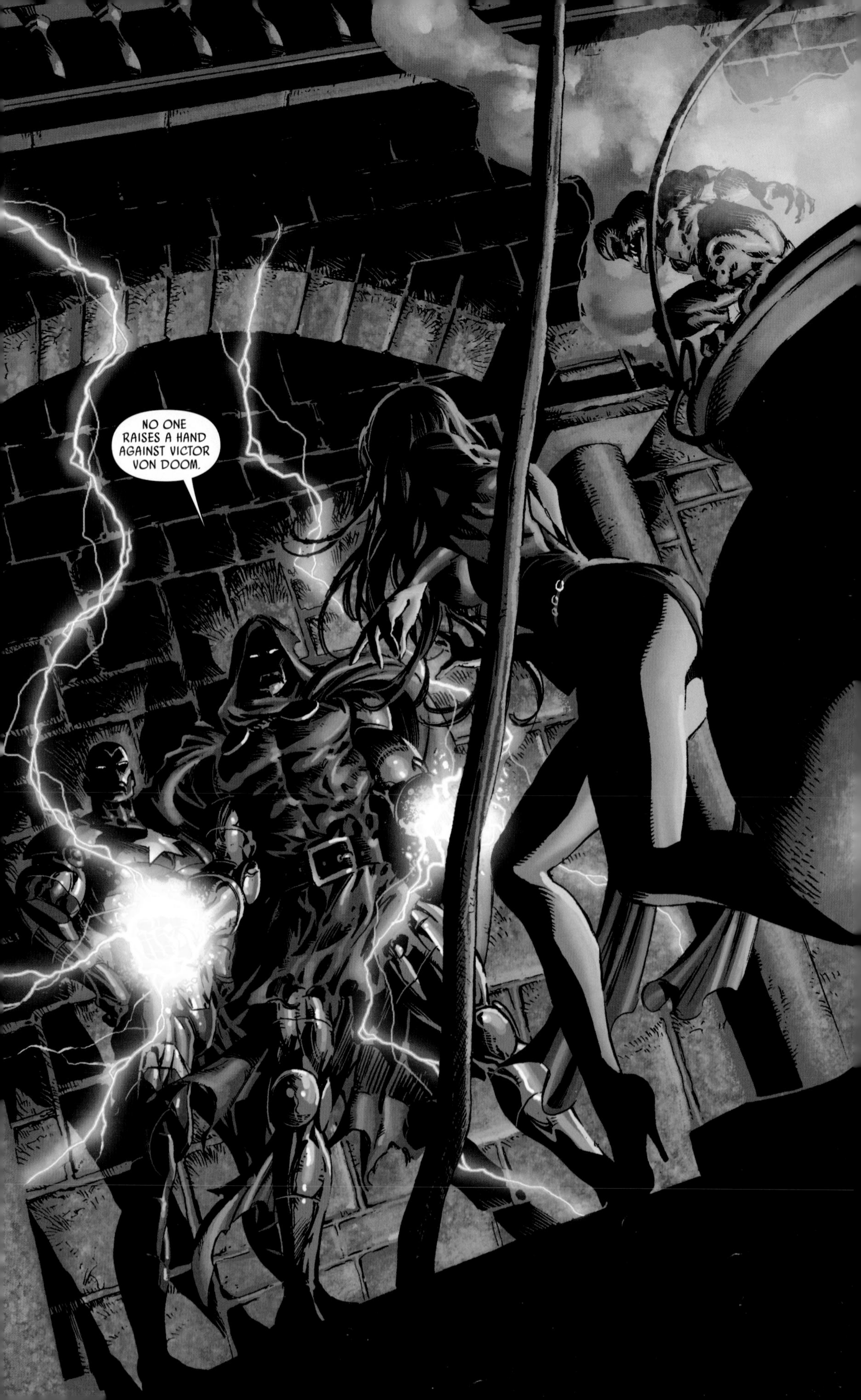
NO ONE RAISES A HAND AGAINST VICTOR VON DOOM.

DARK AVENGERS #4

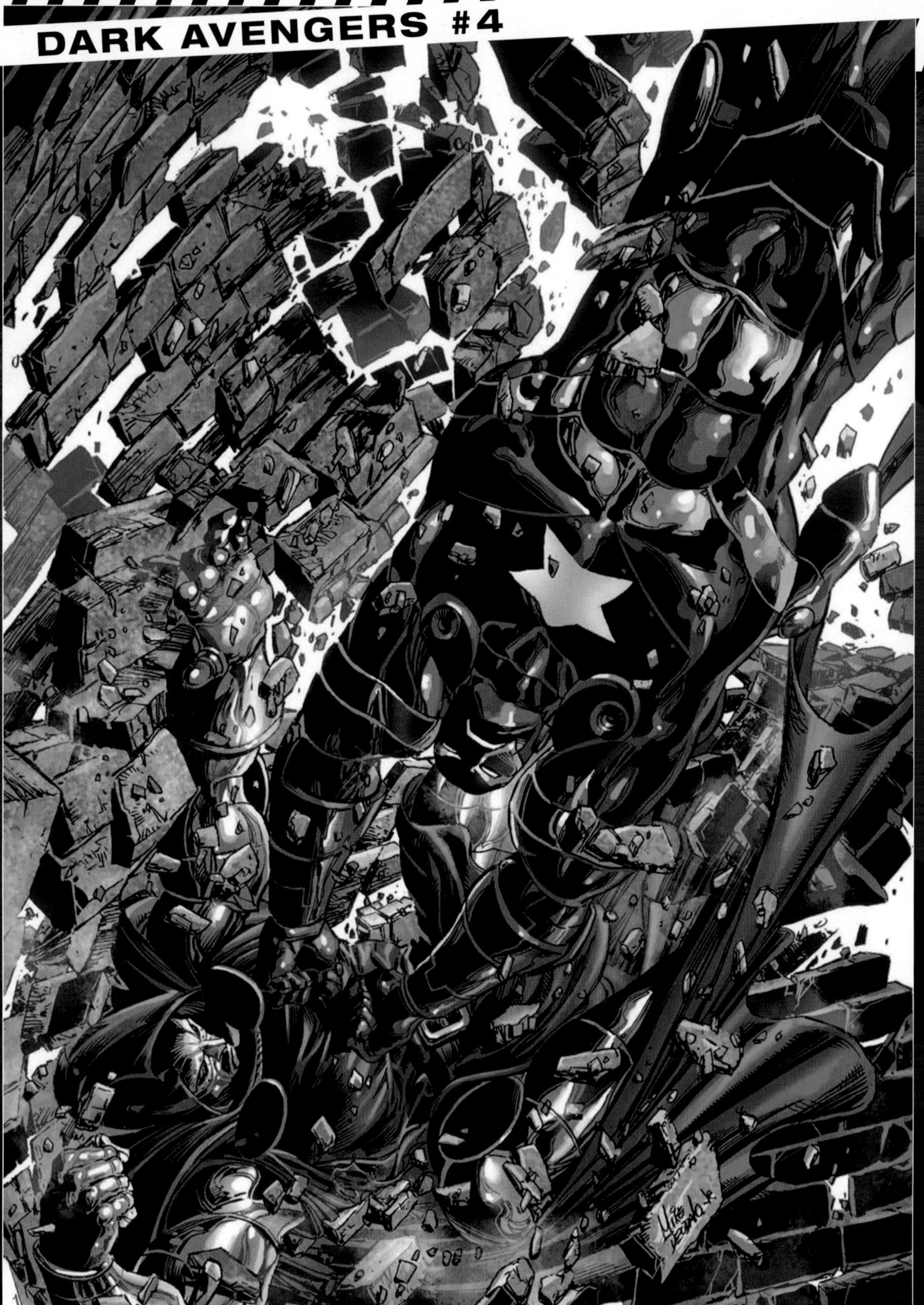

DARK AVENGERS #4 VARIANT

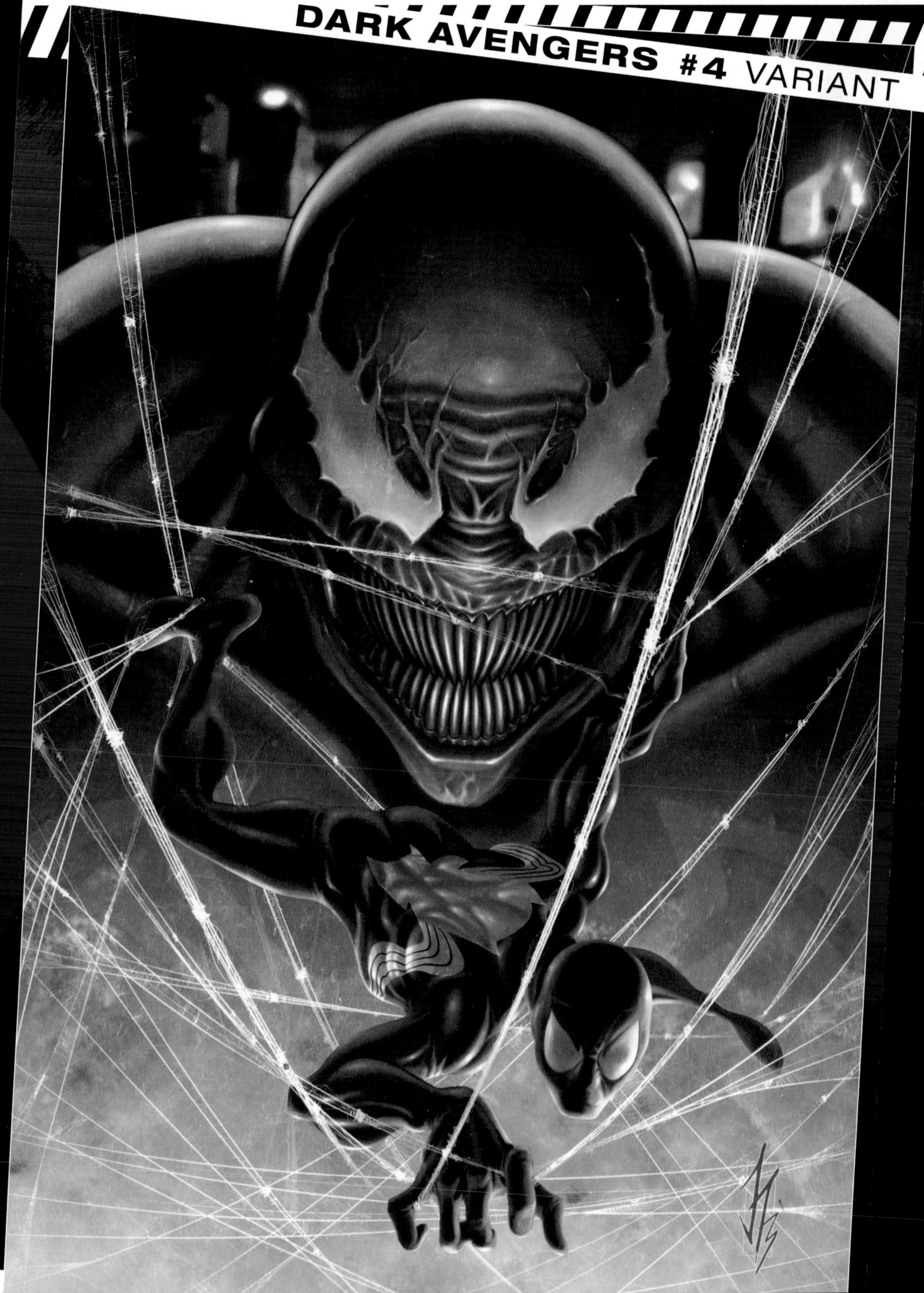

BY STEFANO CASELLI

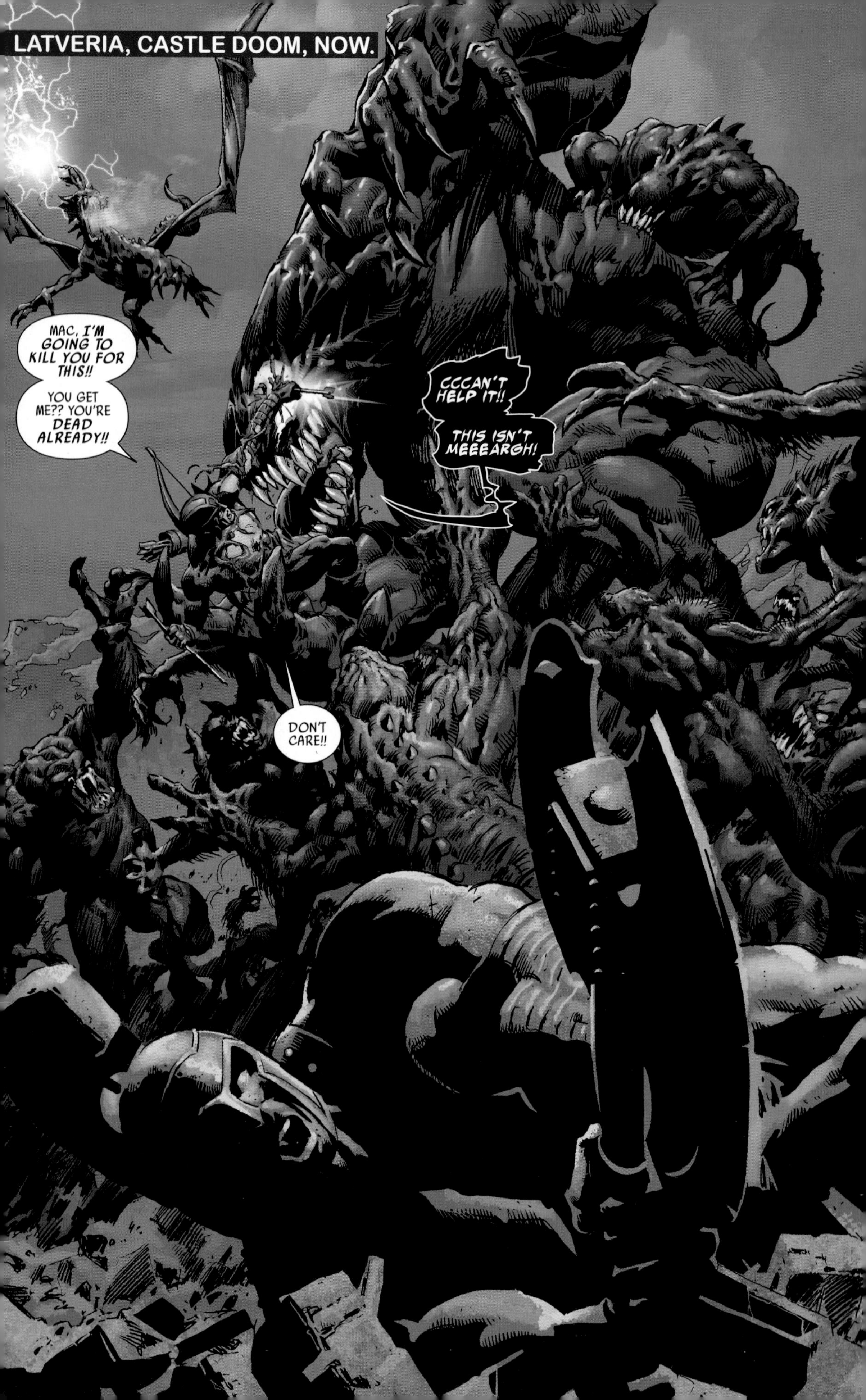
LATVERIA, CASTLE DOOM, NOW.
MAC, I'M GOING TO KILL YOU FOR THIS!!
YOU GET ME?? YOU'RE DEAD ALREADY!!
CCCAN'T HELP IT!!
THIS ISN'T MEEEARGH!
DON'T CARE!!

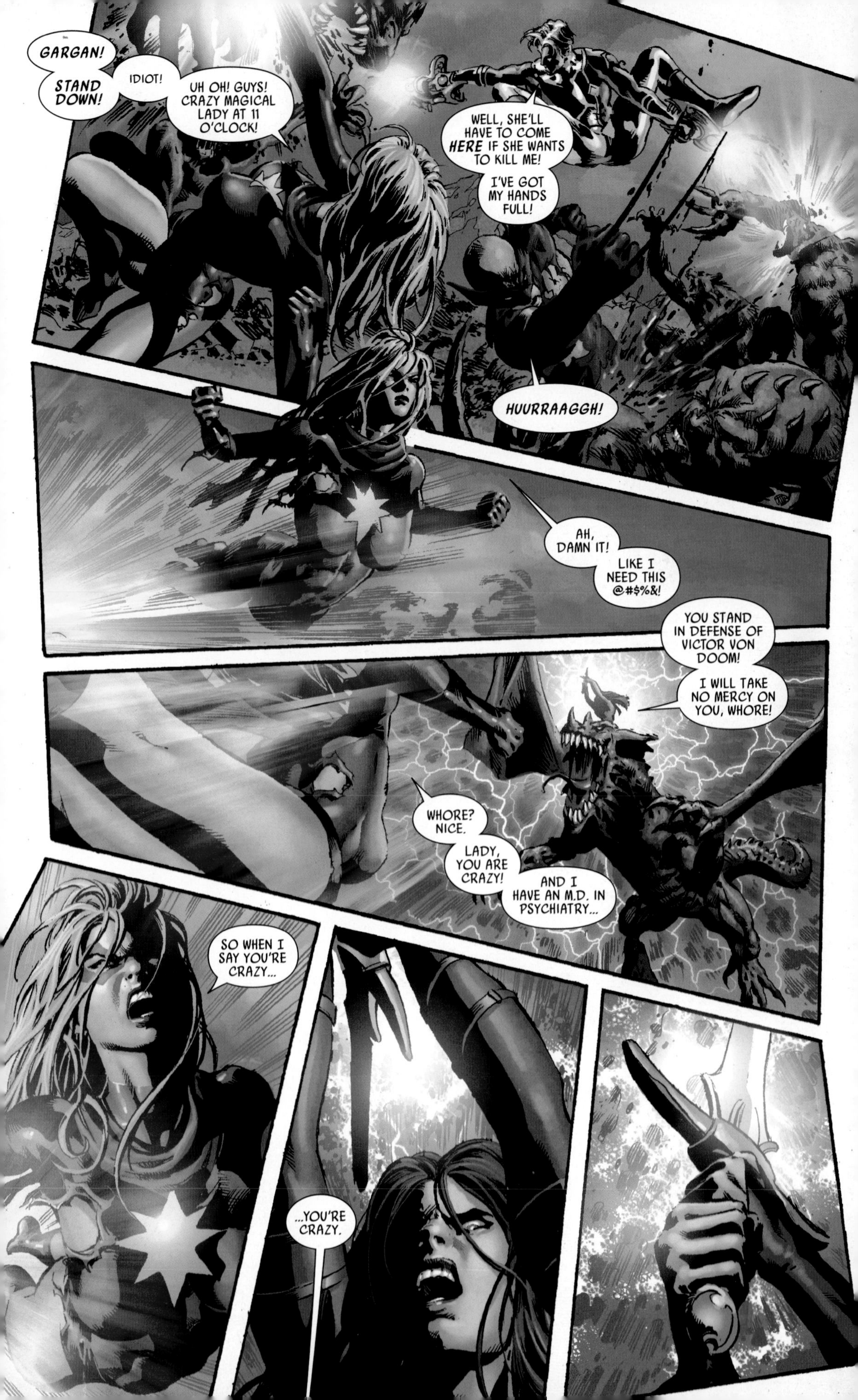
GARGAN!
STAND DOWN!
IDIOT!
UH OH! GUYS! CRAZY MAGICAL LADY AT 11 O'CLOCK!
WELL, SHE'LL HAVE TO COME HERE IF SHE WANTS TO KILL ME!
I'VE GOT MY HANDS FULL!
HUURRAAGGH!
AH, DAMN IT!
LIKE I NEED THIS @#$%&!
YOU STAND IN DEFENSE OF VICTOR VON DOOM!
I WILL TAKE NO MERCY ON YOU, WHORE!
WHORE? NICE.
LADY, YOU ARE CRAZY!
AND I HAVE AN M.D. IN PSYCHIATRY...
SO WHEN I SAY YOU'RE CRAZY...
...YOU'RE CRAZY.

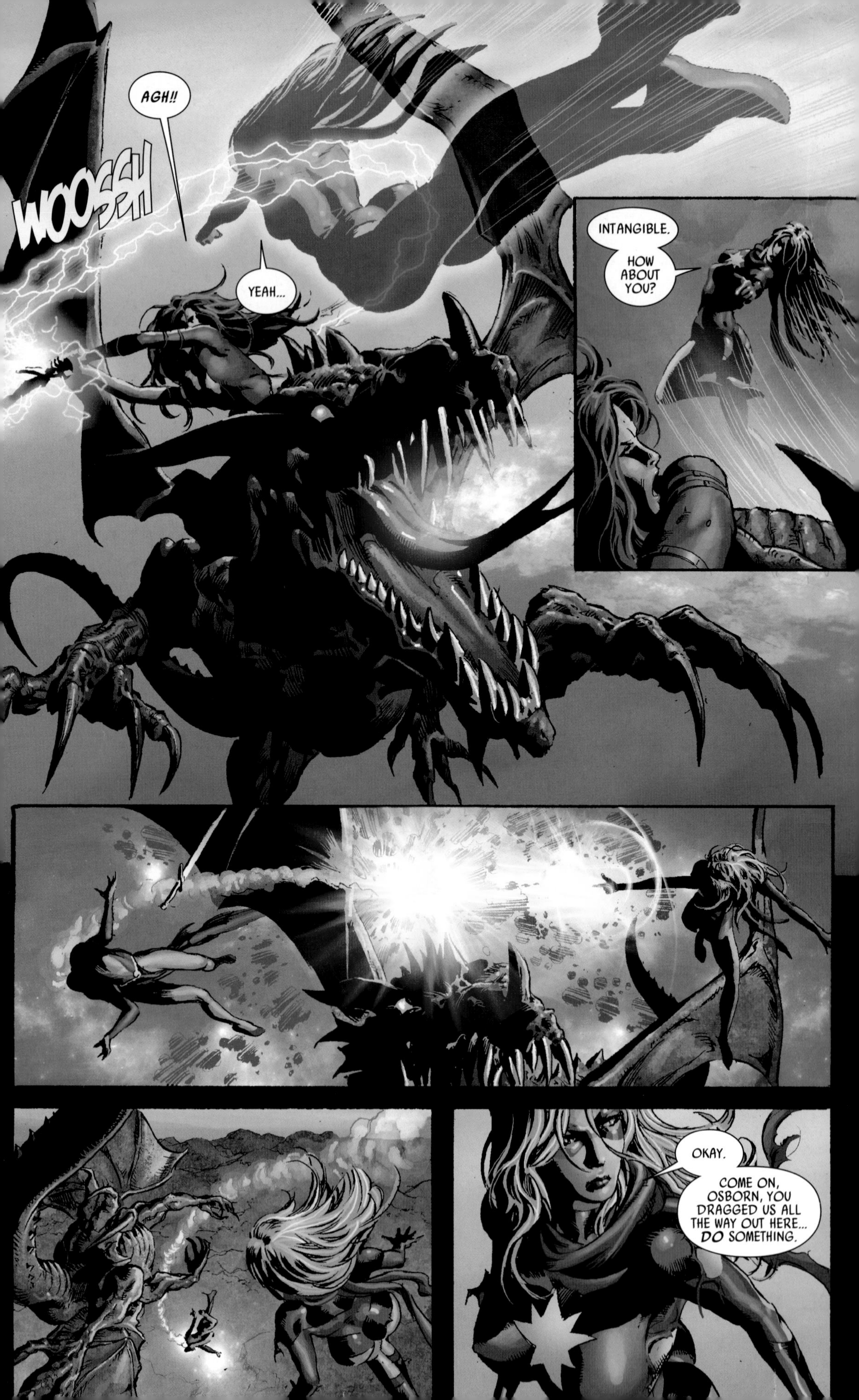
AGH!!
WOOSSH
YEAH...
INTANGIBLE.
HOW ABOUT YOU?
OKAY.
COME ON, OSBORN, YOU DRAGGED US ALL THE WAY OUT HERE... DO SOMETHING.

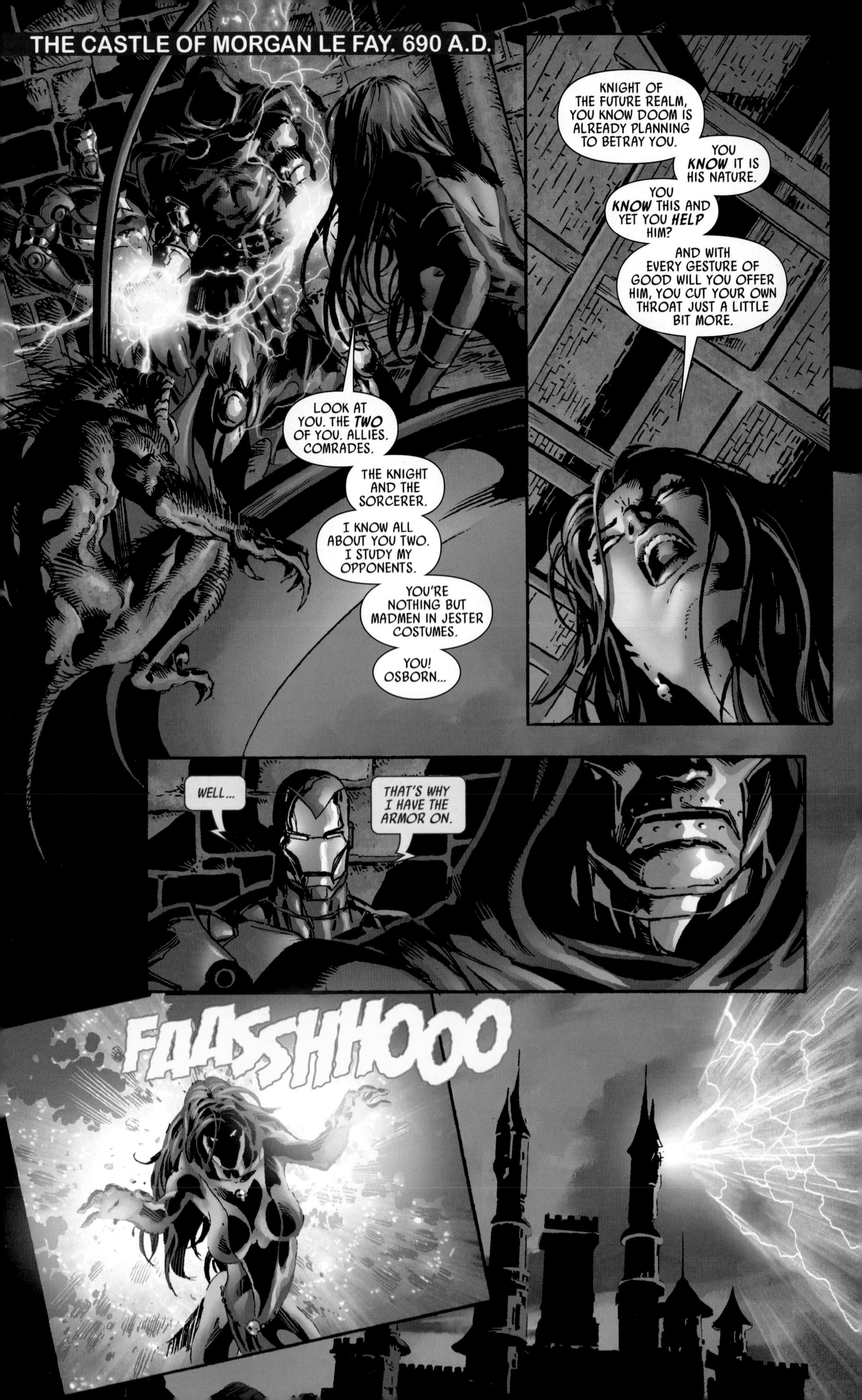
THE CASTLE OF MORGAN LE FAY. 690 A.D.
LOOK AT YOU. THE TWO OF YOU. ALLIES. COMRADES.
THE KNIGHT AND THE SORCERER.
I KNOW ALL ABOUT YOU TWO. I STUDY MY OPPONENTS.
YOU'RE NOTHING BUT MADMEN IN JESTER COSTUMES.
YOU! OSBORN...
KNIGHT OF THE FUTURE REALM, YOU KNOW DOOM IS ALREADY PLANNING TO BETRAY YOU.
YOU KNOW IT IS HIS NATURE.
YOU KNOW THIS AND YET YOU HELP HIM?
AND WITH EVERY GESTURE OF GOOD WILL YOU OFFER HIM, YOU CUT YOUR OWN THROAT JUST A LITTLE BIT MORE.
WELL...
THAT'S WHY I HAVE THE ARMOR ON.
FAASSHHOOO

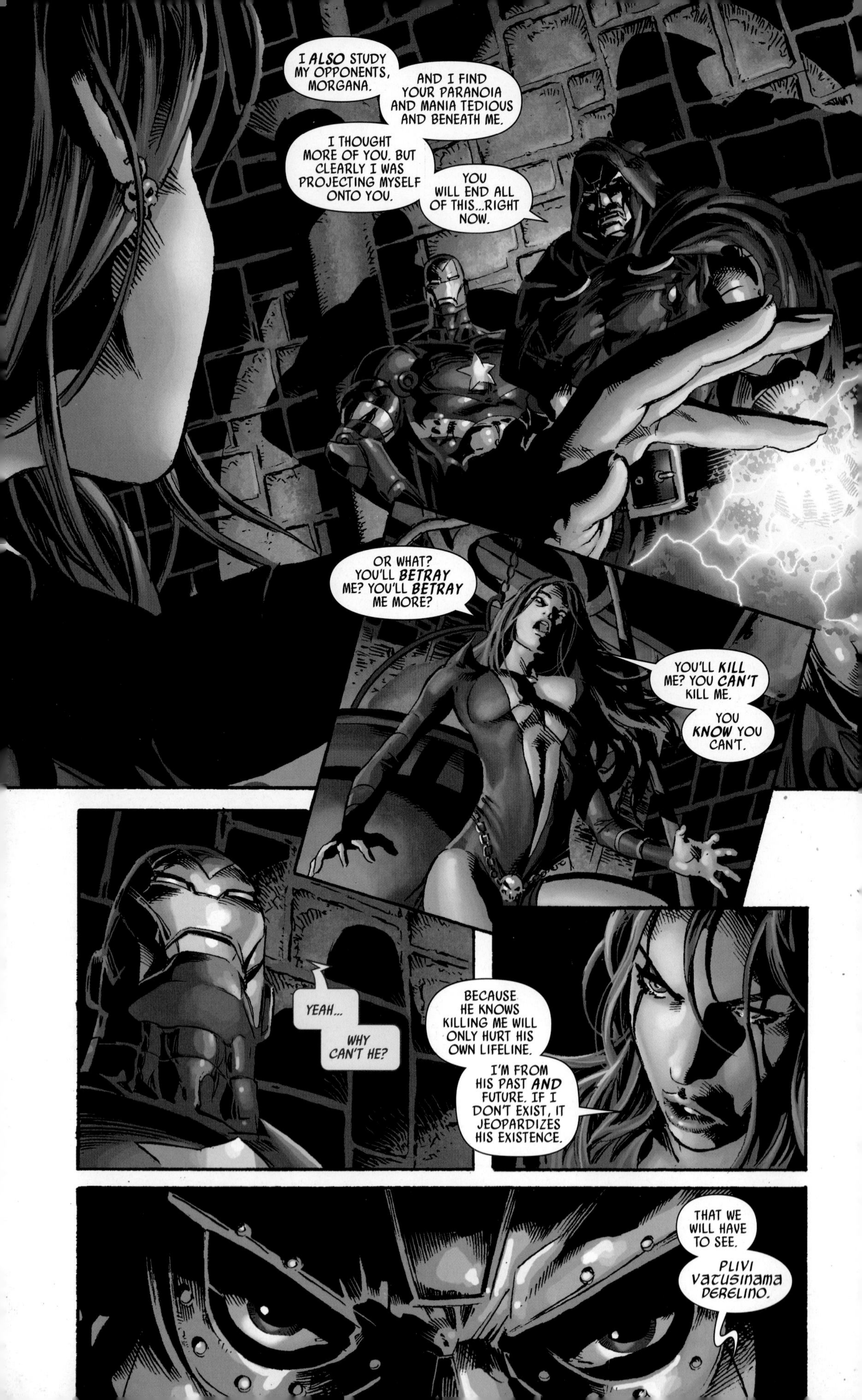

I ALSO STUDY MY OPPONENTS, MORGANA.
AND I FIND YOUR PARANOIA AND MANIA TEDIOUS AND BENEATH ME.
I THOUGHT MORE OF YOU. BUT CLEARLY I WAS PROJECTING MYSELF ONTO YOU.
YOU WILL END ALL OF THIS...RIGHT NOW.
OR WHAT? YOU'LL BETRAY ME? YOU'LL BETRAY ME MORE?
YOU'LL KILL ME? YOU CAN'T KILL ME.
YOU KNOW YOU CAN'T.
YEAH...
WHY CAN'T HE?
BECAUSE HE KNOWS KILLING ME WILL ONLY HURT HIS OWN LIFELINE.
I'M FROM HIS PAST AND FUTURE. IF I DON'T EXIST, IT JEOPARDIZES HIS EXISTENCE.
THAT WE WILL HAVE TO SEE.
PLIVI VATUSINAMA DERELINO.

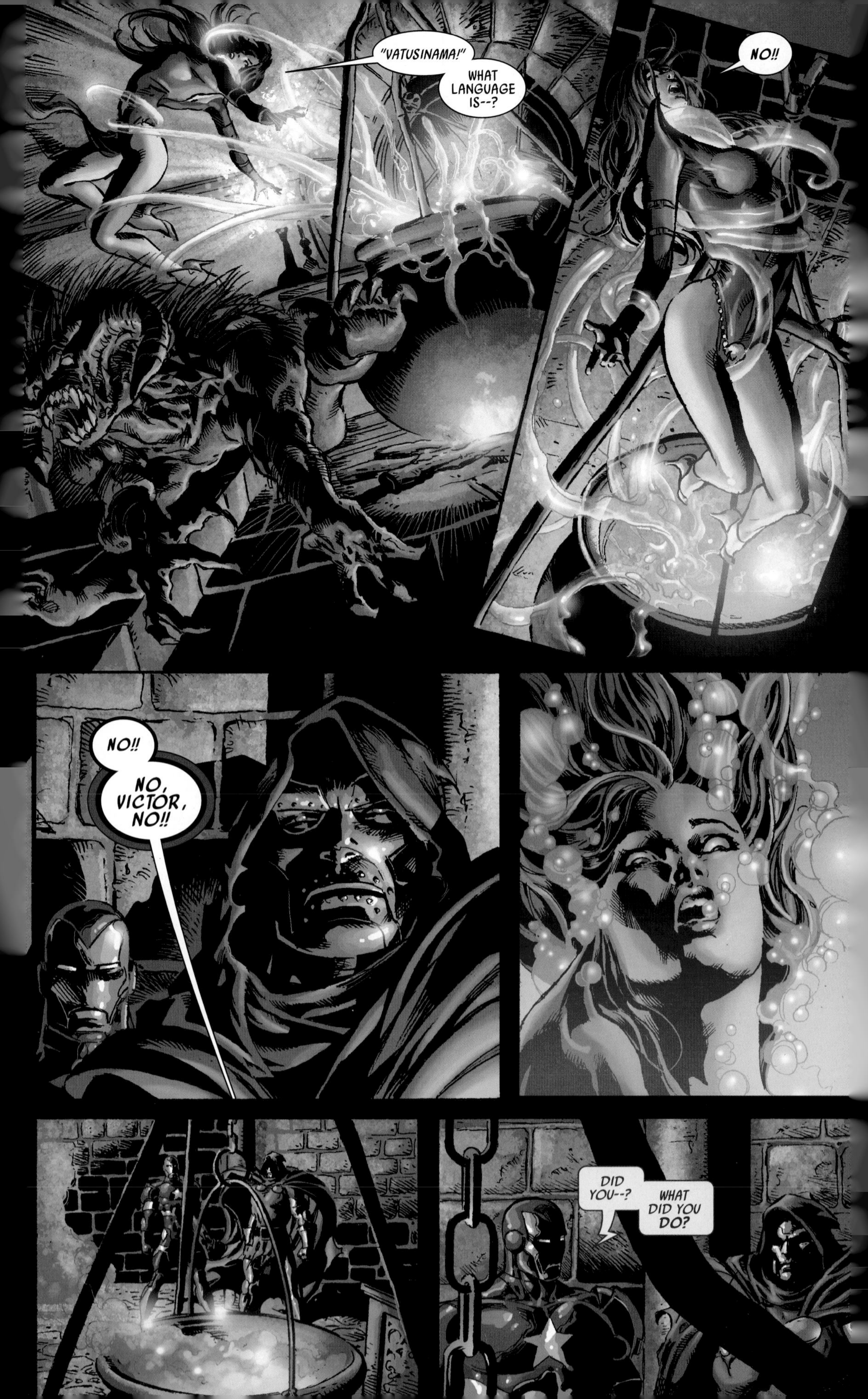
"VATUSINAMA!"
WHAT LANGUAGE IS--?
NO!!
NO!!
NO, VICTOR, NO!!
DID YOU--?
WHAT DID YOU DO?

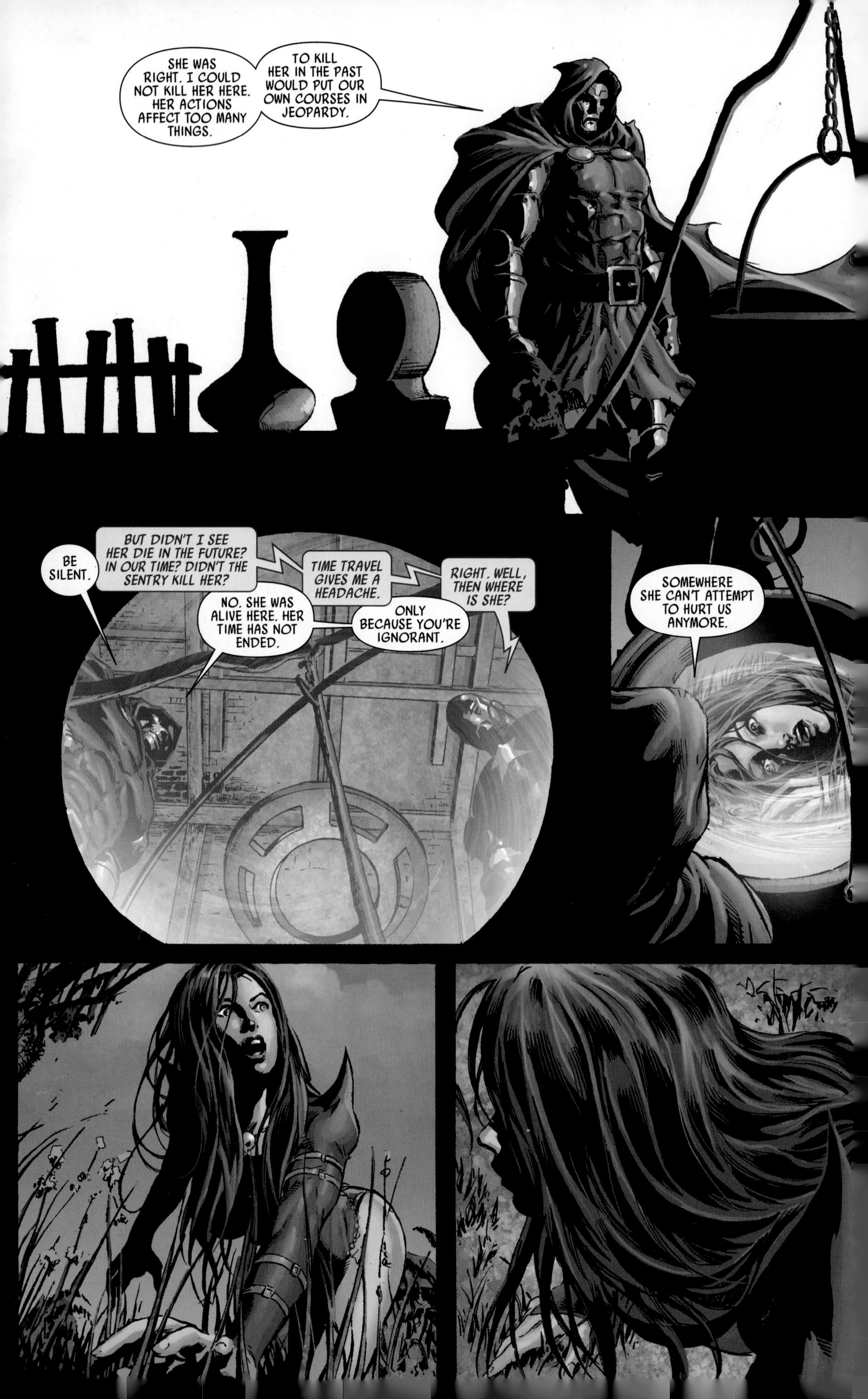
SHE WAS RIGHT. I COULD NOT KILL HER HERE. HER ACTIONS AFFECT TOO MANY THINGS.
TO KILL HER IN THE PAST WOULD PUT OUR OWN COURSES IN JEOPARDY.
BE SILENT.
BUT DIDN'T I SEE HER DIE IN THE FUTURE? IN OUR TIME? DIDN'T THE SENTRY KILL HER?
NO. SHE WAS ALIVE HERE. HER TIME HAS NOT ENDED.
TIME TRAVEL GIVES ME A HEADACHE.
ONLY BECAUSE YOU'RE IGNORANT.
RIGHT. WELL, THEN WHERE IS SHE?
SOMEWHERE SHE CAN'T ATTEMPT TO HURT US ANYMORE.

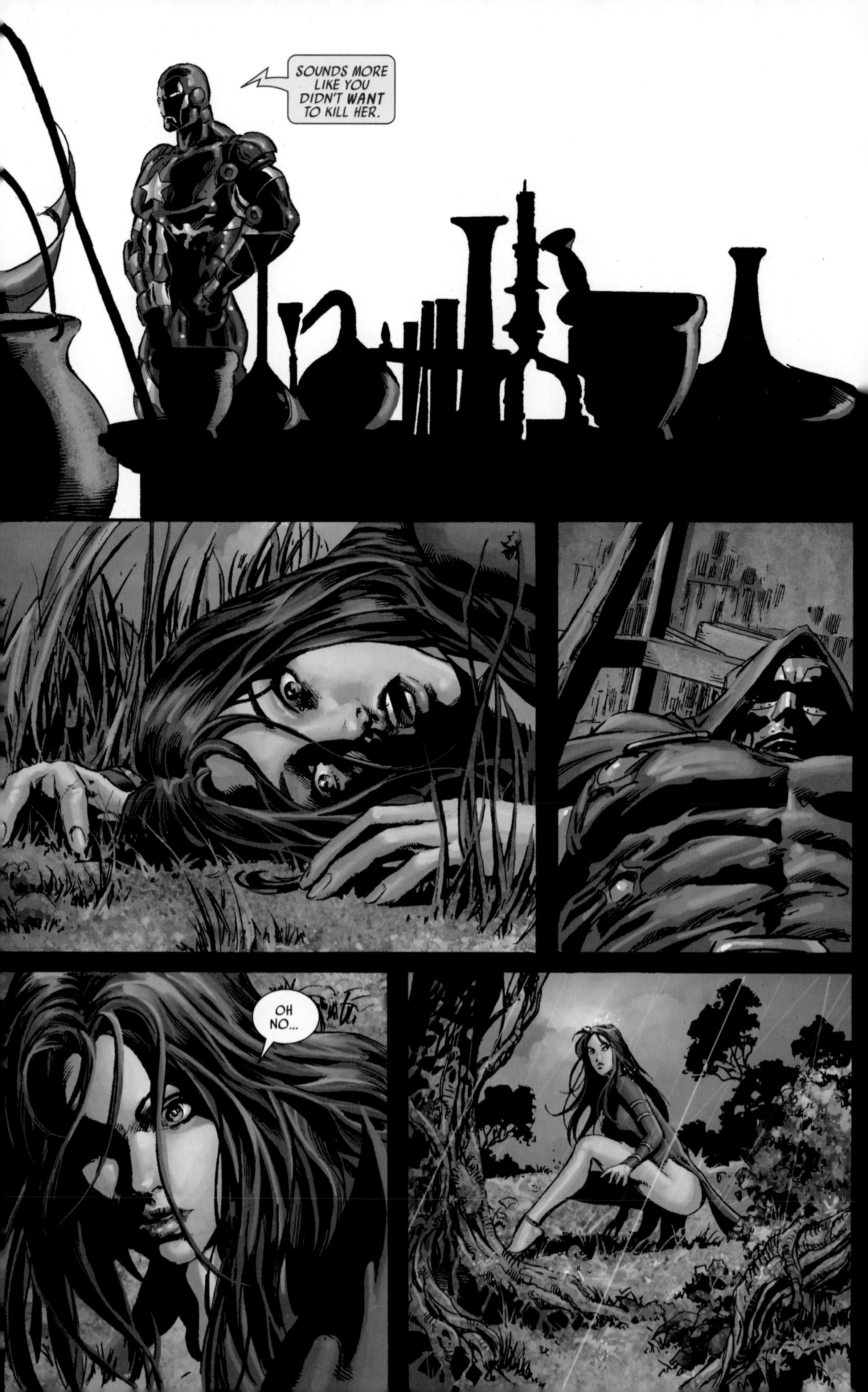
SOUNDS MORE LIKE YOU DIDN'T WANT TO KILL HER.
OH NO...

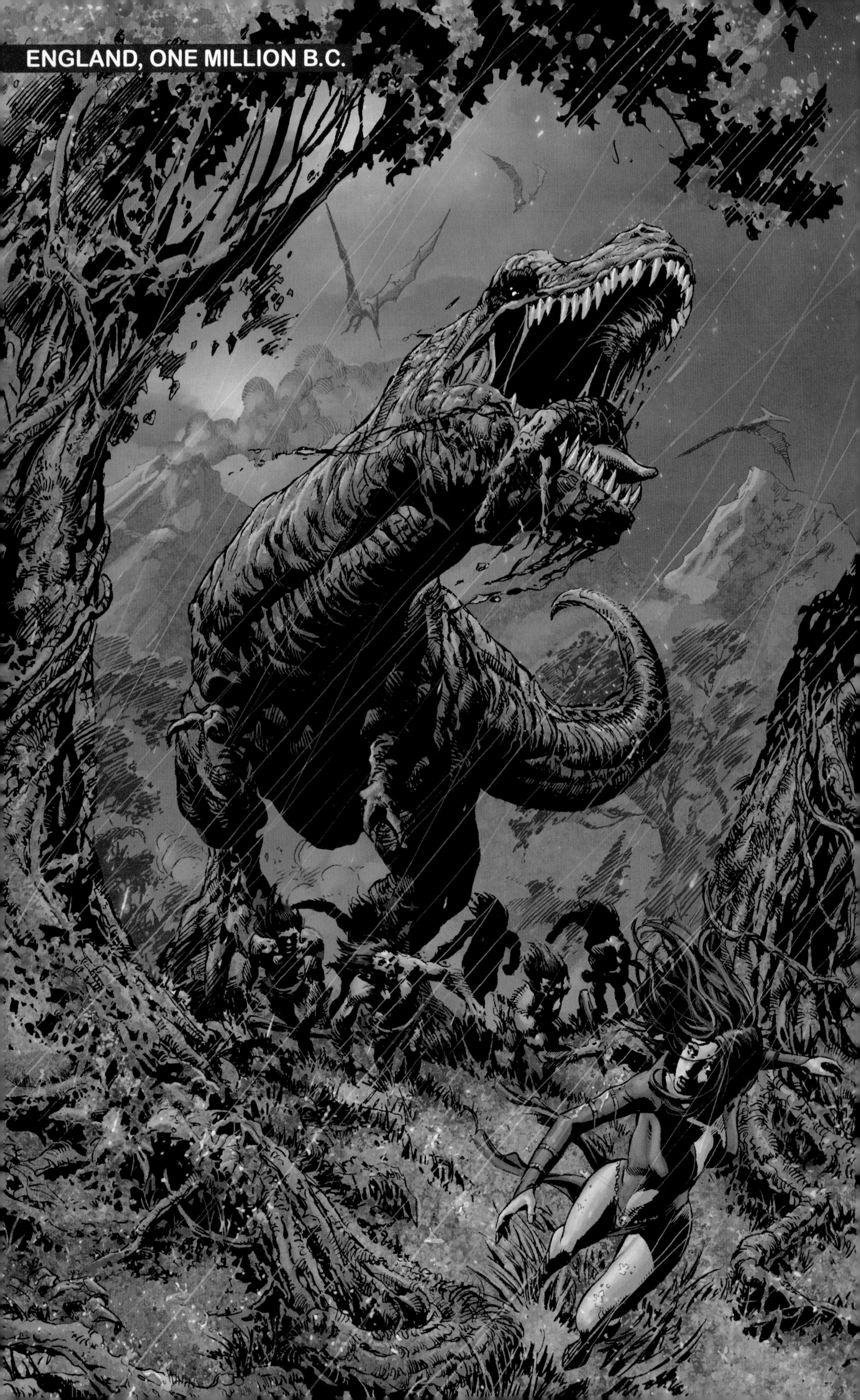
ENGLAND, ONE MILLION B.C.

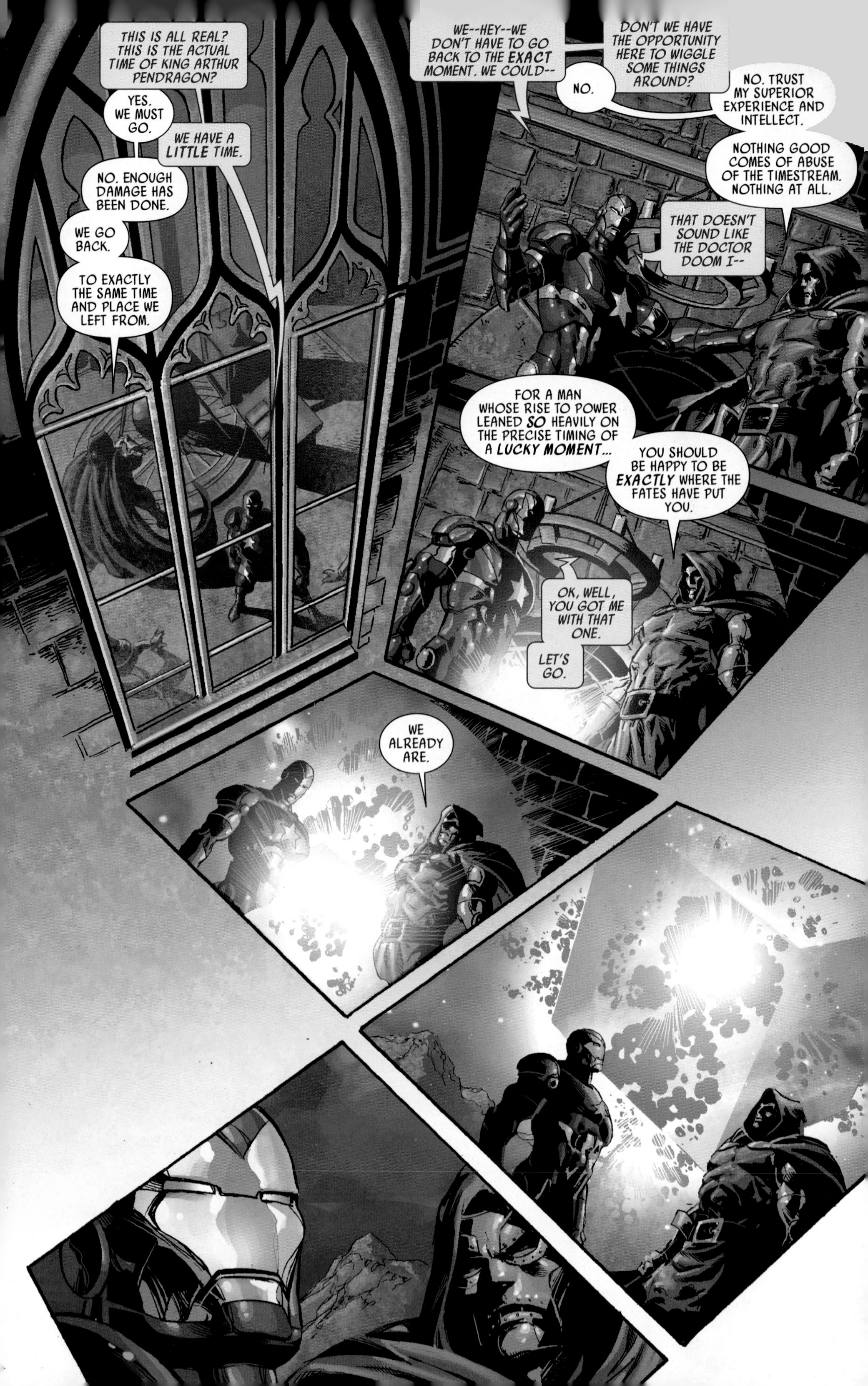
THIS IS ALL REAL? THIS IS THE ACTUAL TIME OF KING ARTHUR PENDRAGON?
YES. WE MUST GO.
WE HAVE A LITTLE TIME.
NO. ENOUGH DAMAGE HAS BEEN DONE.
WE GO BACK.
TO EXACTLY THE SAME TIME AND PLACE WE LEFT FROM.
WE--HEY--WE DON'T HAVE TO GO BACK TO THE EXACT MOMENT. WE COULD--
NO.
DON'T WE HAVE THE OPPORTUNITY HERE TO WIGGLE SOME THINGS AROUND?
NO. TRUST MY SUPERIOR EXPERIENCE AND INTELLECT.
NOTHING GOOD COMES OF ABUSE OF THE TIMESTREAM. NOTHING AT ALL.
THAT DOESN'T SOUND LIKE THE DOCTOR DOOM I--
FOR A MAN WHOSE RISE TO POWER LEANED SO HEAVILY ON THE PRECISE TIMING OF A LUCKY MOMENT...
YOU SHOULD BE HAPPY TO BE EXACTLY WHERE THE FATES HAVE PUT YOU.
OK, WELL, YOU GOT ME WITH THAT ONE.
LET'S GO.
WE ALREADY ARE.

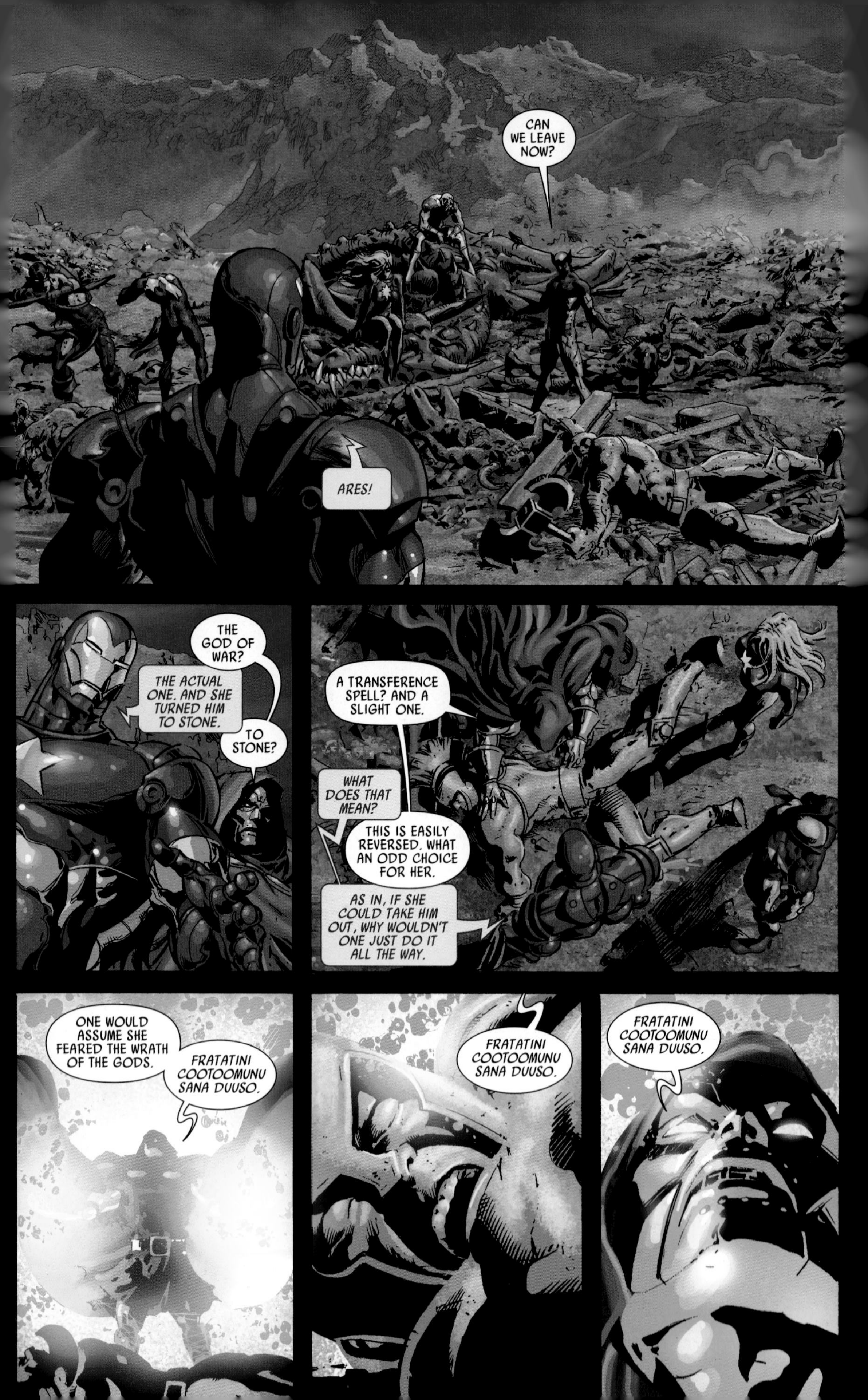
CAN WE LEAVE NOW?
ARES!
THE GOD OF WAR?
THE ACTUAL ONE. AND SHE TURNED HIM TO STONE.
TO STONE?
A TRANSFERENCE SPELL? AND A SLIGHT ONE.
WHAT DOES THAT MEAN?
THIS IS EASILY REVERSED. WHAT AN ODD CHOICE FOR HER.
AS IN, IF SHE COULD TAKE HIM OUT, WHY WOULDN'T ONE JUST DO IT ALL THE WAY.
ONE WOULD ASSUME SHE FEARED THE WRATH OF THE GODS.
FRATATINI COOTOOMUNU SANA DUUSO.
FRATATINI COOTOOMUNU SANA DUUSO.
FRATATINI COOTOOMUNU SANA DUUSO.

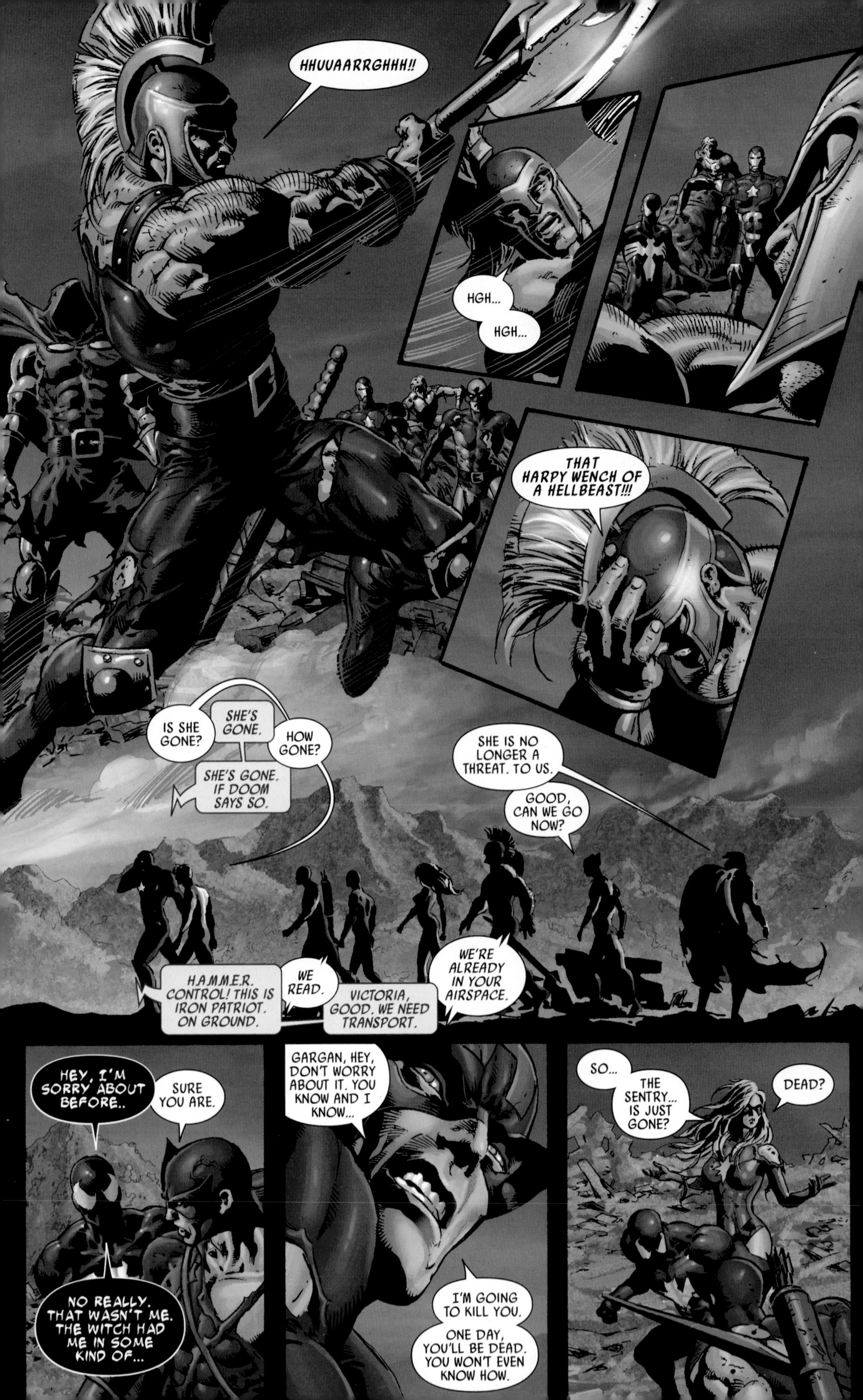
HHUUAARRGHHH!!
HGH...
HGH...
THAT HARPY WENCH OF A HELLBEAST!!!
IS SHE GONE?
SHE'S GONE.
HOW GONE?
SHE'S GONE. IF DOOM SAYS SO.
SHE IS NO LONGER A THREAT. TO US.
GOOD, CAN WE GO NOW?
H.A.M.M.E.R. CONTROL! THIS IS IRON PATRIOT. ON GROUND.
WE READ.
VICTORIA, GOOD. WE NEED TRANSPORT.
WE'RE ALREADY IN YOUR AIRSPACE.
HEY, I'M SORRY ABOUT BEFORE..
SURE YOU ARE.
NO REALLY. THAT WASN'T ME. THE WITCH HAD ME IN SOME KIND OF...
GARGAN, HEY, DON'T WORRY ABOUT IT. YOU KNOW AND I KNOW...
I'M GOING TO KILL YOU.
ONE DAY, YOU'LL BE DEAD. YOU WON'T EVEN KNOW HOW.
SO...
THE SENTRY... IS JUST GONE?
DEAD?

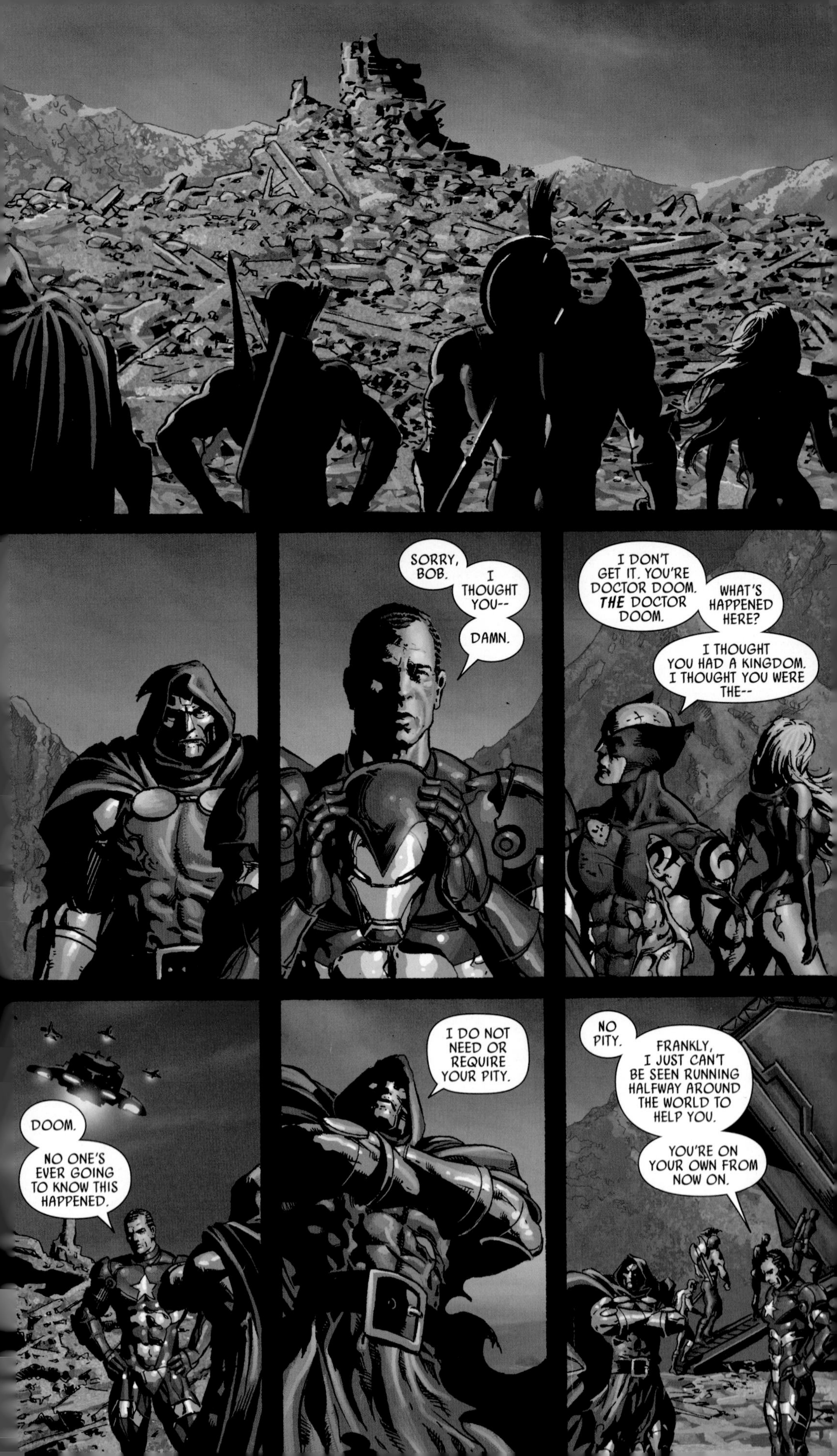
SORRY, BOB.
I THOUGHT YOU--
DAMN.
I DON'T GET IT. YOU'RE DOCTOR DOOM. THE DOCTOR DOOM.
WHAT'S HAPPENED HERE?
I THOUGHT YOU HAD A KINGDOM. I THOUGHT YOU WERE THE--
DOOM.
NO ONE'S EVER GOING TO KNOW THIS HAPPENED.
I DO NOT NEED OR REQUIRE YOUR PITY.
NO PITY.
FRANKLY, I JUST CAN'T BE SEEN RUNNING HALFWAY AROUND THE WORLD TO HELP YOU.
YOU'RE ON YOUR OWN FROM NOW ON.

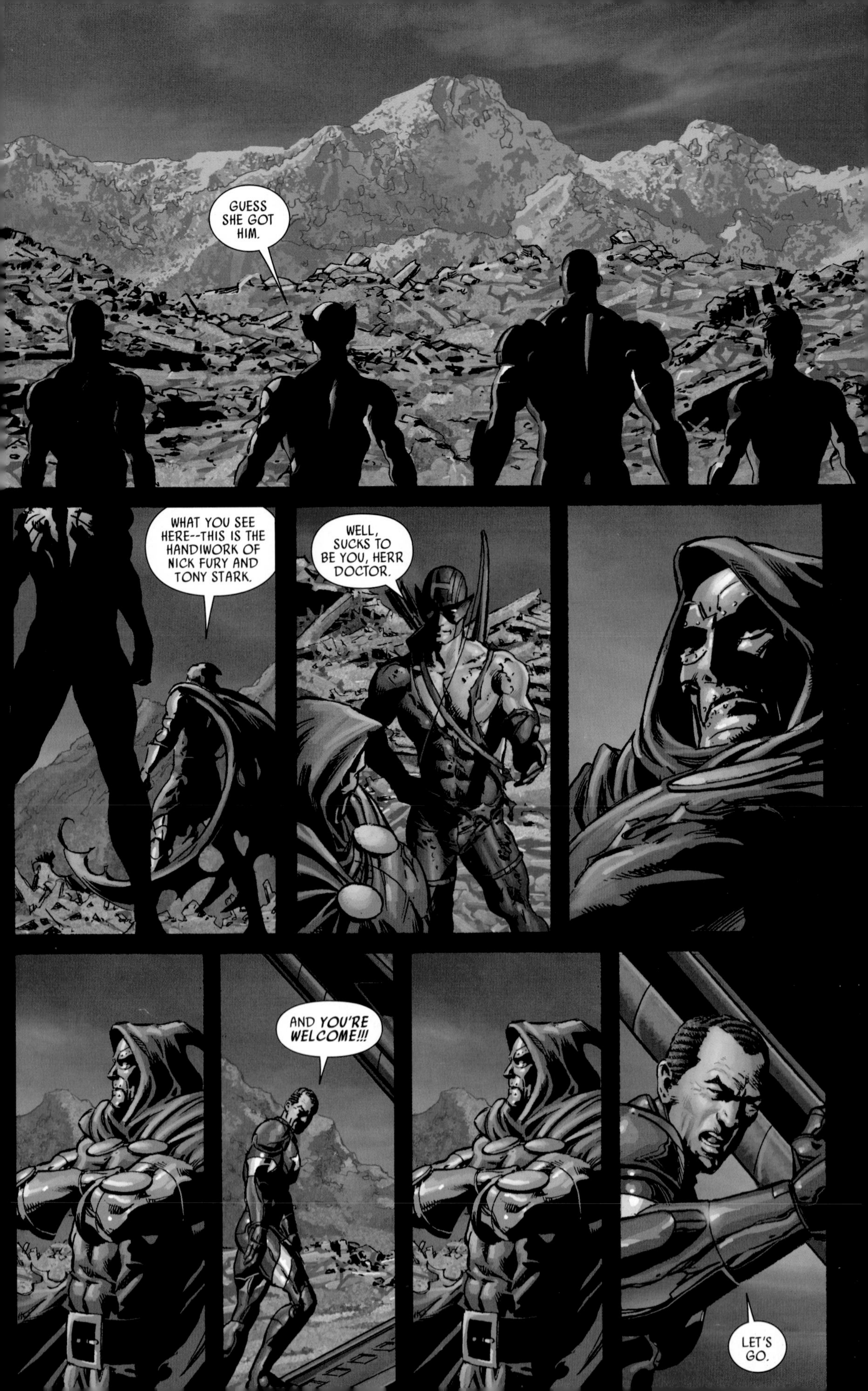
GUESS SHE GOT HIM.
WHAT YOU SEE HERE--THIS IS THE HANDIWORK OF NICK FURY AND TONY STARK.
WELL, SUCKS TO BE YOU, HERR DOCTOR.
AND *YOU'RE WELCOME!!!*
LET'S GO.

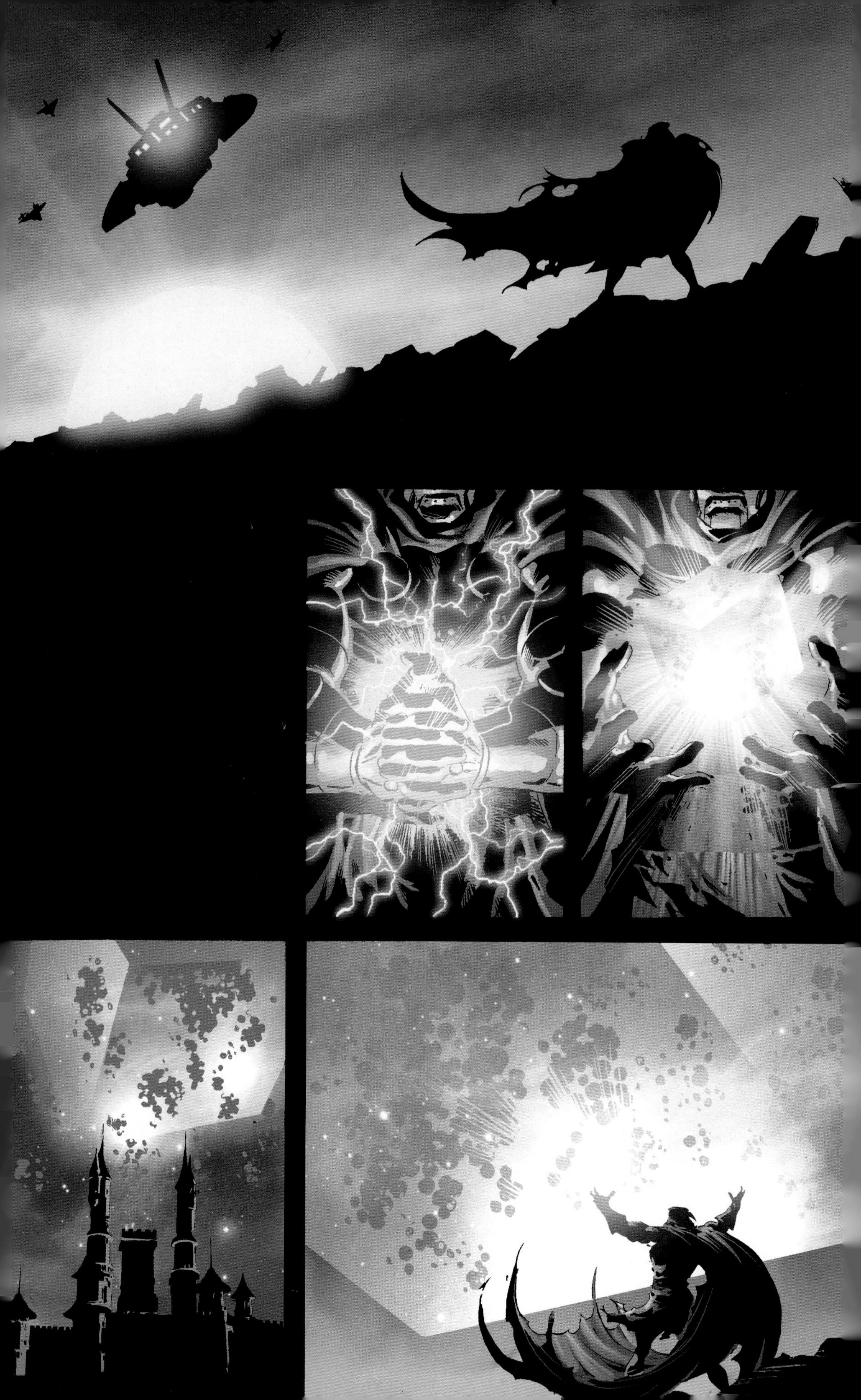

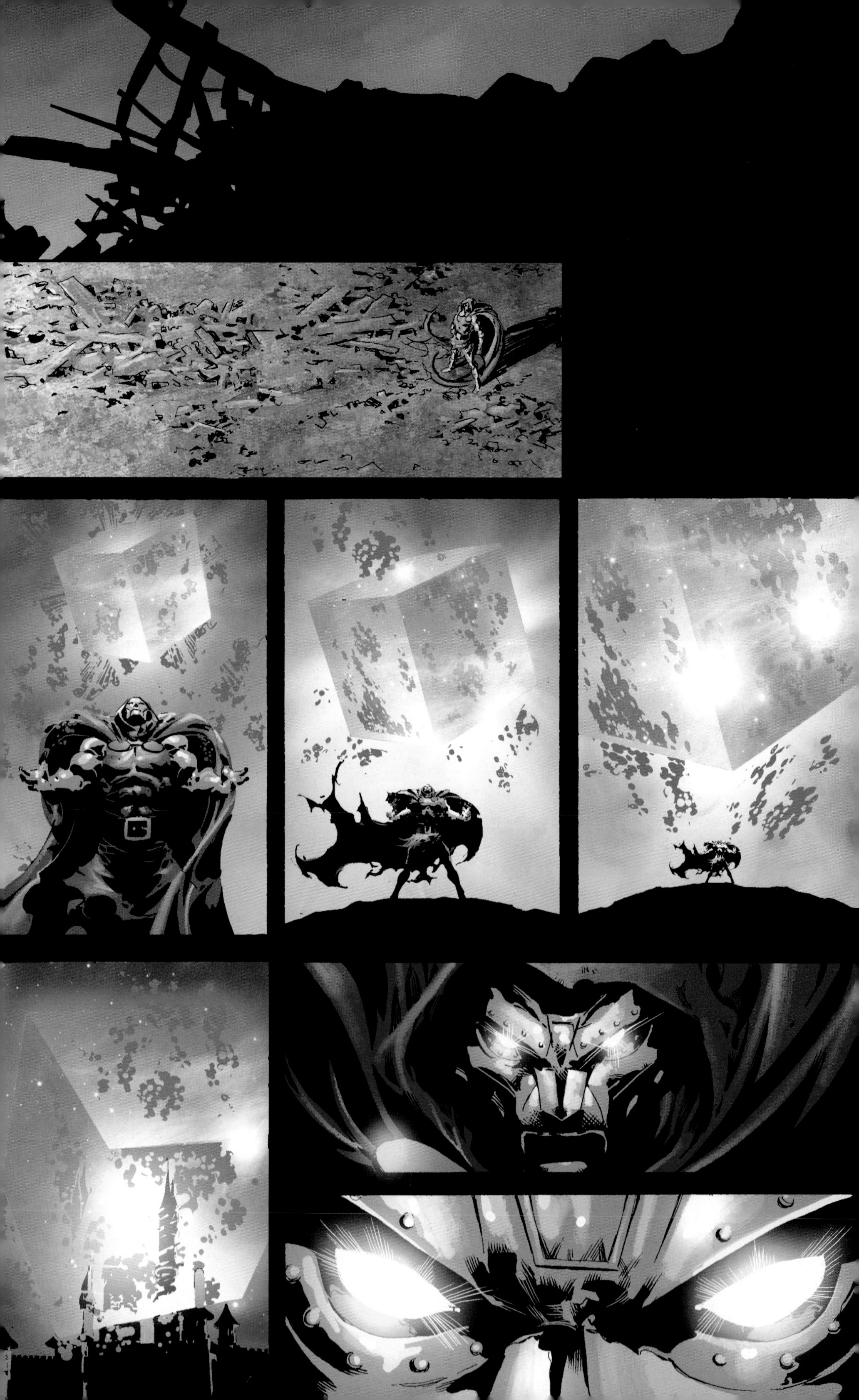

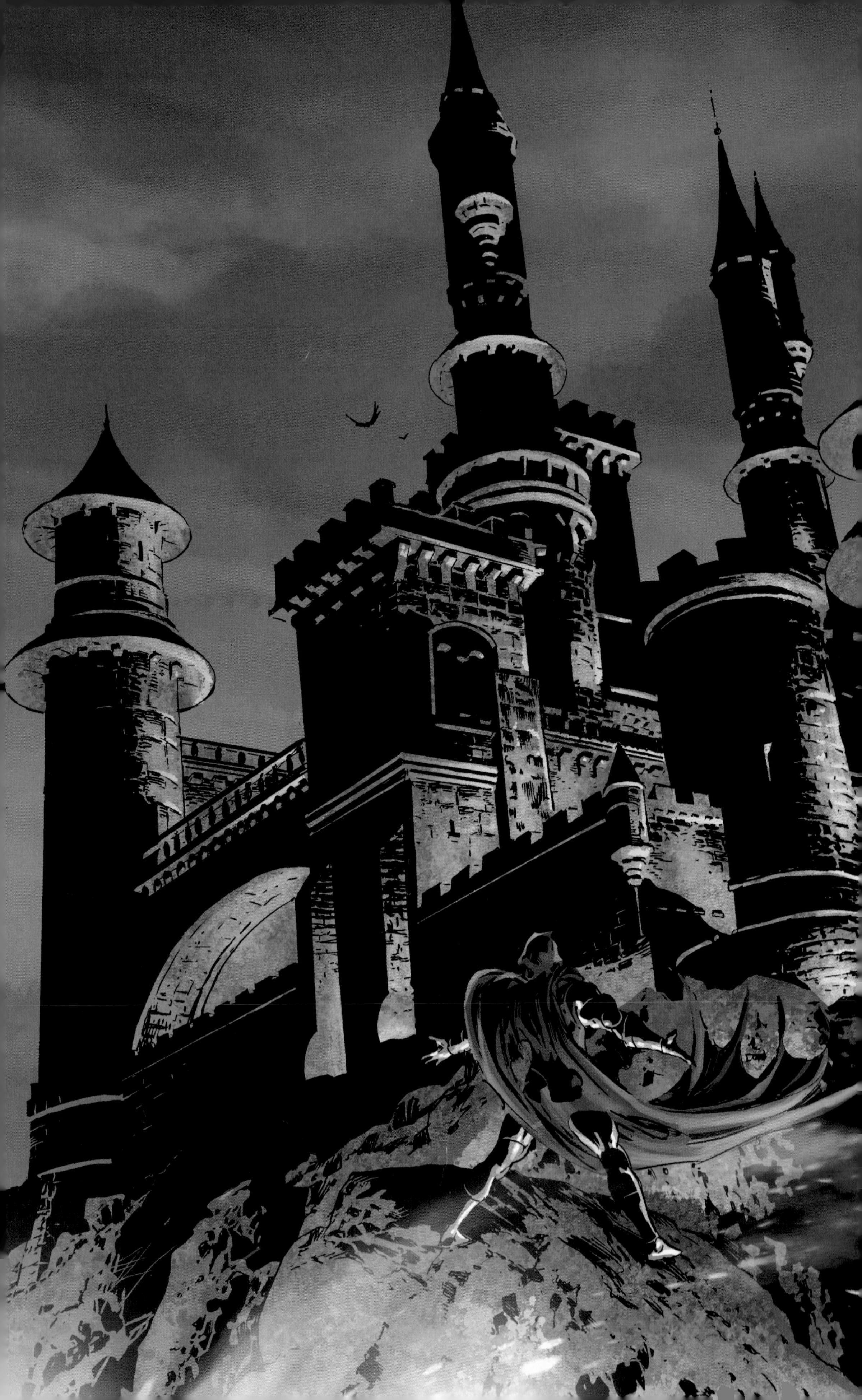

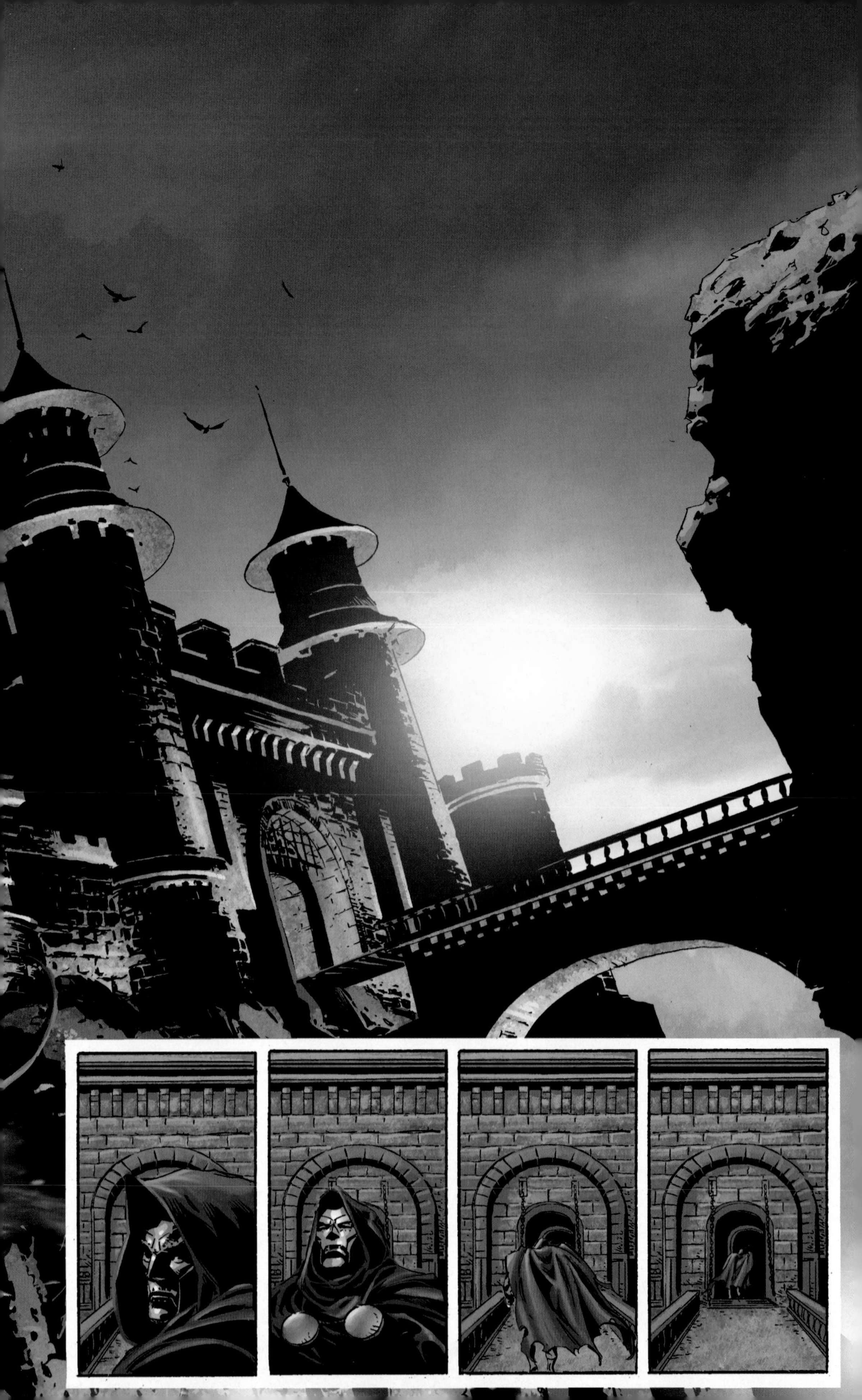

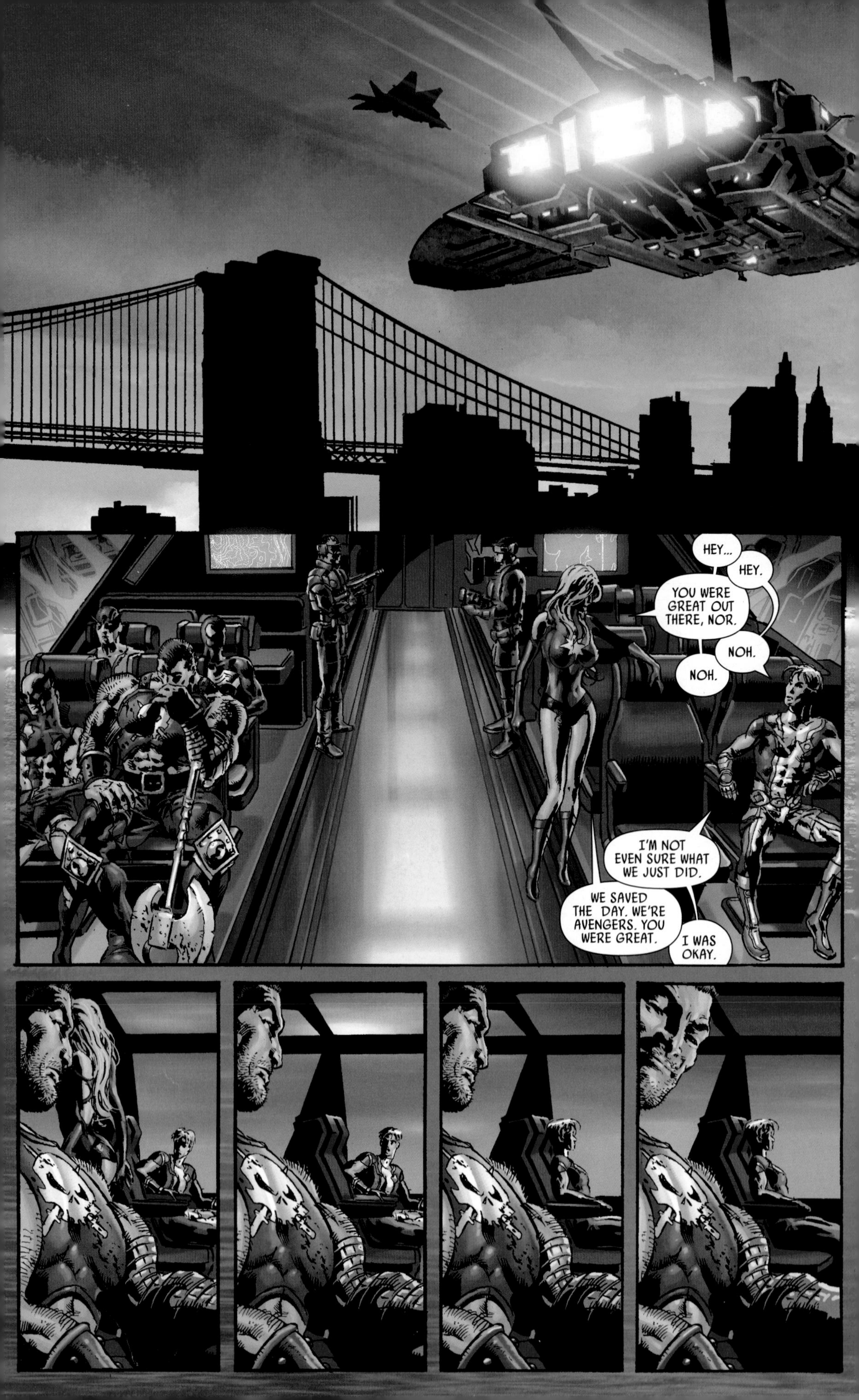
HEY...
HEY.
YOU WERE GREAT OUT THERE, NOR.
NOH.
NOH.
I'M NOT EVEN SURE WHAT WE JUST DID.
WE SAVED THE DAY. WE'RE AVENGERS. YOU WERE GREAT.
I WAS OKAY.

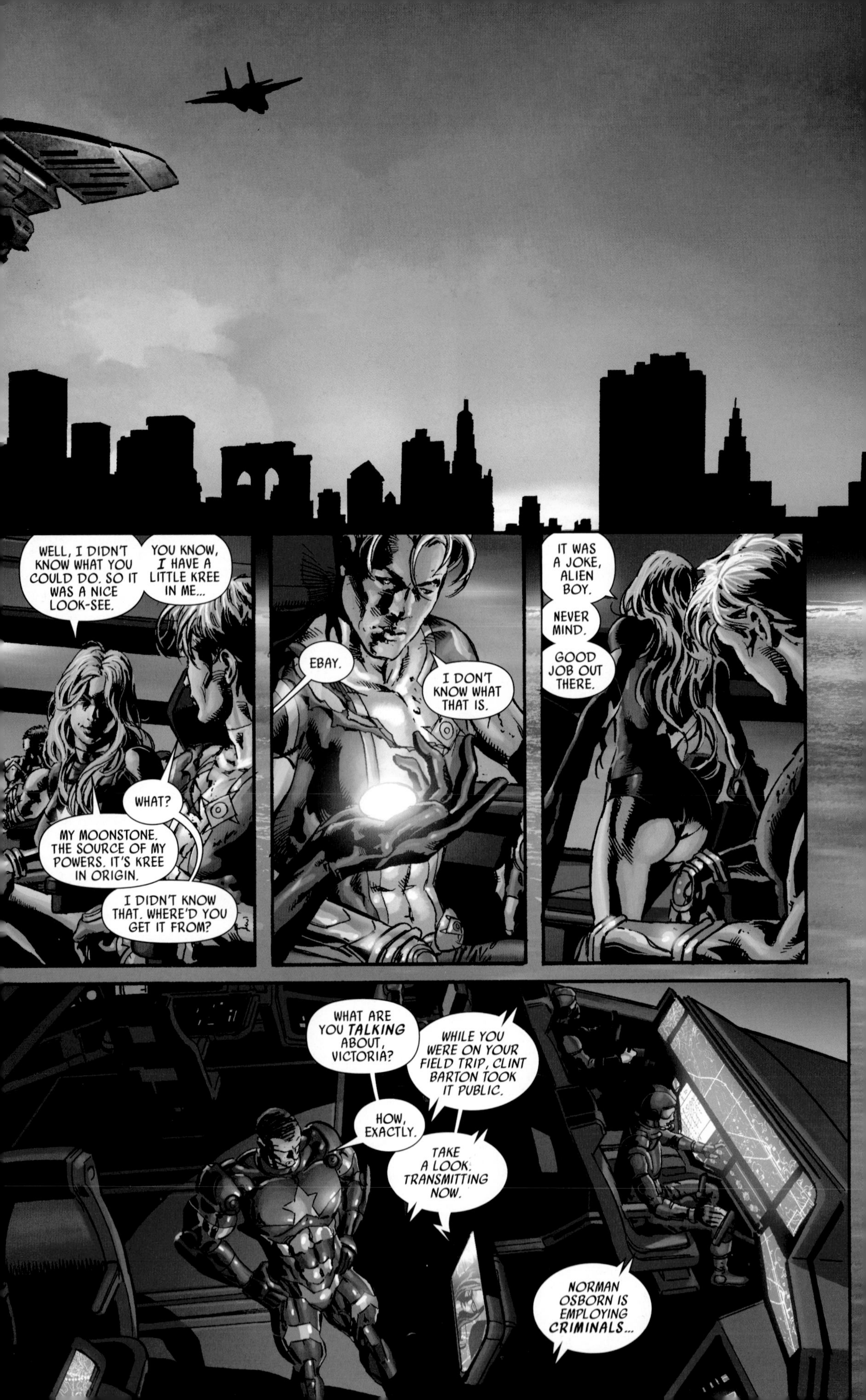
WELL, I DIDN'T KNOW WHAT YOU COULD DO. SO IT WAS A NICE LOOK-SEE.
YOU KNOW, I HAVE A LITTLE KREE IN ME...
WHAT?
MY MOONSTONE. THE SOURCE OF MY POWERS. IT'S KREE IN ORIGIN.
I DIDN'T KNOW THAT. WHERE'D YOU GET IT FROM?
EBAY.
I DON'T KNOW WHAT THAT IS.
IT WAS A JOKE, ALIEN BOY.
NEVER MIND.
GOOD JOB OUT THERE.
WHAT ARE YOU TALKING ABOUT, VICTORIA?
WHILE YOU WERE ON YOUR FIELD TRIP, CLINT BARTON TOOK IT PUBLIC.
HOW, EXACTLY.
TAKE A LOOK. TRANSMITTING NOW.
NORMAN OSBORN IS EMPLOYING CRIMINALS...

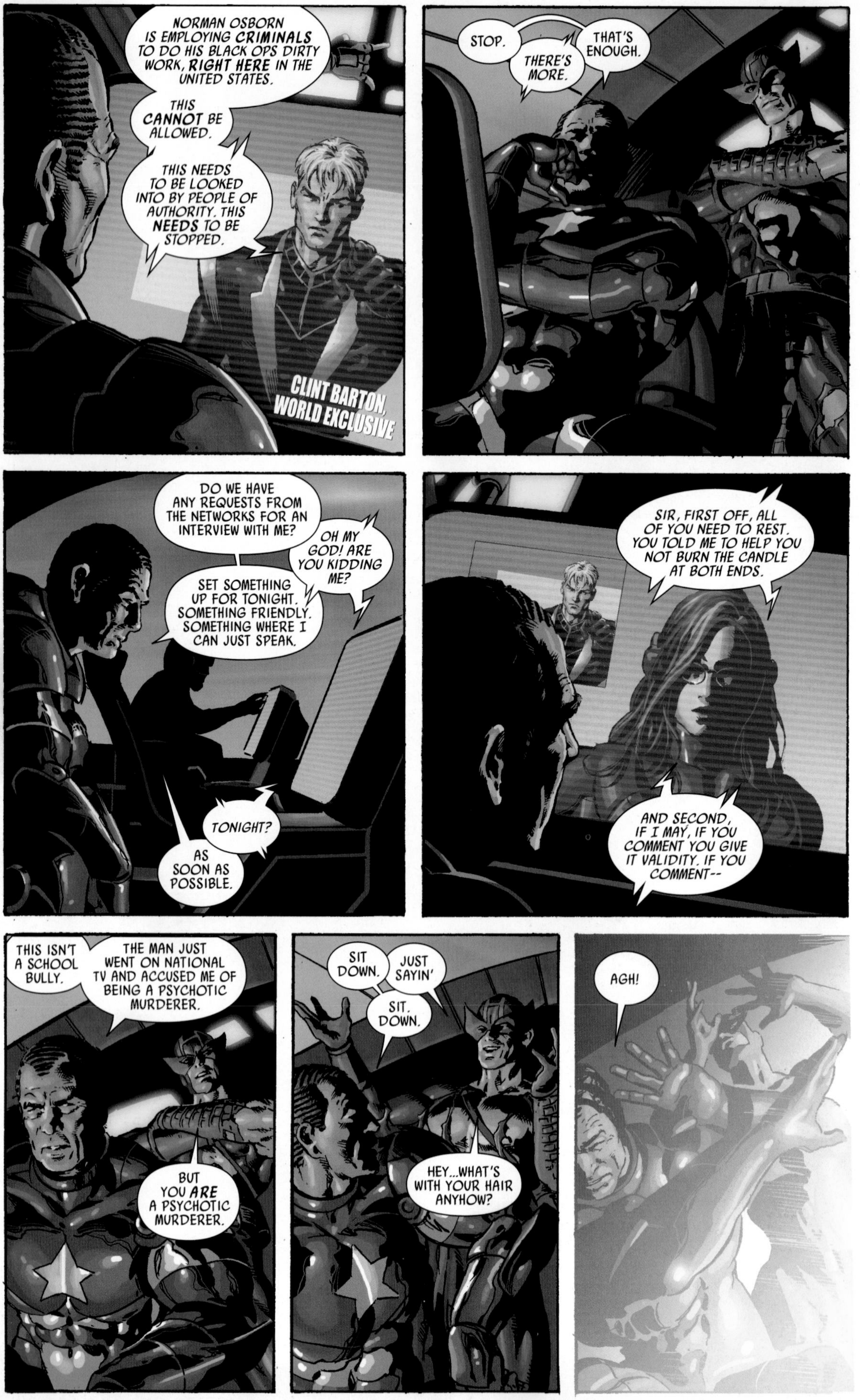
NORMAN OSBORN IS EMPLOYING CRIMINALS TO DO HIS BLACK OPS DIRTY WORK, RIGHT HERE IN THE UNITED STATES.
THIS CANNOT BE ALLOWED.
THIS NEEDS TO BE LOOKED INTO BY PEOPLE OF AUTHORITY. THIS NEEDS TO BE STOPPED.
CLINT BARTON, WORLD EXCLUSIVE
STOP.
THERE'S MORE.
THAT'S ENOUGH.
DO WE HAVE ANY REQUESTS FROM THE NETWORKS FOR AN INTERVIEW WITH ME?
OH MY GOD! ARE YOU KIDDING ME?
SET SOMETHING UP FOR TONIGHT. SOMETHING FRIENDLY. SOMETHING WHERE I CAN JUST SPEAK.
TONIGHT?
AS SOON AS POSSIBLE.
SIR, FIRST OFF, ALL OF YOU NEED TO REST. YOU TOLD ME TO HELP YOU NOT BURN THE CANDLE AT BOTH ENDS.
AND SECOND, IF I MAY, IF YOU COMMENT YOU GIVE IT VALIDITY. IF YOU COMMENT--
THIS ISN'T A SCHOOL BULLY.
THE MAN JUST WENT ON NATIONAL TV AND ACCUSED ME OF BEING A PSYCHOTIC MURDERER.
BUT YOU ARE A PSYCHOTIC MURDERER.
SIT DOWN.
JUST SAYIN'
SIT. DOWN.
HEY...WHAT'S WITH YOUR HAIR ANYHOW?
AGH!

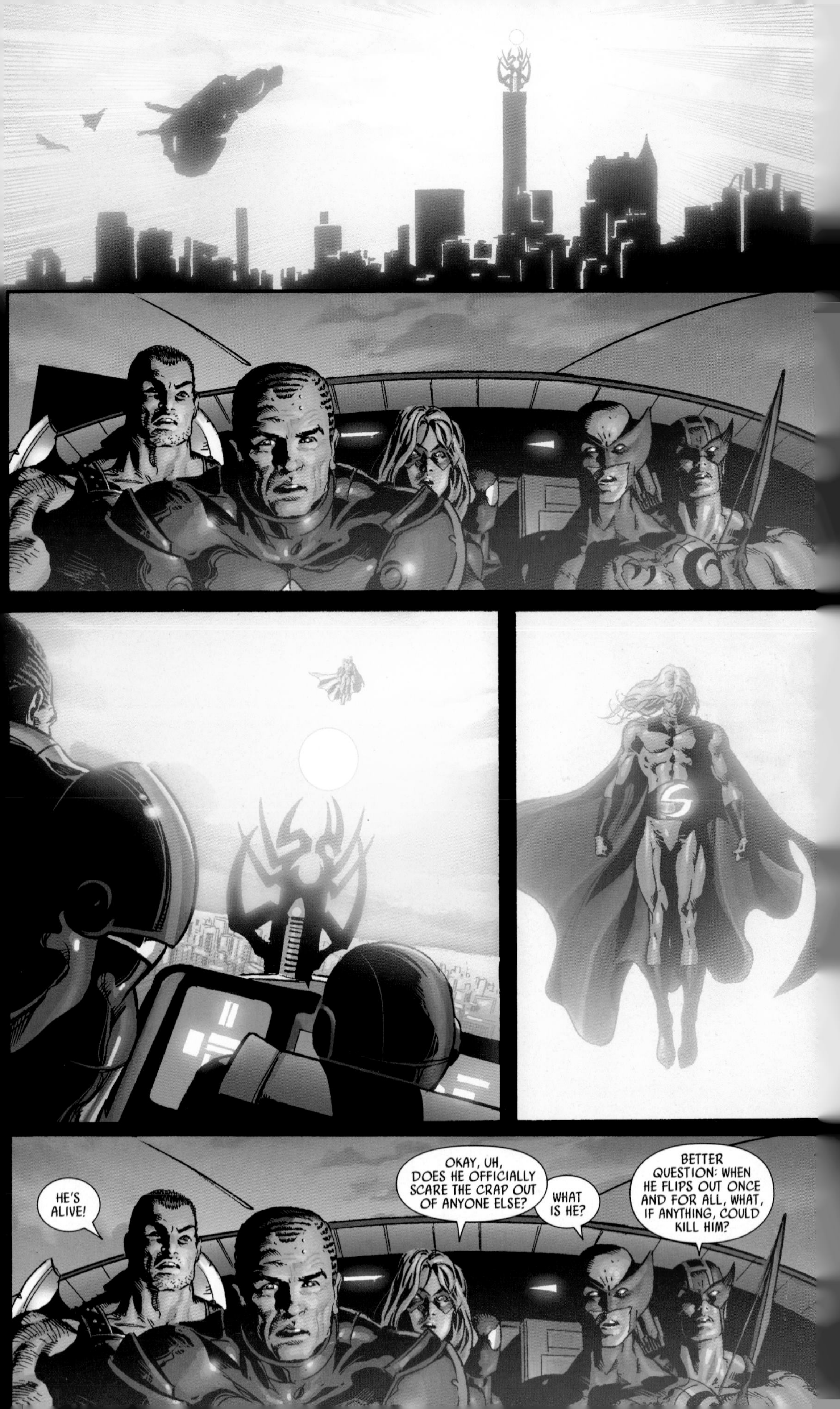
HE'S ALIVE!
OKAY, UH, DOES HE OFFICIALLY SCARE THE CRAP OUT OF ANYONE ELSE?
WHAT IS HE?
BETTER QUESTION: WHEN HE FLIPS OUT ONCE AND FOR ALL, WHAT, IF ANYTHING, COULD KILL HIM?

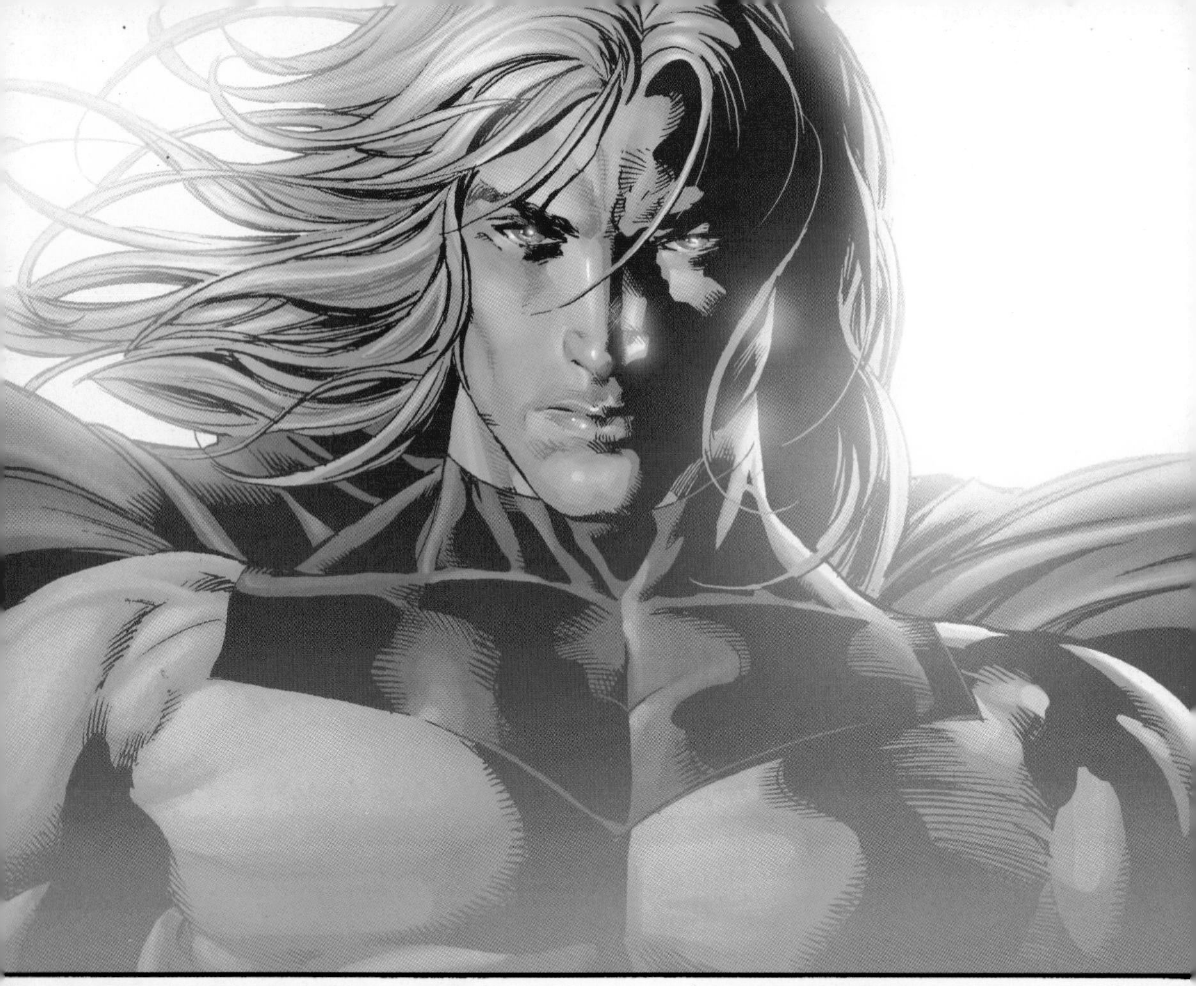

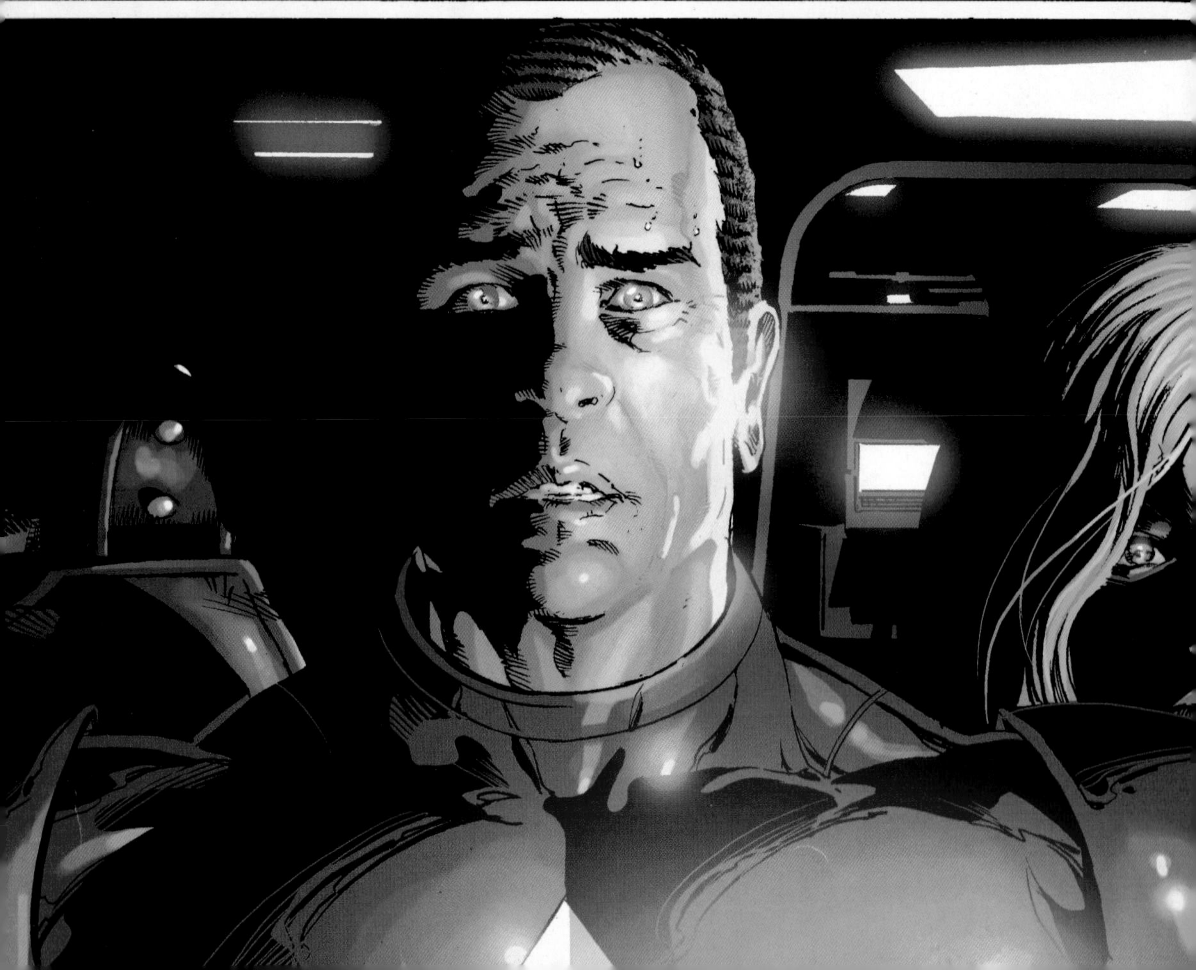

DARK AVENGERS #5

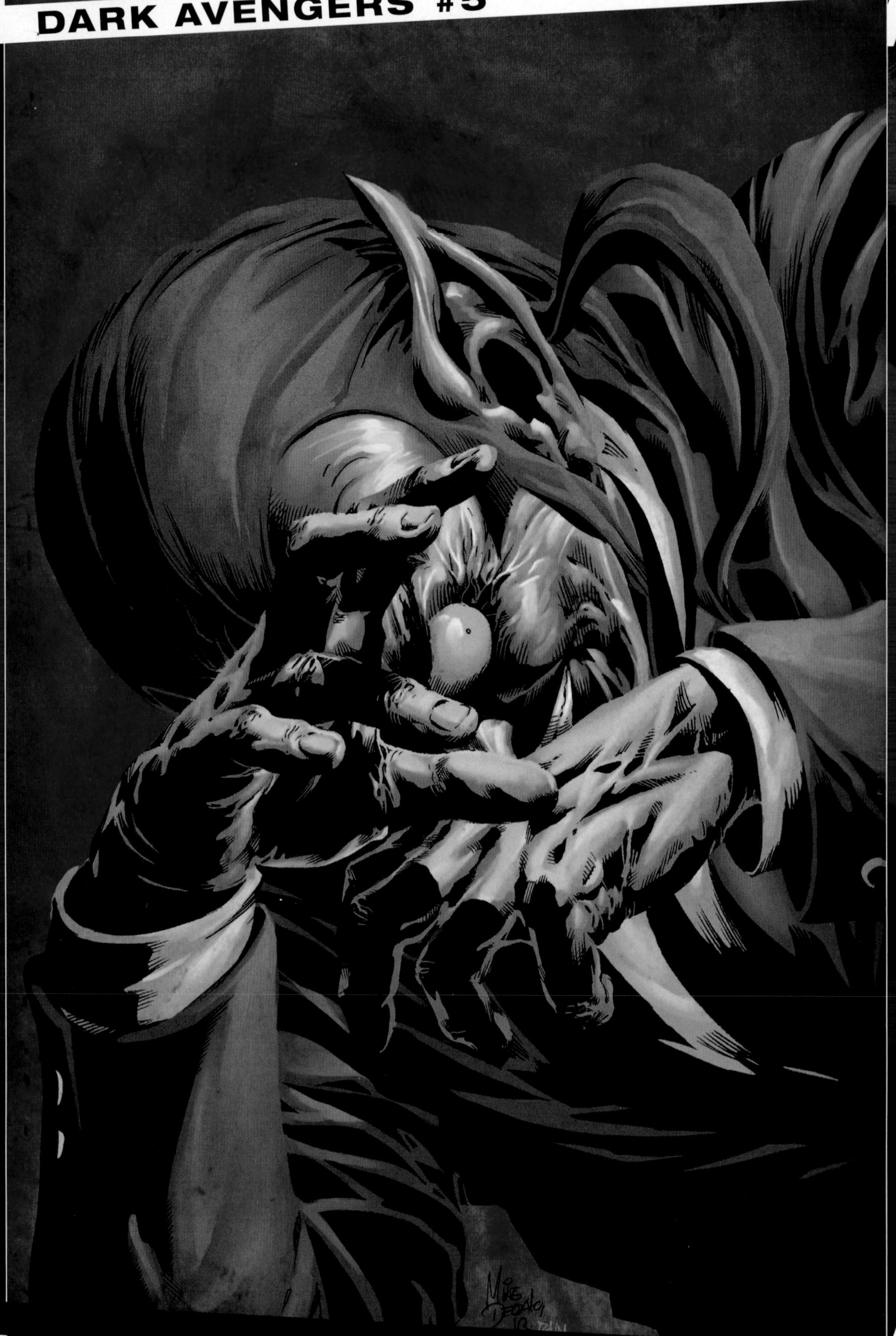

DARK AVENGERS #5 VARIANT

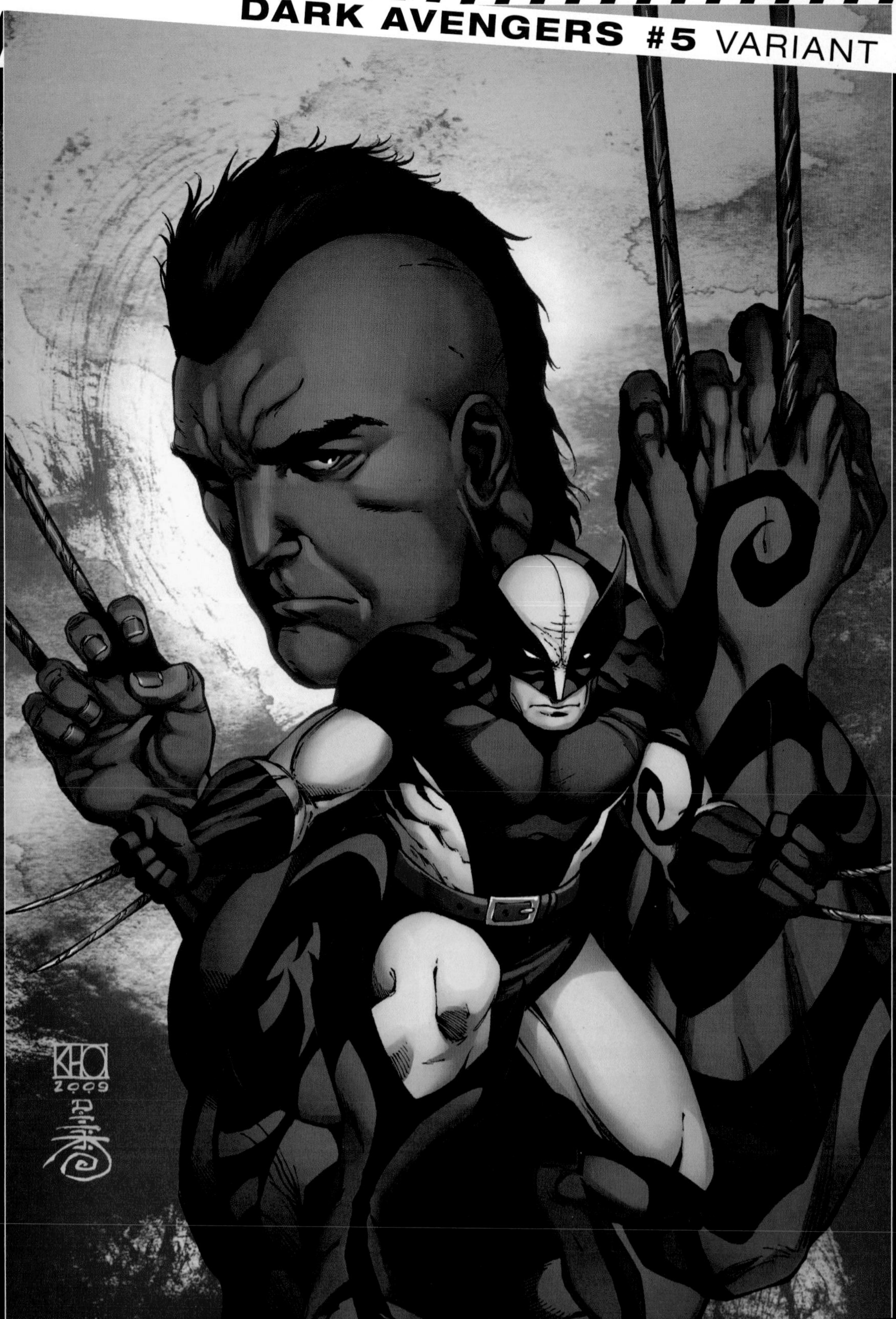
KHOI
2009

BY KHOI PHAM

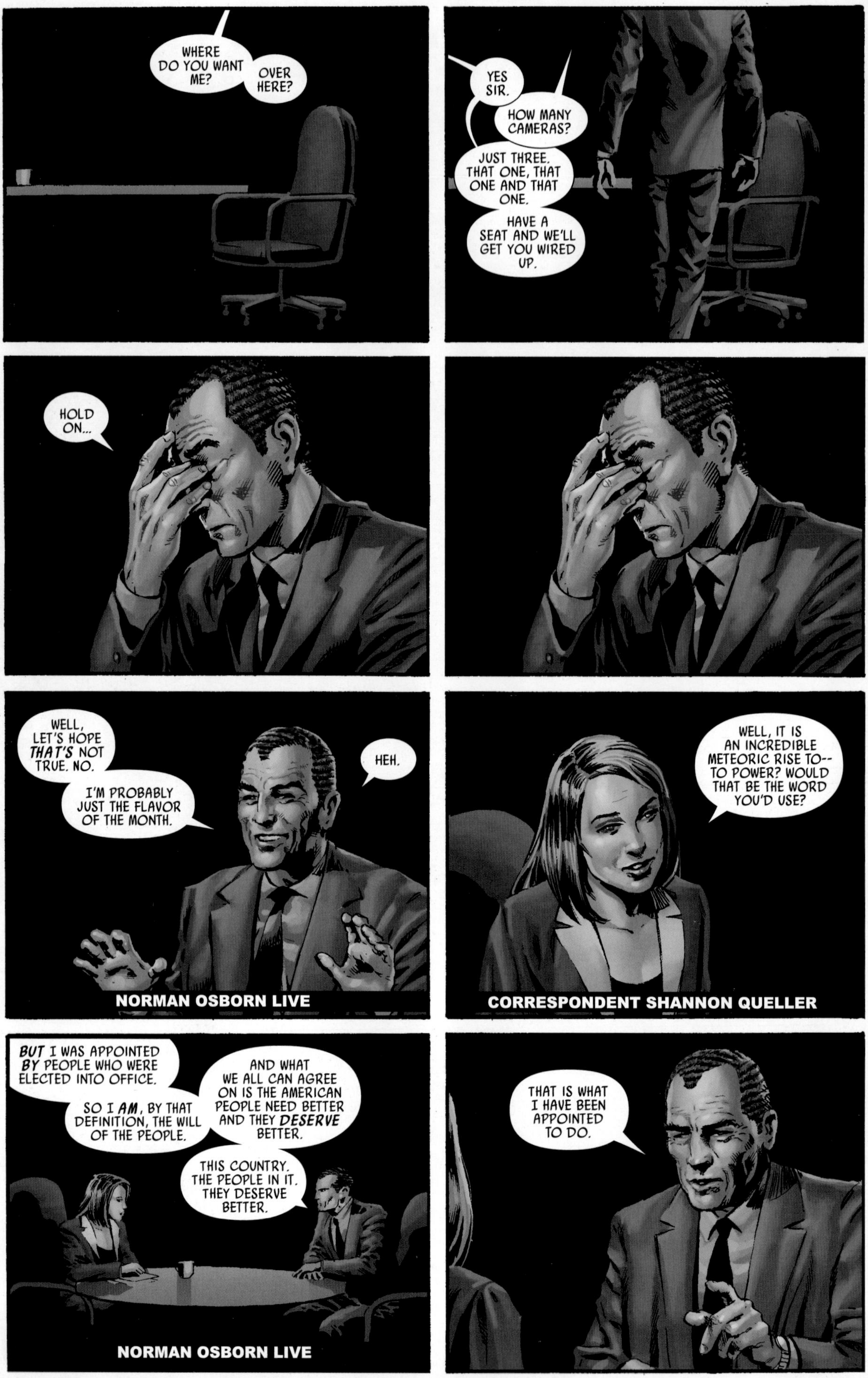
WHERE DO YOU WANT ME?
OVER HERE?
YES SIR.
HOW MANY CAMERAS?
JUST THREE. THAT ONE, THAT ONE AND THAT ONE.
HAVE A SEAT AND WE'LL GET YOU WIRED UP.
HOLD ON...
WELL, LET'S HOPE THAT'S NOT TRUE. NO.
I'M PROBABLY JUST THE FLAVOR OF THE MONTH.
HEH.
NORMAN OSBORN LIVE
WELL, IT IS AN INCREDIBLE METEORIC RISE TO-- TO POWER? WOULD THAT BE THE WORD YOU'D USE?
CORRESPONDENT SHANNON QUELLER
BUT I WAS APPOINTED BY PEOPLE WHO WERE ELECTED INTO OFFICE.
SO I AM, BY THAT DEFINITION, THE WILL OF THE PEOPLE.
AND WHAT WE ALL CAN AGREE ON IS THE AMERICAN PEOPLE NEED BETTER AND THEY DESERVE BETTER.
THIS COUNTRY. THE PEOPLE IN IT. THEY DESERVE BETTER.
NORMAN OSBORN LIVE
THAT IS WHAT I HAVE BEEN APPOINTED TO DO.

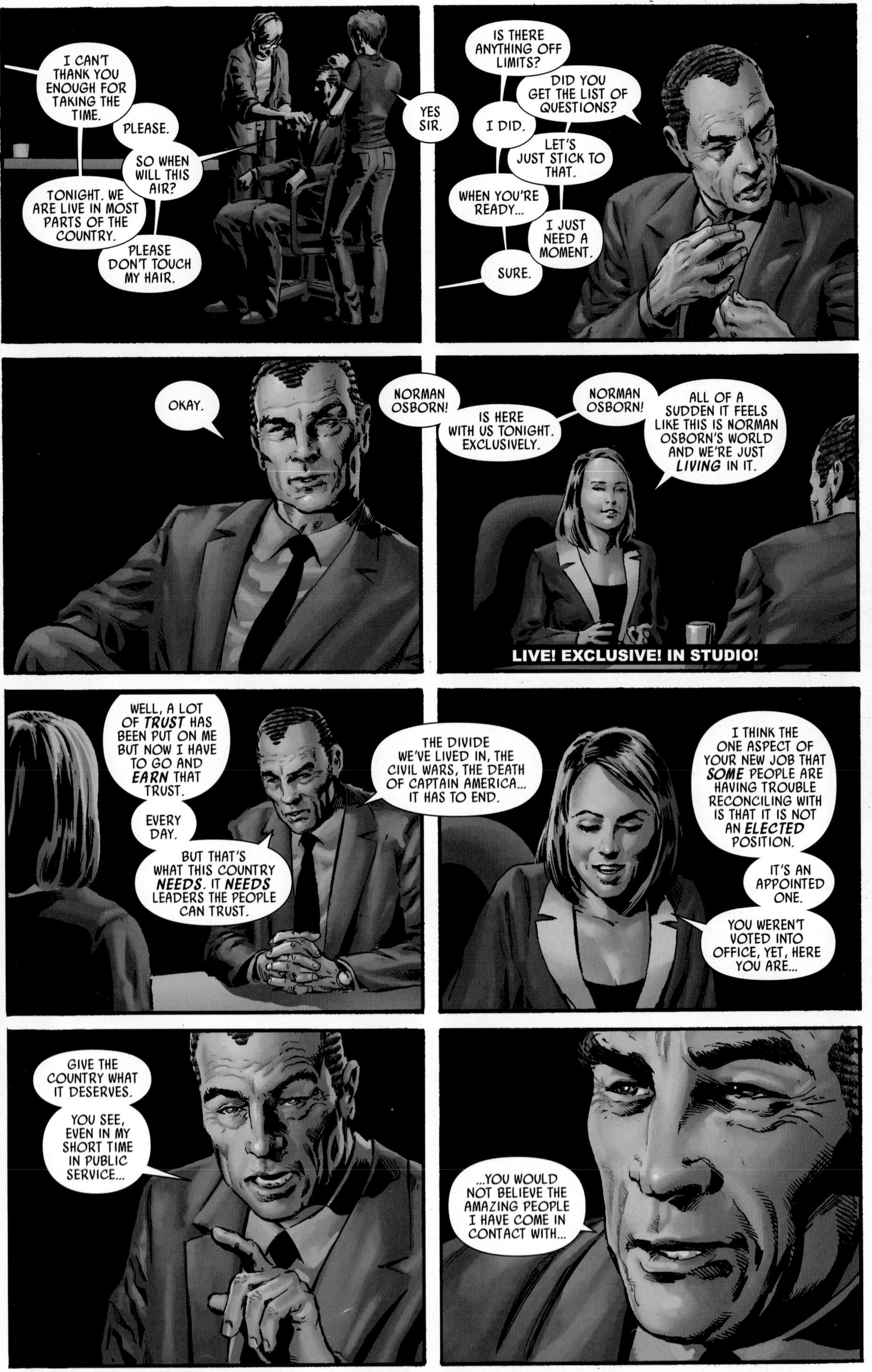
I CAN'T THANK YOU ENOUGH FOR TAKING THE TIME.
PLEASE.
SO WHEN WILL THIS AIR?
TONIGHT. WE ARE LIVE IN MOST PARTS OF THE COUNTRY.
PLEASE DON'T TOUCH MY HAIR.
YES SIR.
IS THERE ANYTHING OFF LIMITS?
DID YOU GET THE LIST OF QUESTIONS?
I DID.
LET'S JUST STICK TO THAT.
WHEN YOU'RE READY...
I JUST NEED A MOMENT.
SURE.
OKAY.
NORMAN OSBORN!
IS HERE WITH US TONIGHT. EXCLUSIVELY.
NORMAN OSBORN!
ALL OF A SUDDEN IT FEELS LIKE THIS IS NORMAN OSBORN'S WORLD AND WE'RE JUST LIVING IN IT.
LIVE! EXCLUSIVE! IN STUDIO!
WELL, A LOT OF TRUST HAS BEEN PUT ON ME BUT NOW I HAVE TO GO AND EARN THAT TRUST.
EVERY DAY.
BUT THAT'S WHAT THIS COUNTRY NEEDS. IT NEEDS LEADERS THE PEOPLE CAN TRUST.
THE DIVIDE WE'VE LIVED IN, THE CIVIL WARS, THE DEATH OF CAPTAIN AMERICA... IT HAS TO END.
I THINK THE ONE ASPECT OF YOUR NEW JOB THAT SOME PEOPLE ARE HAVING TROUBLE RECONCILING WITH IS THAT IT IS NOT AN ELECTED POSITION.
IT'S AN APPOINTED ONE.
YOU WEREN'T VOTED INTO OFFICE, YET, HERE YOU ARE...
GIVE THE COUNTRY WHAT IT DESERVES.
YOU SEE, EVEN IN MY SHORT TIME IN PUBLIC SERVICE...
...YOU WOULD NOT BELIEVE THE AMAZING PEOPLE I HAVE COME IN CONTACT WITH...

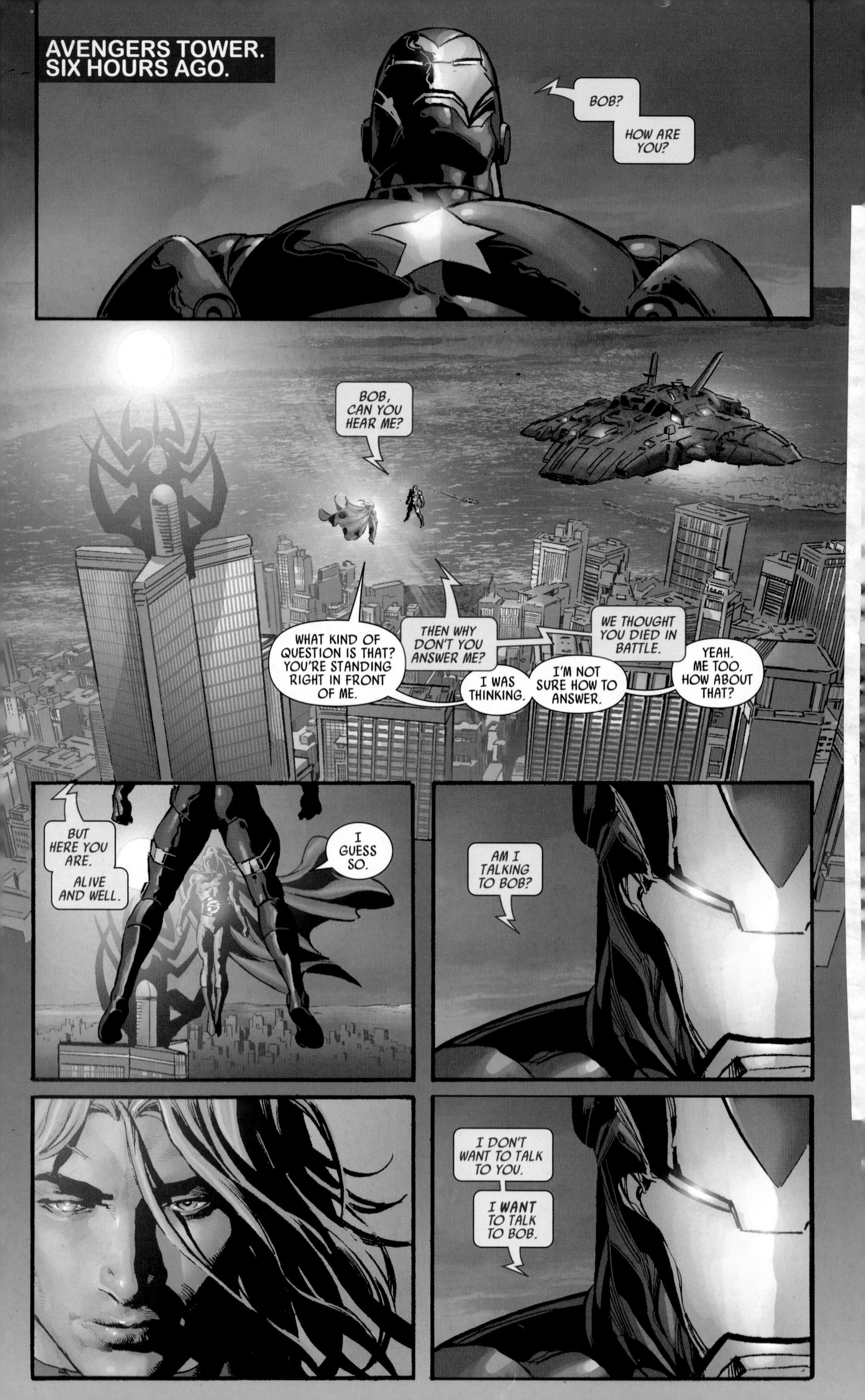
AVENGERS TOWER. SIX HOURS AGO.
BOB?
HOW ARE YOU?
BOB, CAN YOU HEAR ME?
WHAT KIND OF QUESTION IS THAT? YOU'RE STANDING RIGHT IN FRONT OF ME.
THEN WHY DON'T YOU ANSWER ME?
I WAS THINKING.
I'M NOT SURE HOW TO ANSWER.
WE THOUGHT YOU DIED IN BATTLE.
YEAH. ME TOO. HOW ABOUT THAT?
BUT HERE YOU ARE.
ALIVE AND WELL.
I GUESS SO.
AM I TALKING TO BOB?
I DON'T WANT TO TALK TO YOU.
I WANT TO TALK TO BOB.

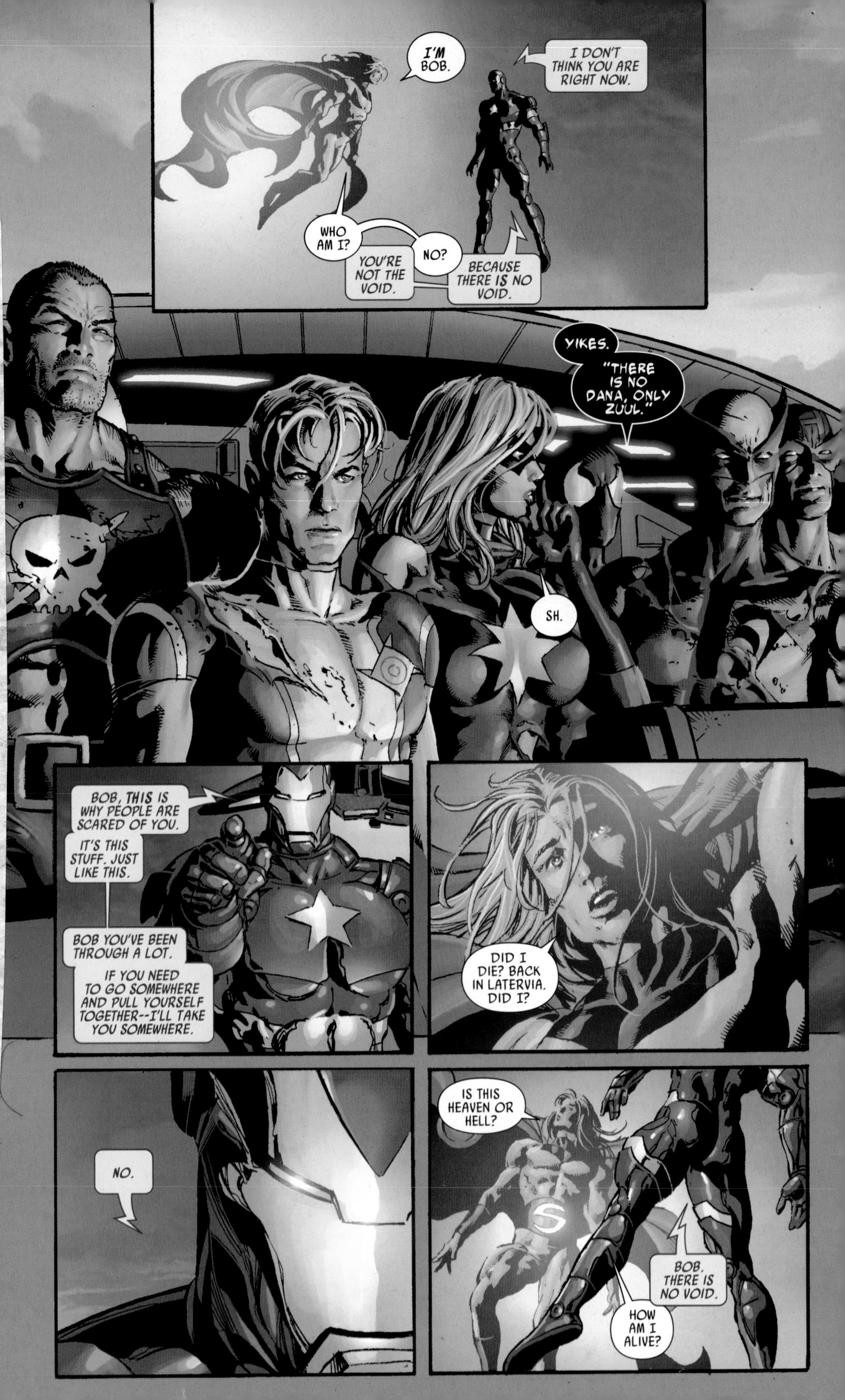

I'M BOB.
I DON'T THINK YOU ARE RIGHT NOW.
WHO AM I?
NO?
YOU'RE NOT THE VOID.
BECAUSE THERE IS NO VOID.
YIKES.
"THERE IS NO DANA, ONLY ZUUL."
SH.
BOB, THIS IS WHY PEOPLE ARE SCARED OF YOU.
IT'S THIS STUFF. JUST LIKE THIS.
BOB YOU'VE BEEN THROUGH A LOT.
IF YOU NEED TO GO SOMEWHERE AND PULL YOURSELF TOGETHER--I'LL TAKE YOU SOMEWHERE.
DID I DIE? BACK IN LATERVIA. DID I?
NO.
IS THIS HEAVEN OR HELL?
BOB. THERE IS NO VOID.
HOW AM I ALIVE?

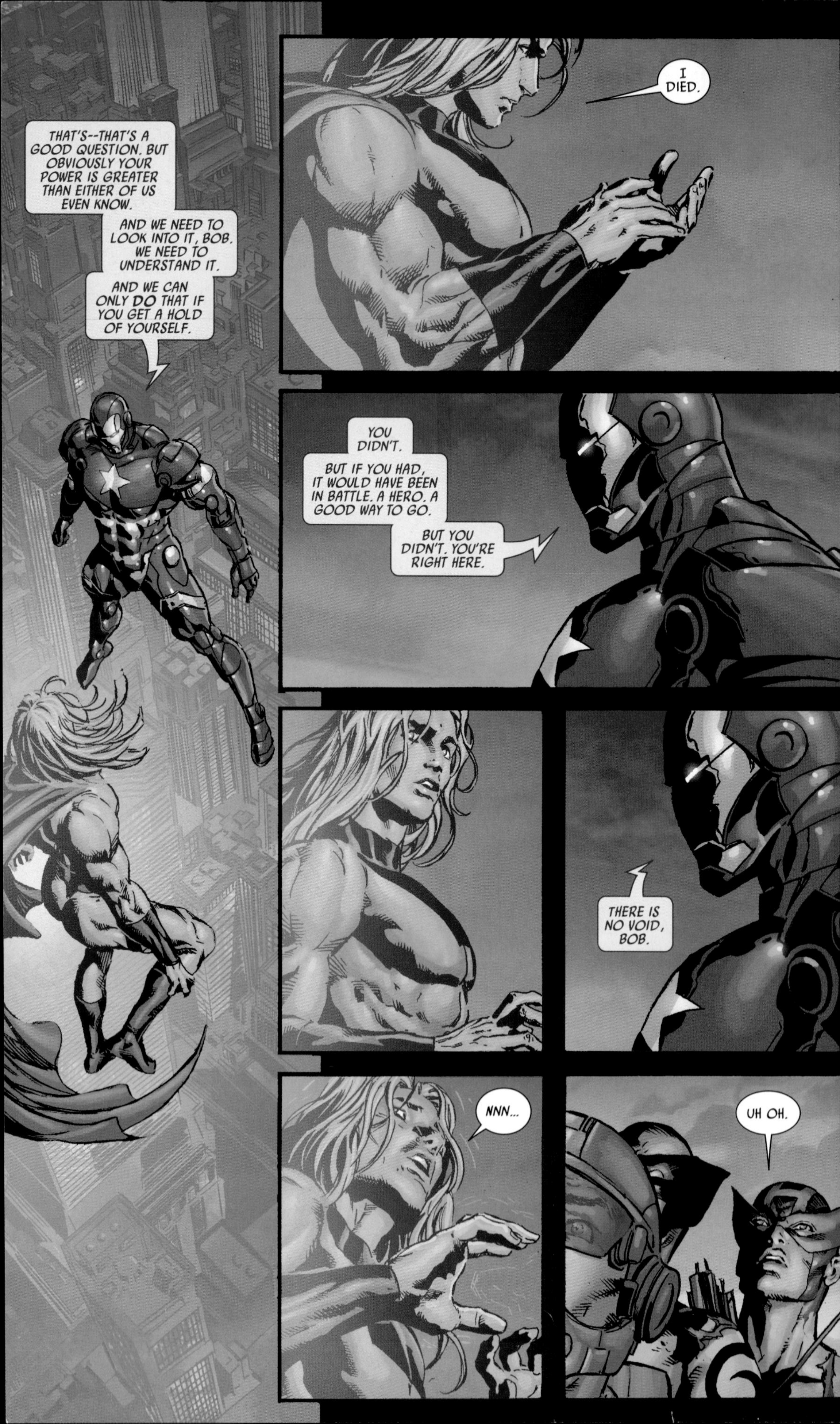
THAT'S--THAT'S A GOOD QUESTION. BUT OBVIOUSLY YOUR POWER IS GREATER THAN EITHER OF US EVEN KNOW.
AND WE NEED TO LOOK INTO IT, BOB. WE NEED TO UNDERSTAND IT.
AND WE CAN ONLY DO THAT IF YOU GET A HOLD OF YOURSELF.
I DIED.
YOU DIDN'T.
BUT IF YOU HAD, IT WOULD HAVE BEEN IN BATTLE. A HERO. A GOOD WAY TO GO.
BUT YOU DIDN'T. YOU'RE RIGHT HERE.
THERE IS NO VOID, BOB.
NNN...
UH OH.

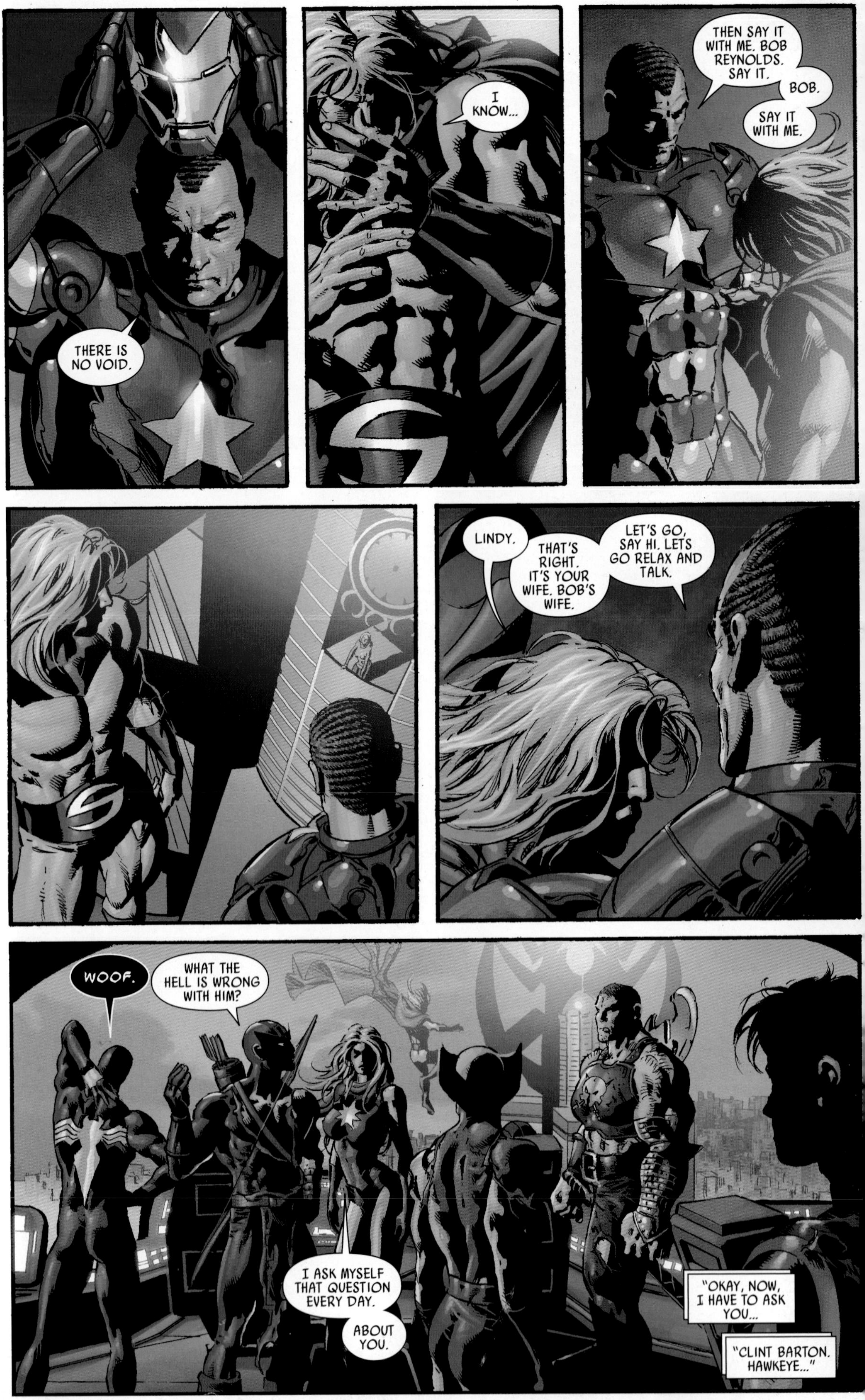
THERE IS NO VOID.
I KNOW...
THEN SAY IT WITH ME. BOB REYNOLDS. SAY IT.
BOB.
SAY IT WITH ME.
LINDY.
THAT'S RIGHT. IT'S YOUR WIFE. BOB'S WIFE.
LET'S GO, SAY HI. LETS GO RELAX AND TALK.
WOOF.
WHAT THE HELL IS WRONG WITH HIM?
I ASK MYSELF THAT QUESTION EVERY DAY.
ABOUT YOU.
"OKAY, NOW, I HAVE TO ASK YOU...
"CLINT BARTON. HAWKEYE..."

HE WENT ON TELEVISION...

THIS IS WHAT I HEAR.

AND MADE SOME DAMNING ACCUSATIONS.

YES, HE DID.

WE HAVE A CLIP.

OH, GOOD.

NORMAN OSBORN IS A CRIMINAL SOCIOPATH.

MOST PEOPLE DON'T EVEN KNOW, OR SEEM TO HAVE FORGOTTEN, BUT HE USED TO BE THE MURDERER KNOWN AS THE GREEN GOBLIN.

HE WENT TO JAIL AND A MENTAL INSTITUTION BECAUSE OF THIS.

HAWKEYE COMES CLEAN, WORLD EXCLUSIVE

I BRING THIS UP BECAUSE SOMEHOW ALL THIS IS BEING GLOSSED OVER BY THE MEDIA SO HE CAN TAKE TONY STARK AND NICK FURY'S OLD JOB.

THE FACT THAT THIS IS BEING GLOSSED OVER IS ONE OF THE MOST INSANE THINGS I HAVE EVER SEEN.

AND THOSE AVENGERS OF HIS... THOSE CHARACTERS DRESSED AS AVENGERS WHOSE SECRET IDENTITIES ARE BEING KEPT UNDER WRAPS AS A POINT OF "NATIONAL SECURITY..."

CLINT BARTON, WORLD EXCLUSIVE

THOSE ARE CRIMINALS AS WELL. FELONS. KNOWN ASSASSINS AND MURDERERS.

THEY AREN'T AVENGERS. THEY AREN'T HEROES.

CLINT BARTON, WORLD EXCLUSIVE

NOW, OF COURSE THIS BRINGS UP MANY QUESTIONS. THE--

WAS I THE GREEN GOBLIN?

YES.

NORMAN OSBORN LIVE

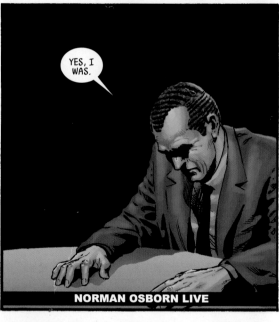

YES, I WAS.

NORMAN OSBORN LIVE

THIS IS NOT A SECRET. THIS IS NOT SOMETHING I AM TRYING TO HIDE.

BUT IT IS SOMETHING I AM TRYING TO PUT **BEHIND** ME. AND I **DO** WISH IT NEVER HAPPENED.

SO WHAT THIS REALLY IS--IS AN ATTEMPT TO DREDGE UP CONSPIRACY IN WHAT IS SUPPOSED TO BE A TIME OF HOPE AND CHANGE.

NORMAN OSBORN LIVE

WHY IS CLINT BARTON DOING THIS? I DON'T KNOW. I DON'T KNOW THE MAN.

BUT WHAT IS IMPORTANT, VERY IMPORTANT, FOR THE PEOPLE AT HOME TO KNOW IS THAT I **WAS** A VERY ILL MAN.

I WAS NOT OF, AS THEY SAY, SOUND MIND AND BODY...

FILE FOOTAGE

I WAS SUFFERING FROM A SEVERE CHEMICAL IMBALANCE. ONE I WAS BORN WITH. LIKE MILLIONS OF AMERICANS.

AND IN MY TERRIBLE STATE I WAS TAKEN ADVANTAGE OF.

I WAS ENGAGED BY UNSAVORY PEOPLE. I WAS PUSHED INTO VIOLENCE. I WAS TAKEN ADVANTAGE OF.

NORMAN OSBORN LIVE

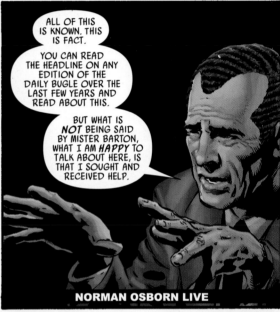

ALL OF THIS IS KNOWN. THIS IS FACT.

YOU CAN READ THE HEADLINE ON ANY EDITION OF THE DAILY BUGLE OVER THE LAST FEW YEARS AND READ ABOUT THIS.

BUT WHAT IS **NOT** BEING SAID BY MISTER BARTON, WHAT I AM **HAPPY** TO TALK ABOUT HERE, IS THAT I SOUGHT AND RECEIVED HELP.

NORMAN OSBORN LIVE

I AM CURED.

I AM NO LONGER THIS GREEN GOBLIN, **OBVIOUSLY** I AM NOT.

BUT, YES, WHAT IS SO ODD ABOUT THIS STORY IS, AFTER I GOT MY ACT TOGETHER, OTHER PEOPLE, MUTANTS, SPIDER-MAN, WHAT HAVE YOU, DONNED THE GREEN GOBLIN PERSONA.

MOST OF WHAT PEOPLE THINK OF WHEN THEY THINK OF THE GREEN GOBLIN, THAT WAS ACTUALLY **NOT** ME.

AND I CAN PROVE IT BECAUSE THE GREEN GOBLIN VERY PUBLICLY ATTACKED ME AND MY LOVED ONES.

THERE'S AN ENTIRE EPISODE OF NIGHTLINE DEDICATED TO IT.

AS YOU SEE NOW, I AM A WELL MAN.

I HAVE SIGNED DOCUMENTS BY NOBEL PRIZE-WINNING DOCTORS TO BACK THAT UP. I AM WELL.

AND REALLY, DO YOU THINK FOR A SECOND THAT THE PRESIDENT OF THE UNITED STATES AND THE JOINT CHIEFS OF STAFF WOULD ALLOW A MURDEROUS COSTUMED MANIAC TO LEAD AN IMPORTANT INITIATIVE IN THIS, THE MOST IMPORTANT TIME IN OUR HISTORY?

FILE FOOTAGE

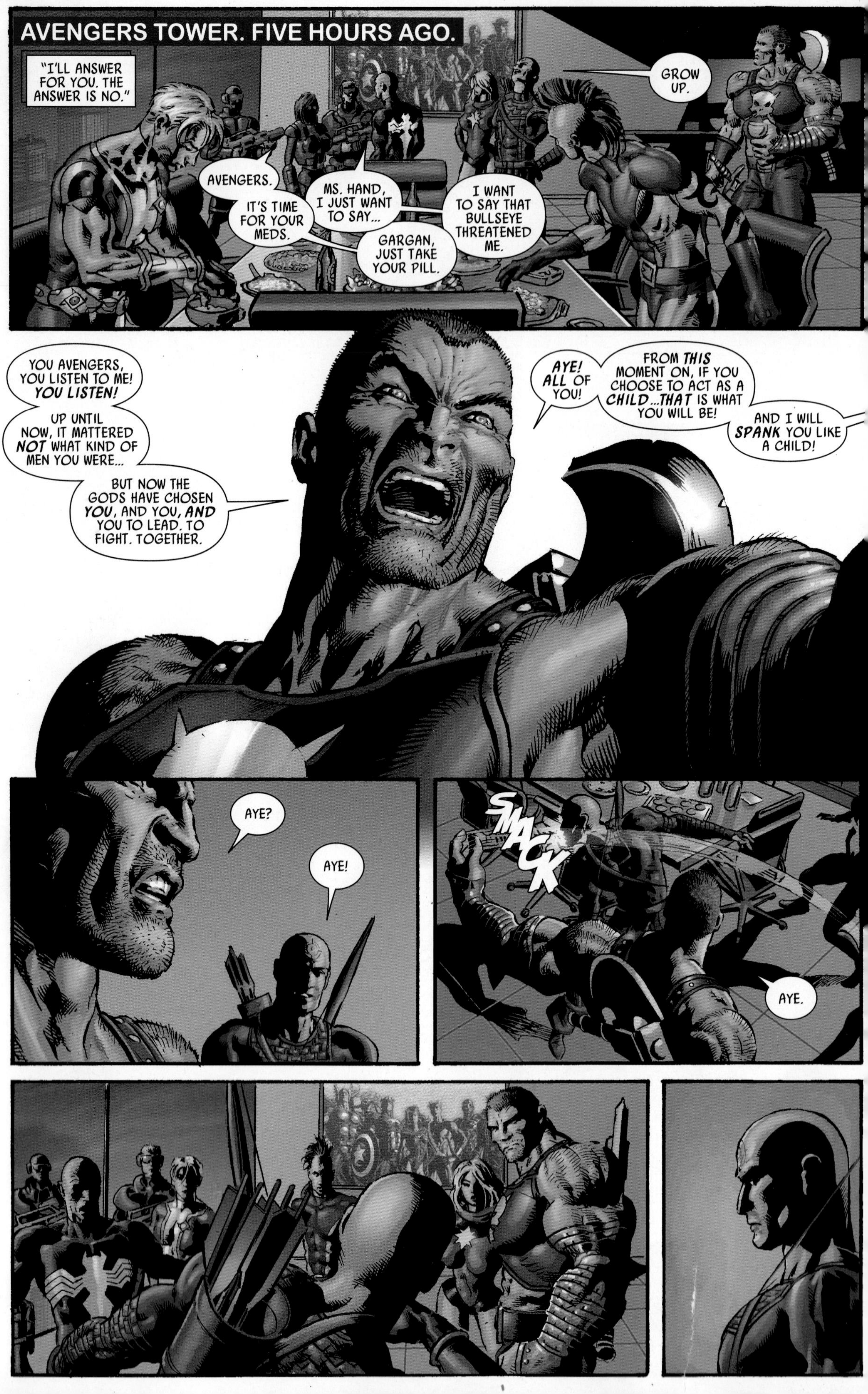
AVENGERS TOWER. FIVE HOURS AGO.
"I'LL ANSWER FOR YOU. THE ANSWER IS NO."
GROW UP.
AVENGERS.
IT'S TIME FOR YOUR MEDS.
MS. HAND, I JUST WANT TO SAY...
GARGAN, JUST TAKE YOUR PILL.
I WANT TO SAY THAT BULLSEYE THREATENED ME.
YOU AVENGERS, YOU LISTEN TO ME! YOU LISTEN!
UP UNTIL NOW, IT MATTERED NOT WHAT KIND OF MEN YOU WERE...
BUT NOW THE GODS HAVE CHOSEN YOU, AND YOU, AND YOU TO LEAD. TO FIGHT. TOGETHER.
AYE! ALL OF YOU!
FROM THIS MOMENT ON, IF YOU CHOOSE TO ACT AS A CHILD...THAT IS WHAT YOU WILL BE!
AND I WILL SPANK YOU LIKE A CHILD!
AYE?
AYE!
SMACK
AYE.

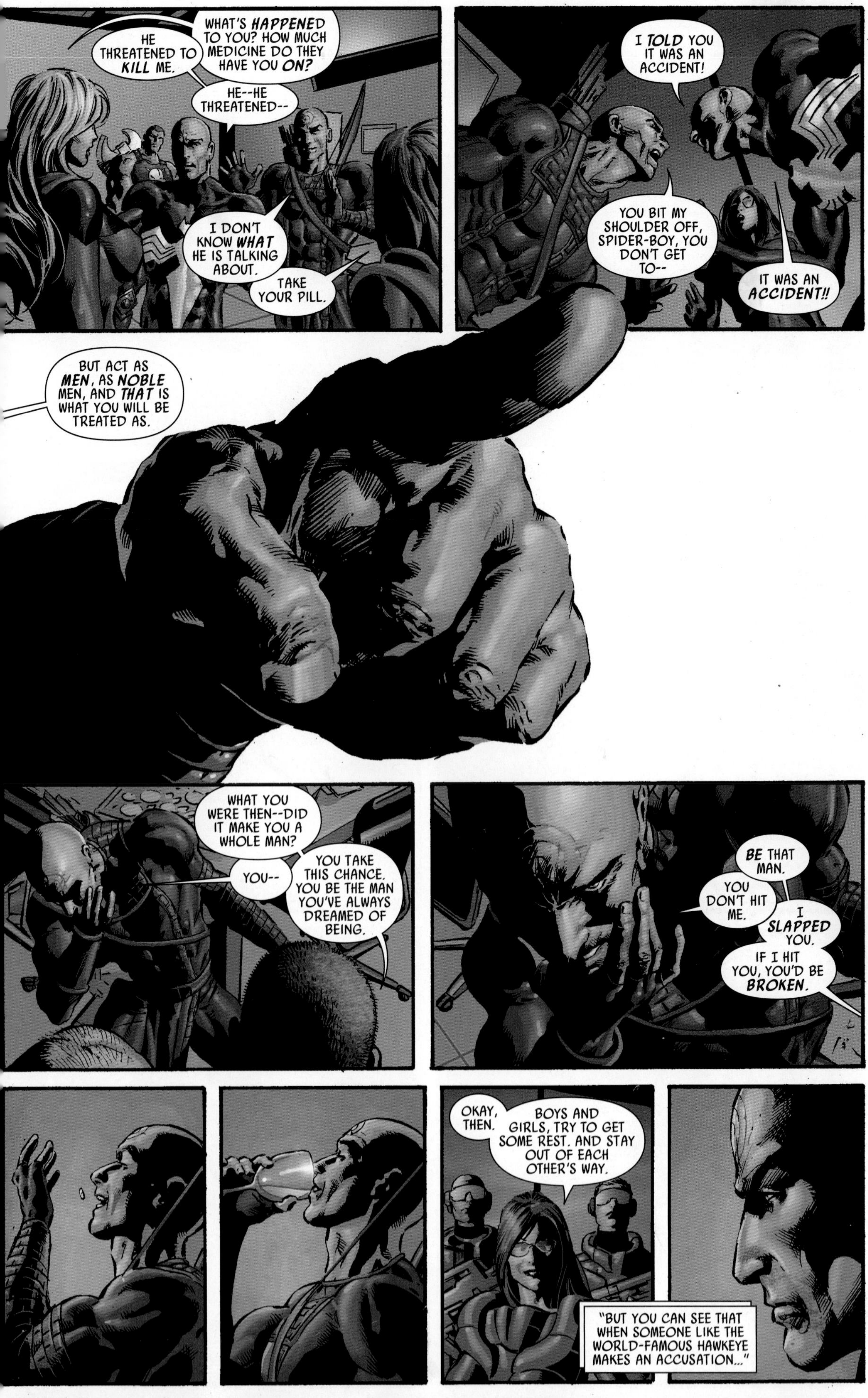

WHAT'S HAPPENED TO YOU? HOW MUCH MEDICINE DO THEY HAVE YOU ON?
HE THREATENED TO KILL ME.
HE--HE THREATENED--
I DON'T KNOW WHAT HE IS TALKING ABOUT.
TAKE YOUR PILL.
I TOLD YOU IT WAS AN ACCIDENT!
YOU BIT MY SHOULDER OFF, SPIDER-BOY, YOU DON'T GET TO--
IT WAS AN ACCIDENT!!
BUT ACT AS MEN, AS NOBLE MEN, AND THAT IS WHAT YOU WILL BE TREATED AS.
WHAT YOU WERE THEN--DID IT MAKE YOU A WHOLE MAN?
YOU--
YOU TAKE THIS CHANCE. YOU BE THE MAN YOU'VE ALWAYS DREAMED OF BEING.
BE THAT MAN.
YOU DON'T HIT ME.
I SLAPPED YOU.
IF I HIT YOU, YOU'D BE BROKEN.
OKAY, THEN.
BOYS AND GIRLS, TRY TO GET SOME REST. AND STAY OUT OF EACH OTHER'S WAY.
"BUT YOU CAN SEE THAT WHEN SOMEONE LIKE THE WORLD-FAMOUS HAWKEYE MAKES AN ACCUSATION..."

YES. HAWKEYE. WHAT'S FUNNY ABOUT CLINT BARTON'S ACCUSATION OF ME...

...IS THAT WHEN HE FIRST JOINED THE AVENGERS, WAY BACK WHEN, IT WAS QUITE A CONTROVERSY.

SOME PROBABLY DON'T REMEMBER, BUT HE *WAS* A CONVICTED FELON.

AND HE JOINED THE TEAM WITH TWO MUTANTS WHO WERE KNOWN *TERRORISTS.*

THE CHILDREN OF MAGNETO. THE MUTANT TERRORIST.

REFORMED TERRORISTS, YES, BUT TERRORISTS.

BUT *HE* WAS GIVEN A SECOND CHANCE IN LIFE AND WITH THAT SECOND CHANCE HE SERVED THIS NATION. AND THE WORLD.

AVENGERS ASSEMBLE/ HAWKEYE'S FIRST PUBLIC APPEARANCE AS HERO

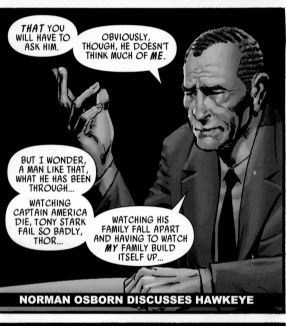

THAT YOU WILL HAVE TO ASK HIM.

OBVIOUSLY, THOUGH, HE DOESN'T THINK MUCH OF *ME.*

BUT I WONDER, A MAN LIKE THAT, WHAT HE HAS BEEN THROUGH...

WATCHING CAPTAIN AMERICA DIE, TONY STARK FAIL SO BADLY, THOR...

WATCHING HIS FAMILY FALL APART AND HAVING TO WATCH *MY* FAMILY BUILD ITSELF UP...

NORMAN OSBORN DISCUSSES HAWKEYE

IT MUST BE HARD.

AND WHO KNOWS WHAT KIND OF TRAUMA A MAN LIKE THAT HAS BEEN THROUGH, DEATHS AND NEAR-DEATHS...

WHAT DO YOU THINK IT *DOES* TO A MAN AFTER A WHILE? LIKE A PRIZE FIGHTER. NO MATTER HOW GREAT...

FILE FOOTAGE. HAWKEYE AT LARGE

BECAUSE, AND THIS IS THE POINT, THE LORD GAVE HIM A SECOND CHANCE ONCE, AND LOOK AT THE GREAT GOOD HE DID.

AND NOW THE LORD HAS GIVEN THE *SAME* TO ME. A SECOND CHANCE.

AND I LOOK AROUND THIS COUNTRY, I LOOK AROUND THE WORLD...

WE, AS A PEOPLE, ALMOST *FELL.* ALMOST.

AND NOW WE'RE, *ALL* OF US, WE'VE *ALL* BEING GIVEN THIS ASTONISHING SECOND CHANCE.

NORMAN OSBORN COMES CLEAN

WHEN I WAS AT MY WORST, I USED TO PRAY TO *GOD* HE WOULD LET ME HAVE THIS SECOND CHANCE.

NORMAN OSBORN COMES CLEAN

WHEN ONE THINKS OF THE GLORY DAYS OF THE AVENGERS, ONE THINKS OF CLINT BARTON...

BUT SHOULD WE JUDGE HIM FOR HIS PAST EVEN THOUGH HE PAID HIS DUES?

NO. THAT'S WHY HE WAS OFFERED A PLACE IN THE INITIATIVE.

BUT HE TURNED IT DOWN.

NORMAN OSBORN REFUTES CRITICS

WHY DID HE TURN IT DOWN?

NORMAN OSBORN REFUTES CRITICS

I MEAN, WHAT IS HE DOING NOW? HIDING IN THE SHADOWS? CONCOCTING CONSPIRACIES?

A MAN LIKE *THAT?* IT'S SO SAD.

I SAW THAT INTERVIEW. IT FELT LIKE A CRY FOR HELP.

FACTOID: CLINT BARTON WAS GOLIATH

AND *I* WOULD HELP HIM, ABSOLUTELY!

I WANT TO FIND HIM AND BRING HIM IN IF ONLY TO HELP HIM BEFORE HE HURTS HIMSELF.

NORMAN OSBORN COMES CLEAN

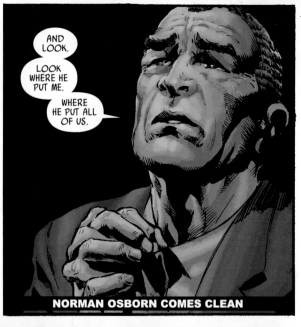

AND LOOK.

LOOK WHERE HE PUT ME.

WHERE HE PUT ALL OF US.

NORMAN OSBORN COMES CLEAN

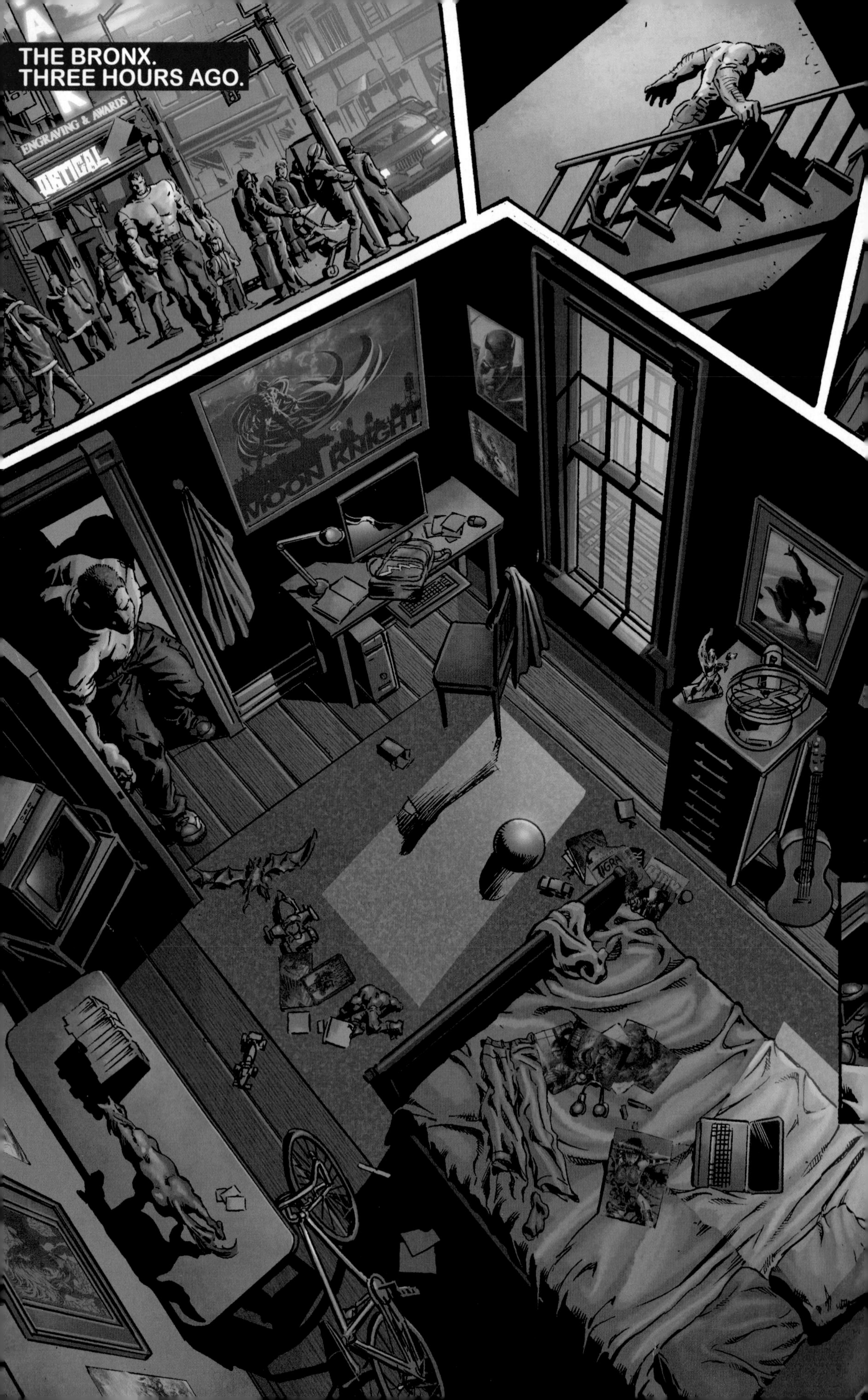
THE BRONX.
THREE HOURS AGO.
ENGRAVING & AWARDS
OPTICAL
MOON KNIGHT

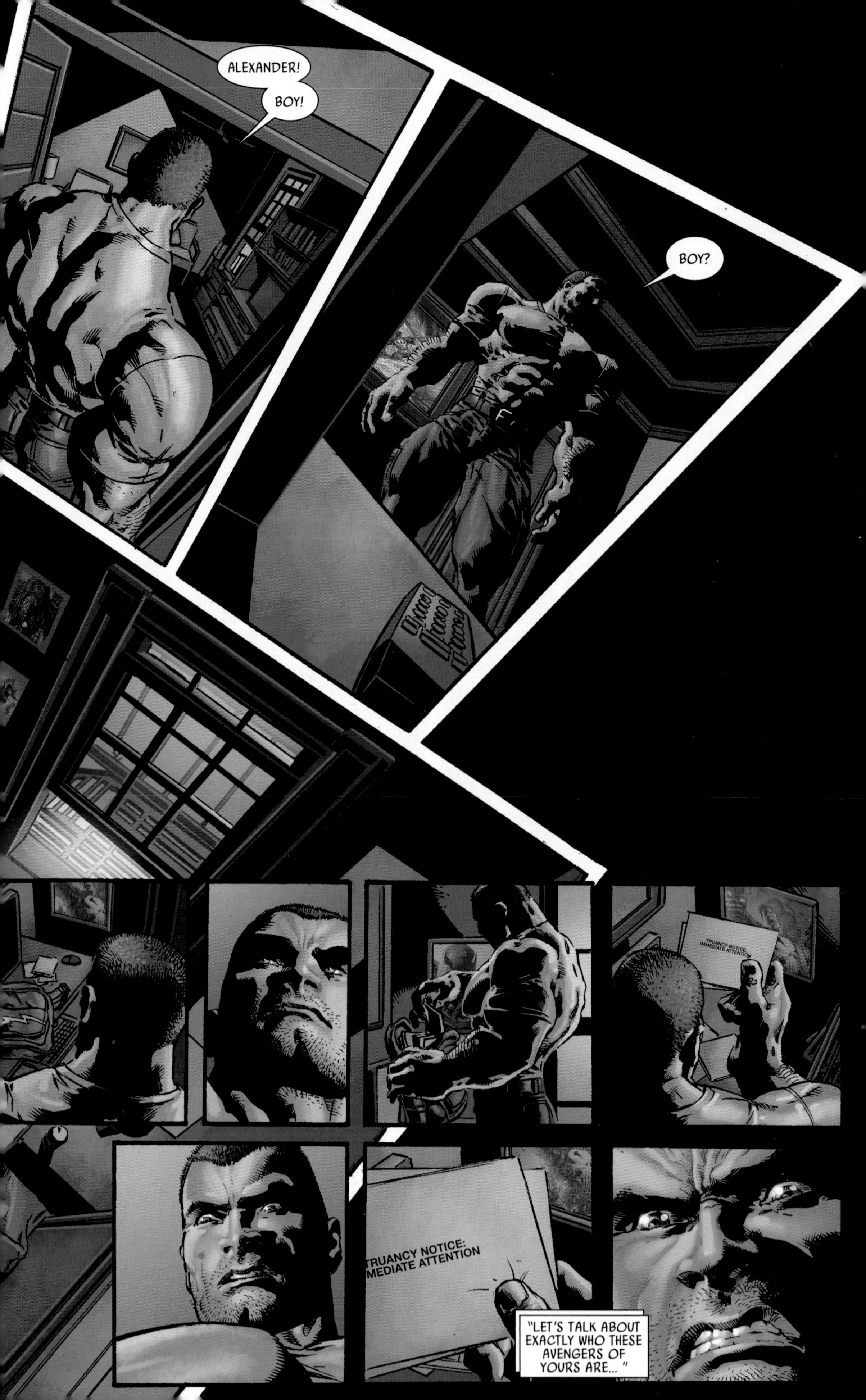
ALEXANDER!
BOY!
BOY?
TRUANCY NOTICE:
IMMEDIATE ATTENTION
TRUANCY NOTICE:
IMEDIATE ATTENTION
"LET'S TALK ABOUT EXACTLY WHO THESE AVENGERS OF YOURS ARE..."

YOU PUT TOGETHER THIS TEAM. YOUR TEAM.

YOU SURPRISED THE WORLD WITH IT.

BUT WHO ARE THEY?

FILE FOOTAGE/ AVENGERS TOWER/ THE OSBORN AVENGERS

THAT...I'M NOT GOING TO TELL YOU.

NORMAN OSBORN LIVE

YOU SEE WHERE *SOME* MIGHT HAVE A PROBLEM WITH THAT?

NOT REALLY.

DO PEOPLE CARE *WHO* IS IN THE ARMY OR THE NAVY?

OR DO THEY JUST WANT ONE?

ALL THEY CARE ABOUT IS THAT THEY ARE BEING *PROTECTED*.

AND THE AVENGERS WILL BE *PROTECTING* YOU.

NORMAN OSBORN LIVE

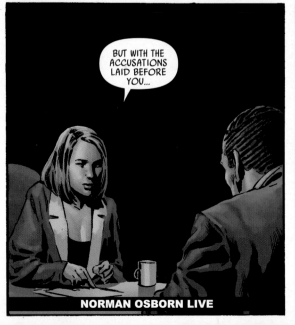

BUT WITH THE ACCUSATIONS LAID BEFORE YOU...

NORMAN OSBORN LIVE

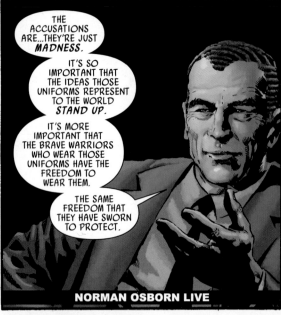

THE ACCUSATIONS ARE...THEY'RE JUST *MADNESS*.

IT'S SO IMPORTANT THAT THE IDEAS THOSE UNIFORMS REPRESENT TO THE WORLD *STAND UP*.

IT'S MORE IMPORTANT THAT THE BRAVE WARRIORS WHO WEAR THOSE UNIFORMS HAVE THE FREEDOM TO WEAR THEM.

THE SAME FREEDOM THAT THEY HAVE SWORN TO PROTECT.

NORMAN OSBORN LIVE

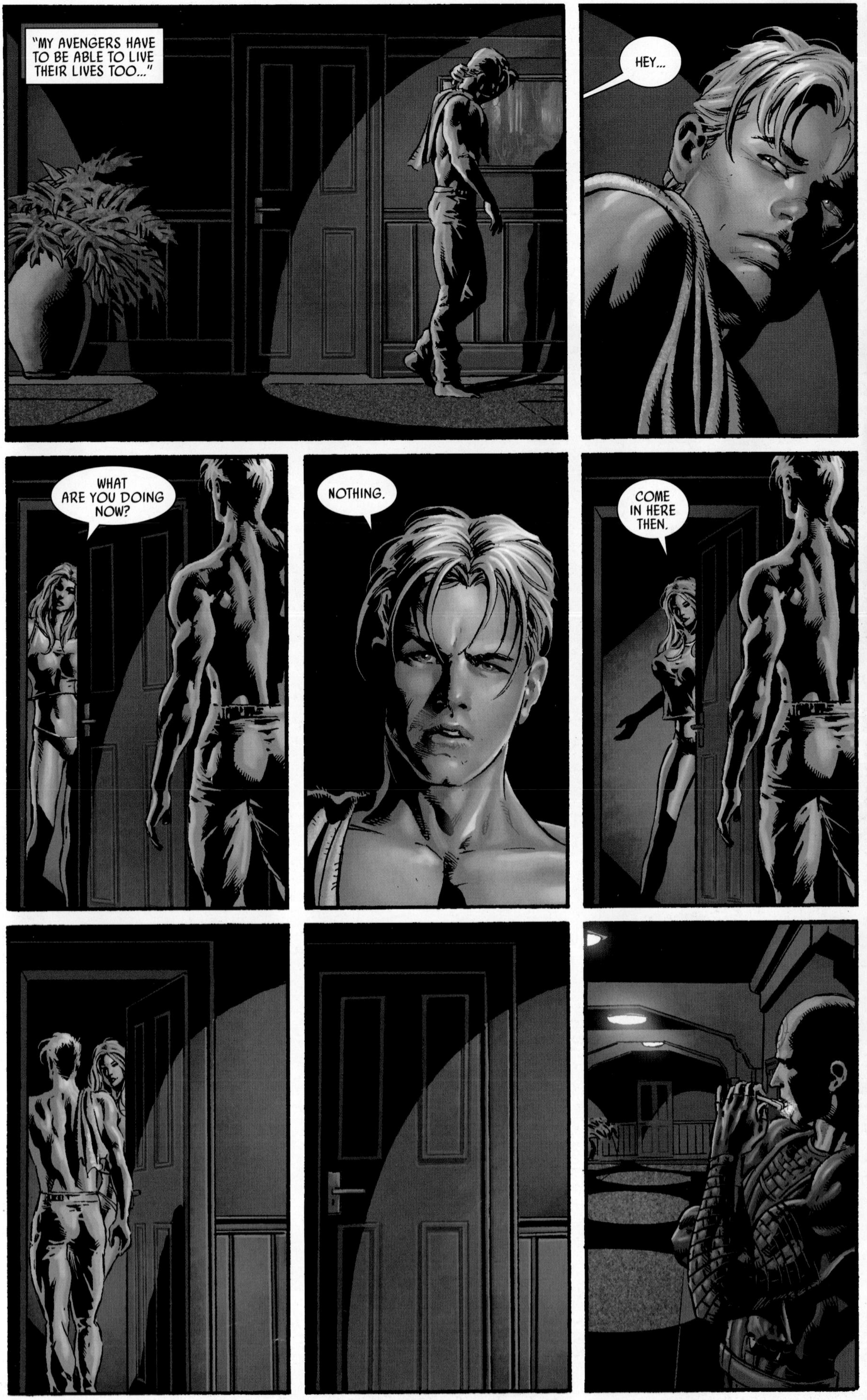
"MY AVENGERS HAVE TO BE ABLE TO LIVE THEIR LIVES TOO..."
HEY...
WHAT ARE YOU DOING NOW?
NOTHING.
COME IN HERE THEN.

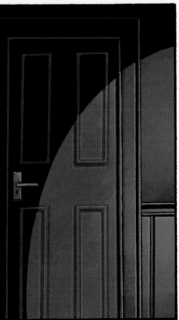

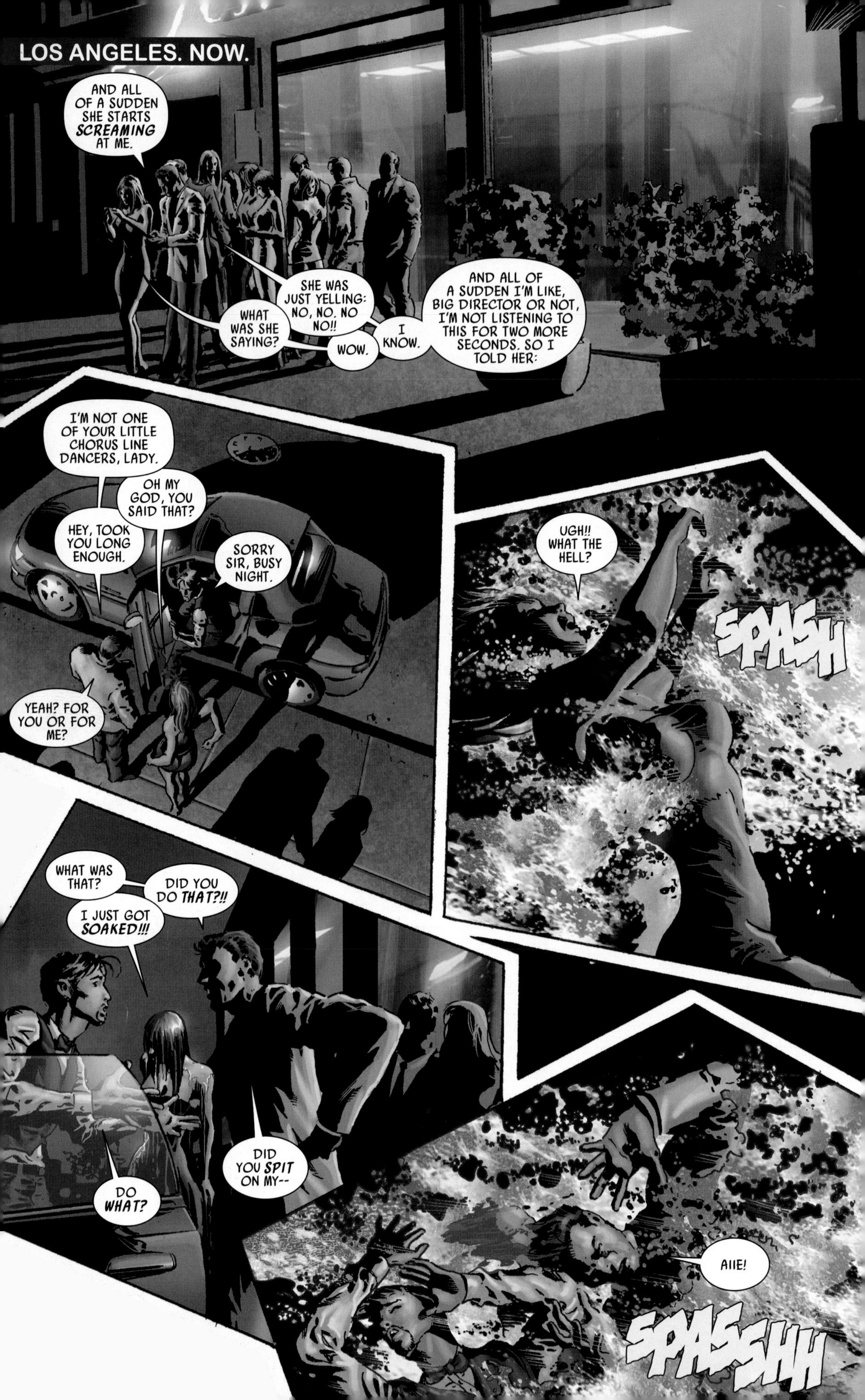
LOS ANGELES. NOW.
AND ALL OF A SUDDEN SHE STARTS SCREAMING AT ME.
WHAT WAS SHE SAYING?
SHE WAS JUST YELLING: NO, NO. NO NO!!
WOW.
I KNOW.
AND ALL OF A SUDDEN I'M LIKE, BIG DIRECTOR OR NOT, I'M NOT LISTENING TO THIS FOR TWO MORE SECONDS. SO I TOLD HER:
I'M NOT ONE OF YOUR LITTLE CHORUS LINE DANCERS, LADY.
OH MY GOD, YOU SAID THAT?
HEY, TOOK YOU LONG ENOUGH.
SORRY SIR, BUSY NIGHT.
YEAH? FOR YOU OR FOR ME?
UGH!! WHAT THE HELL?
SPASH
WHAT WAS THAT?
DID YOU DO THAT?!!
I JUST GOT SOAKED!!!
DID YOU SPIT ON MY--
DO WHAT?
AIIE!
SPASSHH

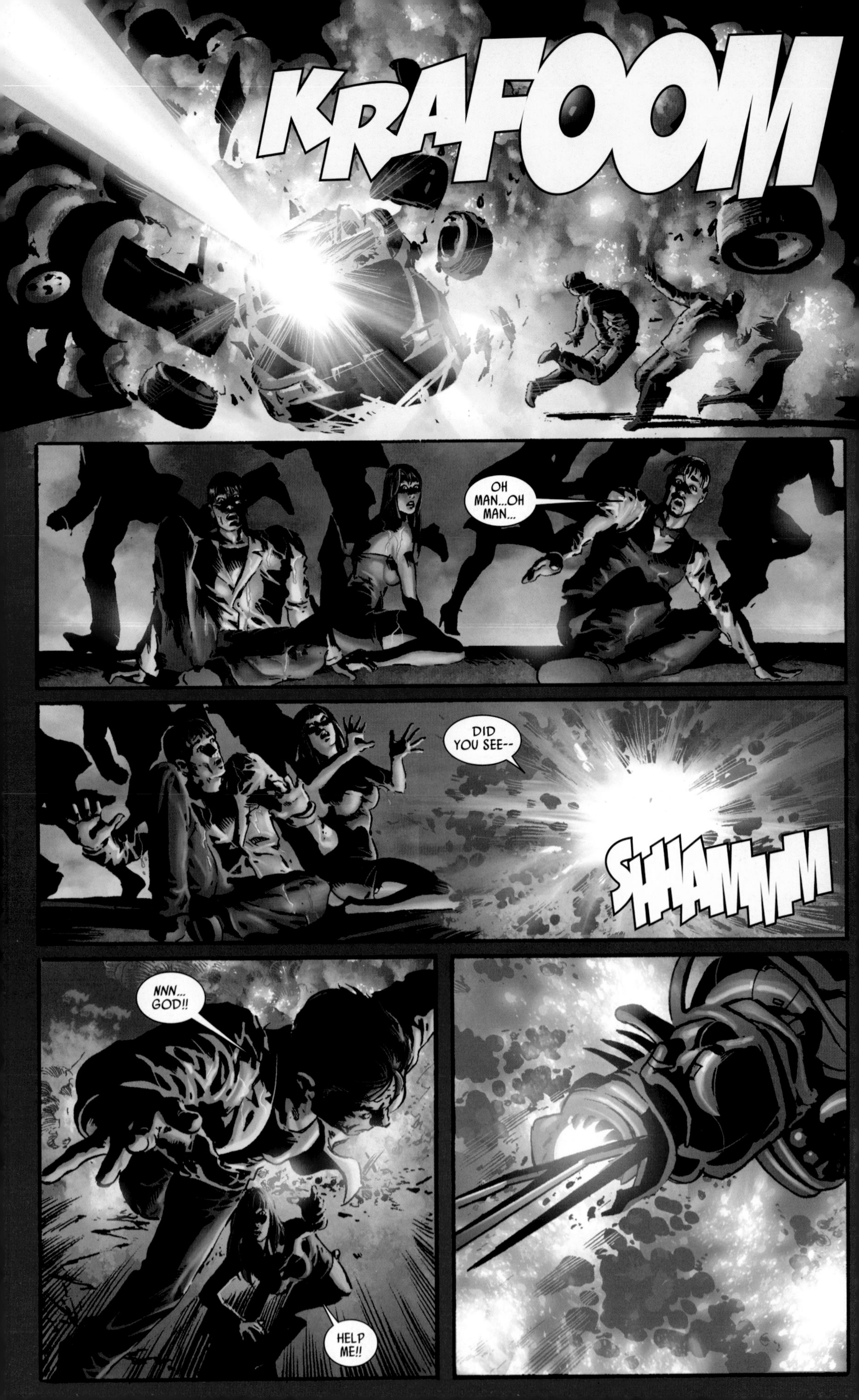
KRAFOOM
OH MAN...OH MAN...
DID YOU SEE--
SHHAMMM
NNN... GOD!!
HELP ME!!

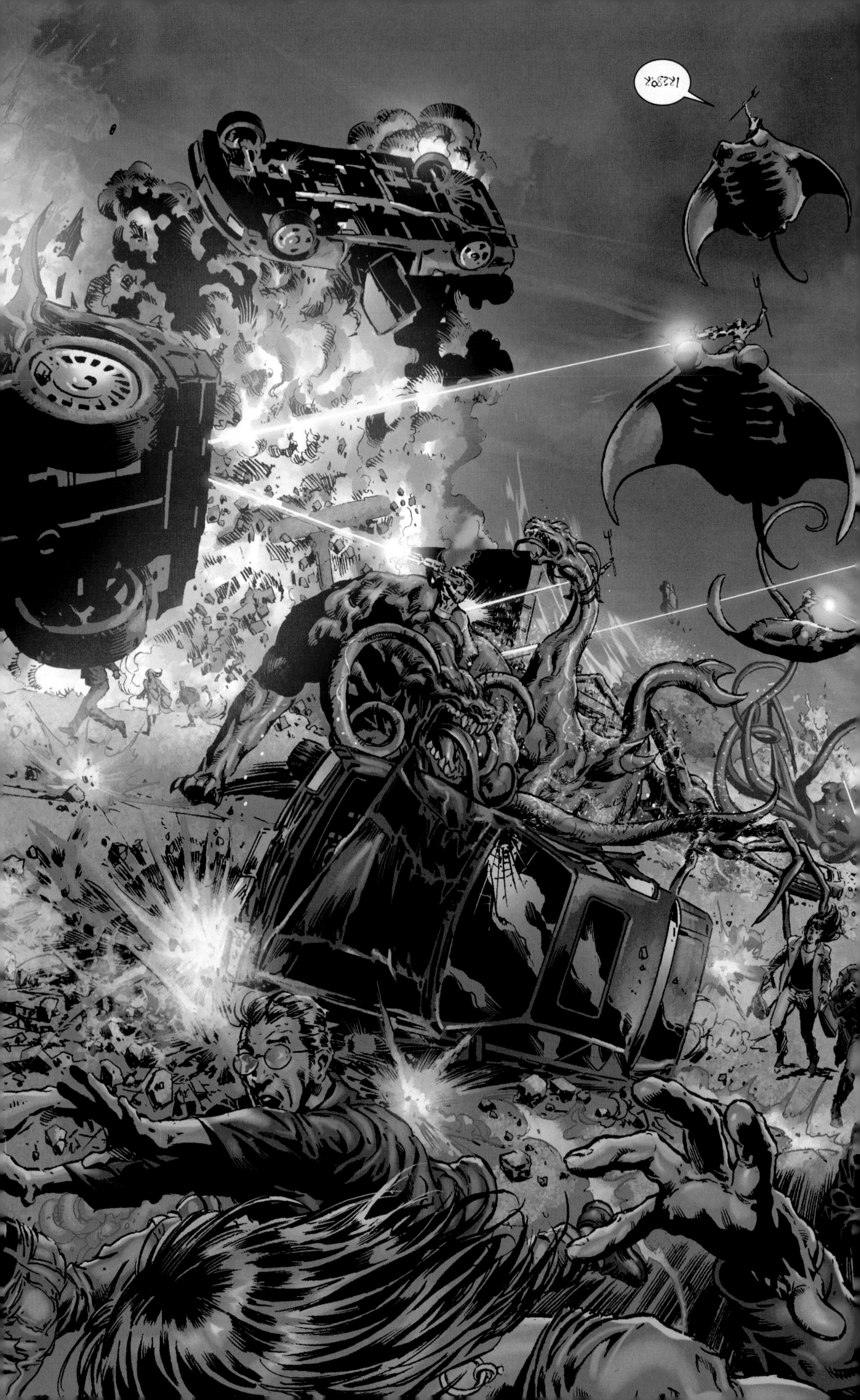

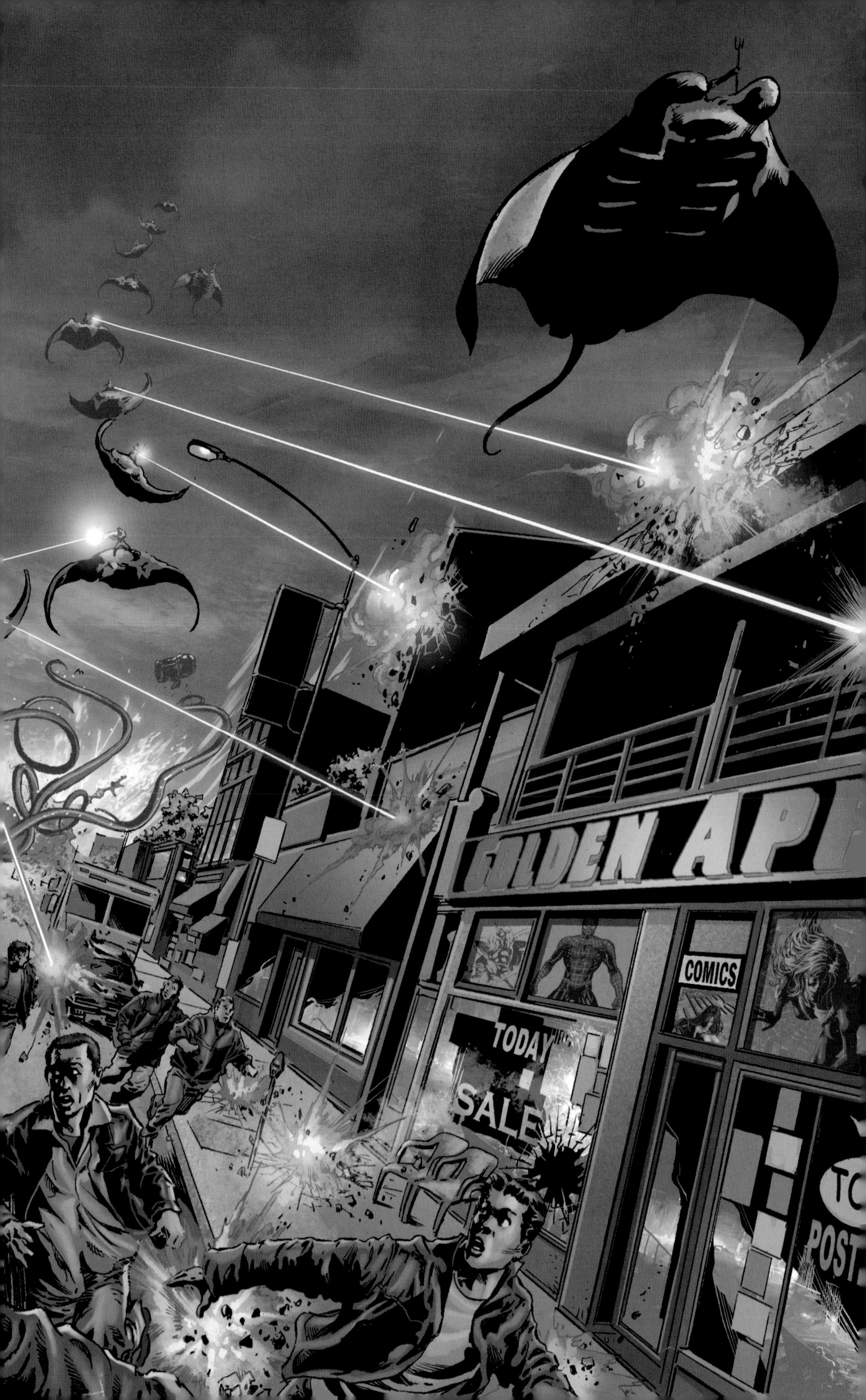

GOLDEN AP
COMICS
TODAY
SALE
TO
POST

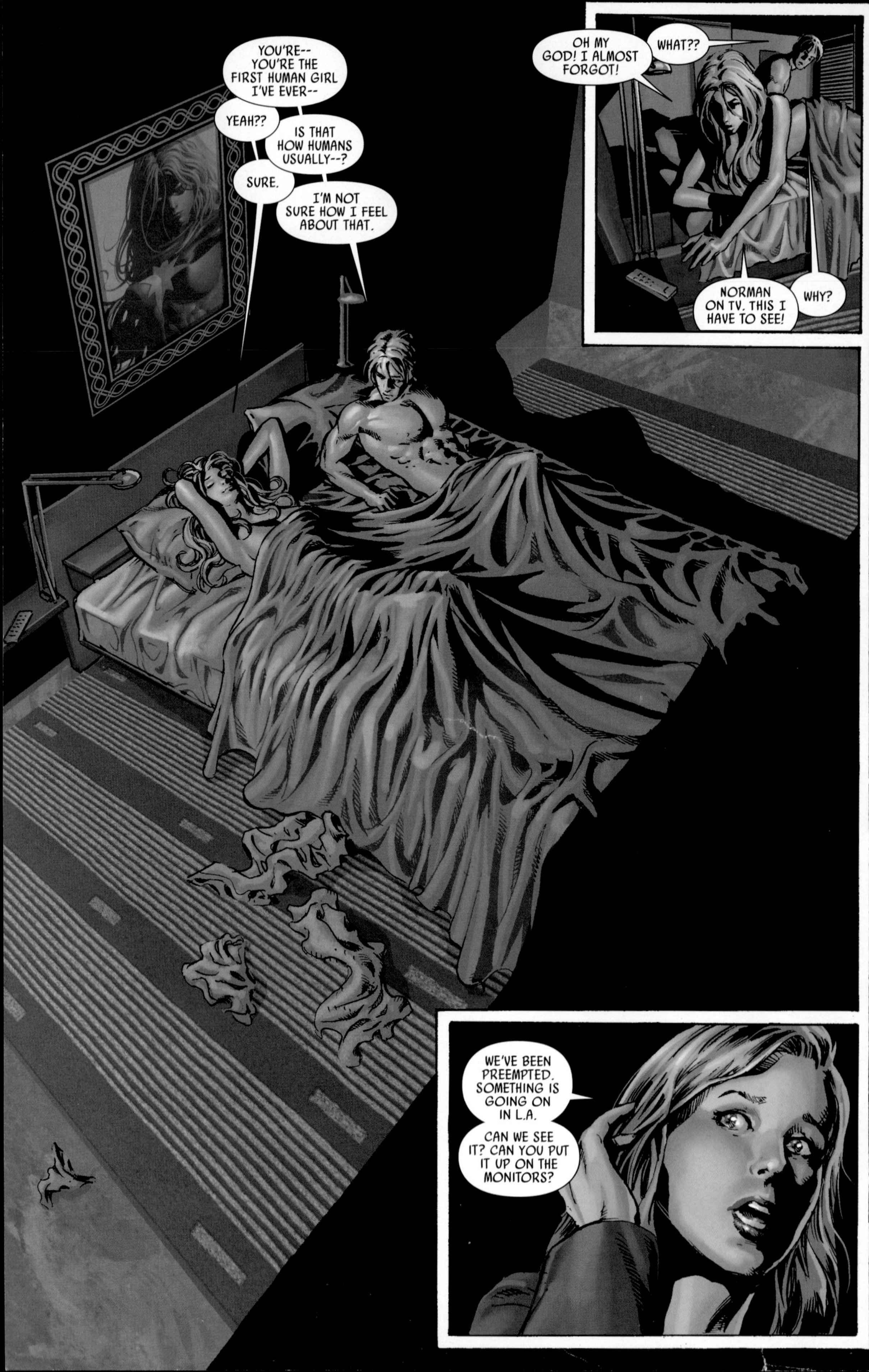
YOU'RE-- YOU'RE THE FIRST HUMAN GIRL I'VE EVER--
YEAH??
IS THAT HOW HUMANS USUALLY--?
SURE.
I'M NOT SURE HOW I FEEL ABOUT THAT.
OH MY GOD! I ALMOST FORGOT!
WHAT??
NORMAN ON TV. THIS I HAVE TO SEE!
WHY?
WE'VE BEEN PREEMPTED. SOMETHING IS GOING ON IN L.A.
CAN WE SEE IT? CAN YOU PUT IT UP ON THE MONITORS?

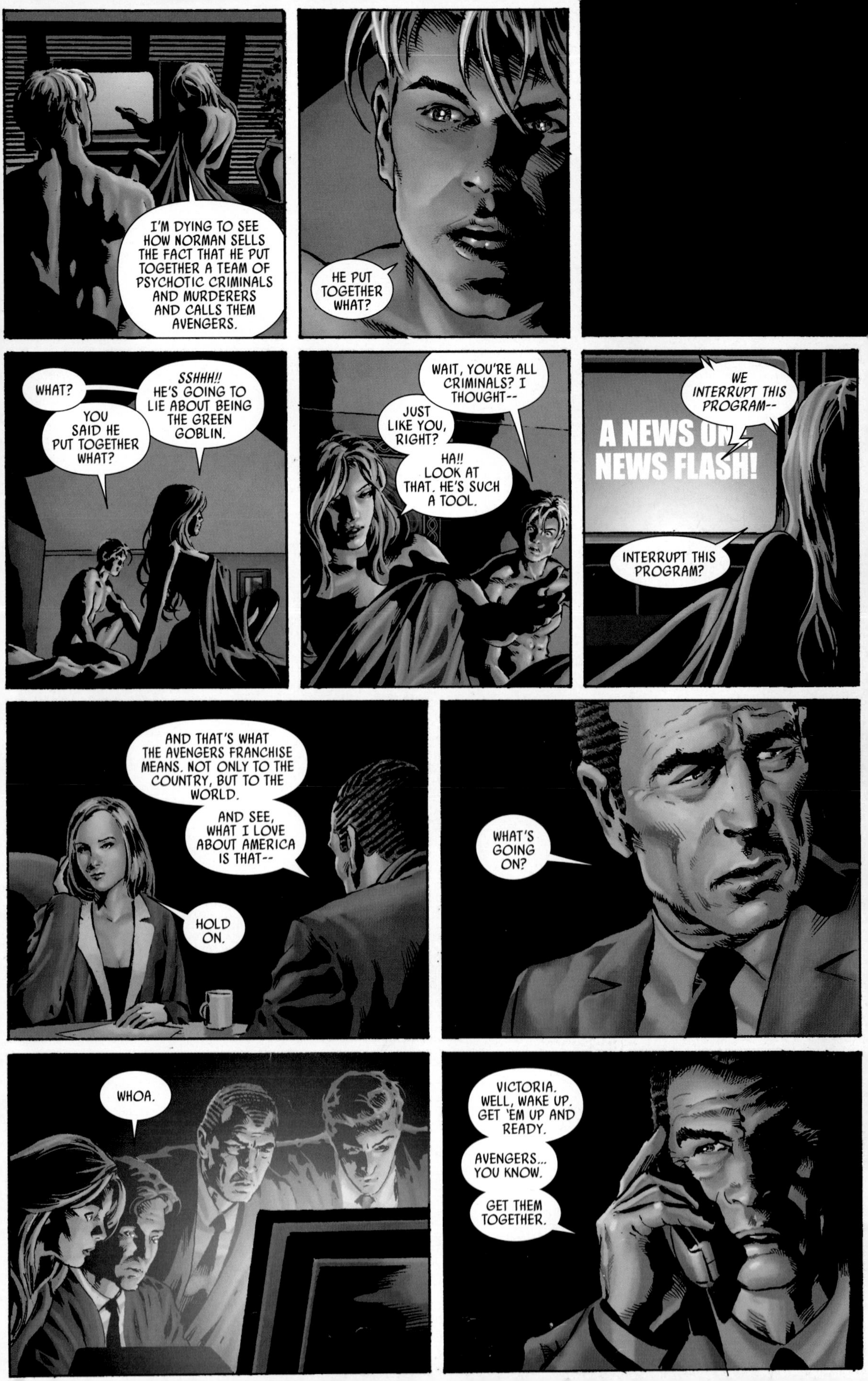
I'M DYING TO SEE HOW NORMAN SELLS THE FACT THAT HE PUT TOGETHER A TEAM OF PSYCHOTIC CRIMINALS AND MURDERERS AND CALLS THEM AVENGERS.
HE PUT TOGETHER WHAT?
WHAT?
SSHHH!! HE'S GOING TO LIE ABOUT BEING THE GREEN GOBLIN.
YOU SAID HE PUT TOGETHER WHAT?
WAIT, YOU'RE ALL CRIMINALS? I THOUGHT--
JUST LIKE YOU, RIGHT?
HA!! LOOK AT THAT. HE'S SUCH A TOOL.
WE INTERRUPT THIS PROGRAM--
A NEWS ON, NEWS FLASH!
INTERRUPT THIS PROGRAM?
AND THAT'S WHAT THE AVENGERS FRANCHISE MEANS. NOT ONLY TO THE COUNTRY, BUT TO THE WORLD.
AND SEE, WHAT I LOVE ABOUT AMERICA IS THAT--
HOLD ON.
WHAT'S GOING ON?
WHOA.
VICTORIA. WELL, WAKE UP. GET 'EM UP AND READY.
AVENGERS... YOU KNOW.
GET THEM TOGETHER.

DARK AVENGERS #6

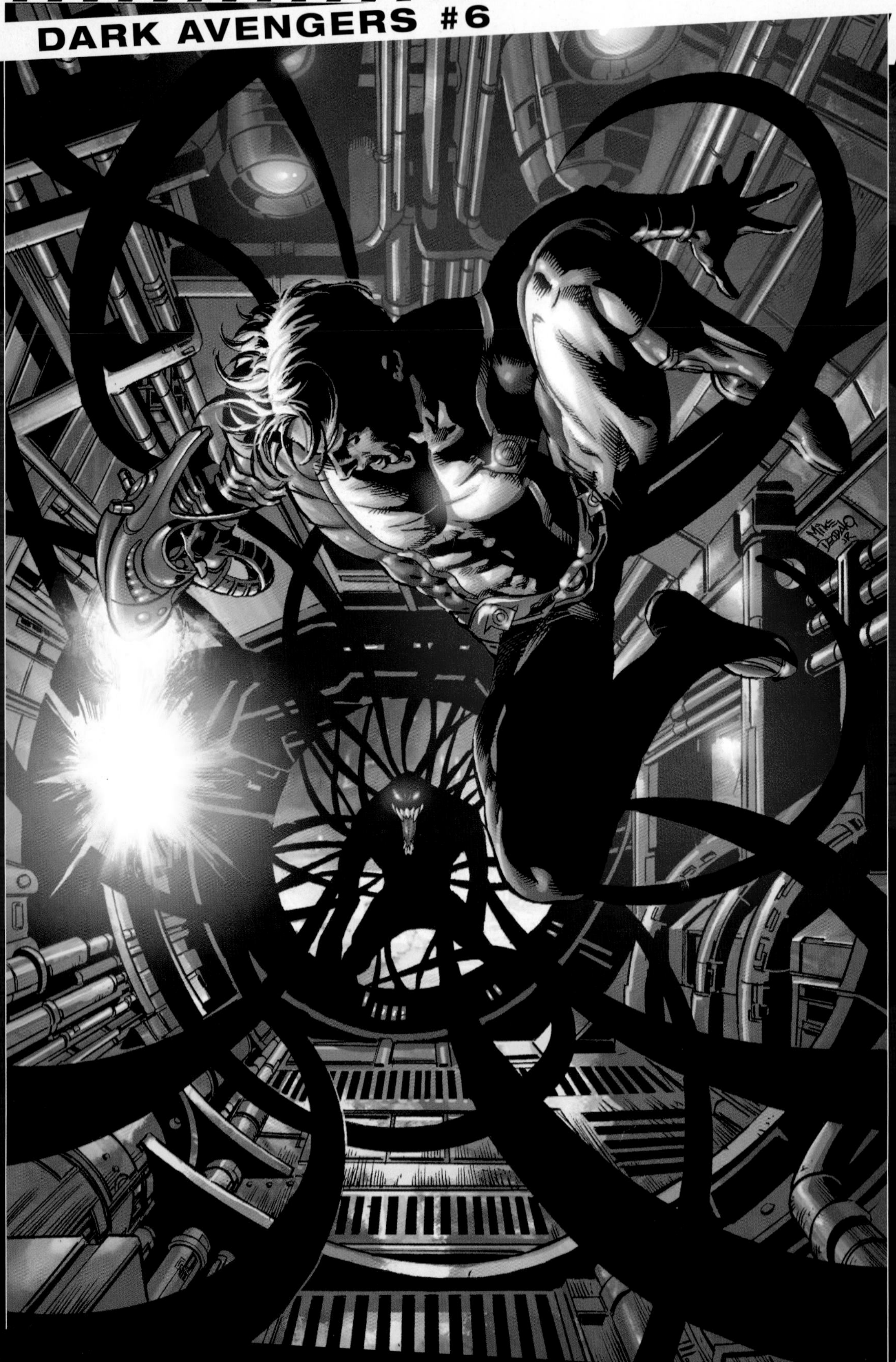

DARK AVENGERS #6 VARIANT

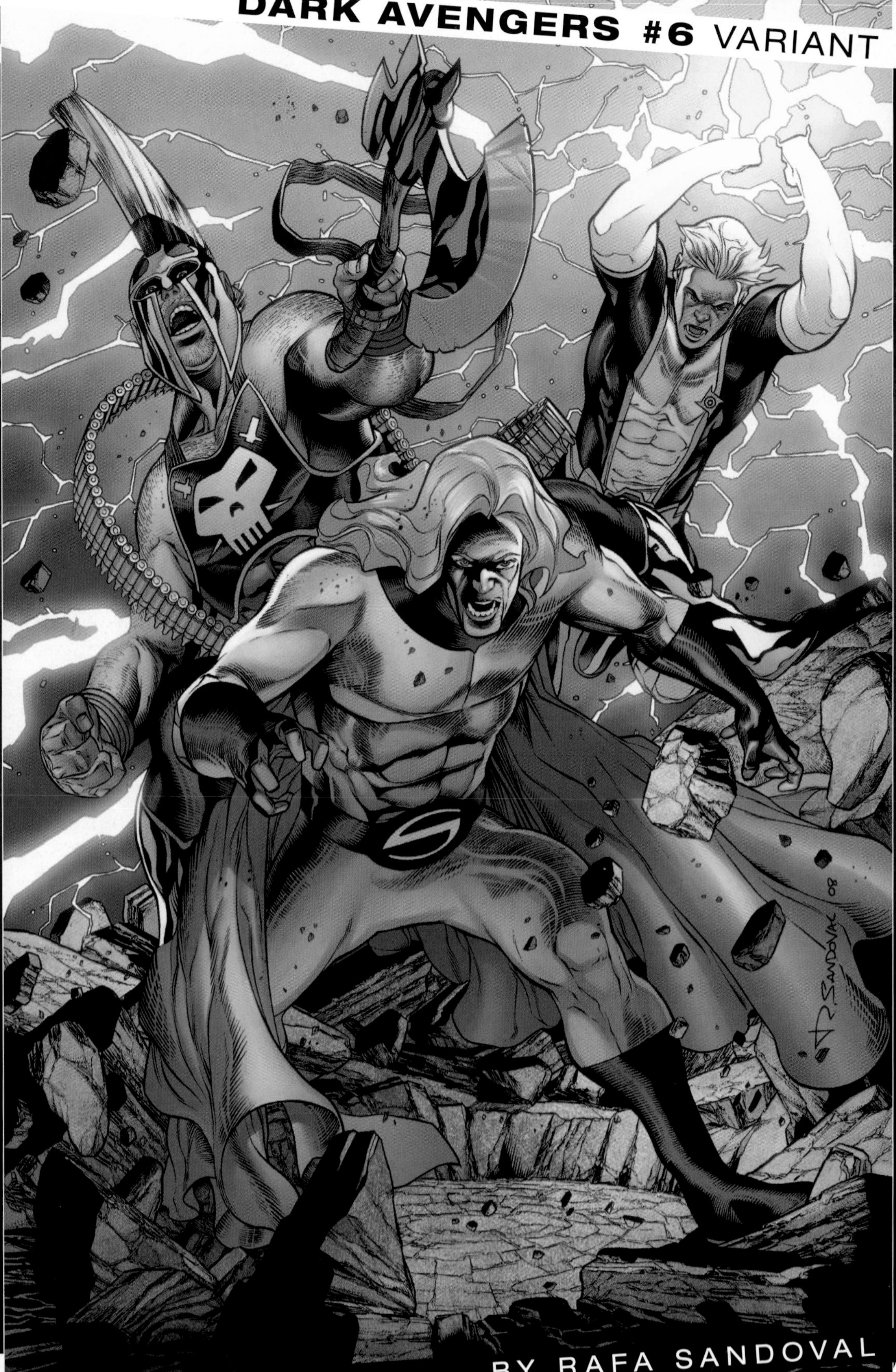

BY RAFA SANDOVAL

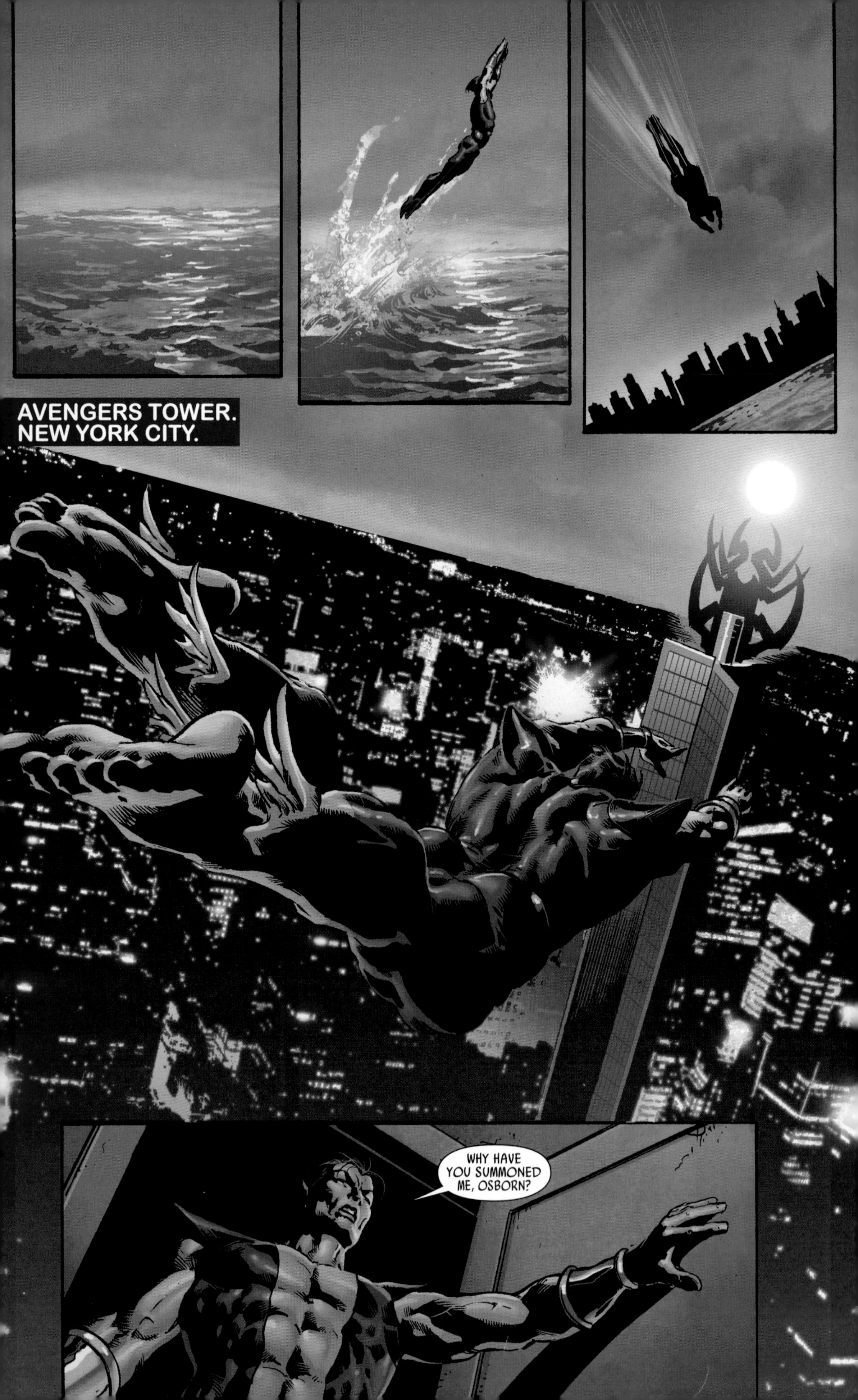
AVENGERS TOWER. NEW YORK CITY.
WHY HAVE YOU SUMMONED ME, OSBORN?

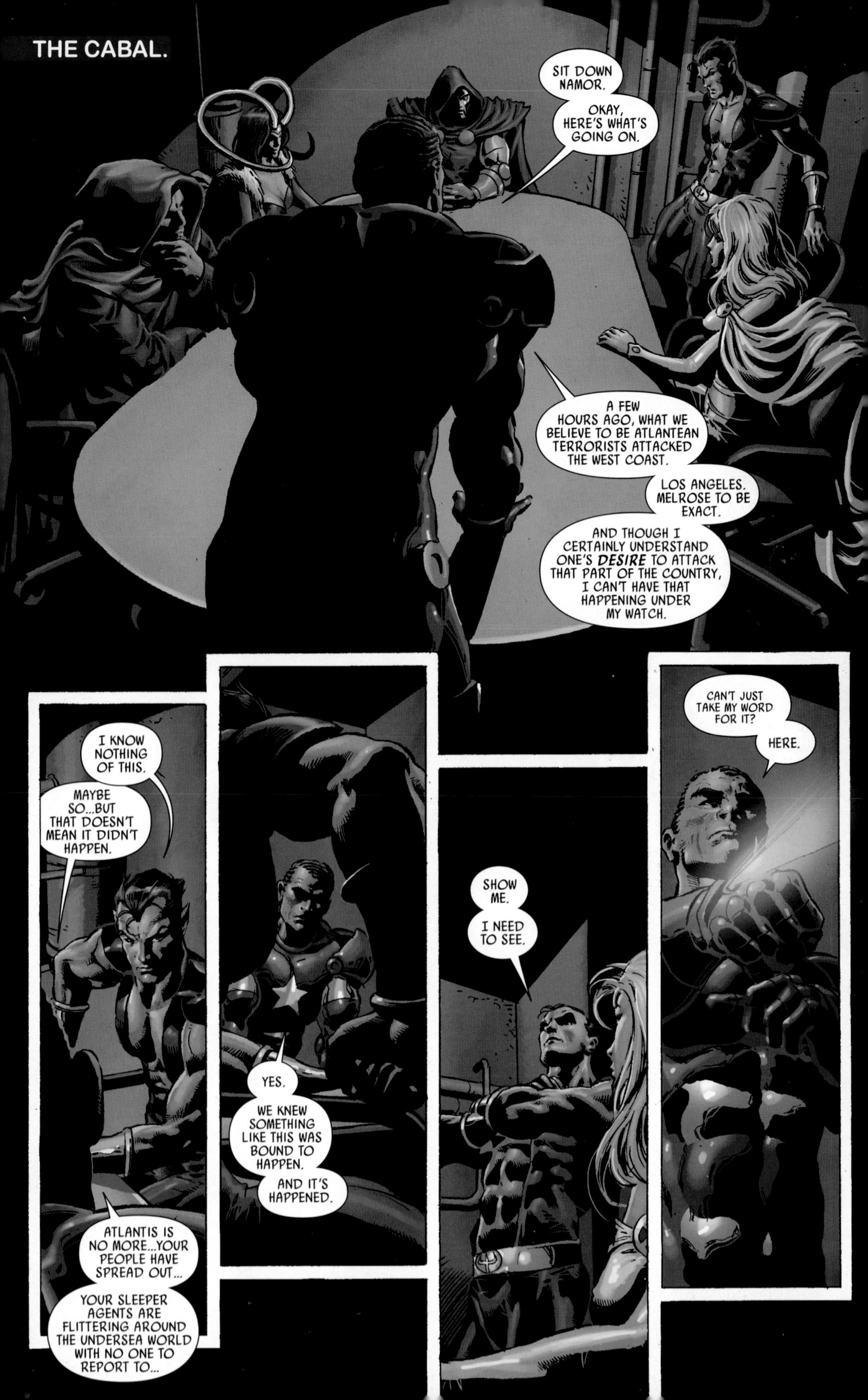
THE CABAL.
SIT DOWN NAMOR.
OKAY, HERE'S WHAT'S GOING ON.
A FEW HOURS AGO, WHAT WE BELIEVE TO BE ATLANTEAN TERRORISTS ATTACKED THE WEST COAST.
LOS ANGELES. MELROSE TO BE EXACT.
AND THOUGH I CERTAINLY UNDERSTAND ONE'S DESIRE TO ATTACK THAT PART OF THE COUNTRY, I CAN'T HAVE THAT HAPPENING UNDER MY WATCH.
I KNOW NOTHING OF THIS.
MAYBE SO...BUT THAT DOESN'T MEAN IT DIDN'T HAPPEN.
ATLANTIS IS NO MORE...YOUR PEOPLE HAVE SPREAD OUT...
YOUR SLEEPER AGENTS ARE FLITTERING AROUND THE UNDERSEA WORLD WITH NO ONE TO REPORT TO...
YES.
WE KNEW SOMETHING LIKE THIS WAS BOUND TO HAPPEN.
AND IT'S HAPPENED.
SHOW ME.
I NEED TO SEE.
CAN'T JUST TAKE MY WORD FOR IT?
HERE.

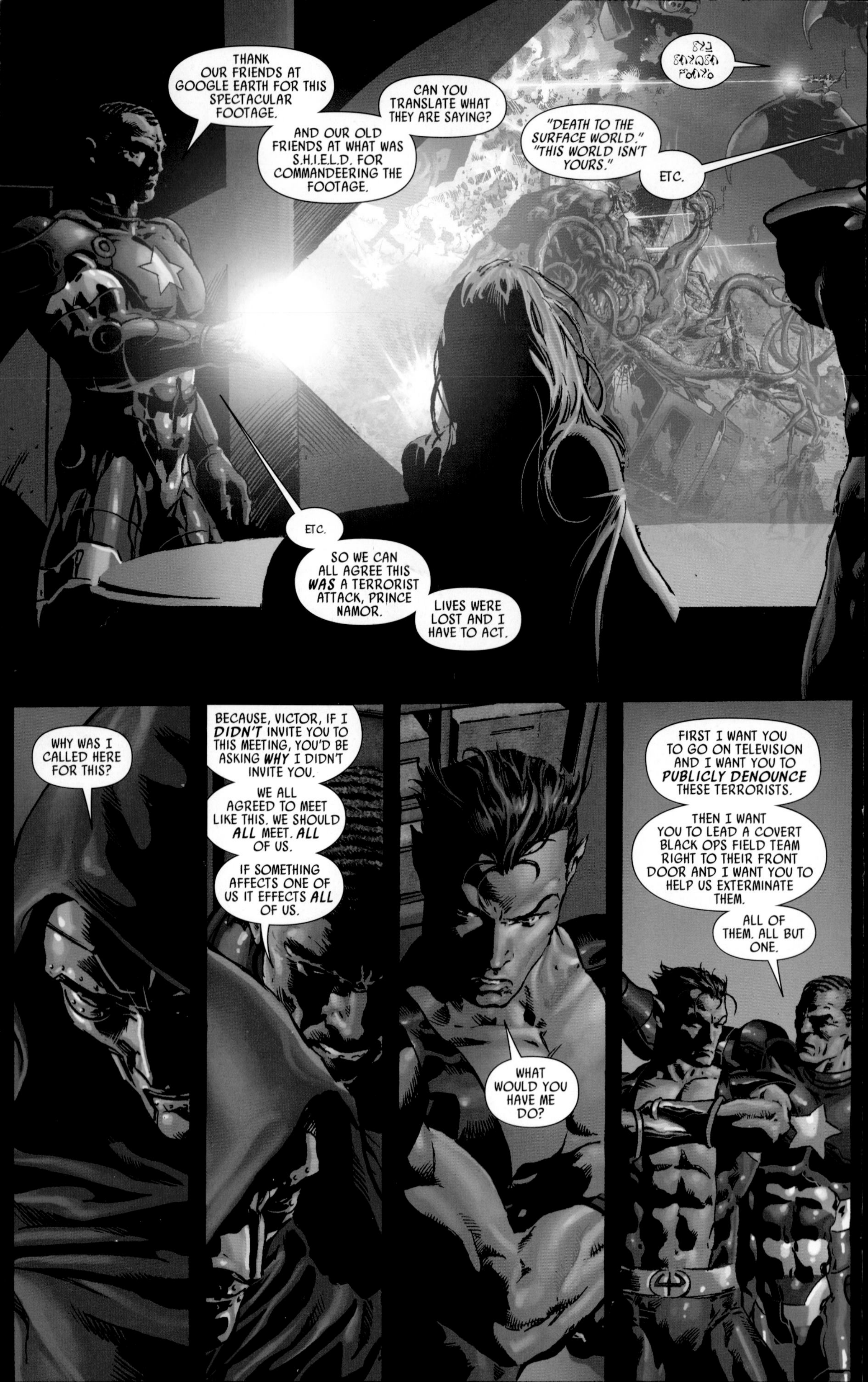
THANK OUR FRIENDS AT GOOGLE EARTH FOR THIS SPECTACULAR FOOTAGE.
AND OUR OLD FRIENDS AT WHAT WAS S.H.I.E.L.D. FOR COMMANDEERING THE FOOTAGE.
CAN YOU TRANSLATE WHAT THEY ARE SAYING?
"DEATH TO THE SURFACE WORLD." "THIS WORLD ISN'T YOURS."
ETC.
ETC.
SO WE CAN ALL AGREE THIS *WAS* A TERRORIST ATTACK, PRINCE NAMOR.
LIVES WERE LOST AND I HAVE TO ACT.
WHY WAS I CALLED HERE FOR THIS?
BECAUSE, VICTOR, IF I *DIDN'T* INVITE YOU TO THIS MEETING, YOU'D BE ASKING *WHY* I DIDN'T INVITE YOU.
WE ALL AGREED TO MEET LIKE THIS. WE SHOULD *ALL* MEET. *ALL* OF US.
IF SOMETHING AFFECTS ONE OF US IT EFFECTS *ALL* OF US.
WHAT WOULD YOU HAVE ME DO?
FIRST I WANT YOU TO GO ON TELEVISION AND I WANT YOU TO *PUBLICLY DENOUNCE* THESE TERRORISTS.
THEN I WANT YOU TO LEAD A COVERT BLACK OPS FIELD TEAM RIGHT TO THEIR FRONT DOOR AND I WANT YOU TO HELP US EXTERMINATE THEM.
ALL OF THEM. ALL BUT ONE.

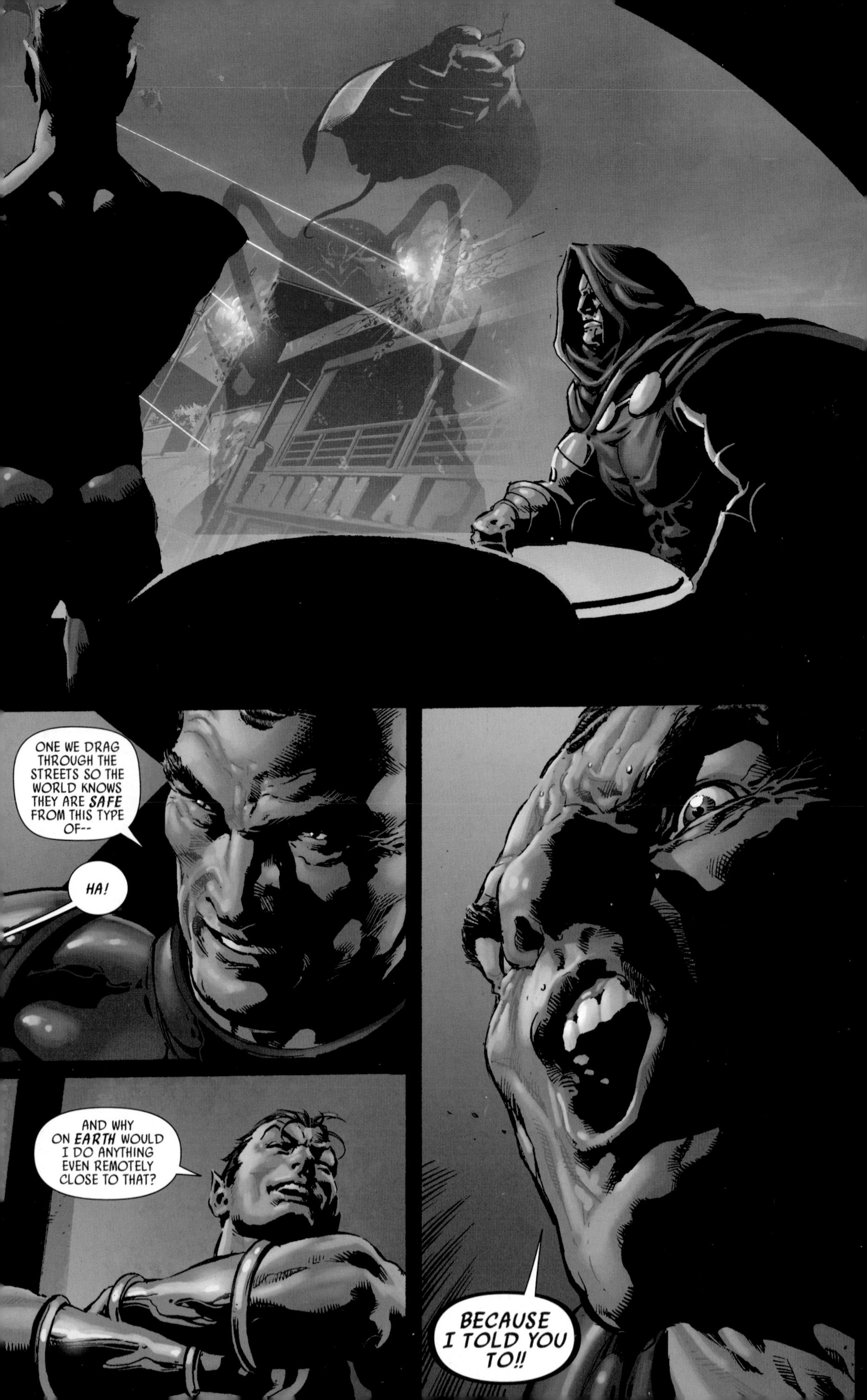
ONE WE DRAG THROUGH THE STREETS SO THE WORLD KNOWS THEY ARE SAFE FROM THIS TYPE OF--
HA!
AND WHY ON EARTH WOULD I DO ANYTHING EVEN REMOTELY CLOSE TO THAT?
BECAUSE I TOLD YOU TO!!

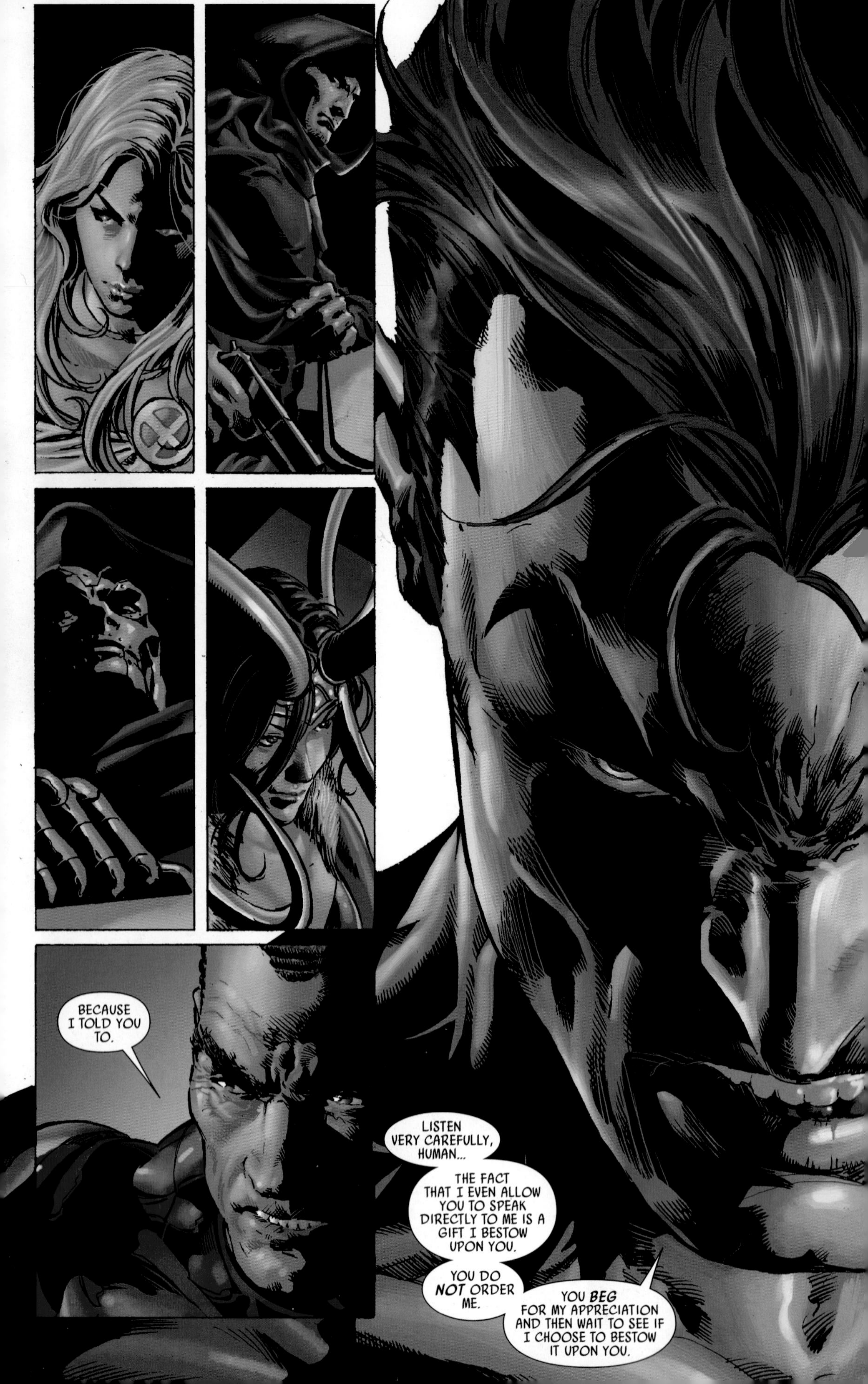
BECAUSE I TOLD YOU TO.
LISTEN VERY CAREFULLY, HUMAN...
THE FACT THAT I EVEN ALLOW YOU TO SPEAK DIRECTLY TO ME IS A GIFT I BESTOW UPON YOU.
YOU DO **NOT** ORDER ME.
YOU **BEG** FOR MY APPRECIATION AND THEN WAIT TO SEE IF I CHOOSE TO BESTOW IT UPON YOU.

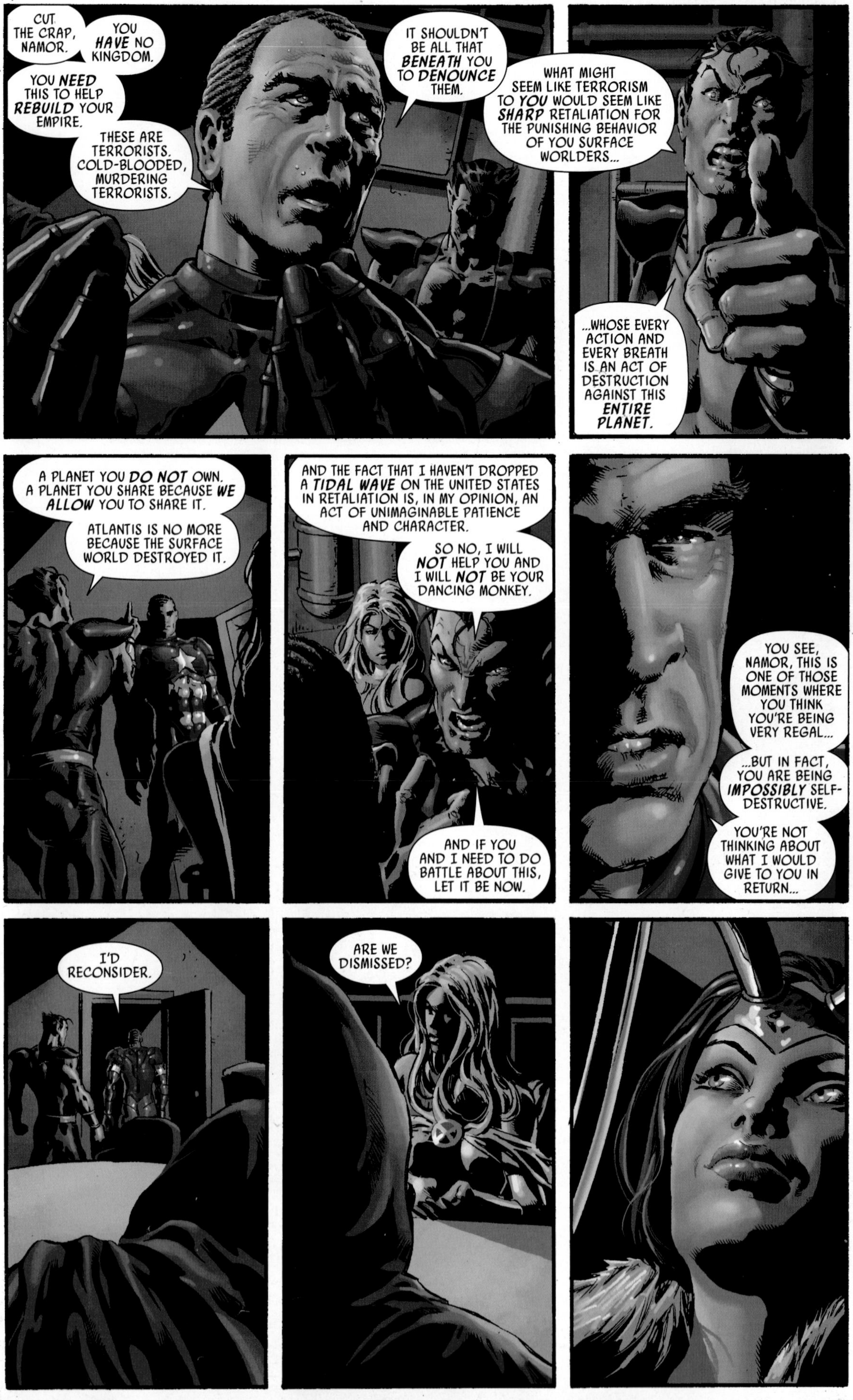
CUT THE CRAP, NAMOR.
YOU HAVE NO KINGDOM.
YOU NEED THIS TO HELP REBUILD YOUR EMPIRE.
THESE ARE TERRORISTS. COLD-BLOODED, MURDERING TERRORISTS.
IT SHOULDN'T BE ALL THAT BENEATH YOU TO DENOUNCE THEM.
WHAT MIGHT SEEM LIKE TERRORISM TO YOU WOULD SEEM LIKE SHARP RETALIATION FOR THE PUNISHING BEHAVIOR OF YOU SURFACE WORLDERS...
...WHOSE EVERY ACTION AND EVERY BREATH IS AN ACT OF DESTRUCTION AGAINST THIS ENTIRE PLANET.
A PLANET YOU DO NOT OWN. A PLANET YOU SHARE BECAUSE WE ALLOW YOU TO SHARE IT.
ATLANTIS IS NO MORE BECAUSE THE SURFACE WORLD DESTROYED IT.
AND THE FACT THAT I HAVEN'T DROPPED A TIDAL WAVE ON THE UNITED STATES IN RETALIATION IS, IN MY OPINION, AN ACT OF UNIMAGINABLE PATIENCE AND CHARACTER.
SO NO, I WILL NOT HELP YOU AND I WILL NOT BE YOUR DANCING MONKEY.
AND IF YOU AND I NEED TO DO BATTLE ABOUT THIS, LET IT BE NOW.
YOU SEE, NAMOR, THIS IS ONE OF THOSE MOMENTS WHERE YOU THINK YOU'RE BEING VERY REGAL...
...BUT IN FACT, YOU ARE BEING IMPOSSIBLY SELF-DESTRUCTIVE.
YOU'RE NOT THINKING ABOUT WHAT I WOULD GIVE TO YOU IN RETURN...
I'D RECONSIDER.
ARE WE DISMISSED?

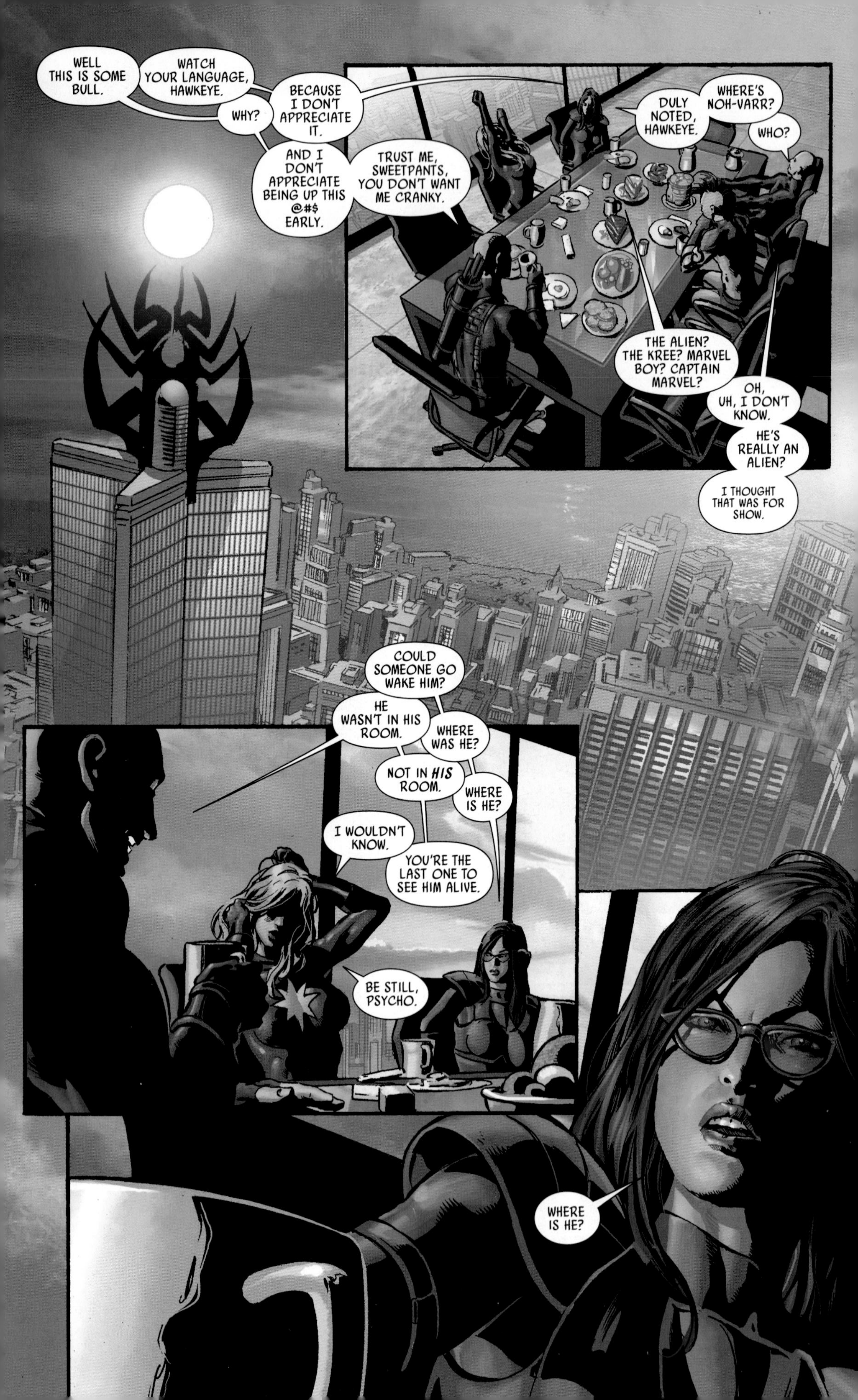
WELL THIS IS SOME BULL.
WATCH YOUR LANGUAGE, HAWKEYE.
WHY?
BECAUSE I DON'T APPRECIATE IT.
AND I DON'T APPRECIATE BEING UP THIS @#$ EARLY.
TRUST ME, SWEETPANTS, YOU DON'T WANT ME CRANKY.
DULY NOTED, HAWKEYE.
WHERE'S NOH-VARR?
WHO?
THE ALIEN? THE KREE? MARVEL BOY? CAPTAIN MARVEL?
OH, UH, I DON'T KNOW.
HE'S REALLY AN ALIEN?
I THOUGHT THAT WAS FOR SHOW.
COULD SOMEONE GO WAKE HIM?
HE WASN'T IN HIS ROOM.
WHERE WAS HE?
NOT IN HIS ROOM.
WHERE IS HE?
I WOULDN'T KNOW.
YOU'RE THE LAST ONE TO SEE HIM ALIVE.
BE STILL, PSYCHO.
WHERE IS HE?

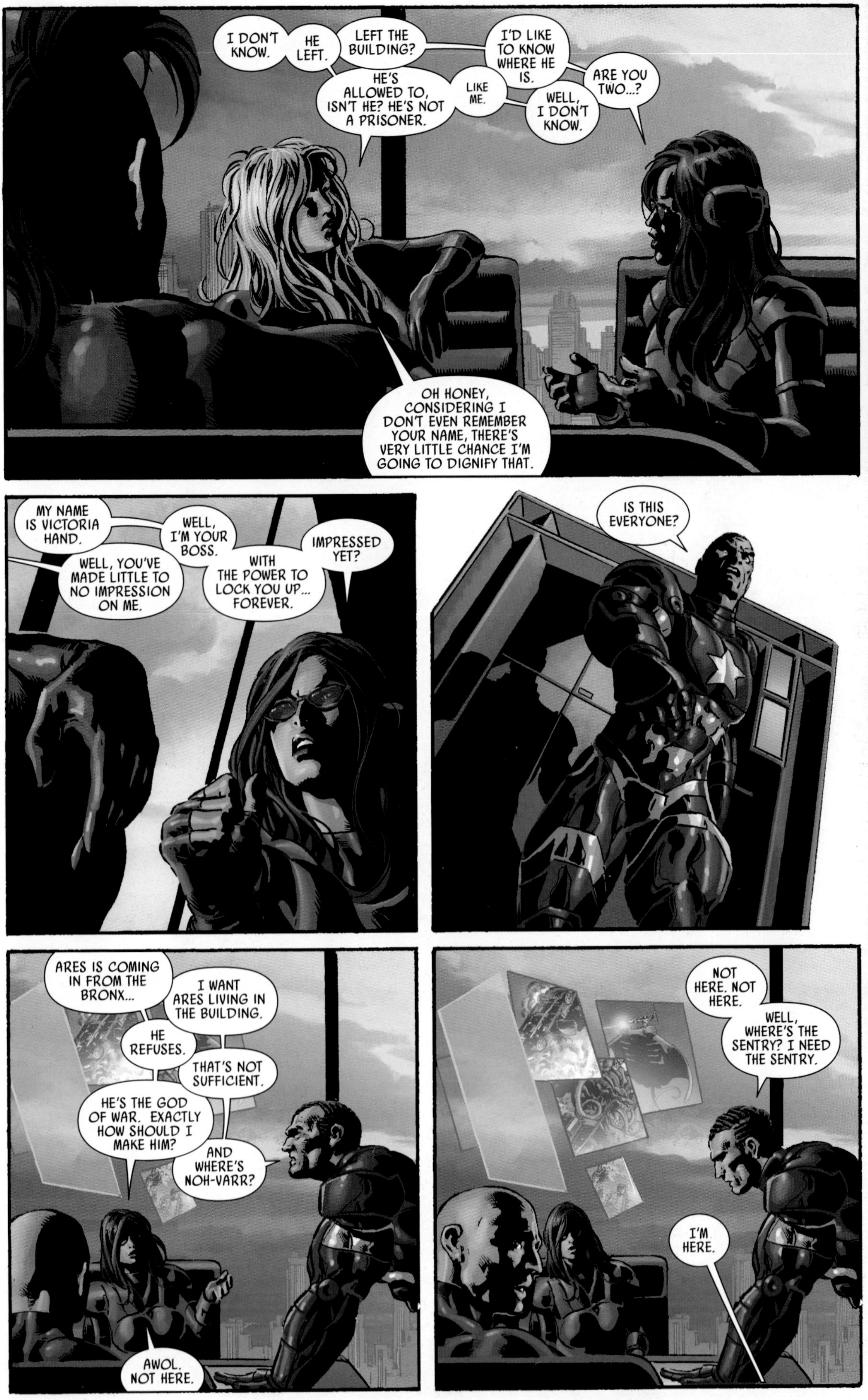
I DON'T KNOW.
HE LEFT.
LEFT THE BUILDING?
HE'S ALLOWED TO, ISN'T HE? HE'S NOT A PRISONER.
LIKE ME.
I'D LIKE TO KNOW WHERE HE IS.
WELL, I DON'T KNOW.
ARE YOU TWO...?
OH HONEY, CONSIDERING I DON'T EVEN REMEMBER YOUR NAME, THERE'S VERY LITTLE CHANCE I'M GOING TO DIGNIFY THAT.
MY NAME IS VICTORIA HAND.
WELL, YOU'VE MADE LITTLE TO NO IMPRESSION ON ME.
WELL, I'M YOUR BOSS.
WITH THE POWER TO LOCK YOU UP... FOREVER.
IMPRESSED YET?
IS THIS EVERYONE?
ARES IS COMING IN FROM THE BRONX...
I WANT ARES LIVING IN THE BUILDING.
HE REFUSES.
THAT'S NOT SUFFICIENT.
HE'S THE GOD OF WAR. EXACTLY HOW SHOULD I MAKE HIM?
AND WHERE'S NOH-VARR?
AWOL. NOT HERE.
NOT HERE. NOT HERE.
WELL, WHERE'S THE SENTRY? I NEED THE SENTRY.
I'M HERE.

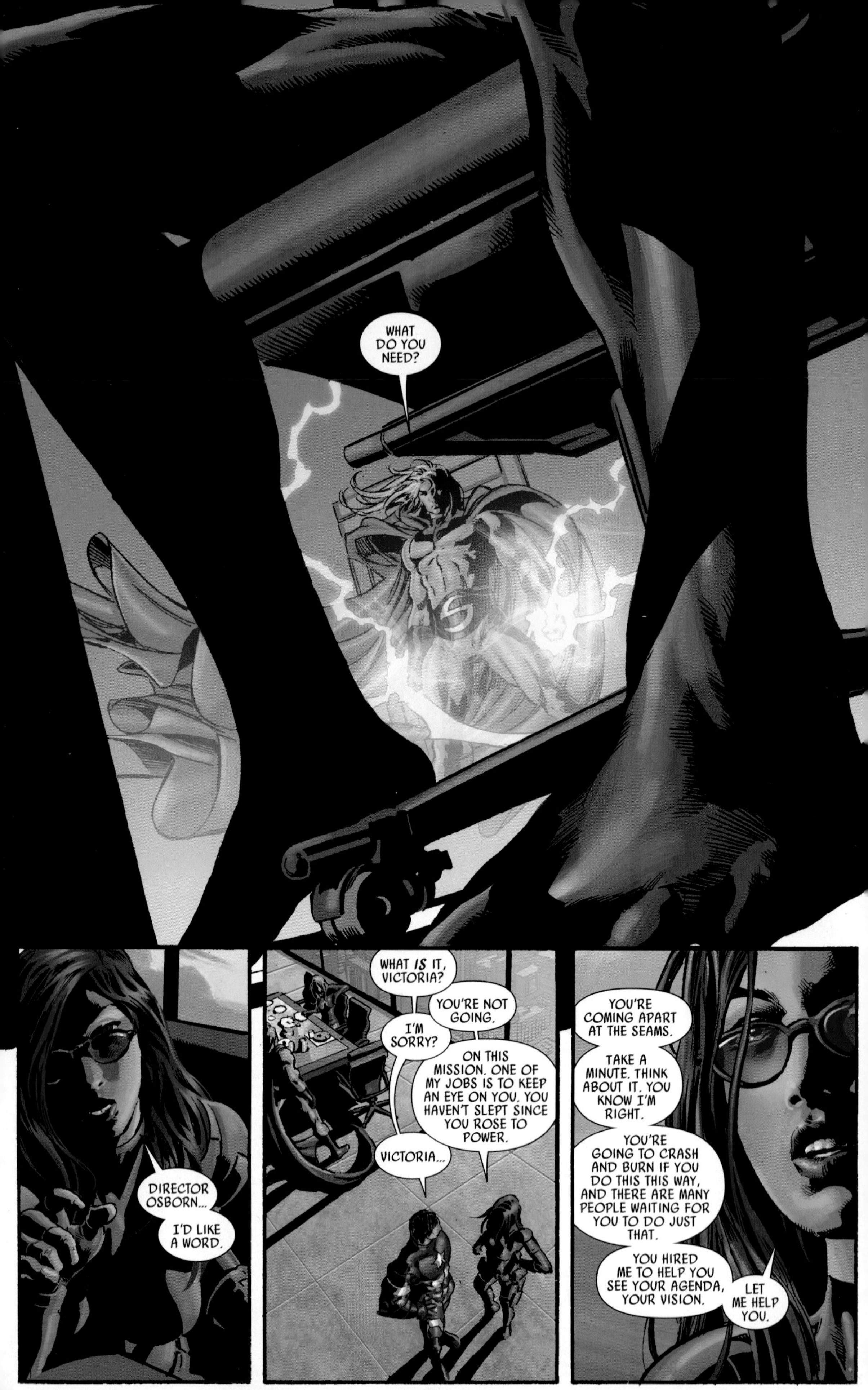

WHAT DO YOU NEED?
DIRECTOR OSBORN...
I'D LIKE A WORD.
WHAT IS IT, VICTORIA?
YOU'RE NOT GOING.
I'M SORRY?
ON THIS MISSION. ONE OF MY JOBS IS TO KEEP AN EYE ON YOU. YOU HAVEN'T SLEPT SINCE YOU ROSE TO POWER.
VICTORIA...
YOU'RE COMING APART AT THE SEAMS.
TAKE A MINUTE. THINK ABOUT IT. YOU KNOW I'M RIGHT.
YOU'RE GOING TO CRASH AND BURN IF YOU DO THIS THIS WAY, AND THERE ARE MANY PEOPLE WAITING FOR YOU TO DO JUST THAT.
YOU HIRED ME TO HELP YOU SEE YOUR AGENDA, YOUR VISION.
LET ME HELP YOU.

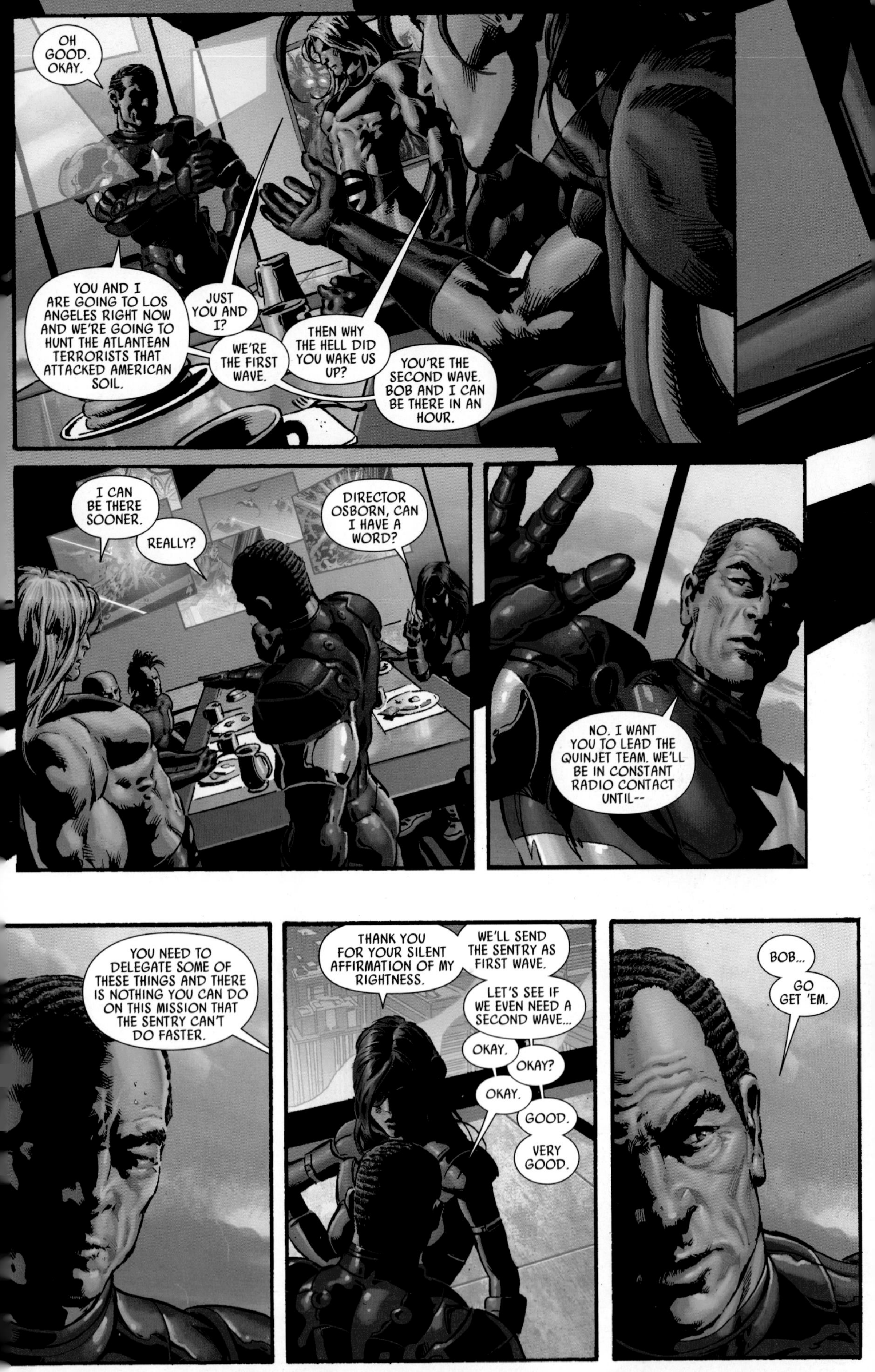
OH GOOD. OKAY.
YOU AND I ARE GOING TO LOS ANGELES RIGHT NOW AND WE'RE GOING TO HUNT THE ATLANTEAN TERRORISTS THAT ATTACKED AMERICAN SOIL.
JUST YOU AND I?
WE'RE THE FIRST WAVE.
THEN WHY THE HELL DID YOU WAKE US UP?
YOU'RE THE SECOND WAVE. BOB AND I CAN BE THERE IN AN HOUR.
I CAN BE THERE SOONER.
REALLY?
DIRECTOR OSBORN, CAN I HAVE A WORD?
NO. I WANT YOU TO LEAD THE QUINJET TEAM. WE'LL BE IN CONSTANT RADIO CONTACT UNTIL--
YOU NEED TO DELEGATE SOME OF THESE THINGS AND THERE IS NOTHING YOU CAN DO ON THIS MISSION THAT THE SENTRY CAN'T DO FASTER.
THANK YOU FOR YOUR SILENT AFFIRMATION OF MY RIGHTNESS.
WE'LL SEND THE SENTRY AS FIRST WAVE.
LET'S SEE IF WE EVEN NEED A SECOND WAVE...
OKAY.
OKAY?
OKAY.
GOOD.
VERY GOOD.
BOB...
GO GET 'EM.

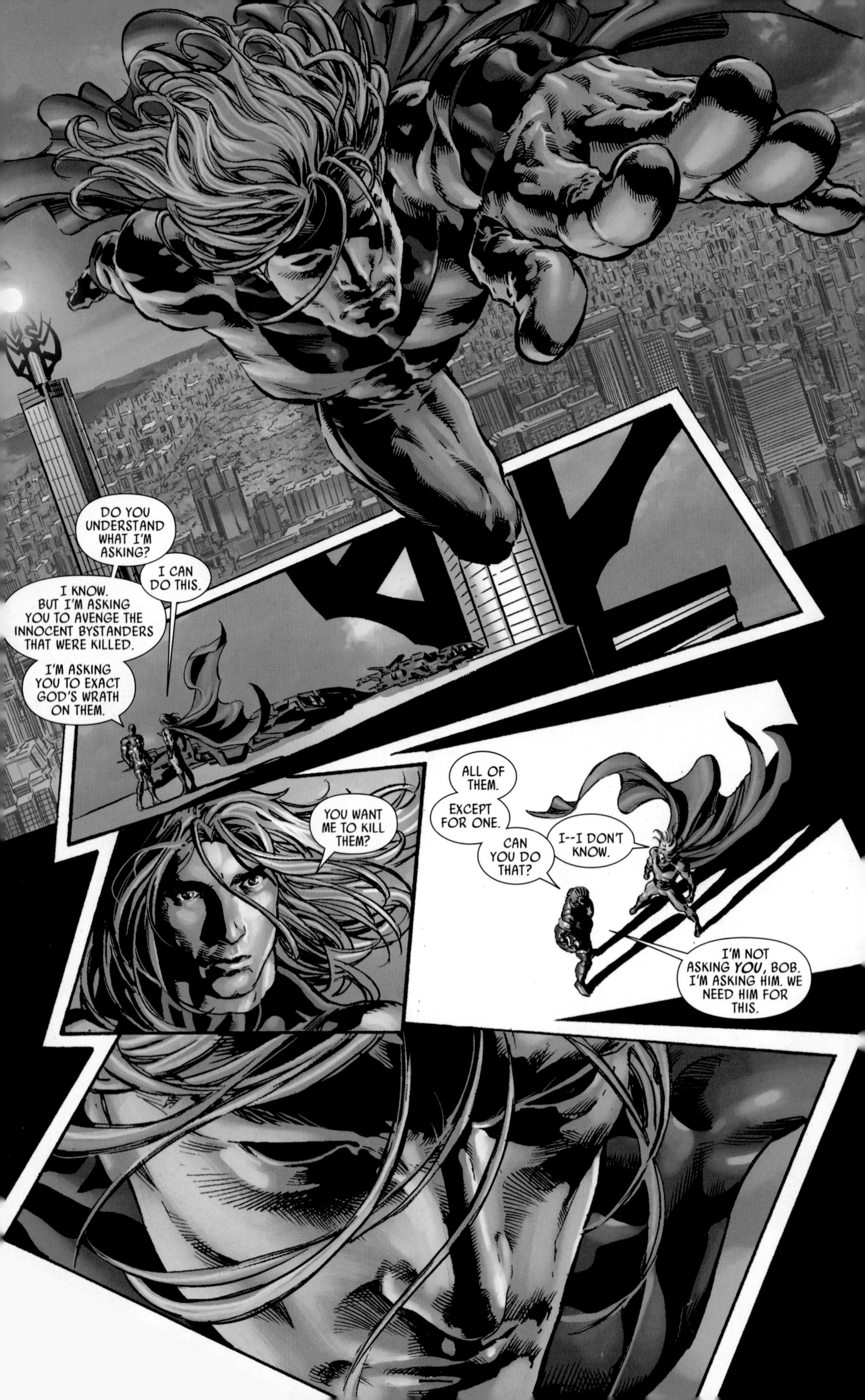
DO YOU UNDERSTAND WHAT I'M ASKING?
I CAN DO THIS.
I KNOW. BUT I'M ASKING YOU TO AVENGE THE INNOCENT BYSTANDERS THAT WERE KILLED.
I'M ASKING YOU TO EXACT GOD'S WRATH ON THEM.
YOU WANT ME TO KILL THEM?
ALL OF THEM.
EXCEPT FOR ONE.
CAN YOU DO THAT?
I--I DON'T KNOW.
I'M NOT ASKING *YOU*, BOB. I'M ASKING HIM. WE NEED HIM FOR THIS.

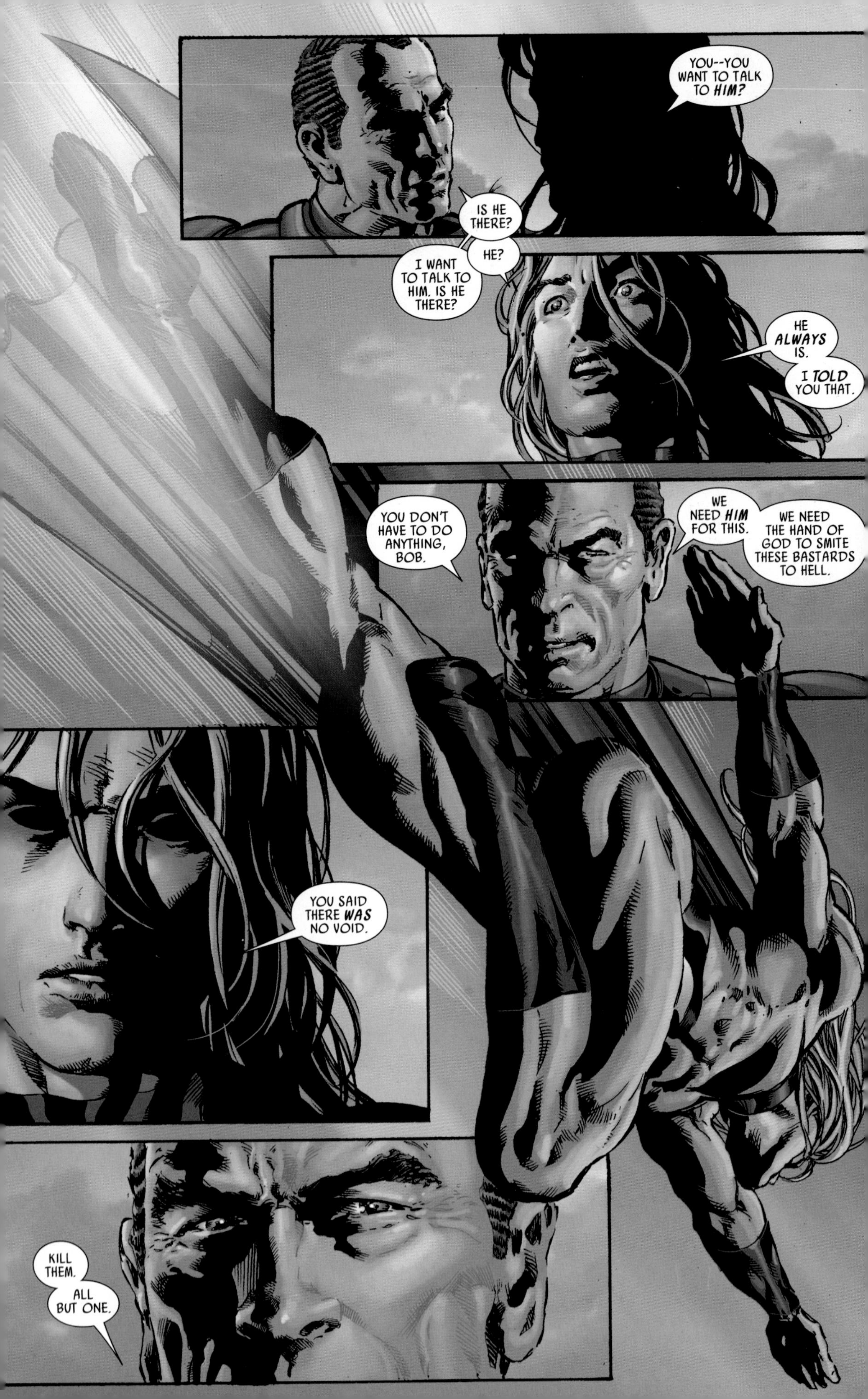
YOU--YOU WANT TO TALK TO HIM?
IS HE THERE?
HE?
I WANT TO TALK TO HIM. IS HE THERE?
HE ALWAYS IS.
I TOLD YOU THAT.
YOU DON'T HAVE TO DO ANYTHING, BOB.
WE NEED HIM FOR THIS.
WE NEED THE HAND OF GOD TO SMITE THESE BASTARDS TO HELL.
YOU SAID THERE WAS NO VOID.
KILL THEM.
ALL BUT ONE.

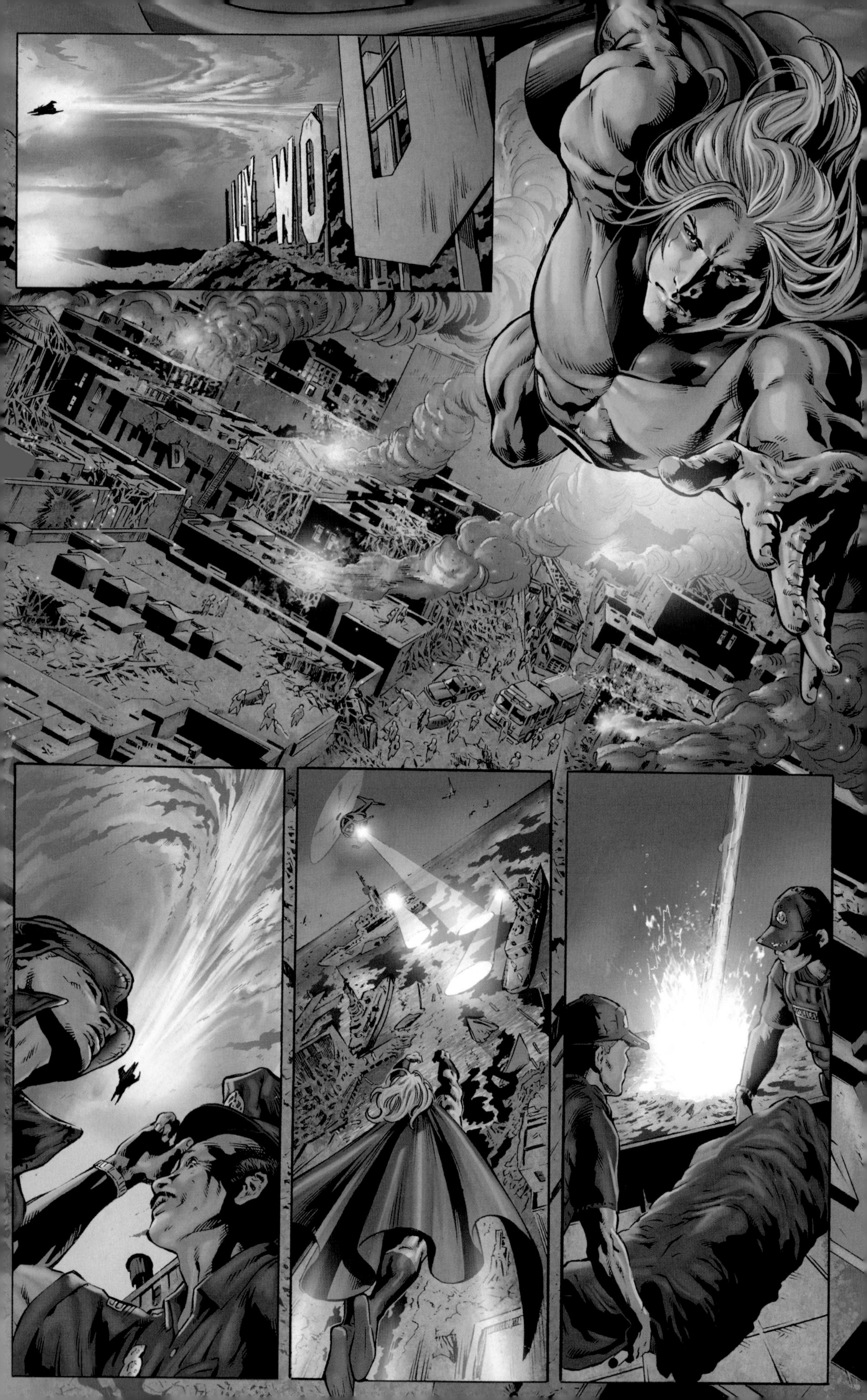

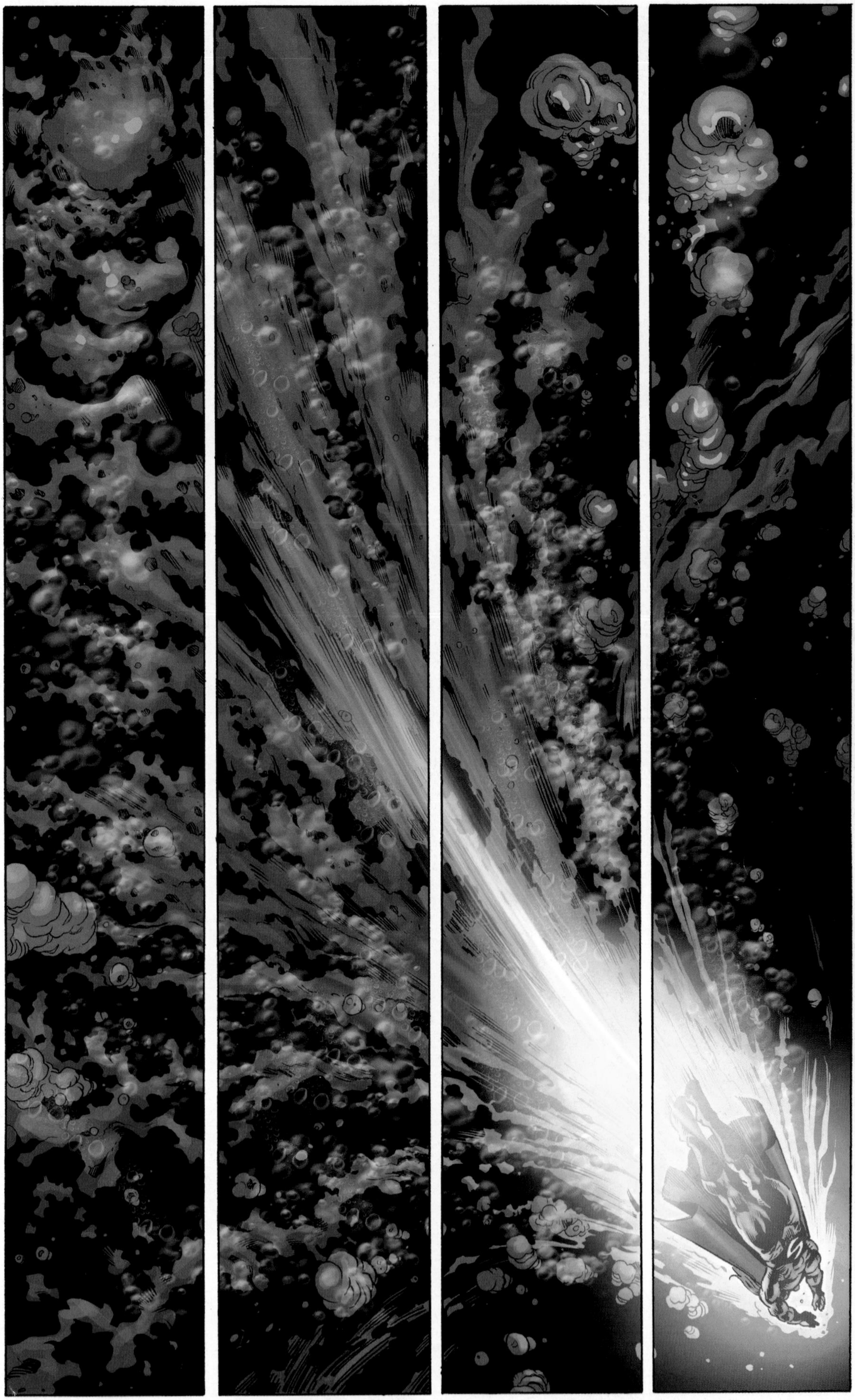

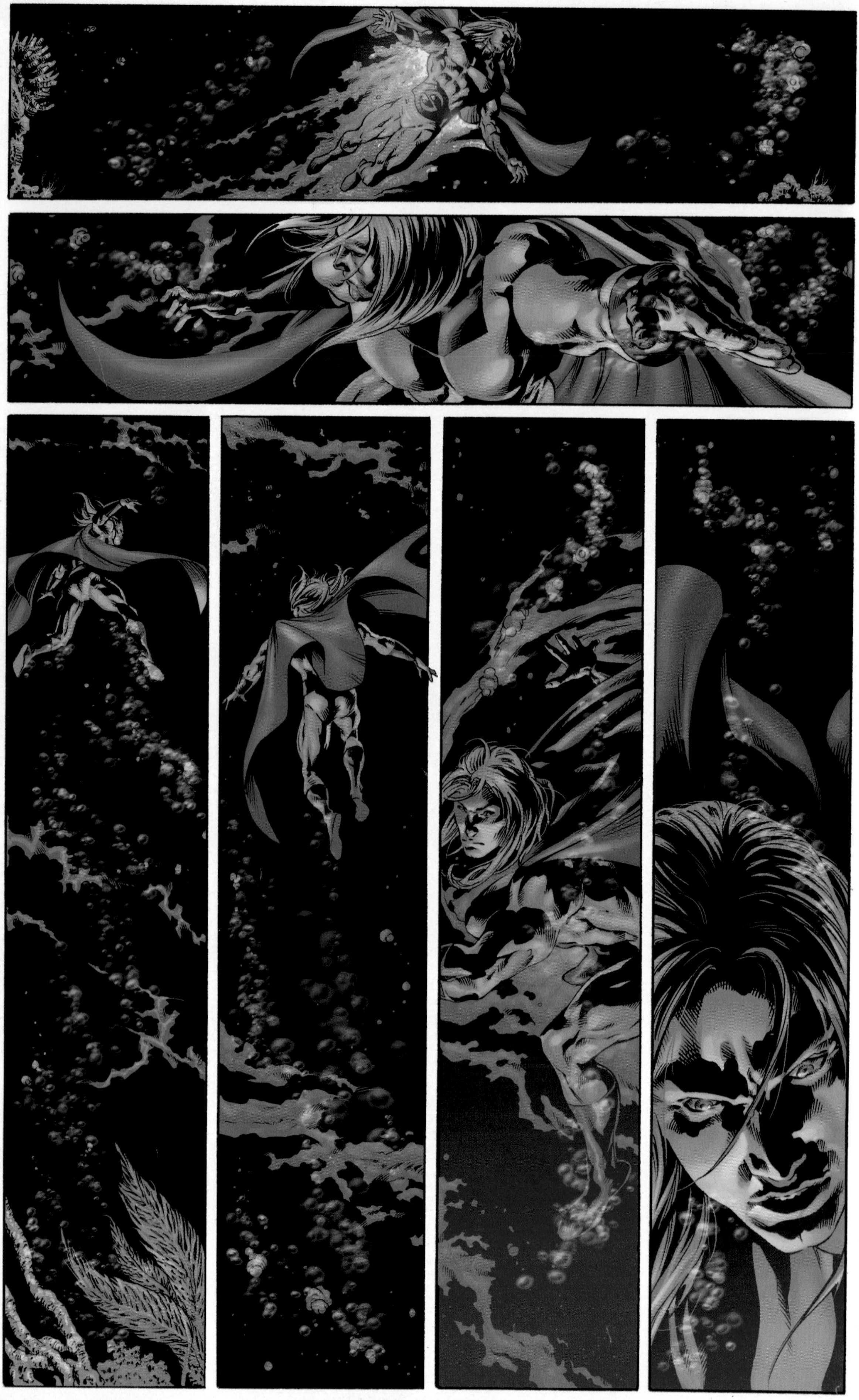

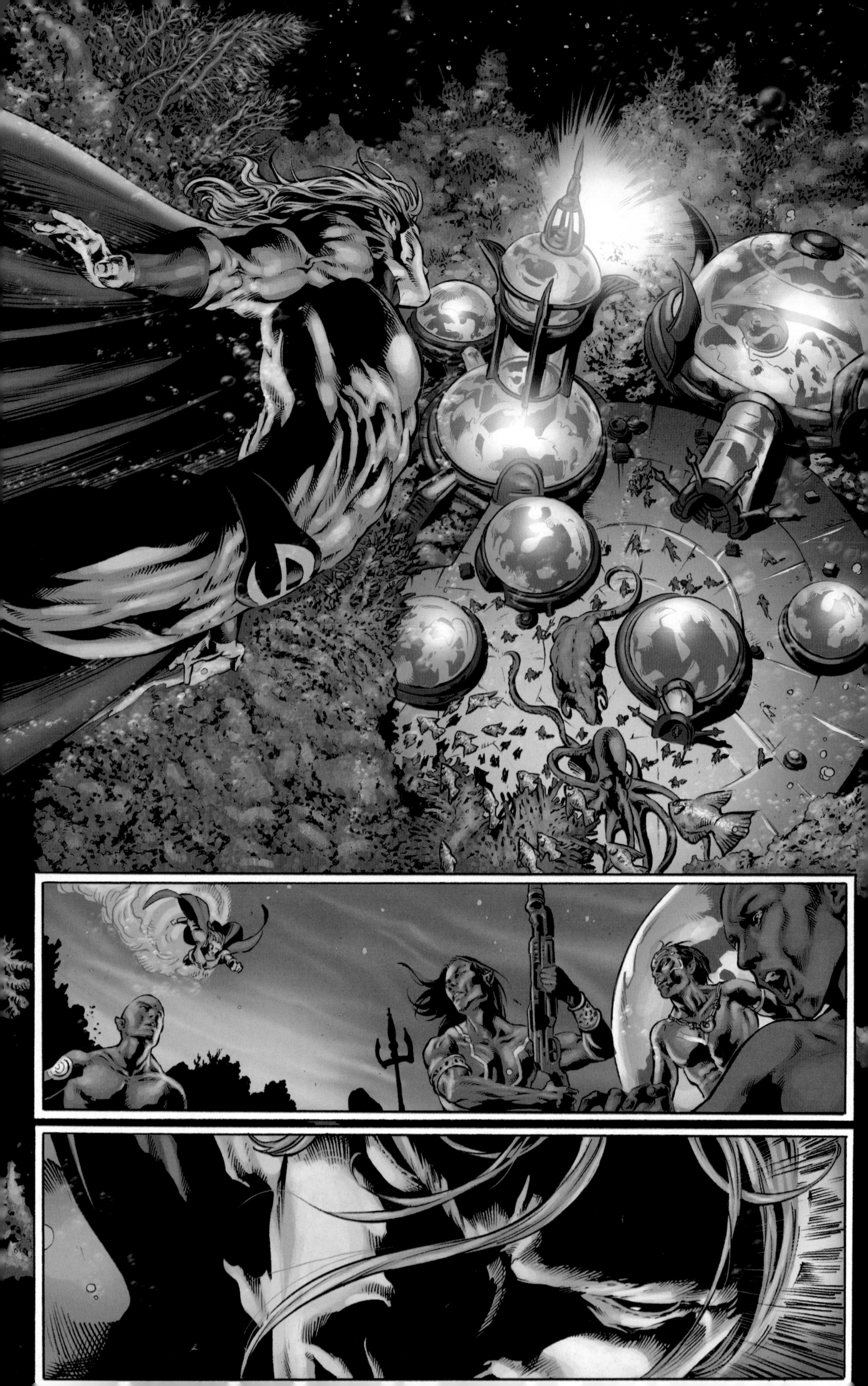

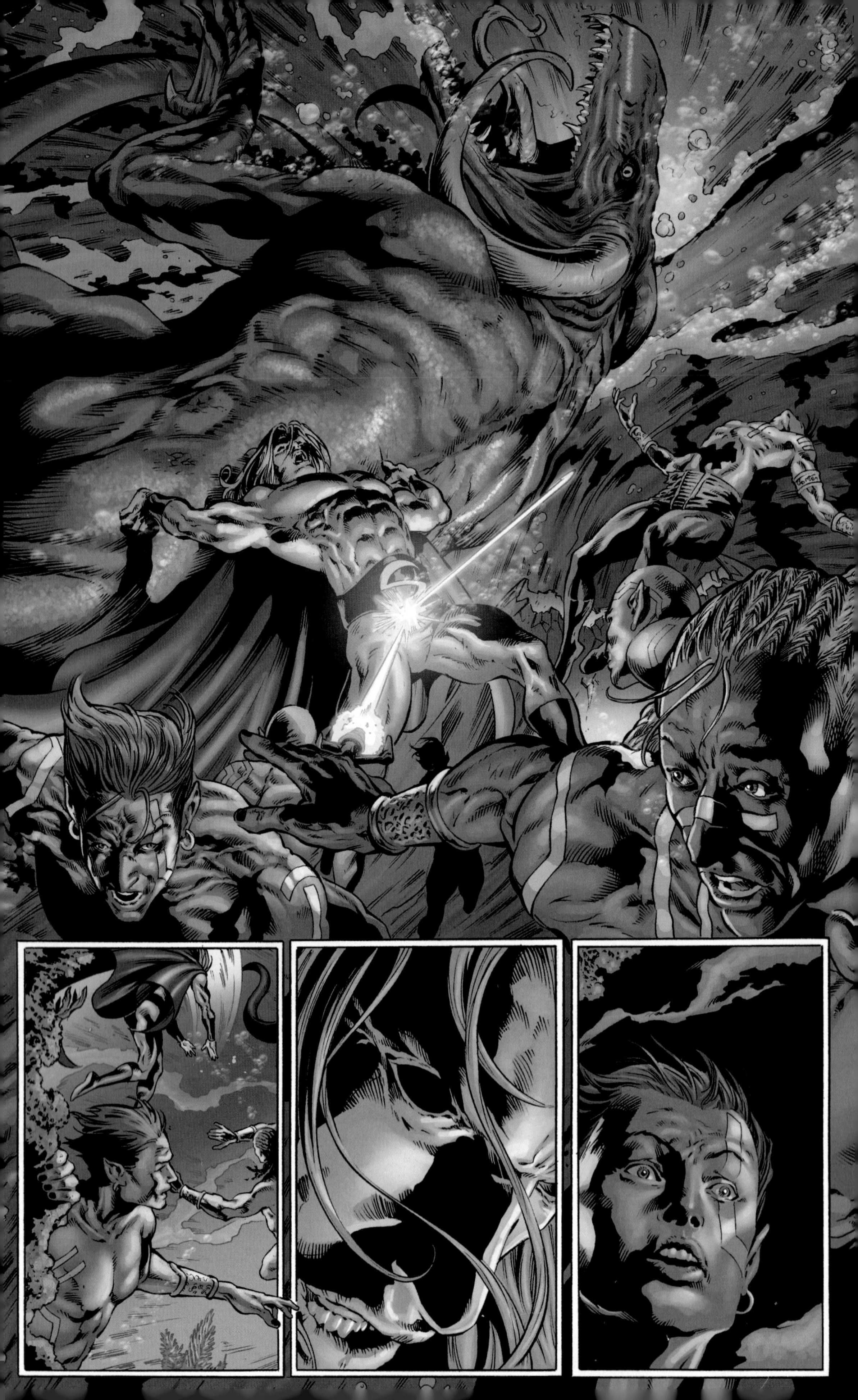

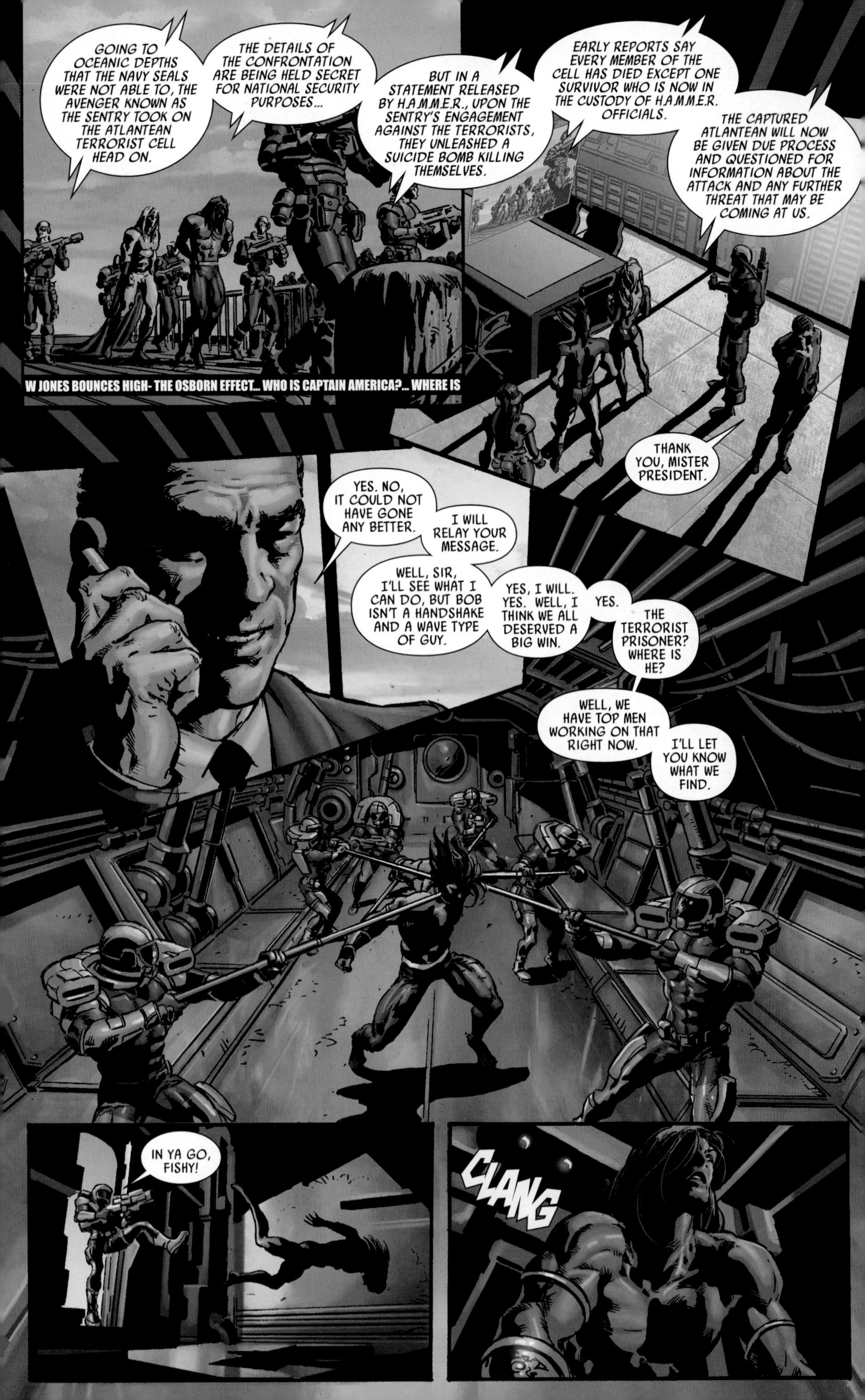
GOING TO OCEANIC DEPTHS THAT THE NAVY SEALS WERE NOT ABLE TO, THE AVENGER KNOWN AS THE SENTRY TOOK ON THE ATLANTEAN TERRORIST CELL HEAD ON.
THE DETAILS OF THE CONFRONTATION ARE BEING HELD SECRET FOR NATIONAL SECURITY PURPOSES...
BUT IN A STATEMENT RELEASED BY H.A.M.M.E.R., UPON THE SENTRY'S ENGAGEMENT AGAINST THE TERRORISTS, THEY UNLEASHED A SUICIDE BOMB KILLING THEMSELVES.
EARLY REPORTS SAY EVERY MEMBER OF THE CELL HAS DIED EXCEPT ONE SURVIVOR WHO IS NOW IN THE CUSTODY OF H.A.M.M.E.R. OFFICIALS.
THE CAPTURED ATLANTEAN WILL NOW BE GIVEN DUE PROCESS AND QUESTIONED FOR INFORMATION ABOUT THE ATTACK AND ANY FURTHER THREAT THAT MAY BE COMING AT US.
W JONES BOUNCES HIGH- THE OSBORN EFFECT... WHO IS CAPTAIN AMERICA?... WHERE IS
THANK YOU, MISTER PRESIDENT.
YES. NO, IT COULD NOT HAVE GONE ANY BETTER.
I WILL RELAY YOUR MESSAGE.
WELL, SIR, I'LL SEE WHAT I CAN DO, BUT BOB ISN'T A HANDSHAKE AND A WAVE TYPE OF GUY.
YES, I WILL. YES. WELL, I THINK WE ALL DESERVED A BIG WIN.
YES.
THE TERRORIST PRISONER? WHERE IS HE?
WELL, WE HAVE TOP MEN WORKING ON THAT RIGHT NOW.
I'LL LET YOU KNOW WHAT WE FIND.
IN YA GO, FISHY!
CLANG

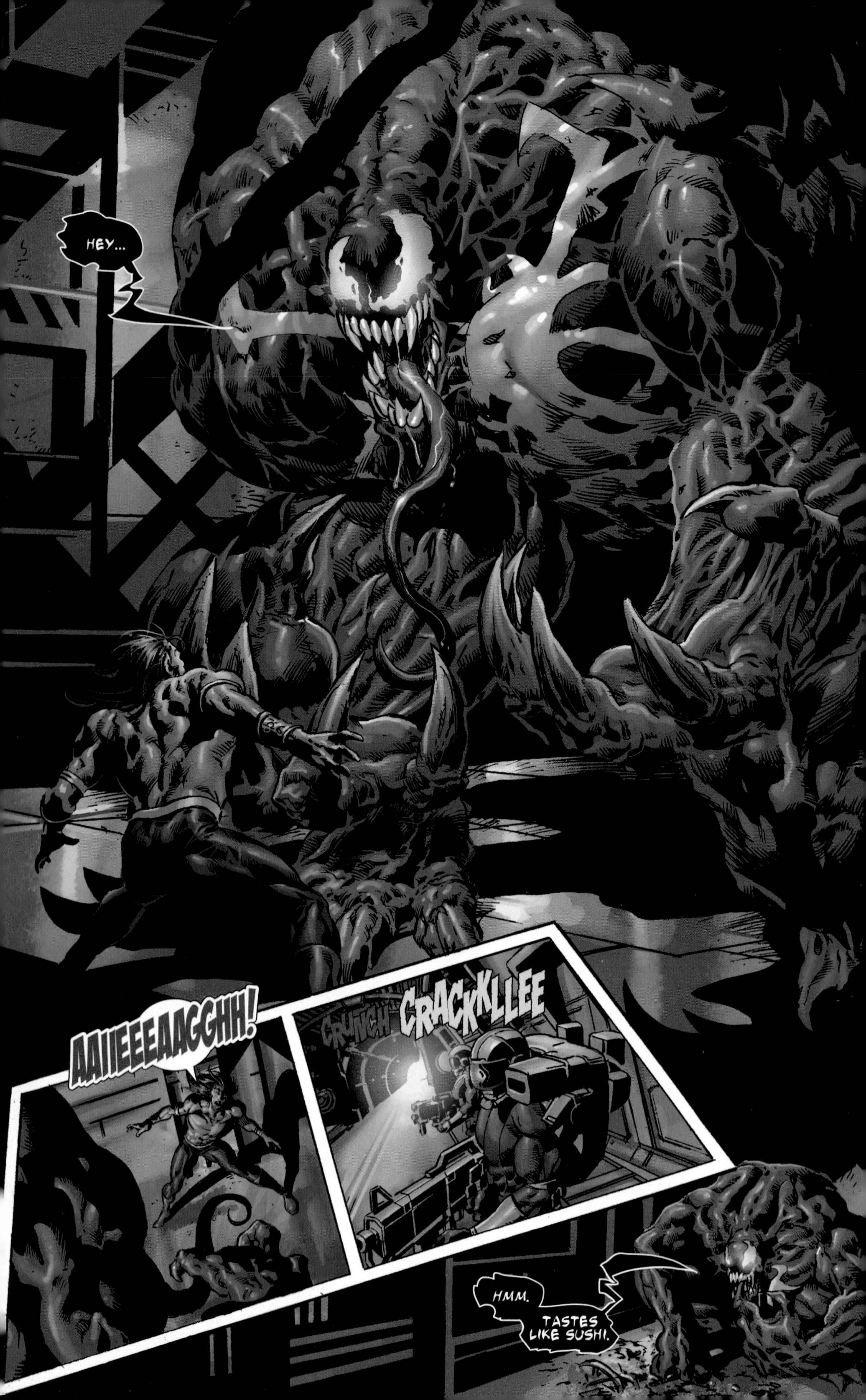
HEY...
AAIIEEEAAGGHH!
CRUNCH
CRACKKLLEE
HMM.
TASTES LIKE SUSHI.

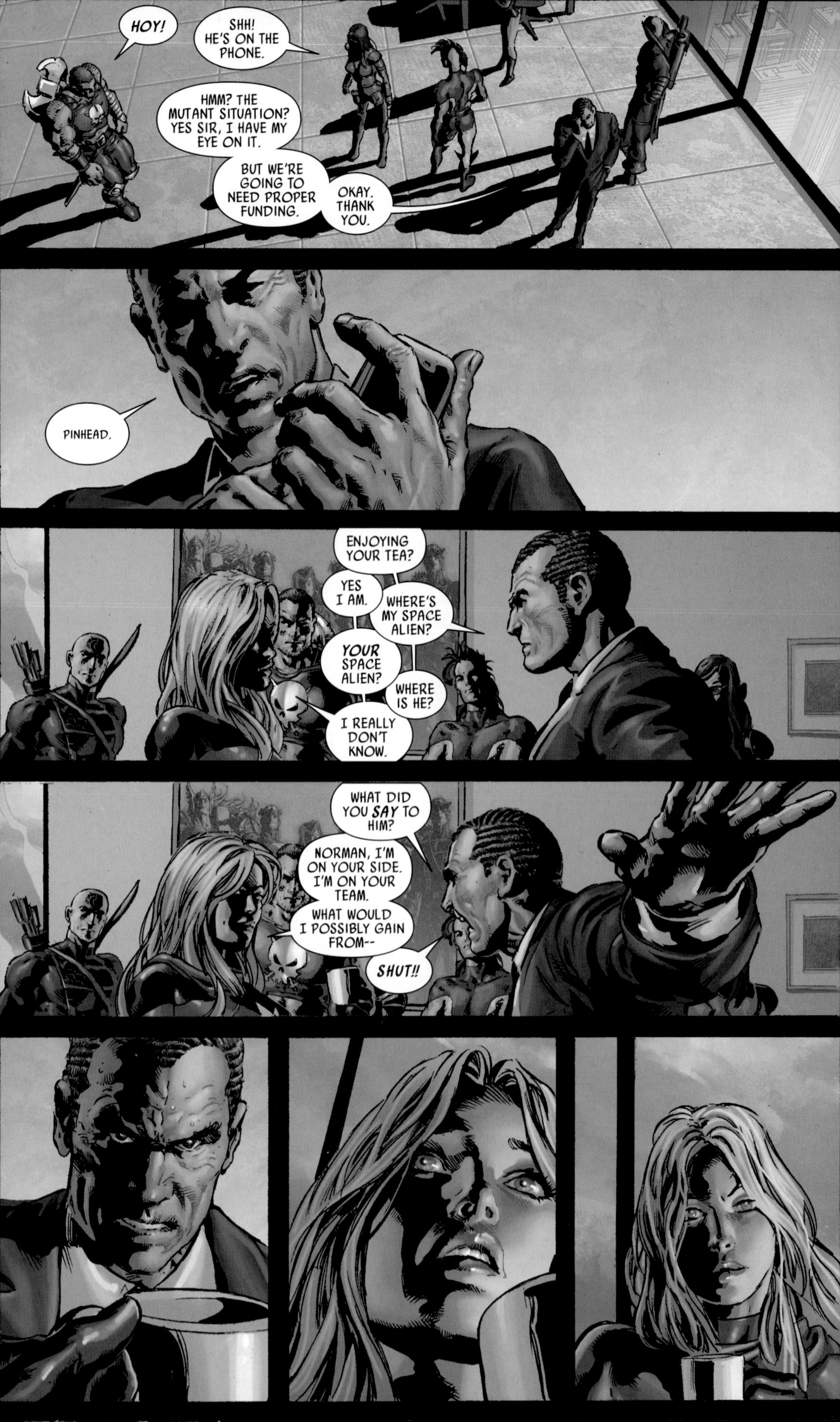
HOY!
SHH! HE'S ON THE PHONE.
HMM? THE MUTANT SITUATION? YES SIR, I HAVE MY EYE ON IT.
BUT WE'RE GOING TO NEED PROPER FUNDING.
OKAY. THANK YOU.
PINHEAD.
ENJOYING YOUR TEA?
YES I AM.
WHERE'S MY SPACE ALIEN?
YOUR SPACE ALIEN?
WHERE IS HE?
I REALLY DON'T KNOW.
WHAT DID YOU SAY TO HIM?
NORMAN, I'M ON YOUR SIDE. I'M ON YOUR TEAM.
WHAT WOULD I POSSIBLY GAIN FROM--
SHUT!!

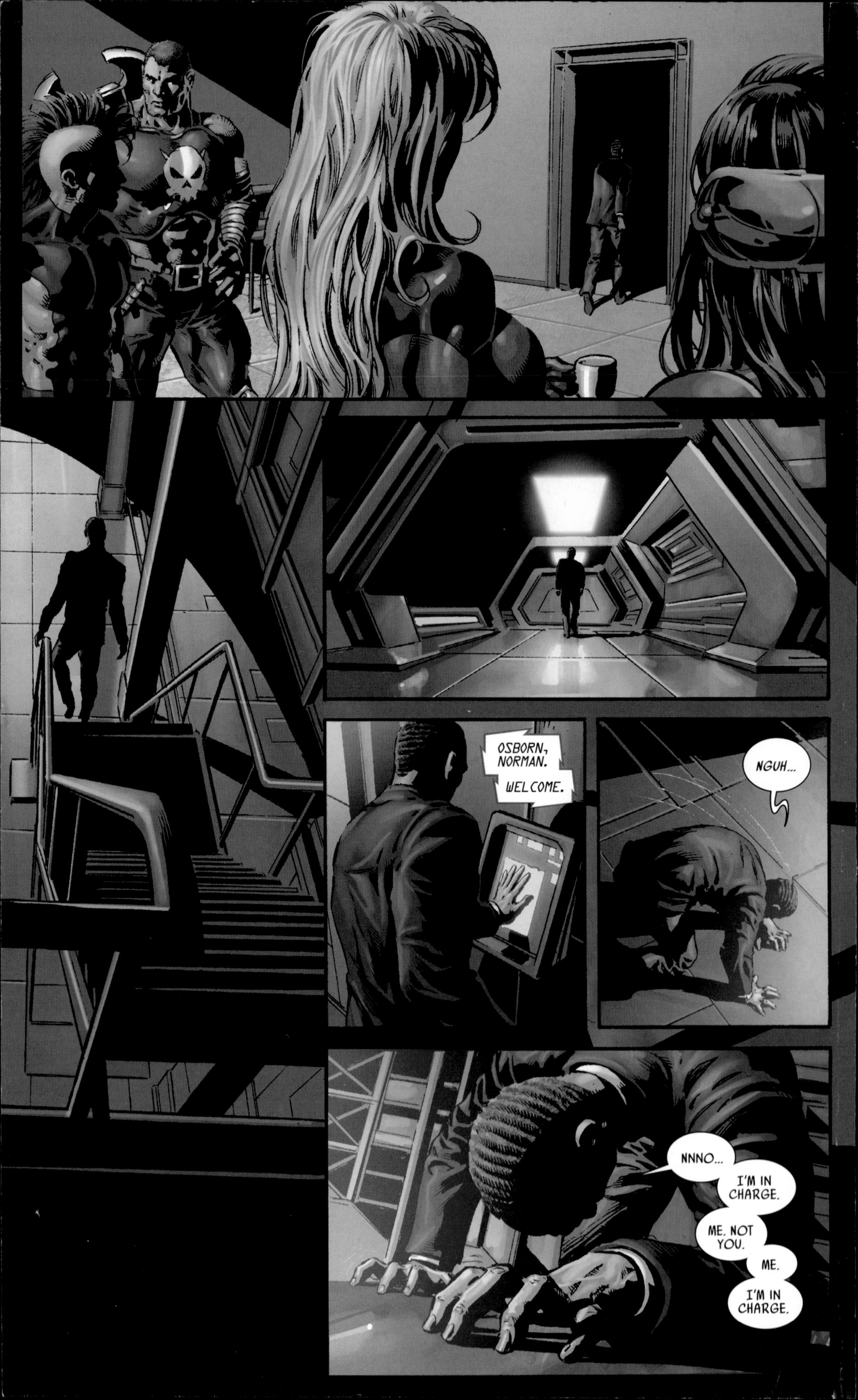
OSBORN, NORMAN.
WELCOME.
NGUH...
NNNO...
I'M IN CHARGE.
ME. NOT YOU.
ME.
I'M IN CHARGE.

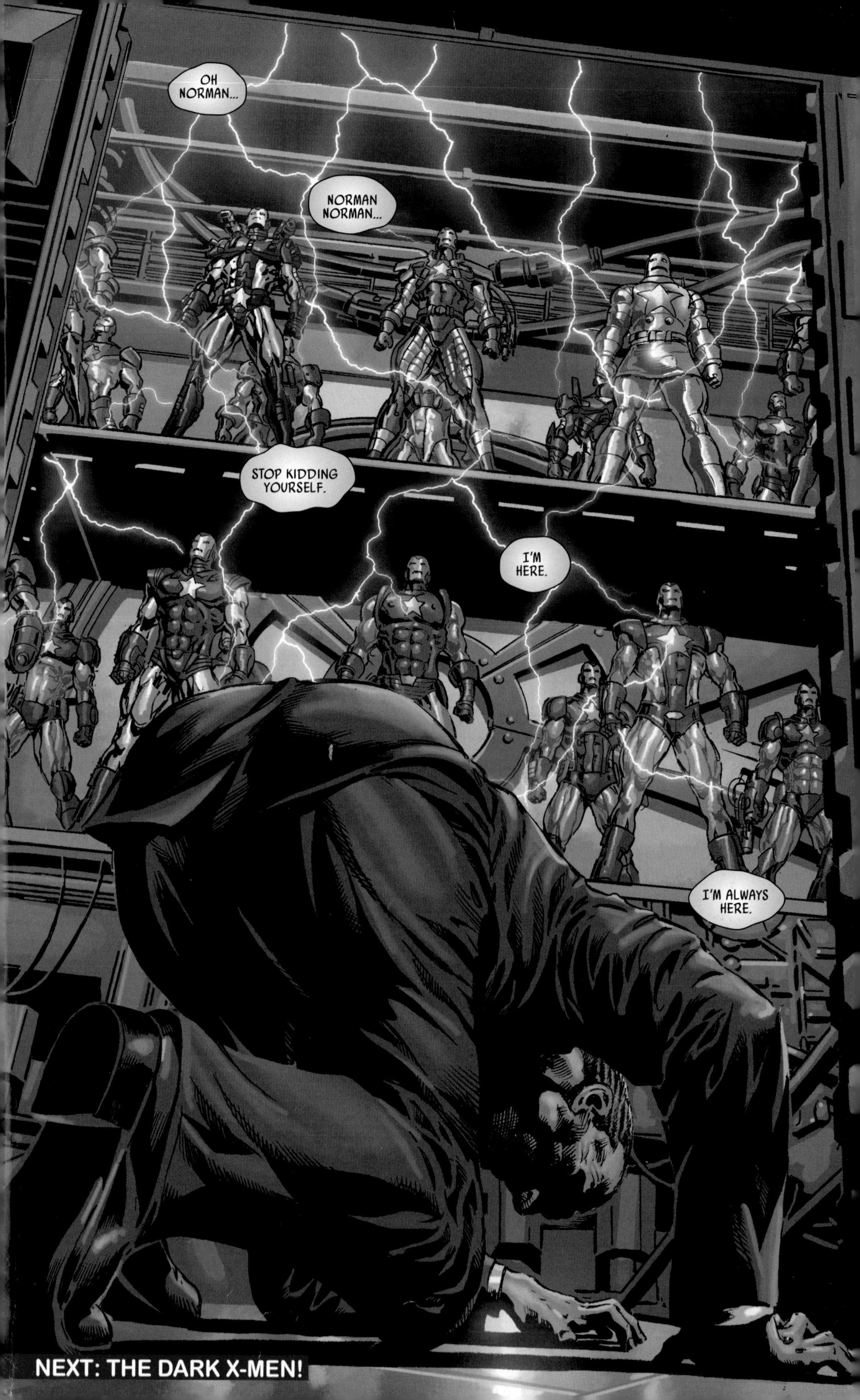
OH NORMAN...
NORMAN NORMAN...
STOP KIDDING YOURSELF.
I'M HERE.
I'M ALWAYS HERE.

NEXT: THE DARK X-MEN!

DARK AVENGERS #1 2ND PRINTING VARIANT

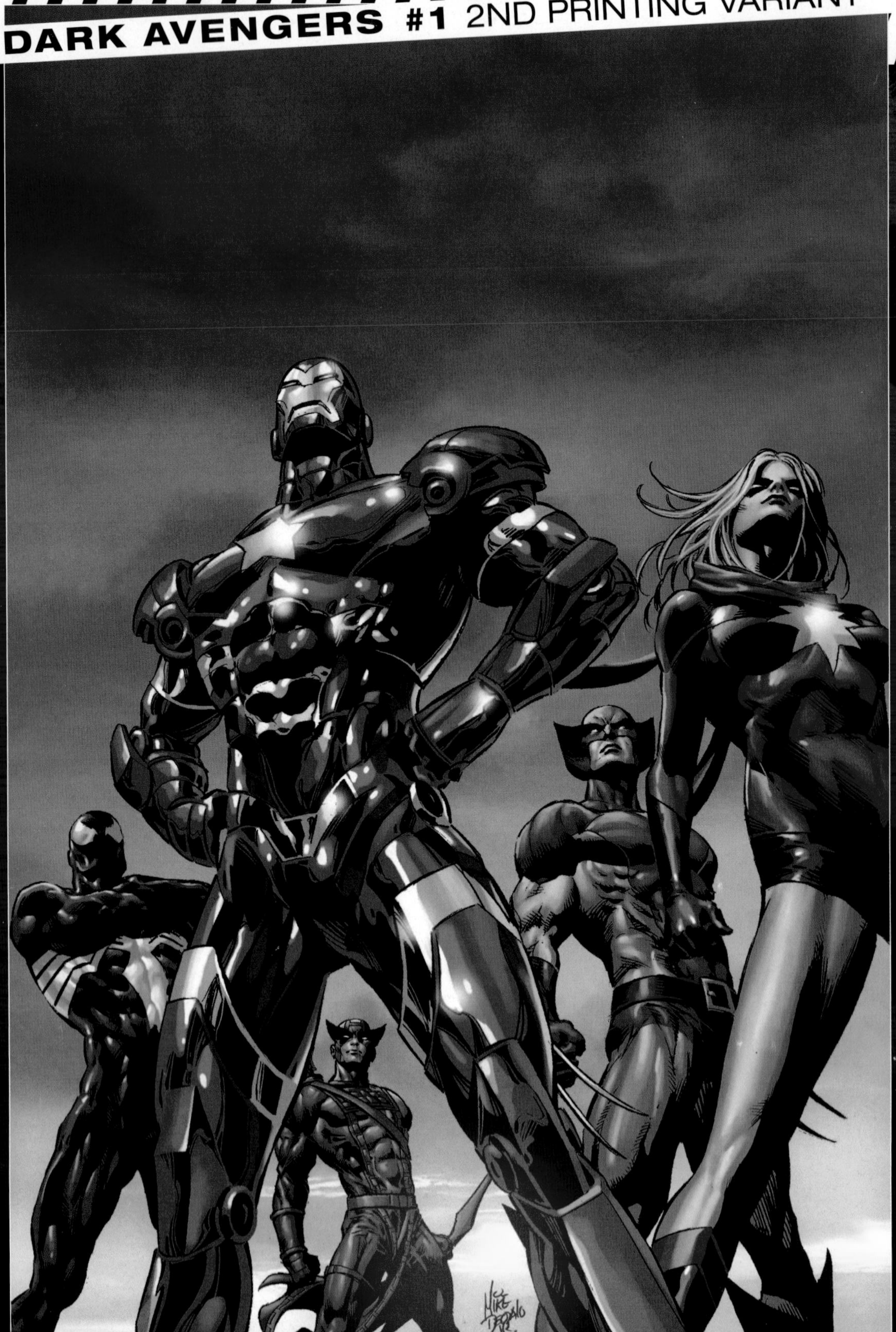

BY MIKE DEODATO